Oxford Practice Grammar
Advanced

Oxford Practice Grammar

Advanced

With answers

George Yule

OXFORD

UNIVERSITY PRESS

OXFORD
UNIVERSITY PRESS

Great Clarendon Street, Oxford OX2 6DP

Oxford University Press is a department of the University of Oxford.
It furthers the University's objective of excellence in research, scholarship,
and education by publishing worldwide in

Oxford New York

Auckland Cape Town Dar es Salaam Hong Kong Karachi
Kuala Lumpur Madrid Melbourne Mexico City Nairobi
New Delhi Shanghai Taipei Toronto

With offices in

Argentina Austria Brazil Chile Czech Republic France Greece
Guatemala Hungary Italy Japan Poland Portugal Singapore
South Korea Switzerland Thailand Turkey Ukraine Vietnam

OXFORD and OXFORD ENGLISH are registered trade marks of
Oxford University Press in the UK and in certain other countries

ISBN-13: 978 0 19 432754 1
ISBN-13: 978 0 19 430916 5   (Pack)

Cover illustration by Joanna Usherwood
Index by Sue Lightfoot

Printed in China

For advice and encouragement during the writing of this book, I
would like to thank Maryann Overstreet, Elaine Tarone, Henry
Widdowson, Annie Yule and the excellent editorial team, led by
Glynnis Chantrell and Helen Ward, at Oxford University Press.

ACKNOWLEDGEMENTS

*The authors and publisher are grateful to those who have given permission to
reproduce the following extracts and adaptations of copyright material*: pp13,
28, 71, 91, 135, 175 *Oxford Guide to British and American Culture*
published by Oxford University Press © Oxford University Press, 1999.
Reproduced by permission. p15 *The Restraints of Beasts* by Magnus Mills.
Copyright © 1998 Magnus Mills. Reproduced by permission of the
author c/o Rogers, Coleridge & White Ltd., 20 Powis Mews, London
W11 1JN. p26 From *Alice in Wonderland*, Norton Critical Edition-Second
edition by Lewis Carroll, edited by Donald J. Gray. Copyright © 1992,
1971 by W. W. Norton & Company, Inc. Used by permission of W. W.
Norton & Company, Inc. p68 'Traveling by modern jet safer than
going by car' by Dr Vernon Ansdell published 7 November 1997, *The
Honolulu Advertiser* © Vernon Ansdell 1997. Reproduced by permission.
p79 From 'Homage to Switzerland'. Reprinted with permission of
Scribner, an imprint of Simon & Schuster Adult Publishing Group,
and The Random House Group Ltd from *The Short Stories of Ernest
Hemingway*, published by Jonathan Cape. Copyright 1933 by Charles
Scribner's Sons. Copyright renewed © 1961 by Mary Hemingway. p80
Extract from *In Patagonia* by Bruce Chatwin published by Jonathan
Cape. Copyright © Bruce Chatwin 1977. Used by permission of The
Random House Group Limited and Gillon Aitken Associates Ltd. p96
'The Kid from Kogarah' from *Unreliable Memoirs* by Clive James
published by Picador (Pan Books). Reproduced by permission of
Macmillan UK. p96 Brief quotation from *That's Not What I Meant* by
Deborah Tannen. Copyright © 1986 by Deborah Tannen. Reprinted by
permission of HarperCollins Publishers Inc., William Morrow and
Virago Press (part of Time Warner Book Group UK). p96 From *Libra* by
Don DeLillo (Viking, 1988) copyright © Don DeLillo, 1988. p124
'Missing out on "the experience"' by Jennifer Currie published in *The
Times Higher Educational Supplement*, 16 July 1999. Reproduced by
permission of the THES. p138 Adapted from 'Saying what's hard to
say' by Sara Shandler published in *Seventeen Magazine*. Reproduced by
permission of Seventeen Magazine. p169 *You Just Don't Understand* by
Deborah Tannen © 1990 Deborah Tannen. Reproduced by permission
of the author c/o Rogers, Coleridge & White Ltd., 20 Powis Mews,
London W11 1JN. p170 From *Whales, Candelight and Stuff Like That* by
Maryann Overstreet, copyright 2000 by Oxford University Press, Inc.
Used by permission of Oxford University Press, Inc. p171 From 'Has
this chimp taught himself to talk' published by *New Scientist*, 6
December 2003. Reproduced by permission of *New Scientist*. p188 'The
Rum Tum Tugger' from *Old Possum's Book of Practical Cats*, copyright
1939 by T.S. Eliot and renewed 1967 by Esme Valerie Eliot. Reprinted
by permission of Harcourt, Inc. and Faber and Faber. p191 Modified
from *I Can't Accept Not Trying* by Michael Jordan. Copyright © 1994 by
Rare Air, Ltd. Text © 1994 by Michael Jordan. Reprinted by permission
of HarperCollins Publishers Inc. p194 From *Heartburn* by Nora
Ephron. Reproduced by permission of International Creative
Management, Inc. Copyright © 1983 by Nora Ephron. p123 Extract
from *Memoirs of a Geisha* by Arthur Golden published by Chatto &
Windus/Vintage. Used by permission of The Random House Group
Limited and Random House, Inc.

Credit Source: p2 Adapted from article 'Runaway bus stopped by
teacher' published in the *E L Gazette*, September 2001. p131 From
The English Patient by Michael Ondaatje published by Vintage Books.

Illustrations by: Adrian Barclay pp28, 64; Mark Duffin pp79, 91, 187,
196; Chris Pavely pp68, 131, 135

*We would also like to thank the following for permission to reproduce the
following photographs*: Getty Images pp16, 131; Punchstock p16; John
Walmsley/Education Photos p13

Contents

Introduction

The Oxford Practice Grammar series

The *Oxford Practice Grammar* is a series of three books, each written at the right level for you at each stage in your study of English. The series is intended for your use either in a classroom or when working independently in your own time.

The books are divided into units, each of which covers an important grammar topic. Each unit starts with an explanation of the grammar and this is followed by a set of practice exercises. Tests at the end of each unit or section of units give the opportunity for more practice and enable you to assess how much you have learned. Answers to the exercises and the tests are given at the back of the book.

You may want to choose the order in which you study the grammar topics, perhaps going first to those giving you problems. (Topics are listed in the Contents page at the front of each book and in the Index at the back.) Alternatively you may choose to start at the beginning of each book and work through to the end.

An interactive CD-ROM is included at each of the three levels, offering alternative ways to practise. You can recognize and correct written mistakes, and you can also take part in spoken dialogues; you can record and listen to your own voice and learn to speak more naturally.

Exam practice

The first level in the series is *Oxford Practice Grammar – Basic*. This is suitable for elementary to pre-intermediate learners, and those working for the PET exam and IELTS. The second is *Oxford Practice Grammar – Intermediate*, for students who are no longer beginners but are not yet advanced in their use of English. It is suitable for those studying for the Cambridge FCE. *Oxford Practice Grammar – Advanced* is for those who have progressed beyond the intermediate level and who wish to increase their knowledge of English grammar and become more confident when using it. It helps students prepare for CAE, CPE, TOEFL, and other advanced-level exams.

Oxford Practice Grammar – Advanced is for more advanced students who have already studied English grammar at the middle or intermediate level. It can be used by students working alone, in study groups, or while attending classes.

The book consists of seventeen units, providing a complete review of the grammar of contemporary English. Within each unit there are separate sections on specific features (e.g. 'The uses of the passive') and problem areas (e.g. 'Present Perfect or Past Simple?'). Each section consists of explanations of grammar points, with examples, plus a number of exercises on the same page or the facing page. At the end of each unit there is a two-page test. Answers for all the exercises and tests are provided in the Answer key (page 220). There is also a Glossary (page 265) explaining the meaning of all grammatical terms used.

Using this book

This book can be used in a number of ways.

- You can use it as a reference guide for clear and concise explanations of particular points of English grammar. Each explanation is followed by examples of correct use in context, with advice on common errors to avoid. For easy reference, each separate topic is presented in a heading at the top of the page. All unit and section topics are listed in the Contents (page V) and in the Index (page 273).

- You can use the book as a workbook in which you write answers to complete the exercises. You can then check in the Answer key to see whether your answers are correct. If you find you have an incorrect answer, you can look at the relevant grammatical point on the accompanying page for an explanation, with examples of what is correct.

- You can use the book as a textbook, beginning on the first page and working at your own pace to the end. This allows you to treat each topic as equally important in a comprehensive review of English grammar. The unit topics are not presented in order of difficulty, but follow a sequence similar to that used in many textbooks.

- You can also use the book to create your own grammar course, working through all or part of a section or unit and completing selected exercises or tests. You can use the cross-references at the bottom of each page of explanation to guide you to other relevant sections. Because the grammar topics are not presented in order of difficulty, you can work on the topics in any order you choose.

Special features

In addition to traditional types of exercises, there are a number of innovative grammar exercises in this book, specifically designed for students who are becoming more advanced in English.

- In the **summary exercises**, you choose appropriate grammatical forms from a longer text in order to complete a short summary of that text. These exercises help you to improve your ability to create grammatically accurate reports of what you have read (page 2, Exercise 2).

- In the **dictionary exercises**, you choose appropriate grammatical forms to complete definitions of words and phrases. These exercises expand your vocabulary and help to develop your ability to create clear and grammatically accurate descriptions (page 7, Exercise 8).

- In the **matching exercises**, you add appropriate grammatical forms to a sentence, part of a sentence, or a question, in order to create a meaningful connection with another sentence. These exercises improve your ability to produce more complex spoken and written English while ensuring that it is grammatically accurate (page 7, Exercise 9).

- In the **editing exercises**, you read through a paragraph, checking for grammatical mistakes and providing corrections where necessary. These exercises help to develop your ability to write longer texts in English with increased grammatical accuracy (page 9, Exercise 13).

- In the **numbering exercises**, you complete the connection between explanation and example by choosing the number of the example that best illustrates the explanation. These exercises provide an opportunity to take a more interactive role in creating a connection between your ability to understand English and your knowledge of the grammatical rules of English (page 12, Exercise 17).

- In the **test exercises**, you provide answers in a range of different formats used in examinations such as the TOEFL, the Michigan Test, and the Cambridge Proficiency. These exercises allow you to become more familiar with examinations at the advanced level and to work with authentic texts by authors such as Lewis Carroll, Bruce Chatwin, Nora Ephron, Magnus Mills, and many others (pages 14–15).

1 Sentences

We can form simple sentences with a subject and a verb in a single clause (*Jenny laughed*). We can include auxiliary verbs (*be, do, have* and modals) as part of the verb phrase and an adverbial after the verb (*She was sitting at the table*). We can use verbs with an object (*She was drawing a picture*), without an object (*She giggled*) or with two objects (*She showed me the picture*). We can also use linking verbs with complements (*It looked very silly*).

We form compound sentences with clauses joined by the coordinating conjunctions *and*, *but* and *or* (*I made some coffee, but Jenny wanted orange juice*). We form complex sentences with clauses joined by subordinating conjunctions such as *after*, *because*, *if* and *while* (*We chatted in the kitchen while I cooked breakfast*).

1 Read through this newspaper report and find:

1 another simple sentence
2 a complex sentence with two conjunctions

A YOUNG ENGLISH TEACHER saved the lives of 30 students when he took control of a bus after its driver suffered a fatal heart attack. Guy
5 Harvold, 24, had collected the students and three course leaders from Gatwick airport and they were travelling to Bournemouth to meet their host families. They were going to start a course at the International Language
10 Academy in Bournemouth where Harvold works as a teacher.

Harvold, who has not passed his driving test, said, 'I realized the bus was out of control when I was speaking to the students on the
15 microphone.' The bus collided with trees at the side of the road and he noticed the driver was slumped over the wheel. The driver didn't move. He was unconscious.

'We hit a barrier and swerved to the other
20 side of the road and I grabbed the wheel,' Harvold explained. 'The driver's legs were over the pedals and I had difficulty reaching the brake. We hit a lamp post and it shattered the glass on the front door before I managed
25 to bring the bus to a halt.' Police praised the young teacher's quick thinking. If he hadn't reacted quickly, there could have been a terrible accident.

The bus driver never regained
30 consciousness. He was later pronounced dead at East Surrey hospital. He had worked regularly with the school and was very well regarded by staff. Harvold said, 'I was so relieved that no one else was hurt, but I hoped
35 the driver would survive. It was only later I heard he had died. That's a terrible tragedy.'

The Language Academy's principal told the Gazette that the school is going to send Harvold on a weekend trip to Dublin with a
40 friend, as a gesture of thanks for his bravery. A local driving school has also offered him six free driving lessons. ■

2 Using verbs and conjunctions from the newspaper report above, complete this summary.

English teacher Guy Harvold, 24, ...saved.......... the lives of 30 students on a bus from Gatwick to Bournemouth (1) .... the driver (2) .... a heart attack. The bus went out of control. It (3) .... trees, a barrier and a lamp post (4) .... Harvold could stop it. The driver (5) ...., (6) .... no-one else (7) .... hurt. Harvold, who hasn't passed his driving test, was (8) .... by police (9) .... was (10) .... free driving lessons by a local driving school.

2

Simple sentences and verbs

Simple sentences

A simple sentence is a single clause with a subject and a verb.
> 1 *Mary sneezed.* • *Somebody coughed.* • *The train didn't come.* • *People were waiting.*

Simple sentences can also have an object (2) and/or an adverbial, such as an adverb (3) or a prepositional phrase (4).
> 2 *Mr Owen made **lunch**.* • *I brought **some cakes**.* • *We drank **tea**.* • *Everyone enjoyed **it**.*
> 3 ***Suddenly** the weather changed.* • *We **quickly** closed the windows.* • *It **often** rains **there**.*
> 4 *Shakespeare married Anne Hathaway **in 1582**. He moved **to London in 1588**.*

Simple sentences with linking verbs, such as *be* or *look*, have complements that describe the subject.
> 5 *Cathy is **a nurse**.* • *She wasn't **ready**.* • *Her hair looked **wet**.* • *The room felt **like an oven**.*

Verbs

Most verbs are action verbs, used to describe actions (what we do) and events (what happens).
> 6 *Richard **eats** a lot of pasta. It **gives** him energy. He **runs** every night. I **saw** him in the park.*

Some verbs are state verbs rather than action verbs. They are used to describe states: what we think (7), how we feel (8) and relationships, especially those concerned with inclusion and possession (9).
> 7 *I **know** what you **mean**.* • *My parents **understood** everything.* • *They **believe** in fate.*
> 8 *I **appreciate** all your help.* • *Some people **hate** cucumber in sandwiches.*
> 9 *The city guide **contains** useful information.* • *That old suitcase **belongs** to me.*

We don't usually use state verbs in the continuous. (NOT ~~That suitcase is belonging to me.~~)
Other state verbs include: consist of, exist, include, matter, own, prefer, realize, remember, resemble

We also use linking verbs (*be, seem*, etc.) to describe states: how things are or seem to be.
> 10 *These flowers **are** beautiful.* • *Everything **seems** fine.* • *Your friend **appears** to be nervous.*

We can use some verbs, such as *taste* or *weigh*, as state verbs (11) or as action verbs (12).
> 11 *Flowers don't usually **taste** very good.* • *The box **weighs** two kilos.*
> 12 *Have you **tasted** this soup?* • *They **weighed** it at the post office.*

We use the auxiliary verbs *be, do* and *have* with other verbs when we form different tenses (13), questions and negatives (14) and for emphasis (15).
> 13 *The boys **have been** waiting for you. I think they**'ve** gone outside. They**'re** playing football.*
> 14 *What **did** Josh say? ~ He **didn't** say anything.* • ***Does** he want coffee? ~ I **don't** think so.*
> 15 *You **aren't** working very hard. ~ I **AM** working hard!* • *You **don't** miss me. ~ I **DO** miss you!*

We also use *be, do* and *have* as main verbs: *He **is** lazy. He **does** nothing. He **has** no money.*

We use modal auxiliary verbs (modals) such as *can, must, should* or *will* with other verbs to express concepts such as permission, obligation, necessity, prediction, etc.
> 16 ***Can** I leave now?* • *You **shouldn't** go yet.* • *I **must** catch the next bus or I**'ll** be late for work.*

3 Find an example of each of the following in the newspaper report on page 2.

1 a simple sentence with a linking verb: ....
2 a clause with an action verb and an adverb: ....
3 a clause with a modal: ....

Subjects and verbs

Subjects

The subject of a sentence is usually the first noun phrase or pronoun identifying who or what is performing an action expressed by the verb (1). It can identify who or what is experiencing something (2). It can also be the focus of a description (i.e. who or what the complement is linked to) (3).

1 **Tony** lost his keys. • **The dog** ate my homework. • **You** are working too hard these days.
2 **The children** heard a loud noise. • **The audience** enjoyed the concert. • **Meg** doesn't like coffee.
3 **Lions** are large and powerful. • **Her new classmates** seem friendly. • **Your hair** looks great.

We usually put the subject before the verb except in questions (4) and sentences using inversion (5).

4 Where has **she** been? • Does **this bus** go to the university? • Isn't **Oslo** in southern Norway?
5 In front of us and blocking the way stood **a large dog**. Never had **I** seen such a fierce animal.

The subject can also be a gerund (6), an infinitive (7) or a clause (8).

6 **Reading comics** is her favourite thing. • **Studying** always makes me sleepy.
7 **Just to complete the classes** has become my new goal. • **To go without you** wouldn't be any fun.
8 **That Labour would win the election** was never in doubt. • **What he said** wasn't very polite.

Subject-verb agreement

It is the subject that determines whether the verb is singular or plural (9). It is the main noun as subject, not a prepositional phrase, that makes the verb singular (10) or plural (11).

9 Gregory's **sister lives** in Scotland. His **parents live** near London.
10 A new pair of shoes **doesn't** cost a lot. • A woman with three children **was** waiting outside.
11 New shoes **don't** always feel comfortable at first. • The children **were** crying.

We use singular verbs after indefinite pronouns (*everybody, nobody*, etc.) as subjects (12). We usually use singular verbs after subjects beginning with *none of* and *neither of* in formal situations (13). We sometimes use plural verbs in informal situations (14).

12 Everybody in the country **wants** one of these. • Nobody except his parents **was** willing to help.
13 None of the candidates **has** much support. • Neither of King Henry's sons **was** born in France.
14 She shouted, 'None of you **have** a chance.' • He's complaining that neither of them **were** asked .

We use singular verbs after some subjects that seem to be plural: some nouns ending in *-s* (15), phrases describing an amount (16) and some combinations with *and* (17). There are some nouns such as *people* and *police* which appear to be singular, but which are used with a plural verb (18).

15 The news **wasn't** too bad. • Cards **is** more than a game for some people. • Measles **is** a disease.
16 Fifty pounds **is** too much. • Twenty miles **was** too far and two days **wasn't** enough time.
17 Tom and Jerry **is** a rather violent cartoon. • Sausage and beans **doesn't** cost very much.
18 The police **are** trying to stop speeding in the city, but people **are** still driving too fast.

We can use a group noun as subject to refer to several people, with a plural verb (19), or to refer to the group as a single unit, with a singular verb (20), depending on our point of view.

19 The Welsh team **are** getting tired. • The committee **have** not expressed all their views.
20 The Welsh team **is** in second place. • The committee **hasn't** reached a decision yet.

Other group nouns include: audience, class, crowd, enemy, family, government, orchestra, staff
Note that, in American English, a singular verb is typically used after a group noun:
My wife's family always has a big get-together with a barbecue on July 4th.

---

4 Find an example of each of the following in the newspaper report on page 2.

1 a clause with an indefinite pronoun ....
2 a clause with a noun referring to a group ....

Group nouns 75 Indefinite pronouns 98 Infinitives and gerunds 139 Inversion 216

5 Add one of these verbs to each of the sentences.

✓does doesn't has have is isn't are aren't was wasn't won't

                              does
Example: Excuse me, but this train stop at Croydon?

1 To get an A in every class be easy.

2 Lord of the Flies the name of the book we had to read last year?

3 My new pair of jeans pockets on the side of the legs.

4 What they're doing in Parliament interest me.

5 Being absent from class a lot going to improve his chances of passing.

6 Jan got really angry with us and screamed, 'None of you my friends any more!'

7 Never I had to listen to so many boring people!

8 I watched Dances with Wolves, which about dancing at all.

9 Statistics more difficult than Economics?

10 These new sunglasses made of glass or plastic or anything like that.

6 Choose an ending (a–e) for each beginning (1–5) and add appropriate forms of the verb be.

Example: The Simpsons ..... is .... (.f.)
1 Romeo and Juliet .... (...)
2 Last night's news .... (...)
3 Twenty-five kilos .... (...)
4 Billy as well as all his friends .... (...)
5 The audience .... (...)

a a lot to carry by yourself, don't you think?
b usually in their seats before the play starts.
c written by Shakespeare.
d going camping this weekend.
e rather exciting, I thought.
f the name of a television programme.

7 Complete each sentence with one of these words plus *has* or *have*.

committee darts ✓diabetes eggs everybody nobody orchestra police teachers

Example: ..Diabetes has.. become a more common disease, mainly because of the way we eat.
1 The conductor and the .... had very little time to rehearse for the concert.
2 Security is just something that .... to go through in airports nowadays.
3 .... from the new student group .... volunteered to help with the Christmas party.
4 The planning .... all been given individual copies of the agenda for the meeting.
5 .... always been a popular game in English pubs.
6 According to the rules, none of the .... the right to make students stay after school.
7 The .... no idea how the robbers got into the bank.
8 Bacon and .... been the Sunday breakfast in our house for years.

Verbs and objects

Verbs with objects (transitive verbs)

Transitive verbs have objects, usually noun phrases or pronouns.
  1 *He **kicked** a small stone. It **hit** me.* • *We **discussed** the problems. They **affected** all of us.*

We use a transitive verb to describe an action that affects an object (**2**) or to describe a feeling or experience caused by an object (**3**).
  2 *Are they **building** a wall?* • *I'll **cut** the grass.* • *Elizabeth **bought** an old Volkswagen.*
Others include: carry, catch, fix, heat, prepare, protect, rob, scratch, sell, trim
  3 *Did you **enjoy** the concert?* • *One of our old teachers **remembered** us.* • *I don't **like** onions.*
Others include: admire, believe, fear, hate, hear, love, need, please, prefer, receive

Only transitive verbs can be used in the passive.
  4 *Someone **stole** my bag.* → *My bag was stolen.* • *They **caught** the thief.* → *The thief was caught.*

We usually use a prepositional phrase after the object of a transitive verb such as *put*.
  5 *He **put** the keys <u>in the drawer</u>.* • *We **crammed** all our boxes <u>into the back of Jane's car</u>.*

Verbs without objects (intransitive verbs)

Intransitive verbs are used without an object.
  6 *I can't **sleep**.* • *Everyone was **waiting**, but he didn't **care**.* (NOT ~~He didn't care it.~~)
Others include: arrive, depart, disappear, happen, hesitate, occur, pause, rain

We use intransitive verbs when we talk about simple events, actions and sounds.
  7 *The roof **collapsed**.* • *She **sighed** and **yawned**.* • *A lot of people **were screaming**.*
Others include: cough, faint, fall, growl, moan, scream, shiver, sneeze

Intransitive verbs are not used in the passive.
  8 *The thief **escaped**.* (NOT ~~The thief was escaped. The police were escaped by the thief.~~)

We often use prepositional phrases after intransitive verbs (**9**), especially verbs describing movement (**10**).
  9 *Darwin **died** in 1882.* • *I **slept** until noon.* • *They are **kneeling** on mats and **praying** to God.*
  10 *It **came** from Argentina.* • *Let's **go** to bed.* • *We **walk** to the park and then we **run** round it.*

Verbs used with and without objects

We can use some verbs, such as *eat* or *read,* with objects (**11**) or without objects (**12**).
  11 *She **read** his note.* • *I don't **eat** fish.* • *We **won** the match.* • *Do you **speak** English?*
  12 *He always **reads** when he's **eating**.* • *Did you **win**?* • *She was so upset she couldn't **speak**.*
Others include: cook, draw, dress, drink, drive, hurt, paint, spread, study, write

There are some verbs, such as *die* or *smile,* that we usually use without an object (**13**), but which can also be used with one particular object (**14**).
  13 *Miss Reynolds **smiled** and said she was quite certain that none of us would ever **die**.*
  14 *Nina **smiled** her bright smile. She seemed unconcerned that she might **die** a painful death.*
Others include: dance, dream, laugh, live, sigh

We can use some verbs, such as *fight* or *meet,* with objects (**15**). We can also use them without objects after plural subjects when *each other* (**16**) or *with each other* (**17**) is understood.
  15 *When I **met** Sergio in Madrid, he **embraced** me like a brother.* • *John had to **fight** two thugs.*
  16 *We **met** in Rome.* • *Our fingers **touched**.* • *The old women **embraced**.* • *They **hugged** and **kissed**.*
  17 *John and I always **fight**.* • *Two of Australia's major wine producers **have merged**.*

8 Using a dictionary if necessary, complete these definitions with the nouns and appropriate forms of the verbs. Add the word *things* after any verb that needs an object.

hallucination	hinge		behave	close	go	seize
✓ hassle	holdall		carry	demand	pretend	swing
hijacker	hypocrite		✓ cause	✓ do	see	travel

Example: A ....*hassle*.... is something that is annoying because it ....*causes*.... problems or difficulties when you try to ..*do things*........

A (1) .... is a large soft bag in which you can (2) .... when you (3)

....

A (4) .... is a small piece of metal on which a door (5) .... as it opens and (6) ....

A (7) .... is a feeling or belief that you are (8) .... when nothing is there.

A (9) .... is a person who (10) .... to have high values that are not matched by the way he or she (11) ....

A (12) .... is a person who (13) .... control of a vehicle, especially an aircraft, in order to (14) .... to a new destination or to (15) .... from a government in return for the safety of those in the vehicle.

9 Choose an answer (a–d) for each question (1–4) and add appropriate forms of these verbs. If necessary, add the pronoun *it* and/or a preposition.

believe   go   hear   like   put   shiver   take   wait

1 Did Andreas .... the key? (...)
2 Do you .... old towns? (...)
3 Could you .... outside? (...)
4 Have you .... the latest rumour? (...)

a Yes, but I don't ....
b Yes, he .... his pocket.
c Yes, that's why I'm .... Edinburgh.
d No, it's too cold and I'm ....

10 Add the correct pair of intransitive verbs to each sentence. Use appropriate forms.

breathe / snore	✓ dream / sleep	eat / hibernate	fall / lie
get / move	go / sing	happen / talk	nap / rest

Example: When you .....*dream*....., you see and experience things while you are ....*sleeping*..... .

1 Someone who .... up and .... around while asleep is called a sleepwalker.

2 When people in hot countries .... or .... after lunch, it's called having a siesta.

3 Animals that .... don't .... at all while they spend the winter in a deep sleep.

4 When you .... awake at night and you can't .... asleep, you have insomnia.

5 If someone .... about a place as 'sleepy', it means that nothing much .... there.

6 When you .... softly to help a child .... to sleep, you are singing a lullaby.

7 People who .... very noisily when they are sleeping.

Verbs with indirect objects and clauses

Verbs with indirect objects

We use two objects after some verbs: an indirect object and a direct object. With a verb such as *send*, we can put the indirect object after the verb: (**1**) or after the preposition *to* (**2**). The indirect object (*you, Joe, everyone*) receives the direct object (*postcard, note, form*).
   1 *I'll send* **you** *a postcard.* • *She handed* **Joe** *the note.* • *Did you give* **everyone** *a form?*
   2 *I'll send a postcard* **to you.** • *She handed the note* **to Joe.** • *Did you give a form* **to everyone?**
Others include: bring, lend, offer, pass, post, read, sell, show, teach, tell, throw, write
We don't put *to* + indirect object before a direct object (NOT *Did you give to everyone a form?*)

With a verb such as *buy*, we can put the indirect object after the verb (**3**) or after the preposition *for* (**4**). The indirect object (*him, me, you*) benefits from the action of the verb (*buy, do, make*).
   3 *She bought* **him** *a tie.* • *Can you do* **me** *a favour?* • *I'll make* **you** *a sandwich.*
   4 *She bought a tie* **for him.** • *Can you do a favour* **for me?** • *I'll make a sandwich* **for you.**
Others include: build, cook, cut, draw, fetch, find, get, keep, leave, order, pick, save
We don't put *for* + indirect object before a direct object (NOT *I'll make for you a sandwich.*)

We put shorter objects, especially pronouns, before longer objects (**5**). When we use pronouns for both objects after the verb, we put the indirect object pronoun first (**6**).
   5 *Show* **me** *the prize you won.* • *Show* **it** *to everyone who said you couldn't do it.* • *Show* **it** *to them!*
   6 *Show* **me** *it.* (NOT *Show it me.*) • *I'll make* **you** *one.* (NOT *I'll make one you.*)

With verbs such as *describe* or *explain*, we put the indirect object after a preposition, not after the verb. But compare (**14**) below.
   7 *He described the man* **to them.** • *He explained the plan* **to us.** (NOT *He explained us the plan.*)
Others include: admit, announce, mention, murmur, report, shout, suggest, whisper
Note that these are often verbs of speaking: *He said 'Hello'* **to me.** (NOT *He said me 'Hello'.*)

With a verb such as *cost*, we must put the indirect object after the verb.
   8 *The mistake cost* **us** *a lot of money.* • *They fined* **him** *£250.* • *I bet* **you** *£5.* (NOT *I bet £5 to you.*)
Others include: deny, forgive, grudge, refuse

Verbs with clauses

We can use *that*-clauses as direct objects after 'thinking' verbs such as *believe* or *think* (**9**) and after 'reporting' verbs such as *explain* or *say* (**10**).
   9 *They believed that the sun went round the earth.* • *He thinks that the students are lazy.*
  10 *She said that she would be late.* • *He explained that there was no money left.*
Note that the word *that* is often omitted: *He thinks the students are lazy.*

After verbs reporting questions, we can begin the clause with *if, whether* (**11**) or a *wh*-word (**12**).
  11 *The teacher asked if anyone was absent.* • *They enquired whether it was legal or not.*
  12 *We should ask what it costs.* • *I wonder when they'll make the decision.*

After reporting verbs such as *remind* or *tell*, we must have an indirect object before the clause.
  13 *I'll remind* **him** *that you're here.* • *You told* **me** *that he was ill.* (NOT *You told that he was ill.*)
Others include: assure, convince, inform, notify, persuade

After a reporting verb such as *admit*, we must use *to* before an indirect object before a clause.
  14 *He admitted* **to the police** *that he had stolen the money.* (NOT *He admitted the police that he had stolen the money.*)
     She mentioned **to me** *that she hated her job.* (NOT *She mentioned me that she hated her job.*)
Others include: boast, confess, declare, hint, propose, reveal

11 Complete each sentence in such a way that it is as similar as possible in meaning to the sentence or sentences before it.

Example: They had it. Now we have it. → .....They gave *it to us.*.... (OR .....They gave *us it.*....)

1 She quietly wished him, 'Good luck.'

She whispered ....

2 She was ordered by the judge to pay £500 for speeding.

The judge fined ....

3 The farmer wouldn't give permission to us to walk across his field.

The farmer refused ....

4 James took Caroline's book. He told me.

James confessed ....

12 Using a dictionary if necessary, complete these sentences with appropriate forms of these verbs. Add appropriate pronouns and prepositions if necessary.

| *find* | *offer* | *reserve* | *sell* | *spread* | *transmit* |
| *keep* | *require* | *retrieve* | ✓*send* | *transfer* | ✓*transport* |

Example: Your boxes will be ... transported ... by air. We will .. send them to .. you soon.

1 In a restaurant, if a table is ...., that means the restaurant is .... a special person or group.

2 Contagious diseases are easily .... People with contagious diseases can easily .... the rest of the population.

3 Those computer files that I thought I had lost were .... by Andrew. I was so glad that he .... me.

4 In football, when a player is ...., it means that one team .... another team.

5 In a university, if certain courses are ...., it means that all students must take those courses and the university must .... students every year.

13 Editing. Correct the mistakes in this text.

During the psychology class, one student reported u̶s̶ her experiment. ^to us She explained us that it was about communication between husbands and wives. The researcher gave the following information half of the husbands. 'Your wife has described you a holiday trip to China. One of her friends told to her about it. You think sounds like a really good idea, so you ask to her some questions about the cost.' The other group of husbands heard the following information. 'Your wife has suggested you a holiday trip to China. You don't like. You believe is a really bad idea, so you ask some questions her about the cost.' The researcher didn't tell to the wives she said to the husbands. She asked the wives to listen to the tape recording of their husbands' questions and decide the husbands thought it was a good idea or not. A significant number of the wives couldn't decide. That was very surprising.

Linking verbs

Linking verbs and complements

Linking verbs, such as *be* or *seem*, are followed by a complement that describes or identifies the subject of the sentence. Complements can be adjectives (**1**), noun phrases (**2**) or prepositional phrases (**3**).

1 *His parents **were Welsh**.* • *That **isn't funny**! • It doesn't **seem possible**. • You **sound unhappy**.*
2 *I **am a student**. • Anna **became my best friend**. • Despite the scandal, he **remained president**.*
3 *She said she **was on a diet**. • He **seemed in a good mood**. • Sometimes I **feel like an idiot**.*

Linking verbs are also called copulas or copular verbs.

We can use *seem* and *appear* as linking verbs with an infinitive and a complement (**4**). We can also use *seem* with or without *to be* before complements (**5**). *Seem* is less formal than *appear*.

4 *Bill **seems** to have no friends. • There **appears** to be a problem.* (NOT ~~There appears a problem.~~)
5 *The old man **seemed** (to be) lost. • Equal pay for everyone **seems** (to be) the best solution.*

In American English, *to be* is not left out after *seem*: *He seemed to be a hard-working student.*

We can use verbs describing our sense experiences (*feel, smell, taste*) or our opinions (*look, sound*) as linking verbs with adjectives (**6**) or with *like* before noun phrases (**7**).

6 *I **feel** great! • You **look** much better. • The food didn't **smell** good and it **tasted** terrible.*
7 *Her suggestion **sounded like** a good idea. • Your drawing **looks like** a cat.* (NOT ~~Your drawing looks a cat.~~)

With some verbs (*make, find, call*) we can use adjectives and noun phrases as complements after the objects to describe or add information about the objects.

8 *That **makes** me angry. • They **found** the exam difficult. • She **called** him a fool.*

Note the word order: *Let's paint the wall white.* (NOT ~~Let's paint white the wall.~~)

Linking verbs used to express change

We use *become* and *get* as linking verbs to talk about the result of change.

9 *The world is **becoming/getting** more crowded. • Everything will **get** worse before it **gets** better.*

We can use *become* (not *get*) as a linking verb with noun complements (**10**) and *get* (not *become*) in many common phrases describing actions (**11**). *Get* is less formal than *become*.

10 *Traffic delays **have become** a problem. • We **became** friends.* (NOT ~~We became to be friends.~~)
11 *They won't **get** married. • He **got** dressed quickly. • Let's **get** ready.* (NOT ~~Let's become ready.~~)

We can use *go* and *turn* to talk about change (**12**). We use *turn into* before a noun phrase for a complete change of state (**13**).

12 *I'll **go** crazy if I have to wait. • Our dog **is going** blind. • She **turned** pale. • The light **turned** green.*
13 *Joe **turned into** a maniac. • The caterpillar **turned into** a butterfly.* (NOT ~~The caterpillar turned a butterfly.~~)

We use *come* and *grow* as linking verbs with adjectives in phrases that usually express slower change, unless modified by adverbs such as *suddenly* or *unexpectedly* (**14**). We can use *come* and *grow* before infinitives to describe gradual change (**15**).

14 *Dreams **come** true. • People **grow** old. • The days **grew** warmer. • The knot suddenly **came** loose.*
15 *As we **came to know** her better, we **grew to like** her a lot. We **came to see** things as she did.*

We use some verbs (*keep, remain, stay*) as linking verbs to talk about a situation not changing.

16 *Please **keep** quiet. • She **kept** busy. • Everything **remained** the same. • We tried to **stay** warm.*

Note that these verbs are not used with *to be*. (NOT ~~I'll keep to be quiet. We stayed to be awake.~~)

Adjectives 111   Infinitives 139   Passives with *get* 65

14 Choose an answer (a–f) for each question (1–6) and add the linking verbs below. Use the appropriate form.

appear   be   feel   look   sound   taste

1 What .... he like? (...)
2 Who does she .... like? (...)
3 How does it .... ? (...)
4 Did he .... to be happy? (...)
5 How did he .... ? (...)
6 Does it .... fishy? (...)

a Angry and impatient.
b I'm sure he was smiling.
c No, it's more like chicken.
d He's kind and generous.
e Soft and comfortable.
f The actress Meg Ryan.

15 Complete each paragraph with appropriate forms of the verbs from one group.

appear / be / look / turn   ✓seem / smell / taste / ✓think
become / get / make / seem   feel / get / stay / turn

A The writer of the guide book seemed to think that the Maharani restaurant had the best Indian food. In her description, she wrote, 'All the dishes were full of fragrance and flavour.' In other words, she thought the food (1) .... wonderful and (2) .... delicious.

B In her late teens, Diana fell in love with Jim Covington and wanted to (3) .... married, but that topic always (4) .... him uncomfortable. To her intense disappointment, he later decided to (5) .... a priest.

C Elena was reading a novel with a red dragon on the cover. It (6) .... like a large lizard with wings. The novel was a horror story, she said, full of people who (7) .... living normal lives, but were actually vampires, and one character who (8) .... into a werewolf during the night of a full moon.

D I didn't want the bananas to (9) .... too ripe and then (10) .... soft or squishy when I wanted to eat them, so I put them in the fridge. I was just hoping that they would (11) .... firm, but I didn't realize that the skins would (12) .... black.

16 Editing. Correct the mistakes in the use of linking verbs in this text.

One Saturday afternoon when my younger sister Mona and I were teenagers, I was ~~becoming~~ *getting* ready to go to a party. Mona hadn't been invited. It appeared a big problem for her. She went to be crazy because of it. She found some hair-colouring and she just decided to make blonde her hair, but she didn't do it right and her hair turned into bright orange. It also became orange her face, so she looked like really strange. When my mother saw her, she said Mona looked an orange balloon. After that, Mona got to be very upset and she started screaming with her hands over her ears. I just kept to be quiet during all that. My mother eventually calmed her down and we got some darker hair-colour to make it look like better.

Compound and complex sentences

17 Write the numbers of appropriate examples in the spaces.

Compound sentences

A compound sentence has two 2 or more 1 clauses joined by coordinating conjunctions: *and, but, or.*
1 *You can take the bus **or** stay here **and** I'll drive you tomorrow, **but** I'm not driving tonight.*
2 *Dave slept **and** I read. • It wasn't cold, **but** I was shivering. • You must help us **or** we will fail.*

We usually leave out the same subject ☐, the same subject + verb ☐ or the same subject + auxiliary from later clauses in a compound sentence.
3 *They played well, but … lost. (They played well, but they lost.) • Martin smiled, … shrugged his shoulders and … said nothing. (Martin smiled, he shrugged his shoulders and he said nothing.)*
4 *She will come and … get those later. • You can take it or … leave it. • I am waiting and … hoping.*
5 *They have a cat or … a dog. • I like swimming, … football and … watching TV.*
Leaving out the subject and/or other parts of the sentence is called ellipsis.

We usually leave out the same verb + object after an auxiliary verb in later clauses ☐, but we prefer to leave out repeated objects and/or prepositional phrases from the first clause ☐.
6 *I'll wash … and peel the potatoes. • McGregors have lived … and died in Crieff for centuries.*
7 *I wasn't making a noise and the others were … • They may forget you, but I never will …*

We can emphasize the relationship between two clauses in compound sentences by using different combinations of conjunctions. They can express an addition ☐, an alternative ☐, a combination ☐ or a combination of negatives ☐.
8 *They **not only** clean houses, **but also** do repairs, painting and other odd jobs.*
9 *You can **both** turn the TV on **and** change channels with the remote control.*
10 *I will **neither** sleep **nor** rest until this is over. • He **neither** speaks English **nor** understands it.*
11 *You can **either** go with us **or** stay here alone. • They must **either** pay you **or** give you time off.*

Complex sentences

We create complex sentences by joining two or more clauses with subordinating conjunctions such as *because, before, that, which,* etc.
12 *I couldn't sleep **because** I was thinking about all the work **that** I had to do **before** I could leave.*
Note that the same subject is repeated. (NOT ~~I couldn't sleep because was thinking.~~)
Others include: although, as, if, in order that, since, when, who

Complex sentences contain relative clauses ☐, noun clauses ☐, and adverbial clauses ☐. We can put adverbial clauses, followed by a comma, at the beginning of complex sentences ☐.
13 *I didn't realize **that Brian wasn't feeling well**. • Did you know **that he was married**?*
14 *She liked the women **with whom she worked**, but she hated the dirty jobs **which they had to do**.*
15 *I had a shower **after I ran**. • He's still working **although he's 72**. • We won't play **if it rains**.*
16 ***If it rains**, the ground will be too muddy. • **Although he's 72**, he still walks to work every day.*

Compound-complex sentences

We form compound-complex sentences with three or more clauses joined by both coordinating and subordinating conjunctions.
17 *We hit a lamp post **and** it shattered the glass on the front door **before** I managed to bring the bus to a halt.*
18 *Harvold said, 'I was so relieved **that** no one else was hurt, **but** I hoped the driver would survive.'*

Adverbial clauses 197 *Either/Neither* 89 Ellipsis 106 Noun clauses 161 Relative clauses 173

18 Choose an ending (a–d) for each beginning (1–4) and add the conjunctions *and*, *but* or *or*.

1 You can leave now (....)   a .... she can also read .... write it.
2 He says he needs a knife (....)   b .... dries them straight away.
3 She not only speaks Arabic, (....)   c .... stay .... help us finish the job.
4 Bob usually washes the dishes (....)   d .... scissors to open the package.

19 Complete these sentences with a verb or subject + verb from below.

came	got	had	seemed	stopped	talked
she came	*he got*	*we had*	*it seemed*	*it stopped*	*we talked*

1 Police allowed protests outside the meeting, but .... people trying to get inside.
2 When .... about religion or politics, ... very excited.
3 After .... home from her trip, we sat and .... for hours.
4 .... easier in the past because people just met, ... married and .... kids.
5 If she got up early enough and .... downstairs, ... breakfast together.
6 The dog ran over to the door where .... and .... to be waiting for us to open it.

20 Complete the definitions with these nouns and conjunctions.

✓heartache	heartbeat	heartburn		*and* (×2)	*because*	*or*	*who*
heart attack	heartbreak	heart-throb		*as*	✓*or*	*which* (×2)	*whom*

Example: A ....heartache.... is a feeling of great sorrow, anxiety ....or........ worry.
Your (1) .... is the action (2) .... sound of your heart
(3) .... it pumps blood through your body.
(4) .... is a feeling of great sadness (5) .... something bad has happened, such as the end of a love affair or the loss of a life.
A (6) .... is a famous actor or singer (7) .... is very attractive
(8) .... with (9) .... people fall in love.
A (10) .... is a sudden illness in (11) .... the heart beats violently.
It causes great pain (12) .... sometimes death.
(13) .... is a burning sensation in the chest (14) .... is caused by indigestion.

21 Add the conjunctions and appropriate forms of the verbs to this description.

and	*because*	*but*	*if*	*which*
who	*live*	*not like*	*see*	*tell*

A Neighbourhood Watch is an arrangement by
(1) .... people (2) ....
(3) .... in a particular street or area watch each
other's houses (4) .... (5) .... the
police (6) .... they (7) .... anything
suspicious. Many people have formed local Neighbourhood
Watch groups to try to prevent crime, (8) ....
others have refused to join them (9) .... they
(10) .... the idea of being watched by their
neighbours.

Tests

A Choose the word or phrase that best completes each sentence.

1 He couldn't rest or sleep because _____ too much coffee.

   a drinking   b been drinking   c had been drinking   d he had been drinking

2 My brother, together with his friends, always _____ round collecting wood for bonfire night.

   a go   b goes   c going   d gone

3 Some of the girls in my group tease me because I don't wear makeup, but I don't

   _____ .

   a wear   b care   c do   d like

4 The team all wanted coffee so I made _____ .

   a it them   b some it   c some them   d them some

5 The director _____ to us that there had been financial problems earlier in the year.

   a concluded   b offered   c revealed   d told

B Identify the one underlined expression (A, B, C or D) that must be changed in order to correct the sentence.

1 The tour of the palace <u>included</u> a visit to the old kitchen where they <u>were baking</u> bread and the
                   A   B
   huge underground wine cellar which <u>was containing</u> thousands of bottles and <u>felt</u> like a prison.
                                            C   D

2 None of the children <u>wants</u> to be in the group that <u>has</u> to stay inside because everyone <u>prefer</u>
                           A   B   C
   to go outside and <u>play</u>.
                        D

3 The old ladies <u>were collecting money</u> for people who <u>needed some help</u> at Christmas so,
                           A   B
   after my wife and I <u>discussed it</u>, we decided to <u>put £5 their collection box</u>.
                            C   D

4 Elaine <u>handed Dick the letter</u> that someone had <u>sent her</u> and told him to <u>read it to me</u>,
                    A   B   C
   but I asked him to <u>show it me</u> because I wanted to see the signature.
                          D

5 When Fox <u>became president</u>, this <u>seemed to be</u> the first thing that <u>made happy</u> all the young
                        A   B   C
   people, especially those who had <u>felt angry</u> with the old government leaders.
                                            D

C Complete this text with appropriate forms of the verbs. Add the other words in the appropriate places.

begin   catch   give   include   sneeze   fever   in November   it   the flu

Anyone who has a history of health problems and people who are 50 or older should get a flu vaccination every year before the flu season (1) _____ . Flu, or influenza, is a serious infection of the nose, throat and lungs. Symptoms (2) _____ , cough, runny nose, sore throat, headache and tiredness. Anyone can (3) _____ and
(4) _____ to others. It is spread when an infected person coughs or
(5) _____ .

D Complete each sentence in such a way that it is as similar as possible in meaning to the sentence above it.

1 Nick told one of the detectives that he had taken the cashbox.
   Nick admitted _____
2 The police said it was too dangerous and we were convinced.
   The police persuaded _____
3 After the princess kissed the frog, he suddenly became a prince.
   The frog suddenly turned _____
4 Two hours won't be enough to finish the job, he said to us.
   He told _____
5 The wall is white. Someone did it yesterday.
   Someone painted _____

E Complete this text with appropriate forms of the verbs plus a complement in each space.

be (×2)   become   seem   stand   alone   better   clear   quite satisfied   ready

Donald's presence certainly made a big difference to the speed we arose that day. There was no question of Tam lounging about in bed until the last minute, and we (1) _____ for work by half past seven. Donald had his own map of the job, with all the fences marked out in red ink, and the first thing he did was go for a tour of inspection, accompanied by me. We followed the hill up to the summit, and then came down by way of the cross-fence, Donald all the time checking for wire tension and, of course, straightness. When we got to the encircling fence he
(2) _____ with what he'd seen.
'Hmm, quite professional,' he said.
After a while we came to the gateway that (3) _____ . Donald looked at it for a moment, and then said, 'Yes, I always think it (4) _____ to do the gate first and build the fences round it.'
Donald had put on some overalls, and it soon (5) _____ that he intended to work alongside us during his visit.

2 Tenses

Tense is the relationship between the form of the verb and the time of the action or state it describes. We often use the auxiliary verbs *be* and *have* with other verbs when we form different tenses. See page 17 for a table of English verb forms and tenses.

1 Read through this text and find:

1 another sentence with *be* as a main verb

2 a sentence with *be* and a sentence with *have* as auxiliary verbs

A | This October 31st is a scary day for Dylan Barnes, not just because it is Halloween, but because it is a special anniversary for him. | For several years he will have been trying to turn a good idea into a
5 successful business via the Internet. He won't be doing anything special to celebrate the occasion, mainly because his business venture won't have made any money for most of the past year. Like his two business partners before him, he will soon need
10 to do something else.
B When they started, it had seemed like such a great idea. Dylan and his friend, Michael Underwood, had been writing up their lecture notes as complete sets, with review sheets and sample tests, and selling them
15 to other students. They had used that money to pay for complete sets of notes from other big lecture classes, which they then sold to an eager population of new students. They were starting to make a small steady profit when they met Terry Lloyd. Terry had
20 been creating home pages for his friends, then larger websites on the Internet, and he showed them how to do it too. Using the initials of their last names, they created 'Bullnotes', established a website, and set out to become entrepreneurs of the information age.
C They soon found that students were looking for more than lecture notes. They needed to do other things that they weren't learning in their classes. Imagine that you are applying for a scholarship. You have been trying to write a letter of application and you
30 can't get it right. You need an example of the kind of letter you are trying to write. Or maybe someone has asked you to write a letter of recommendation. From the website you could download the basic form of the letter with spaces in it for your

> . . . everyone wants these things, but no one wants to pay for them.

35 own details. 'I am writing this letter in support of
. . . . whom I have known for
. . . . years', and so on.
D Soon there were all kinds of forms available from
40 Bullnotes, from passport application forms to those for making a will. Dylan was working day and night to make the material available, but he didn't think about what he was doing in terms of a business. The big problem, they soon discovered, is that everyone
45 wants these things, but no one wants to pay for them. In what turned out to be a common experience for many people who tried to create Internet businesses, they had a successful website, but they didn't really make any money from it.
50 E Terry quickly found a highly paid job with an investment company and Michael went off to work for a software manufacturer. Dylan is still looking for a way to make Bullnotes work as a business, but these days he is always counting his pennies and he
55 is having a hard time paying his bills. He has thought about taking a teaching job after seeing an ad for a teacher of business writing with business experience. He has lots of experience now and there really won't be a problem with the letter of application.

2 Choose one of the following as the final sentence of each of the paragraphs (A–E) above.

1 They were ready to become millionaires. (...)
2 He also knows where to find some good lecture notes. (...)
3 Everyone acted as if the information was free. (...)
4 He will have to find a job. (...)
5 Writing was a couple of clicks, then a fill-in-the-blanks exercise. (...)

Verbs, auxiliary verbs and tenses

The base form of the verb is listed in the dictionary. It is used in the imperative and the infinitive.
  1 **Stop!** • Please **wait**. • Don't **be** impatient. • **Ask** someone to **help** you. • Let's **try** to **find** a solution.
The base form is also called the bare infinitive or the infinitive without *to*.

Most verbs are used to describe actions or events (2). Some verbs are used for states (3).
  2 Do you **play** chess? • I'll **open** a window. • Someone has **taken** my book. • The crowd is **cheering**.
  3 Do you **know** Mark? • Anil **seems** really nice. • Her parents **own** a shop. • I **believe** you.
We don't usually use state verbs in the continuous form. (NOT ~~I'm believing you.~~)

We use auxiliary *do* with the base form to make questions and negatives in the present and past simple.
  4 What **did** Ann **want** for lunch? ~ She **didn't want** anything. • **Does** she **feel** better? ~ I **don't know**.

We use auxiliary *be* with the present participle (*-ing* form) of the verb to make continuous forms (5) and auxiliary *have* with the past participle (*-ed*) to make perfect forms (6). We use auxiliary *have* + *been* with the present participle to make perfect continuous forms (7).
  5 **Are** you **waiting** for me? • William **isn't using** his computer. • They **were working** all night.
  6 **Have** you **finished** already? • The post **hasn't come** yet. • Andy **had forgotten** to bring the keys.
  7 **Have** you **been sleeping**? • It **hasn't been raining** recently. • We **had been studying** for hours.
The continuous form is also called the progressive.

We use modal auxiliaries (modals) with the base form of the verb or with the auxiliaries *be* and *have*.
  8 They **will help** us. • I'll **be waiting** for you. • We **won't have finished**. (NOT ~~We won't finished.~~)

---

3 Complete this table with one example of each form from the text on page 16.

Imperative or infinitive: base form	*play* ....
Present simple: base form or base form + *s* in third person singular	*play* .... *plays* ....
Present continuous: present *be* + present participle	*am/is/are playing* ....
Present perfect: present *have* + past participle	*has/have played* ....
Present perfect continuous: present *have* + *been* + present participle	*has/have been playing* ....
Past simple: base form + *ed*	*played* ....
Past continuous: past *be* + present participle	*was/were playing* ....
Past perfect: past *have* + past participle	*had played* ....
Past perfect continuous: past *have* + *been* + present participle	*had been playing* ....
Future: *will* + base form	*will play* ....
Future continuous: *will* + *be* + present participle	*will be playing* ....
Future perfect: *will* + *have* + past participle	*will have played* ....
Future perfect continuous: *will* + *have* + *been* + present participle	*will have been playing* ....

For information about irregular verb forms see pages 286–7.

Present and present perfect

Present simple and present continuous

We use the present simple for permanent situations (1) and things that are generally true (2).

1. *Giraffes **live** in Africa. They **have** very long legs and necks. They **feed** on acacia leaves.*
2. *It **rains** more in winter. • Birds **don't sing** at night. • **Do** women **live** longer than men?*

We also use the present simple for habits (3), things that happen regularly (4), with verbs that describe current states (5) and in informal reports or instructions (6).

3. *I **bite** my nails. • She **smokes** cigars. • **Does** he usually **wear** white socks with black shoes?*
4. *They **play** bingo on Monday nights. • Her parents **go** to Majorca every summer.*
5. *She **loves** chocolate. • They **don't believe** us. • He **owns** his flat.* (NOT ~~He is owning his flat.~~)
6. *It **says** here the strike is over. • Baker **passes** to Cook who **shoots**. • You **go** to the end and **turn** left.*

When we perform an action by speaking, for example when we promise to do something, we usually use the present simple, not the present continuous.

7. *I **accept** their decision. • I **promise** to be more careful.* (NOT ~~I'm promising to be more careful.~~)
Other verbs used like this include: admit, apologize, bet, deny, insist, regret

We use the present continuous for actions in progress or to talk about being in the middle of an activity.

8. *Hi. I**'m calling** to let you know I**'m coming**, but it**'s snowing** and the traffic **is moving** slowly.*

We can describe current situations as permanent with the present simple (9) or as temporary with the present continuous (10).

9. *My brother Alan **lives** in London and **works** for a magazine. He **writes** about economics.*
10. *My sister Fiona **is living** with Alan just now. She **isn't working** yet. She**'s looking** for a job.*

We can use *be* and *have* in the present simple for a typical situation or state (11) and in the present continuous for a temporary or special situation (12).

11. *Wendy**'s** normally a quiet person. She **has** a gentle voice.* (NOT ~~She's having a gentle voice.~~)
12. *Wendy**'s being** wild tonight. She**'s having** a graduation party.* (NOT ~~She has a party.~~)

Present perfect and present perfect continuous

We use the present perfect to talk about or describe an action or situation started in the past which connects to the present (13), when we mean 'at any point up to now' (14) and with state verbs (15).

13. *How long **have** you **worked** here? ~ I**'ve worked** here since 1997.* (NOT ~~I work here since 1997.~~)
14. *This is the best coffee I **have** ever **tasted**. • I **haven't been** to an opera, but I**'ve seen** one on TV.*
15. *I **have known** Tony for about five years.* (NOT ~~I know him for five years. / I've been knowing him for five years.~~)

We use the present perfect continuous when we talk about an activity in progress up to the present (16) and to ask about or describe actions which go on over a period of time up to the present (17).

16. *They**'ve been repairing** our street and it**'s been causing** a lot of traffic problems.*
17. ***Have** you **been waiting** long? ~ I**'ve been sitting** here for an hour.* (NOT ~~Are you waiting long?~~)

We use the present perfect continuous to describe something as if it is a continuous action up to the present (18) and the present perfect to describe it as a series of separate actions (19).

18. *He**'s been calling** for you. • It **has been raining** a lot recently.* (NOT ~~It's raining a lot recently.~~)
19. *He **has called** four times and he **has asked** for you each time.* (NOT ~~He has been calling four times.~~)

We can describe an action as a process going on from earlier up to the present (present perfect continuous) (20) or as the present result of an earlier action (present perfect) (21).

20. *We**'ve been making** chicken soup. That's why the kitchen is hot and steamy.*
21. *We**'ve made** chicken soup. That's what everyone is eating. Would you like some?*

4 Complete each paragraph with one set of verbs, using the present simple or present continuous.

know / look / not be / repair / use   be / be / have / say / tell   be / live / look / move / resemble

A   My computer (1) .... very irritating right now. Every time I (2) ....
it to save something, it (3) .... it (4) .... no space in its memory,
which (5) .... ridiculous.

B   Whales and dolphins (6) .... like fish, but they (7) .... mammals
that (8) .... in the ocean and (9) .... through water in ways that
(10) .... the movements of a dog rather than those of a shark.

C   Man: Excuse me. I (11) .... for Mrs Adamson, but she (12) .... in
her usual classroom. (13) .... you .... where she is?
Woman: Oh, they (14) .... her classroom ceiling this week so she
(15) .... the library as her classroom.

5 Using a dictionary if necessary, complete these sentences with the nouns and the verbs in the present perfect.

| *also-ran* | *hat-trick* | *buy* | *not come* | *say* | *train* |
| *has-been* | *no-show* | *hear* | *not finish* | *take* | *win* |

1   Colin .... the race for the second year in a row and he .... that he
will come back and try to make it a .... next year.

2   An '....................' is an informal expression for a person or a horse that ....
part in a competition or a race, but .... first, second or third.

3   Wilson says he .... people describe him negatively as a '....................', but
he .... hard this year to prove that he's still one of the best.

4   A '....................' is an informal expression for someone who .... a ticket for
an event, a journey, etc., but who .... to the event.

6 Choose an answer (a–d) for each question (1–4) and add these verbs in the present perfect or the present perfect continuous.

be   complete   do   know   read   show   swim

1   How long .... she and Mark ....
each other? (...)
2   Why is your hair all wet? (...)
3   .... you .... an application form? (...)
4   .... you .... Keith the report yet? (...)

a   Yes, he .... it for the past hour.
b   I .... just ....
c   They .... friends since school.
d   Yes, I .... already .... that.

7 Editing. Correct the mistakes in this text.

My neighbour is called Jeanine. She ~~is coming~~ ^comes^ from Belgium. She is living here since 1995 and she
says she has been going back to visit her family in Belgium only once. She's having an accent that is
the same as people who are coming from France, but I never ask her if she is speaking French. She is
really liking to go to the theatre and she is inviting me to go with her one Saturday. In the short time
I am knowing her, we become good friends.

Past and past perfect

Past simple and past continuous

We use the past simple for completed actions in the past (1) and past states (2).

1 *Dickens **wrote** Oliver Twist.* • *Edison **invented** the light bulb.* • *The Beatles **sang** 'Yesterday'.*
2 *Life **seemed** easier then.* • *That ring **belonged** to my mother.* (NOT ~~It was belonging to my mother.~~)

We use the past simple for two or more past actions in sequence, especially in narrative.

3 *I **tripped** and **landed** on my knees.* • *He **knocked** her down, **grabbed** her purse and **ran** off.* •
*He **took** off his hat and **came** forward. The floorboards **creaked** under his boots.*

To talk about habits in the past or to make a stronger contrast with the present, we can use the form *used to* (4). The negative is *didn't use to* or (more formally) *used not to* (5). We can also use *would* to talk about typical actions or activities during a period in the past (6).

4 *There **used to be** a shop on the corner.* • *He **used to smoke** a lot.* (NOT ~~He was used to smoke a lot.~~)
5 ***Didn't** they **use to hang** people?* • *We **didn't use to have** a car.* • *They **used not to be** enemies.*
6 *In summer, we **would take** trips to the country. We **would** sometimes **buy** fresh strawberries.*

We use the past continuous to describe actions in progress at a specific time in the past.

7 *What **were** you **doing** at 8.30 last night? ~ I **wasn't doing** anything special. I **was** just reading.* •
*During the 1890s, many people **were leaving** the south and **moving** to the north to look for work.*

We can use the past continuous with some verbs (*wonder, hope*) to make a request more polite.

8 *I **was wondering** when I could talk to you.* • *We **were hoping** you might have a free moment.*

We can use the past simple when we want to describe a past activity as a series of separate actions (9) and the past continuous to describe the past activity as if it was a continuous action (10). In many cases, the past simple and past continuous can be used interchangeably.

9 *Usually she **went** to the library about once a week and only **studied** occasionally for tests.*
10 *Before the final exam, however, she **was going** to the library and **studying** every single day.*

In sentences with *when-* and *while-*clauses, we can use the past continuous to describe an activity in one clause that starts before an action in another clause (11). The activity that starts later may interrupt the first activity (12).

11 *While he **was driving**, I **fell** asleep.* • *We **saw** Henry while we **were walking** in the park.*
12 *I **was listening** to the news when she **phoned**.* • *When I **was running**, I **slipped** and **fell**.*

Note the difference between *When she came back, we were watching TV* (= We were watching before she came back) and *When she came back, we watched TV* (= We watched after she came back).

Past perfect and past perfect continuous

We use the past perfect (or pluperfect) when we are describing an action with the past simple and we want to refer to an action further in the past (13). We also use the past perfect for earlier events after clauses with reporting or thinking verbs in the past (14).

13 *We went to his office, but he **had left**.* • *Susan didn't have the money because she **had spent** it.*
14 *Joe told me our team **had scored** twice.* • *I thought we **had won**.* (NOT ~~I thought we have won.~~)

We use the past perfect continuous for events in progress before another event in the past.

15 *I **had been thinking** about that before you mentioned it.*

State verbs are not used in this way. (NOT ~~I had been knowing about that before you mentioned it.~~)

We can describe an action as a process going on before a past event (past perfect continuous) (16). We can also describe it as the result of an action before a past event (past perfect) (17).

16 *We **had been making** chicken soup so the kitchen was still hot and steamy when she came in.*
17 *We **had made** chicken soup and so we offered her some when she came in.*

Reporting verbs 152 State verbs 3 *When-* and *while*-clauses 198 *Would* 33

8 Complete each paragraph with one set of verbs, using the past simple or past continuous.

miss / not get / wonder   break / see / steal / teach
come / listen / make / say   explain / talk / understand

A We (1) .... to music when one of the neighbours (2) .... to the door and (3) .... she couldn't sleep because we (4) .... too much noise.

B Someone (5) .... into Barbara's office and (6) .... her computer yesterday afternoon while she (7) .... her history class. No one (8) .... the thief.

C Because he never (9) .... anything very clearly, none of us (10) .... what the science teacher (11) .... about most of the time.

D I'm sorry. I (12) .... here on time and I (13) .... the beginning of your presentation, but I (14) .... if you might have an extra handout left.

9 Complete this text with these verbs in the past perfect or past perfect continuous.

be   catch   live   plan   take
break   have   make   remove   worry

The telephone call from the police was a shock, but not a complete surprise. Molly (1) .... constantly about the old house lying empty during the two months since her mother went into hospital. She (2) .... to go round and check the empty place, but she (3) .... extra busy at work recently. According to the police, a homeless man (4) .... into the house. They (5) .... him one morning as he was leaving the building with one of her mother's large paintings. When Molly walked into the house, it was obvious that the man (6) .... there for quite a while. He (7) .... food from the cupboards and throwing empty tins and packages all over the floor. He (8) .... quite a mess. He (9) .... also .... several paintings from the walls. Molly decided not to tell her mother because she (10) .... already .... enough pain in recent weeks and really didn't need any more bad news.

10 Editing. Correct the mistakes in the use of tenses in this text.

A few years ago, when my friend and I were ~~hitchhike~~ hitchhiking through France, we sometimes stop for the night in a park or a field. If it wasn't rain, we just sleep outside in our sleeping bags under the stars. We really enjoying that. If it was rain, we put up our small tent and crawl inside for the night. One night, while we sleep in the tent, I think that the ground moving under me. I sit up and I realize that the tent was try to move and only the weight of our bodies was hold it in place. When we get outside, we discover that we stand ankle-deep in a small stream and our tent slowly floats away. At first, we really surprised and worried, but then we think it is very funny.

Present perfect or past simple?

We use the present perfect when we think a situation has not ended (1) and the past simple when we think the situation ended (2).

1 *I **have lived** in London for a year.* • *She **has known** him since school.* • ***Has** Jason **been** ill?*
2 *I **lived** in London for a year.* • *She **knew** him in school.* • ***Was** Jason ill?*

We use the present perfect with time expressions for a period up to now (*lately, so far*) (3). We use the past simple with time expressions for a period that ended earlier (*last night, yesterday*) (4).

3 ***Have** you **seen** any good films lately?* • *So far the new teacher **hasn't given** us any homework.*
4 ***Did** you **see** that film last night?* • *I **didn't do** the homework yesterday.*
(NOT *Have you seen that film last night? I haven't done the homework yesterday.*)

We use the present perfect when we are talking about actions up to the present which might happen again (5) and the past simple for actions which we don't think will happen again (6).

5 *He **has written** two bestsellers and we hope his next book will do well.* • *He's **been** on TV; he's famous!* • *He **has** often **had** health problems.*
6 *She **wrote** several books of poetry in the last years of her life.* • *She **was** a teacher in Zambia.* • *She **had** three children.*

In clauses beginning with *after, as soon as* and *when*, we can use the present perfect for completed actions in the future (7) and the past simple for completed actions in the past (8).

7 *After/As soon as/When he **has made** his copies, I <u>will do</u> mine.* (= He hasn't made his copies yet. Neither have I.)
8 *As soon as he **made** his copies, I <u>did</u> mine.* (= He made his copies first, then I made mine.)

11 Complete each paragraph with one set of verbs, using the present perfect or past simple.

have / not come / tell   become / have / hear   know / meet / start

A I (1) .... Laura Palmer since we both (2) .... work on the same day at Thames College about five years ago. She is one of the smartest people I (3) .... ever ....

B (4) .... you .... the good news yet? Jenny and Michael (5) .... just .... parents! Jenny (6) .... a baby girl last night.

C The plumber (7) .... me this morning, 'I'll be back to finish the work as soon as I (8) .... some lunch.' But now it's past three o'clock and he still (9) .... back.

12 Complete this dialogue with these verbs in the present perfect or past simple.

ask   be (×2)   have   make   not call   not eat   not know   not seem   say   tell

It's Monday afternoon. Ron is at home, phoning Sue at the office where they both work.
Ron: Hi Sue, it's me.
Sue: Well, hello! Where (1) .... you .... all day? The boss (2) .... me this morning where you (3) ...., but he (4) .... to be looking for you or anything.
Ron: What (5) .... you ....?
Sue: I (6) .... him that I (7) .... Are you okay?
Ron: I'm sorry I (8) .... you this morning. I (9) .... the flu since Saturday. I (10) .... anything for two days and it (11) .... me feel really weak. But I'll probably be there tomorrow.

Past perfect or past simple?

When we are talking about actions in the past, with the past simple (*won*), and we want to refer to actions even further in the past, we use the past perfect (*had won*).

1 *Jenny Fisher* **won** *her first gold medal in 2004. She* **had won** *two silver medals in previous Olympics, but this was her first gold.*

With the past simple (*arrived*) in a *when*-clause, we use the past perfect (*had started*) in the main clause for an earlier action (2) and the past simple (*started*) for a later action (3).

2 *When he arrived in the morning, we* **had started** *work.* (= We started work before he arrived)
3 *When he arrived in the morning, we* **started** *work.* (= We started work after he arrived)

Note that two verbs in the past simple can suggest a cause and effect: *When I* **called***, he* **came***.*

In conditionals, we use the past perfect for something that did not happen (4) and the past simple for something that might happen (5).

4 *If you* **had come***, you could have stayed with us.* • *If I'd* **known***, I certainly would have helped.*
5 *If you* **came***, you could stay with us.* • *If I* **saw** *anyone doing that, I certainly would try to stop it.*

We usually use the past perfect, not the past simple, with some adverbs (*already, just, still*).

6 *An ambulance came quickly, but the crash victim* **had already died***.* (NOT ~~The crash victim already died.~~)
7 *The books* **still hadn't arrived** *when I left.* (NOT ~~They still didn't arrive when I left.~~)
8 *The students* **had just opened** *their books when the fire alarm went off.*

---

13 Choose an ending (a–d) for each beginning (1–4) and add these verbs in the past perfect or past simple.

come   give   need   not finish   say   talk   work

1 He .... the money last week, (...)
2 You .... during the meeting (...)
3 When he .... back later, (...)
4 Ashley could have done much better (...)

a that you .... about that already.
b so I .... it to him then.
c if she .... harder.
d they still .... writing their reports.

---

14 Complete this text with these verbs.

was (×2)   explained   didn't eat   have gone   had cooked   hadn't eaten
were   went   didn't lock   have heard   had reached   hadn't locked

One of the four-year-olds in the reading group suddenly said, 'This is the silliest story I (1) .... ever ....!' I (2) .... in the middle of reading Goldilocks and the Three Bears to the group. We (3) .... just .... the part in the story where Goldilocks goes into the bears' house and eats some of the food from bowls on the table.

'Where (4) .... the bears?' he asked.

'Maybe outside or playing in the woods,' I suggested.

'And their house was wide open? They (5) .... even .... the door before going out?'

'Well, in the old days, people (6) .... their doors.'

'And their food was on the table, but they (7) .... it before they (8) .... outside?'

'Maybe they (9) .... it because it (10) .... too hot .'

'If you (11) .... that meal, you wouldn't (12) .... out and left it, would you?'

'Probably not, but it's just a story,' I (13) .... rather weakly.

Already, etc. 116   Unreal conditionals 186   Past and past perfect 20

Future

15 Write the numbers of appropriate examples in the spaces.

Future: *will* and *shall*

There is no single form used as the future tense. We can use *will* plus the base form of a verb to give or ask for information about the future `2` and to talk about possible future actions when we make promises, requests or threats `  `. We usually use contracted forms after pronouns (*'ll*) or in negatives (*won't*) unless we are being formal or emphatic.

  1 *We'll help you clean up.* • *I won't tell anyone.* • *Will you please go?* • *Stop or I'll call the police.*
  2 *Christmas will be on a Friday.* • *The meeting won't start until 9.30.* • *When will you leave?*

We can use *shall* with *I* or *we* to express determination, or in questions to make offers or suggestions.

  3 *We will forgive, but we shall never forget.* • *Shall I make some tea?* • *Let's talk later, shall we?*
In American English, *will/won't* (not *shall/shan't*) are used with *I* and *we*.

Future continuous, future perfect and future perfect continuous

We can use *will* + *be* + present participle (the future continuous) to talk about future actions in progress at a particular time `  ` and as a way of expressing plans or intentions `  `.

  4 *I'll be sending in my application tomorrow.* • *Will you be using the car later or can I have it?*
  5 *Next week at this time, you will be lying on the beach and we'll all still be slaving away here.*

We can use *will* + *have* + past participle (the future perfect) to say that something will be completed by a particular time `  `. We use *will* + *have been* + present participle (the future perfect continuous) when we look ahead to a future time and imagine an action lasting from a point before that time up to that future time `  `.

  6 *On the 10th of this month, I'll have been living here for exactly two years.*
  7 *By next summer I'll have finished my degree.* • *It's 5.30. Will Jay have left work already?*

Will or *be going to?*

We use *will* for a prediction based on past experience or knowledge `  `, especially in predictive conditionals `  `, and *be going to* for a prediction based on what we feel or think now `  `. We can use *would* or *was/were going to* when we describe a past prediction about the future `  `.

  8 *Oh, no, I think I'm going to be sick.* • *We've just heard that Kim's going to have a baby.*
  9 *If you eat too much ice cream, you'll be sick.* • *We'll do okay if the test isn't too difficult.*
  10 *As soon as the victorious British team lands at Heathrow, thousands of fans will start celebrating.*
  11 *When I was a teenager, I thought I was going to be a rock star and I would never have to work.*

We use *be going to* for a decision already made `  ` and *will* for a decision made at that moment `  `.

  12 *Her parents have said they're going to pay for her tuition.* • *I've decided I'm going to get a new phone.*
  13 *I need someone to take this to the post office. ~ I'll go!* • *That's the phone ringing. ~ I'll get it!*

Present simple and present continuous for the future

We can use the present simple for future events in a schedule or timetable `  `. We also use the present simple for future actions in clauses after subordinating conjunctions `  `. We can use the present continuous to talk about a future action we have planned or arranged `  `.

  14 *I'm seeing the doctor on Friday.* • *We're playing tomorrow.* (NOT *It's snowing tomorrow.*)
  15 *It won't matter what he says later.* • *I'll see you when I get back.* (NOT *I'll see you when I will get back.*)
  16 *The new course starts in January.* • *I think Kate's flight arrives tomorrow morning.*

Predictive conditionals 185 Subordinating conjunctions 12 *Will, would, be going to, shall* 32

16 Choose an ending (a–d) for each beginning (1–4) and add *will*, *will be* or *will have been*.

1 Next April 21st .... my parent's silver anniversary. (..)

2 I'm sure everyone .... want to get an early start. (..)

3 Mr Russell .... teaching his last English classes during May. (..)

4 My life as a student .... over at the end of this term. (..)

a By then, he .... working here for 40 years.

b That means they .... married for 25 years.

c Do you realize that I .... in school for most of my life so far?

d .... you .... ready to leave at about 6 am?

17 Complete this text with the most appropriate forms of the verbs, using *will*, *be going to* or the present simple.

be   give   have   make   not start   not stop

I was standing at the bus stop reading my horoscope in the newspaper. It said, 'You (1) .... good moments and bad moments today.' I looked up and saw the bus coming. Then I realized it (2) .... because it was already full. 'Oh, no,' I thought. 'If I (3) .... walking fast, I (4) .... late for my first class!' I had just started walking when a car pulled up beside me and one of my classmates leaned out. 'Hey Jean, get in, we (5) .... you a lift.' It's amazing how the bad moments (6) .... the good moments feel so much better.

18 Correct the mistakes in these sentences.

Example: An imminent event is one that ~~happens~~ soon.
                                             will happen

1 Please stop making so much noise or I report you to the supervisor.

2 As I was about to leave his office, Bob said, 'Let's get together for lunch sometime, will we?'

3 They came and asked for people to help immediately, so Jenny jumped up and said, 'I do it!'

4 When he is released next week, Pat McGuire will spend almost five years in prison for a crime he didn't commit.

5 I'm going to work on the report at home last night, but I had left all my notes in the office.

6 It's probably too late to phone Margaret. Do you think she'll go to bed already?

7 I'm not certain, but I guess it's raining later this afternoon.

8 Forthcoming books are those that we think to be available soon.

9 I can't believe that you'll sit on a plane to Malta while I'm driving to work tomorrow morning.

10 If I'll finish before you, I wait for you outside.

11 Will Stefan to get these boxes later or is to take them now?

12 I must get to the post office before it'll close or the parcel doesn't arrive in time for Joy's birthday.

Tests

A Choose the word or phrase that best completes each sentence.

1 I think Mr Wilson _____ in this school since 1990 or maybe earlier.

   a teaches   b is teaching   c has taught   d taught

2 I stopped watching the game before the end, but I thought we _____.

   a had won   b have won   c have been winning   d will have won.

3 That's very sad news. If _____ sooner, I would have tried to help.

   a I know   b I'll know   c I knew   d I'd known

4 My sister _____ to me once or twice since she's been living in Athens.

   a was writing   b has written   c has been writing   d had written

5 According to the memo, we're _____ the meeting at noon tomorrow.

   a having   b have   c going have   d will have

B Identify the one underlined expression (A, B, C or D) that must be changed in order to correct the sentence.

1 My next door neighbour, who <u>is</u> usually shy and <u>doesn't say</u> much, <u>is being</u> very friendly this
                 A   B   C
morning and <u>has</u> a big party tonight for all his friends.
           D

2 Martin <u>was used</u> to smoke a lot when he <u>was studying</u>, but since he <u>has been working</u> in the bank,
         A   B   C
he <u>hasn't been smoking</u> as much.
       D

3 People <u>were slipping</u> on the wet floor because no one <u>had cleaned</u> up the water that all of us
        A   B
<u>were knowing</u> <u>had leaked</u> from the coffee machine.
  C   D

4 When you <u>will make</u> a promise, you <u>tell</u> someone that you <u>will definitely give</u> them something or
        A   B   C
that you definitely <u>will or won't do</u> something.
            D

5 As we <u>were entering</u> the building, I <u>noticed</u> a sign that someone <u>has put</u> above the door
       A   B   C
which <u>said</u>, 'Be alert.'
     D

C Complete this text by choosing only one of the verbs from each pair for each space.

begins	*had*	*will peep*	*reads*	*is thinking*
was beginning	*has had*	*had peeped*	*was reading*	*thought*

Alice (1) _____ to get very tired of sitting by her sister on the bank and of having
nothing to do: once or twice she (2) _____ into the book her sister
(3) _____, but it (4) _____ no pictures or conversations in it, 'and what
is the use of a book,' (5) _____ Alice, 'without pictures or conversations?'

D Complete each sentence in such a way that it is as similar as possible in meaning to the sentence above it.

1 We are spending £300 on repairs before we sell the car.
By the time we sell the car, we _____

2 I never had to think about my health before this.
This is the first _____

3 Juliet started working here about six years ago.
Juliet has _____

4 I didn't think it would be good, but it's really bad.
It's even worse _____

5 I haven't talked to my parents since Christmas.
It was Christmas when _____

E Complete this text with these verbs.

believe	*holds*	*be experiencing*	*had*	*have been changing*
will keep	*lets*	*is happening*	*have been*	*have created*

The world is getting warmer and the oceans are rising. Why (1) _____ this
_____ ? One answer is that it could simply be part of a natural process. After all,
there (2) _____ ice ages and long periods of warmth in the past, so we could just
(3) _____ another warming trend. This kind of answer (4) _____
more supporters a few years ago. What scientists now (5) _____ is that human
activity is the cause. For more than two hundred years, humans (6) _____ gradually
_____ the atmosphere, mainly as a result of industrial pollution. We
(7) _____ an atmosphere around the earth that, like a giant glass container,
(8) _____ heat from the sun through and then (9) _____ it in.
(10) _____ temperatures and sea levels _____ rising? The general
answer is unfortunately yes.

3 Modals

The modals are a group of auxiliary verbs (*can, could, may, might, must, ought, shall, should, will, would*) that we can use with other verbs to say what is possible, permitted, necessary, etc.

The phrasal modals are a group of verb phrases (*be able to, be allowed to, be going to, be supposed to, have to, have got to*) that can be used instead of modals.

1 Read through this text and find:

1 another negative modal
2 a sentence that contains three different modals

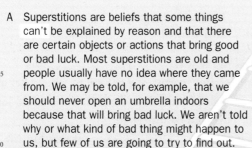

A Superstitions are beliefs that some things can't be explained by reason and that there are certain objects or actions that bring good or bad luck. Most superstitions are old and people usually have no idea where they came from. We may be told, for example, that we should never open an umbrella indoors because that will bring bad luck. We aren't told why or what kind of bad thing might happen to us, but few of us are going to try to find out.

B Everyone knows that thirteen is an unlucky number. Other things that can bring bad luck include breaking a mirror, walking under a ladder or spilling salt. At least when you spill salt, you can avoid the bad luck by immediately throwing some of the salt over your left shoulder with your right hand. Unfortunately, the man sitting behind you at that moment will suddenly get a shower of salt all over him. Obviously, he must have done something earlier that brought him bad luck.

C If you ask people why it is bad luck to walk under a ladder, they usually say that it's because something might fall on your head. It could be a hammer, a brick, a piece of wood, paint or water. It is interesting that the superstition is explained in terms of such ordinary things. The origin of the superstition is much darker and more scary. According to the Oxford Guide to British and American Culture, 'this idea may have developed out of the practice in medieval times of hanging criminals from ladders.'

D More confusing are those superstitions that seem to have different meanings for different people. Some people will tell you that it is bad luck if a black cat walks in front of you. Others will say that seeing a black cat is supposed to be lucky. Other tokens of good luck are a rabbit's foot (not lucky for the rabbit, obviously), a special coin, a four-leaf clover and a horseshoe. If you hang the horseshoe over your front door to bring luck to your house, you must be careful to have the open end pointing upwards. If you hang it the other way, your good luck will just drop out through the gap. You can also wish for good luck by crossing your fingers. You don't have to cross all of them, only the middle finger over the index finger.

E There are special phrases that people use to bring luck. There's 'Good luck', of course. Another expression is 'Touch wood' or 'Knock on wood'. This is usually heard when people talk about their good luck or when they are hoping that they will be able to get or do something they want. By using the expression, the speaker tries to avoid having any bad luck that might be caused by talking about having good luck. If there isn't anything wooden to touch, some people will tap themselves on the head as they say 'Touch wood'. However, acting as if you have a wooden head, touching it with your fingers crossed and saying 'Knock on wood' all at once won't necessarily increase your luck.

2 Choose one of the following as the final sentence of each of the paragraphs A–E above.

1 People will just think you're very superstitious or possibly crazy. (…)
2 That explanation makes the superstition much easier to understand. (…)
3 With your fingers like this, however, it may be hard to nail that horseshoe over your door. (…)
4 We just don't open one until we are outside. (…)
5 Perhaps he had opened an umbrella indoors. (…)

Modals and phrasal modals

Modals

The modals (also called modal auxiliary verbs) are single words that always have the same form.

    1 *We **should** wait for David. He **may** come soon.* (NOT ~~He mays come soon.~~)

Others: can, could, might, must, ought, shall, will, would

We use modals before the base forms of other verbs.

    2 *I **can wait** for him. • You **must leave**.* (NOT ~~I can waiting for him. You must to leave.~~)

Ought is always followed by *to: You **ought to** go home.* (NOT ~~You ought go home.~~)

We do not use *do* with modals in questions (3) or negatives (4).

    3 ***Will** it work? • **Can** you play the piano?* (NOT ~~Do you can play the piano?~~)

    4 *She **might not** want it. • I **couldn't** swim very fast.* (NOT ~~I didn't could swim very fast.~~)

The modals *shall, will* and *would* are usually contracted (5), unless they are being emphasized (6).

    5 *I**'ll** bring you one, shall I? • He**'ll** be there, **won't** he? • She**'d** like to stay, wouldn't she?*

    6 *Do not forget! We **will** leave at 8 a.m. precisely. We **will not** wait for latecomers.*

We usually use the forms *could, might* and *would* in clauses after past tense verbs (7), especially in indirect speech (8).

    7 *I didn't know she **could** speak Spanish. • I was hoping you **might** give me some advice.*

    8 *('Can I help?') She asked if she **could** help. • ('I'll be late.') He said he **would** be late.*

We don't put two modals together before a verb. See (11) below.

    9 *We **can win** this game and we **will win** it!* (NOT ~~We will can win this game!~~)

Phrasal modals

Phrasal modals are verb phrases beginning with *be* or *have* which can be used instead of modals.

    10 *Most old people **are able to** look after themselves.* (= They **can** look after themselves.)

    *However, we **have to** make sure that they can cope.* (= We **must** OR We **should** make sure …)

Others: be allowed to (can/may), be going to (will), be supposed to (should), have got to (must)

We always use phrasal modals instead of modals in five structures: after a modal (11), where an infinitive (12) or a gerund (13) is needed, and in the perfect (14) and continuous (15) forms.

    11 *We **will be able to** win this game! • They **may be going to** increase tuition next year.*

    12 *He seems **to be able to** do everything • I hope **to be allowed to** stay.*

    13 *I love **being able to** sit outside in the sun. • I hate **having to** repeat everything.*

    14 *They **have had to** wait for hours. • They **haven't been allowed to** leave the building.*

    15 *She **is having to** pay extra. • We **aren't being allowed to** take the test early.*

We can use two phrasal modals together: *I**'m going to have to** go to the shop for more bread.*

3   **Find the three sentences in the text on page 28 that contain both a modal and a phrasal modal.**

    ....

    ....

    ....

Complex modals

We form the modal perfect with a modal before *have* plus a past participle.
> 1 Nick **may have taken** your book. He **shouldn't have done** that. (NOT ~~He shouldn't done that.~~) •
> Obviously, he **must have done** something earlier that brought him bad luck.

We form the modal continuous with a modal before *be* plus a present participle.
> 2 Alex **shouldn't be acting** so confident. He **should be studying**. (NOT ~~He should studying.~~)

We form the modal perfect continuous with a modal before *have been* plus a present participle.
> 3 I called, but she didn't answer. She **must have been sleeping**. (NOT ~~She must been sleeping.~~)

We form modal passives with a modal before *be* (4) or *have been* (5) plus a past participle.
> 4 Some things **cannot be explained** by reason. • This shirt **should be washed** by hand.
> 5 People **could have been injured** by falling branches. (NOT ~~People could have injured~~ …)

4 **Complete these sentences with *be*, *have* or *have been*.**

Example: She shouldn't .... *have* .... taken Tom's dictionary. I'm sure he'll .... *be* ....
looking for it later.

1 I was glad that my old computer could .... repaired. I would ....
hated to have to buy a new one.

2 Children may not .... left alone in the playground. They must ....
accompanied by an adult.

3 Where's Tony? He should .... helping you clear out the garage. I guess he must
.... forgotten about it.

4 We weren't tired. We could easily .... chatted for another hour. But we would
probably .... asked to leave the restaurant. It was getting late.

5 **Write the eight completed sentences from Exercise 4 in appropriate spaces in this table.**

Prediction: *will, would, be going to, shall* ·I'm sure he'll be looking for it later.·

1 ....

Willingness, habits and preferences: *will, would*

2 ....

Ability: *can, could, be able to*

3 ....

Permission: *can, could, may, might, be allowed to*

4 ....

Possibility: *may might, can, could*

5 ....

Necessity: *must, have to, have got to, need to, needn't*

6 ....

Deduction: *must, have to, can't, couldn't*

7 ....

Obligation: *should, ought to, be supposed to, had better* She shouldn't have taken Tom's dictionary.

8 ....

6 Choose an ending (a–e) for each beginning (1–5) and add these forms.

able to	will be	must be	ought	going to
can't	won't	must have	should be	may have been

1 You know there .... a test   a so that we .... be late.
   tomorrow (...)
2 Samantha isn't .... study   b so I .... left it somewhere.
   at all (...)
3 I .... find my calculator (...)   c so she .... feeling very confident.
4 We .... to check the   d so he probably isn't .... write.
   timetable (...)
5 Mark's arm .... injured (...)   e so you .... studying tonight.

7 Using a dictionary if necessary, complete these sentences with the adjectives and modals.

advisable	inconceivable	regrettable	can't	should	will
hypothetical	inevitable	reluctant	might	shouldn't	wouldn't

1 Someone who says, 'It is .... that the police didn't do something sooner' feels that
   the police .... have acted sooner.
2 If someone says it is .... to wait, it means that you .... act
   immediately.
3 When you describe something as ...., you are certain that it ....
   happen.
4 It was clear that he was .... to talk and we .... get any information
   from him.
5 If you say that something is ...., you mean that you .... imagine it
   at all.
6 When something is described as ...., it is based on an idea about what
   .... happen and not on a real situation.

8 Editing. Correct the mistakes in the use of modals in this text.

A dilemma is a situation in which you have a choice and you are not sure what you should ~~to.~~ ^do

In my dilemma, I had a good job as a secretary for a big company, but I really wanted to become a

teacher and I didn't could do that without going to university. If I decided to do that, I knew I will

have to quit my job and, as a student, I have much less money. I talked about my dilemma with one

of the other secretaries and she warned me that I don't should give up such a good job. She said that

a young woman supposed to think about getting a husband, not going to university. It really was a

dilemma and I couldn't decided what I ought do. But then I talked to my aunt Maria. She told me

that she should go to university when she was younger. She decided not to go and she regretted it.

She thought that I should to give it a try. She said I didn't should be afraid and that she may can help

me pay for things with some money she had saved. That was the end of my dilemma.

Prediction: *will, would, be going to, shall*

We use *will* for predictions (1) and to say what we think is most likely (2).

1 *It **will** be cold tomorrow.* • *I **won't** finish this before Friday.* • *Who do you think **will** win?*
2 *The phone's ringing. That **will** be Harry.* • *Don't call them now. They**'ll** be sleeping.*

We use *will* for a predictable situation (3) and *would* for a hypothetical situation (4).

3 *He**'ll** look better without that scruffy beard.* (= I think that he's going to shave it off.)
4 *He**'d** look better without that scruffy beard.* (= I don't think that he's going to shave it off.)

We use *will* plus the perfect for a prediction about an event that has already happened at some future time (5). We use *would* plus the perfect for a prediction about an imaginary past event or situation (6).

5 *It's no good phoning at midnight. Everyone **will have gone** to bed.*
6 *Life in the Middle Ages was harsh and cruel. You **would have hated** it.*

We usually use *will* for predictions based on past experience or knowledge (7) and *be going to* for predictions based on what we feel or think now (8).

7 *There **will** be delays because of bad weather.* • *Too much coffee **will** give you a headache.*
8 *Oh, no, I think it**'s going to** rain.* • *He**'s going to** get a headache from drinking all that coffee.*

We use *be going to* for a decision already made (9) or when something is starting to happen (10).

9 *We**'re going to** spend Christmas at home.* • *Paul and Angela **are going to** get married in May.*
10 *Be careful – you**'re going to** drop it!* • *Close your eyes. I**'m going to** give you a big surprise.*
We use *was/were going to* (not *would*) for past plans: *I **was going to** do law, but changed my mind.*

We use *shall* with *I* or *we* in questions when we make offers and suggestions or when we ask for suggestions (11). We can use *shall* (or *will*) to express determination (12).

11 ***Shall** I close the door?* • *Let's try again, **shall** we?* • *Where **shall** we go for lunch today?*
12 *I **shall** (OR I**'ll**) finish this if it kills me!* • *We lost a battle, but we **shall** (OR we**'ll**) never give up!*

9 **Complete this dialogue with these forms.**

will	*I'll*	*I'm going to*	*I'd*	*would*
shall	*you'll*	*I was going to*	*won't*	*would have*

It's 7.30 a.m. on Thursday morning. Pam and Jim are awake, but still in bed. The phone rings.

Pam: Oh, that (1) .... be for me. Hello?

Mum: Hello dear. I was hoping it wasn't too early for you. I have to come into town today and I was wondering if you (2) .... be able to meet me for lunch.

Pam: Oh, (3) .... love to, Mum, but (4) .... get my hair done at lunchtime. I (5) .... been free, but Janet called yesterday and changed my appointment from Friday to today. (6) .... get it cut on Friday so that it would be nice for Dad's birthday this weekend.

Mum: Ah, the birthday party! That's why I have to come to town. (7) .... we just have a coffee later? When do you think (8) .... be finished at the hairdresser's?

Pam: Oh, she (9) .... have finished before 1.30 or 2. And then I have to get back to the office.

Mum: It's okay. I understand. (10) .... talk to you later.

Will, shall and be going to (future) 24 Will, would in conditionals 185–6

Willingness, habits and preferences: *will* and *would*

Willingness: *will* and *would*

We use *will* to say we are definitely willing now (1) and *would* for willingness in the future or in conditional sentences (2). We also use *would* when we mean 'willing, but not able to' (3).

1 I **will** give you one more chance. • There are advisers here who **will** help and guide you.
2 Most people **would** pay more for better health care. • I **would** stay longer if they asked me to.
3 Can you help us carry these boxes? ~ Oh, I **would** help you, but I've injured my back.

We use *won't* (= isn't willing to) or *wouldn't* (= wasn't willing to) to say that a person refuses to do something (4) and to talk about things/machines as if they were people who are/were not willing (5).

4 He's ill, but he **won't** go to the doctor's. • She had a lot of money, but she **wouldn't** lend us any.
5 The door isn't locked, but it **won't** open. • My car **wouldn't** start this morning.

Habits and preferences: *will* and *would*

We can describe present habits or typical behaviour with *will* (6). We can use *would* for habitual actions in the past (7).

6 Her children **will** break everything they touch. • Tim **will** just sit watching TV for hours.
7 I **would** try to stay awake every Xmas to see Santa. • Each summer we **would** visit my cousins.
We say *used to* (not *would*) for past states: I **used to** have a dog. (NOT ~~I would have a dog.~~)

We use *would* (not *will*) with verbs expressing preferences (*like, love, prefer*) (8), especially in offers (9).

8 I **would** prefer an early class. • I'd love to go on a cruise. (NOT ~~I'll love to go on a cruise.~~)
9 **Would** you like some tea or **would** you prefer coffee? (NOT ~~Will you like some tea?~~)

We use *would* (not *will*) after the verb *wish* when we're talking about preferred actions.

10 I wish she **wouldn't** smoke. • Don't you wish they **would** make it easier to recycle things?
We don't use *would* to describe states: I wish I had a car. (NOT ~~I wish I would have a car.~~)

10 **Complete each sentence with one pair of verbs and forms of *will* or *would*, where appropriate.**

be / hate   *be / say*   *eat / need*   *give / go*   *have / like*   *play / stay*   *push / start*

1 Even when she gets the flu, my friend Alice .... to see the doctor because she's afraid that he .... her an injection. She is terrified of needles.
2 We had an old car that .... on cold mornings unless we got out and .... it.
3 Amy: Carla wants to know if you .... a slice of her home-made chocolate cake.
   Bob: Tell her I .... normally .... two slices, but not while I'm on this strict diet.
4 When we were young, we .... always .... outside during the summer holidays, but nowadays children .... just .... inside watching TV or video games all day.
5 I hope I .... never .... asked to work on a night shift because I .... having to go to sleep for most of the following day.
6 I'm sure we .... to cook anything for them because they .... lunch before they come here.
7 When people asked Annie's dad if he had children, his typical answer .... 'And how!' Her mother usually murmured, 'I wish he .... things like that.'

Ability: *can, could, be able to*

We use *can* when we talk about general ability and *could* for general ability in the past.

    1 **Can** you play chess? • Ostriches **can** run very fast. • Their son **could** swim before he **could** walk.

In the negative, *can't* is more usual than *cannot* (written as one word), which is very formal. (NOT ~~I can not go.~~)

We often use *can* and *could* with verbs for mental processes (2) and senses (3).

    2 I **couldn't decide.** • **Can** you **remember** her name? (NOT ~~Are you remembering her name?~~)

    3 We **could hear** a cat, but we **couldn't see** it. • I **can smell** onions. (NOT ~~I'm smelling onions.~~)

We sometimes use these verbs in the present simple (*I smell onions*), but not in the present continuous.

Other verbs used like this include: believe, feel, guess, taste, understand

We use *be able to* (not *can* or *could*) in four of the phrasal modal structures: in infinitives, in gerunds (4), after modals, and in the perfect (5).

    4 They want **to be able to** practise. • She left without **being able to** talk to the teacher.

    5 I won't **be able to** finish. • He hasn't **been able to** study. (NOT ~~He hasn't could study.~~)

We don't use *be able to* in the continuous: He isn't able to walk. (NOT ~~He isn't being able to walk.~~)

We sometimes use *am/is/are able to* instead of *can* for general ability in formal situations (6). We use *was/were able to* (not *could*) for the achievement of something difficult in the past (7).

    6 **Is** the child **able to** tie his or her shoelaces without help?

    7 We had a flat tyre, but we **were able to** fix it and carry on. (NOT … ~~but we could fix it.~~)

We can use *couldn't* to say something difficult was not achieved: We couldn't fix it.

We use *could* (not *can* or *be able to*) plus the perfect to talk about an ability or opportunity not used.

    8 He **could have done** very well, but he was lazy. (NOT ~~He can have done very well.~~)

Note the difference between *I was able to win* (= I won) and *I could have won* (= I didn't win).

11 Using a dictionary if necessary, complete each sentence with one pair of words, plus appropriate forms of *can, could* or *be able to*.

difficult / managed	fly / swimming	stay / unflappable
feel / numb	illiterate / read	successful / tried

1 Penguins are birds that ...., but .... use their wings for

    ....

2 An .... person is someone who .... calm in difficult situations.

3 It was so cold that my fingers were .... and I .... anything.

4 When people are ...., they .... or write.

5 A .... person is someone who has .... do what he or she

    .... to do.

6 If you .... to finish a task, it means you .... do it, even though it

    was ....

12 Complete this joke with appropriate forms of *can* or *could*.

Did you hear about the woman who went fishing, but (1) .... catch anything? On her way home, she stopped at the market so that she (2) .... buy two fish. She then stepped back a few paces and asked the fish seller if he (3) .... throw them to her. The puzzled man asked, 'Why?' The woman answered, 'So that I (4) .... tell my husband that I caught a couple of fish today!'

Permission: *can, could, may, might, be allowed to*

We use *can* and *could* to ask for permission, choosing *could* to be more polite (1). We use *can* (not *could*) to give or refuse permission (2).

 1 **Can** I borrow your dictionary? • **Can** the dog come into the house? • **Could** we leave early today?
 2 *Yes, you* **can**. • *No, it* **can't**. • *I'm sorry, but you* **can't**. (NOT ~~I'm sorry, but you couldn't.~~)

In formal situations, we can use *may* when we ask for (3) or give (4) permission (or not).

 3 **May** we come in? • **May** I take this chair? • **May** I use one of these phones?
 4 *Yes, you* **may**. • *No, you* **may not**, *because I need it*. • *Of course, you* **may** *use any of these phones.*
Might can be used to ask for, but not to give, permission: **Might** *I take one? ~ Yes.* (NOT ~~Yes, you might.~~)

We usually use *can* (not *may*) when we talk about laws and rules (5). *May* (not *might*) is sometimes used in formal rules (6).

 5 *You* **can't** *park here. ~ Why not? ~ I think only buses and taxis* **can** *park here.*
 6 *No food or drinks* **may** *be brought inside.* • *Pedestrians* **may not** *enter this way.*

We use *be allowed to* (not *may* or *might*) when we emphasize getting permission on a specific occasion (7) and in all the phrasal modal structures (8).

 7 *That day was the first time I* **was allowed to** *make my own breakfast.* (NOT ~~I might make ...~~)
 8 *No one* **has been allowed to** *see the test results.* • *We* **aren't being allowed to** *go in yet.*
Note the combination: *You* **may/might be allowed to** *go.* (= It's possible you'll get permission to go.)

---

13 Choose an ending (a–f) for each beginning (1–6) and add *can*, *may* or *be allowed to*.

 1 New students .... not register (...)
 2 Children shouldn't .... (...)
 3 He casually asked, '..................... I see that?' (...)
 4 You might not .... go in (...)
 5 You .... all leave early today (...)
 6 They are unlikely to .... (...)

 a as if he was interested in my drawing.
 b because there's no more work to do.
 c for more than three classes.
 d eat or drink during a test.
 e if you're under 21.
 f play with matches.

---

14 Editing. Correct the mistakes in this text.

My friend Dana ~~can not~~ ^{can't} say 'No'. If another student asks her, 'Can I borrow your pen?', she always

says, 'Of course, you could', and hands it over, even when she only has one pen and it means she isn't

being able to do her own work. After I heard her do that one day, I told her that she can have said,

'Sorry, but you cannot, because I only have one pen.' In reply, she said, 'But how do they could do

their work without a pen?' I knew that I can have tried to answer that question, but somehow I didn't

think I'll can change how she behaved, no matter what I said.

Possibility: *may, might, can, could*

Possibility: *may* and *might*

We can use either *may* or *might* to say that something is possible now or later (1). We use either *may* or *might* plus the perfect to say it is possible that something happened before now (2).

   1 *Taking these pills* **may/might** *cause drowsiness. You* **might/may** *fall asleep at the wheel.*

   2 *I* **may/might have lost** *my key.* • *Tanya* **might/may have met** *James when she was in London.*

In the negative, we can say: *It may not/might not/mightn't happen.* (NOT *It mayn't happen.*)

We use *may* (not *might*) when we say that a possible situation is common or usual (3). We can use *might* (not *may*) in descriptions of what was possible in the past (4) and when we report speech and thoughts after verbs in the past tense (5).

   3 *Peppers* **may** *be green, yellow or red.* • *Measles* **may** *cause a fever and small red spots.*

   4 *In those days, people* **might** *spend their entire lives in the village where they were born.*

   5 ('*I may be late.*') *He said he* **might** *be late.* • *I was wondering if you* **might** *have time to read this.*

Possibility: *can* and *could*

We use *can/could* in general statements to say that a situation is (*can*) or was (*could*) possible.

   6 *Some dogs* **can** *be very dangerous.* • *The old house* **could** *be quite cold, even in summer.*

We use *could* (not *can*) when we speculate about things, meaning 'It's possible that …' (7) and to ask 'Is it possible that …?' (8).

   7 *Your bag* **could** *be in the car.* • *It* **could** *rain this weekend.* (NOT *It can rain this weekend.*)

   8 *Peter is late.* **Could** *he be stuck in traffic?* (NOT *Can he be stuck in traffic?*)

We use *could* (not *can*) plus the perfect when we speculate about the possibility of an earlier event.

   9 *The bank* **could have closed** *already.* • *You* **could have fallen.** (NOT *You can have fallen.*)

May/might or *can/could*?

We use *may, might* or *could* (not *can*) to say that a specific event is possible (10), before phrasal modals (11) and before the continuous or perfect (12). We can use *might* or *could* plus the perfect to express irritation at someone's not having done something (13).

  10 *Ann* **may** *arrive later.* • *There* **could** *be a storm tonight.* (NOT *There can be a storm tonight.*)

  11 *It* **may** *be going to rain.* • *We* **might** *have to leave soon.* (NOT *We can have to leave soon.*)

  12 *The economy* **may be showing** *signs of recovery.* • *Lani* **might have borrowed** *the hair-dryer.*

  13 *You* **might have posted** *my letter when you went out to post yours!*

We use *may* or *might* (not *can* or *could*) when we make a concession before a clause with *but*.

  14 *She* **may** *be seventy,* **but** *she still likes to dance.* • *We* **might** *have lost a battle,* **but** *not the war.*

Note that *It may be old, but it works* is very similar in meaning to *Although it's old, it works.*

We use *can* or *could* (not *may* or *might*) to make suggestions about possible actions (15) and when we ask people to do things (16).

  15 *We have a simple choice. We* **can/could** *wait here for a bus or we* **could/can** *start walking.*

  16 **Can** *you show me where it is?* • **Could** *you take this away?* (NOT *May you take this away?*)

We use *may not* or *might not* when we mean 'possible not' (17). When we mean 'not possible', we use *can't* for the present situation and *couldn't* for the past (18).

  17 *It* **may/might not** *be true.* (= Perhaps not) • *This bill* **may/might not** *be right. It seems too high.*

  18 *That story* **can't** *be true.* (= I'm sure it's not) • *This bill* **can't** *be right. We only had two coffees.* •
     I knew the rumour about your accident **couldn't** *be true because I'd seen you that morning.*

15 Using a dictionary if necessary, complete each sentence with an adjective and a modal.

absurd	feasible	theoretical	may	may be	might
disqualified	potential	undecided	may not (×2)	may have	might not

1 Your uncle .... run in a marathon when he was younger, but it's
.... to keep describing him as 'one of the top runners'.

2 She .... breaking the rules and will possibly be .... from the rest of
the competition.

3 If someone is .... about an action, they .... or ....
do it.

4 We knew about the .... problems and the workmen had said they
.... finish on time.

5 Your plan .... be approved because people don't think it's economically
....

6 From a .... perspective, that .... happen, but nobody thinks it will.

16 Complete this text with appropriate forms of *can* or *could* plus these verbs.

avoid	be	not imagine	pick	save	not send

These days, when we (1) .... up a phone and call anywhere in the world, we really
don't realize, and often (2) .... , how difficult long-distance communication
(3) .... for people in the past. In the early 19th century the Treaty of Ghent
brought an end to the War of 1812 between Britain and the United States. But the news
(4) .... across the Atlantic fast enough to stop General Andrew Jackson attacking and
defeating the British forces in New Orleans a full three weeks after the treaty was signed. With
better communication, the battle (5) .... and the lives of more than two thousand
people (6) ....

17 Correct the mistakes in these sentences using *may*, *might*, *can* or *could*.

Example: It was a bad accident. We ~~can~~ could have been killed.

1 They can be going to increase airport fees to pay for increased security.

2 Don't turn off the computer yet. Someone can still be using it.

3 In late 18th century Scotland, you may be hanged for stealing a sheep.

4 These people can have a lot of money, but it doesn't make them interesting.

5 By Friday I can have finished the book, but if I get too busy, I can not.

6 May someone tell me where the main office is?

7 We know he doesn't tell the truth, so we really might not believe any of his stories.

8 He asked me last night if you may be willing to talk to Margaret for him.

9 According to the forecast, the weather can be a bit warmer today.

10 This switch isn't working. May the children have broken it?

Necessity: *must, have to, have got to, need to, needn't*

Necessity: *must* and *mustn't*

We use *must* to say that something is necessary (1), especially in orders and rules (2). We use the negative *mustn't/must not* to tell people not to do things or to say something is a bad idea (3).

  1 *Plants* **must** *have light.* • *Your basic needs are the things you* **must** *have to live a normal life.*
  2 *You* **must** *come to class on time.* • *Safety helmets* **must** *be worn.* • *All visitors* **must** *sign in.*
  3 *You* **mustn't** *come late.* • *Empty boxes* **must not** *be stacked in front of the emergency exit.*

We also use *must* to encourage someone to do something we think is important (4) or to emphasize a strong feeling or opinion (5).

  4 *We* **must** *have a party at the end of term.* • *You and I* **must** *get together for lunch soon.*
  5 *I* **must** *disagree with that. We* **must not** *accept new regulations that restrict our civil rights.*

Necessity: *have to, don't have to* and *have got to*

We usually use *have to* instead of *must* when we are not in control of what is necessary or required.

  6 *My mother* **has to** *have an operation on her knee.* • *I* **have to** *wear glasses for reading.*

We usually use *have to* (with auxiliary *do*) instead of *must* in questions.

  7 *Why* **does** *everyone* **have to** *sign?* • **Don't** *you* **have to** *wear a seat belt?* • **Do** *I* **have to** *do it again?*
We can form questions with *must*, but they sound more formal: *Must I do it again?*

We use *have to* (not *must*) when we ask or talk about what was required or necessary in the past (8) and in all the phrasal modal structures (9).

  8 **Did** *you* **have to** *wear uniform in school? Colin* **had to** *wear a blazer, a cap and a tie.*
  9 *You* **will have to** *change.* • *I don't want to* **have to** *fight.* • *Nobody likes* **having to** *wash dishes.* •
    I **have had to** *complete three forms already. Now I'm* **having to** *complete another one.*

We use *don't have to* (not *mustn't*) as the opposite of *must* when something is not necessary.

  10 *It's free – you* **don't have to** *pay.* • *The gate was open so we* **didn't have to** *wait outside.*

We can use *have got to* instead of *have to* in informal situations, but only in the present tense (11). We use *have* (not *do*) as an auxiliary with *got to* when we form negatives and questions (12).

  11 *We* **have got to** *find a better way to do this.* • *I've* **got to** *see Ben.* (NOT ~~I had got to see Ben.~~)
  12 *She* **hasn't got to** *wait long.* • **Have** *we* **got to** *buy tickets?* (NOT ~~Do we have got to buy tickets?~~)

Necessity: *need to, don't need to* and *needn't*

We can use *need to* like *have to* to say that something is necessary (13) or not necessary (14).

  13 *Jim* **needs to/has to** *leave soon.* • *I'll* **need to/have to** *take an umbrella.* (NOT ~~I'll need take an umbrella.~~)
  14 *We* **don't need to/have to** *wait.* • *Because it rained, I* **won't need to/have to** *water the garden.*

We can also use *needn't* or *need not* (without *to*) to say that something is not necessary on a particular occasion (15). We usually use *don't need to* for things that are not necessary in general (16).

  15 *You* **needn't** *pay me now.* • *It's still early so we* **needn't** *rush.* (NOT ~~We needn't to rush.~~)
  16 *Students* **don't need to** *pay to use the library.* (NOT ~~Students needn't pay to use the library.~~)
In American English, only *don't need to* (not *needn't*) is used.

We use *didn't need to* when we mean it was not necessary to do something (17). We use *needn't have* plus a past participle when we mean something unnecessary was done (18).

  17 *I knew there wouldn't be a test, so I* **didn't need to** *study. I watched TV instead.*
  18 *I studied all night, then found out the test was cancelled. I* **needn't have** *studied at all.*

Auxiliary verbs 17 *Must, have to, have got to* (deduction) 40 Phrasal modals 29

18 Using a dictionary if necessary, complete the sentences with these words and appropriate forms of *must* or *have to*.

command   duty-free   evil   extra   fruit   obligation   step   taboo

1 An optional .... in a new car is something that is available, but you .... get it.
2 An essential .... is a part of a procedure you'll .... do in order for it to be successful.
3 Forbidden .... is something that you .... touch or have, even though you really want it.
4 In the army, soldiers .... always obey a .... given by a senior officer.
5 If you are under no .... to do something, you .... do it.
6 When you buy things that are ...., you .... pay tax on them.
7 If a topic is .... in a particular culture, it means that you .... talk about it because it is considered offensive.
8 A necessary .... is something you don't like or want, but which you may .... accept in order to achieve your goal.

19 Complete these sentences with the verbs and adjectives.

didn't have to   must   need to   allowed   official   significant
having to   mustn't   needn't have   impossible   required   unnecessary

1 I .... wear a jacket and tie last night. Formal attire was not ....
2 You .... made so much noise. All that shouting was quite ....
3 People .... have dogs in their rooms. Pets are not .... in the hotel.
4 You won't .... fill in forms. All the .... paperwork will be complete.
5 Not .... pay to use the pool is a .... benefit of being a student here.
6 Everyone .... have a valid passport because it will be .... to enter the country without one.

20 Correct the mistakes in these sentences.

1 We have already washed all the dinner dishes so you mustn't clean them tonight.

2 Everyone will have got to go through metal detectors every time they enter the building.

3 I'll need get some aspirin because I've got a terrible headache and I have to keep working.

4 The part that broke is a crucial component and I must to find a replacement immediately.

5 Whenever service is included in a bill, customers needn't to leave a tip for the waiter.

6 Our train arrived rather late and so we had got to take a taxi to get to our meeting on time.

7 I don't want to be the one to must have to tell him that he failed the entrance exam again.

8 I'm sure you don't need be over twenty-one to go into a pub here, but we must ask someone.

9 When we stayed with my grandmother, we must go to church with her every Sunday.

10 We didn't know that our friends had already gone into the theatre so we needn't have to wait all that time for them outside in the cold.

Deduction: *must, have to, have got to, can't* and *couldn't*

We use *must* to say that a particular idea or deduction is very likely or certain, based on the evidence (1). We use *must* in the modal continuous for a deduction about what is happening now (2).

   1 *You're shivering – you* **must** *be cold.* • *Look at that car! Ali's parents* **must** *have a lot of money!*
   2 *Listen. It* **must be raining** *outside.* • *I think I* **must be getting** *the flu.* (NOT ~~I must get the flu.~~)

We use *must* plus the perfect when we want to express a deduction about what has happened already (3) and when we report deductions in clauses after past tense verbs (4).

   3 *Someone* **must have taken** *the key because it isn't here.* (NOT ~~Someone must take the key.~~)
   4 *We realized he* **must have lied**. • *I thought at first that someone* **must have made** *a mistake.*

We use *must* in indirect speech when the information is still true: *He said she* **must** *be Italian.*

We can also use *have to* or *have got to* instead of *must* for a deduction in informal situations.

   5 *I didn't order ten books. This* **has to** *be a mistake.* • *These aren't mine – they***'ve got to** *be yours.*

We use *can't* or *couldn't* (not *mustn't*) as the opposite of *must* in negative deductions (6). We use *can't* or *couldn't* plus the perfect for negative deductions about earlier events (7).

   6 *The bill is over £50 – that* **can't** *be right.* • *You* **can't** *be 21!* (NOT ~~You mustn't be 21!~~)
   7 *You* **can't have finished** *already!* • *If he wasn't there, he* **couldn't have committed** *the murder.*

21 Choose an ending (a–e) for each beginning (1–5) and add appropriate forms of *must* or *can't*.

1 Julia goes to Malta every summer. (...)
2 What she's asking for is ridiculous. (...)
3 The hands on the clock weren't moving. (...)
4 Their daughter was only three this year. (...)
5 Those are two contradictory statements. (...)

a She .... started school yet.
b If one is correct, the other .... be.
c It's crazy. She .... joking.
d She .... really like it there.
e It .... stopped working.

22 Complete this dialogue with *must* or *couldn't* plus appropriate forms of the verbs.

be   carry   do   lose   put   take

Mum (putting on her coat): I'm going to have to go down to the shop for more bread.

Alan: Why?

Mum: I'm not sure what happened. I made some sandwiches earlier and left them on the table when I went to answer the phone. But someone (1) .... them because they're gone.

Alan: Oh, it (2) .... Dad. I'm sure he was in the kitchen earlier.

Mum: No, he went off to his tennis match before I finished making them, so he (3) .... it. Anyway, he (4) .... a plate of sandwiches as well as all his tennis stuff, so I'm sure it wasn't him.

Alan (opening fridge door): Well, it wasn't me. But Mum, look! Are these your sandwiches here on the bottom shelf of the fridge?

Mum: Are they in there? Oh, my goodness. I (5) .... them in there when the phone rang. Oh, dear. I really (6) .... my mind. Now, why did I put on my coat?

Obligation and advice: *should, ought to, be supposed to, had better*

Obligation and advice: *should*

We use *should* to express an obligation (1), to talk about what is expected (2) and generally to say what we think is a good or appropriate idea (3).

1 *The police **should** crack down on speeding.* • *At election time, everyone **should** vote.*
2 *You're a student. You **should** be studying!* • *Nurses and doctors **shouldn't** smoke.*
3 *Teachers **should** get more pay.* • *Children **should** learn to say 'Please' and 'Thank you'.*

We use *should* when we ask for and give advice (4) or warnings (5).

4 *What **should** I do?* • *You **should** take notes during lectures.* • *You **should** get to the airport early.*
5 *You **shouldn't** go swimming right after eating.* • *You **shouldn't** go through the park at night.*

We can use *should* to say that something is likely because we have planned it or expect it.

6 *If all goes well, we **should** be there before it gets dark.* • *The bus **should** come soon.*

We use *should* plus the perfect when we think that something good or desirable did not happen (7), often as a way of expressing regret (8).

7 *They **should have rehearsed** before playing.* • *We **should have left** a tip for our waiter.*
8 *We **should have been** more careful with our money.* • *I **shouldn't have told** anyone about it.*

Obligation and advice: *ought to, be supposed to* and *had better*

We can use *ought to* instead of *should* with no difference in meaning.

9 *Neighbours **ought to/should** help each other.* • *You really **ought to/should** be more careful.* • *He **should/ought to** have completed the work before he left.* (NOT *He ought have completed the work.*)

The negatives are *oughtn't to* or *ought not to*: *You ought not to wait.* (NOT *You ought not wait.*)

We can also use *be supposed to* instead of *should*, usually in informal situations (10). We can use *be supposed to* (not *should*) when we report what others think is true (11).

10 *You **are supposed to/should** be sleeping.* (NOT *You supposed to be sleeping.*)
11 *Killing a spider **is supposed to** be unlucky.* (NOT *Killing a spider should be unlucky.*)

We can use *had better* as a stronger version of *should* when we recommend (12) or warn against (13) doing something.

12 *You have failed two tests. You **had better** start working harder or you won't pass the course.*
13 *Johnny's going to take your bike. ~ He**'d better not** do that!* (NOT *He'd not better do that.*)

23 Add these nouns and verbs to these sentences.

cat	mirror	shoulder	had better	ought not	should be
ladder	person	umbrella	is supposed to	shouldn't	should have

If you listen to the advice of a superstitious (1) ...., you (2) ....
be ready to pay a lot of attention to what you're doing each day. Be careful with that
(3) .... You'll be told that you (4) .... open it indoors. When you're
walking along the street, watch out for a (5) .... You (6) .... careful
not to walk under one. Did you spill any salt recently? You know that you (7) ....
immediately thrown some of it over your (8) ...., don't you? And remember that you
(9) .... to be careless with a (10) ...., because if you break one, you'll
have seven years of bad luck. However, if you see a black (11) ...., that's good,
because it (12) .... be lucky.

Tests

A Choose the word or phrase that best completes each sentence.

1 You're 18! You're _____ to be able to look after yourself by now.

   a have   b ought   c should   d supposed

2 A permit is a document which states that you _____ to do something.

   a are allowed   b cannot   c may   d shall

3 He _____ have helped us if he'd really wanted to.

   a could   b may   c must   d will

4 My computer _____ be old, but it still works really well.

   a can   b could   c may   d would

5 _____ someone please tell me where the library is?

   a Can   b May   c Must   d Should

B Identify the one underlined expression (A, B, C or D) that must be changed in order to correct the sentence.

1 They say it <u>can be going to</u> rain later so you <u>should</u> take an umbrella or you <u>might</u> get wet.
              A   B   C   D

2 I <u>was going to ask</u> you if you <u>would read</u> over my essay before I <u>have to hand</u> it in, but when you
     A   B   C

   read it, you <u>ought not be</u> too critical or negative.
                D

3 His right hand <u>may have been</u> badly injured and he probably <u>won't be able to</u> type, so I thought
               A   B   C

   that I <u>will</u> offer to do some typing for him.
        D

4 Andy was so generous. If I asked him, '<u>Could</u> I borrow your car?', he <u>would</u> always say,
                                     A   B

   'Of course, you <u>could!</u>', and he <u>would</u> immediately start looking for the keys.
                    C   D

5 I really wish I <u>would have</u> a car of my own so that I <u>could</u> go for a drive in the country and I
               A   B

   <u>would be able to</u> go when I want to and not <u>have to</u> wait for a bus or a train.
       C   D

C Combine one modal and one verb phrase to fill each space in this text.

can	may not	must	be charged	be paid	be used
will	won't		be familiar	be required	

Note: Credit cards are used instead of cash, interest is charged and part payment is allowed. Charge cards are used instead of cash, but no interest is charged and full payment is required.

As a new customer of the bank, you (1) _____ with the difference between a charge card and a credit card. Both cards (2) _____ instead of cash in most places to pay for goods and services. Later, when you receive your charge card bill, the total (3) _____ in full every time. However, when you receive your monthly credit card bill, you (4) _____ to pay the total amount. If you choose to pay only part of the bill, you (5) _____ interest on the amount not paid.

D Complete each sentence in such a way that it is as similar as possible in meaning to the sentence above it.

1 Students may not park here.
Students are _____

2 It's possible that his trip was cancelled at the last minute.
His trip may _____

3 She had to get up at five every morning and she didn't enjoy it.
She didn't enjoy _____

4 It was impossible for him to have committed the crime, according to the report.
He _____

5 It was a bad idea to put this shirt in the washing machine.
This shirt _____

E Complete this text with these words.

be able to	couldn't	might	was able to	would (×2)
be willing to	had to	should	was going to	

'Hello! Mr Appleton!'

The voice was some distance behind him. He stopped raking the leaves and turned to see two women struggling up the driveway towards him. They were wearing identical white T-shirts which had MADD in large black letters across the front. He had a sudden strange thought that they (1) _____ be crazy people who (2) _____ spell. But they didn't look crazy. As they came closer, he (3) _____ make out smaller letters under each of the big letters, spelling out the words 'Mothers Against Drunk Driving'.

'I'm so glad we found you. I'm Nettie Albright and this is Agnes Miller.'

He shook their outstretched hands. Agnes was wearing thin gloves.

'We talked to your wife this morning and she's the one who told us we (4) _____ (5) _____ find you here. She said she hadn't really witnessed the accident, but you had. We were hoping you (6) _____ (7) _____ testify.' She (8) _____ stop and take a deep breath.

'You mean the car crash?'

'Yes, exactly, the crash. We need witnesses. That awful man says it wasn't his fault. He (9) _____ be taken out and shot! He's a menace to society. We need your help to put him away.'

It had happened one early evening in July. I (10) _____ just _____ cross the street when a car came racing through the red light, narrowly missing me, but smashing into another car in the middle of the junction. The woman in that car died. When the man who hit her turned out to be very drunk, it all changed from being an accident to being a criminal case.

4 Negatives and questions

Negatives are usually formed with an auxiliary verb (*be*, *do* or *have*) or a modal plus *not/n't* before the main verb (*I **am not** crying, you **don't** care, he **hasn't** gone, we **shouldn't** wait*).

Questions are usually formed with an auxiliary verb (*be*, *do* or *have*) or a modal before the subject and the main verb (***Has** he gone?* ***Should** we wait?*).

There are yes/no questions (***Are** you crying?* ***Do** they care?*) and *wh*-questions (***Where has** he gone?* ***Why should** we wait?*).

1 Read through this interview and find:

1 another yes/no question
2 the one sentence that contains two negative verbs

A **Why did you start the 'Protect Yourself' programme?** A good friend of mine was attacked and robbed last year on her way home from work. She wasn't seriously injured, but it really frightened her and she wouldn't go out alone. I started talking to her about protecting herself and she thought it would be a good idea to form a group. Eventually we had so many people that it turned into a regular kind of night class.

B **Who can take part?** Anyone who wants to, but mostly it's young women. We meet in an old building that's next to the big church on Wilder Avenue, from 6 to 7 on Mondays.

C **Do you teach karate and stuff like that?** Not really. We tried some of that at first, but it wasn't very successful. There is a real karate class in the same building on Thursdays for people who want that. We still use some of the movements from karate when we talk about ways to escape, but we focus more on not getting into that kind of situation.

D **What do you mean? How don't you get into 'that kind of situation'?** We talk a lot about not becoming a victim and thinking of ways to avoid being attacked. It's really more about awareness and how not to be an easy target. There are some statistics about assault victims that we talk about. For example, women with longer hair are more likely to be attacked than women whose hair is shorter or in a style that can't be grabbed.

E **Is there anything else?** Clothing is another thing. Women in skirts and dresses are attacked more than those wearing jeans or trousers.

F **When and where do most attacks occur?** At night, of course. But surprisingly, a large number of assaults occur in the early morning, before 8.30. They happen in isolated areas, parks, outside schools and office buildings before and after regular working hours. We advise women not to go alone to parking areas and garages in the morning or in the evening. But, if you must, you should carry an umbrella or something like that and, if you're going to your car, have your keys ready.

G **What's the umbrella for? Is it a weapon?** Well, it isn't much of a weapon, is it? But we think it helps you feel more confident. We actually practise using the umbrella to keep someone at a distance while you shout and scream as loud as you can to discourage any attacker who wants you to be an easy victim.

H **What should you do if you're actually attacked?** Be a problem. Grab fingers and bend them backwards. Bite hands. Stomp your foot down hard on the attacker's toes. Grab the skin under the arm above the attacker's elbow and squeeze as hard as you can. Move, twist, kick, scratch, fall down, scream and yell. Be hard to hold and make a lot of noise.

2 Choose one of the following as the final sentence of the last five paragraphs above (D–H)

1 We want you to be a difficult problem. (...)
2 Maybe that's why there are also more attacks in warmer weather. (...)
3 You may be fighting for your life. (...)
4 It isn't wise to stand out there searching for something in your bag. (...)
5 A pony tail can make you very vulnerable. (...)

Word order in negatives and questions

Negatives

With auxiliaries *be*, *have* and modals, we form negatives with *not/n't*. In formal situations we use the full form (*We are not*) (1). In informal situations, we usually contract *not* (*We aren't*) (2) or we contract the auxiliary (*We're not*) and the modal (*We'll not*) (3).

    1 *Dogs **are not** allowed in city parks.* • *Guests **must not** eat or drink outside.*

    2 *They **aren't** listening.* • *We **haven't** forgotten the meeting.* • *Her parents **won't** let her go.*

    3 *We**'re not** ready yet.* • *I**'ve not** been given any instructions.* • *He**'ll not** go unless you ask him.*

With other verbs, we form negatives with *do* plus *not/n't* before the base form of the verb.

    4 *Some people **do not** understand.* • *It **does not** work.* • *I **did not** refuse to pay.* • *They **don't** remember.* • *It **doesn't** help us.* • *We **didn't** see it.* (NOT ~~We didn't saw it.~~)

Negative forms of *do* are not used with modal verbs: *I **can't** swim.* (NOT ~~I don't can swim.~~)

In sentences with infinitives and gerunds, we put *not* before the infinitive or gerund.

    5 *He pretended **not to see** us.* • *I enjoyed **not going** to school for a few days.*

We can use *no* before nouns (6), and negative adverbs such as *no longer* or *never* before verbs (7).

    6 *There were **no** problems.* • *We'll have **no** money for rent.* (NOT ~~We'll no have money for rent.~~)

    7 *She's **no longer** working there.* • *They will **never** be free.* (NOT ~~They will be never free.~~)

Questions

With auxiliaries *be*, *have* and modals, we form questions by putting the auxiliary or modal before the subject. We put the main verb after the subject.

    8 ***Are you** coming?* • ***Have they** finished?* • *Why **must you** leave?* (NOT ~~Why you must leave?~~) • *How **can I** help?* • *Where **was your watch** made?* (NOT ~~Where was made your watch?~~)

With other verbs, we form questions with *do* before the subject and the base form of the verb.

    9 ***Do you** know the answer?* • *What **does she** want?* • ***Did he** break it?* (NOT ~~Did he broke it?~~)

We begin yes/no questions with *be*, *do*, *have* or a modal and usually use them to get *Yes* or *No* as an answer (10). We can use yes/no questions joined by *or* when we offer a choice between two possible answers (11).

    10 ***Am I** the first to arrive?* • ***Are you** feeling okay?* • ***Do you** like it?* • ***Does it** work?* • ***Have you** got a minute?* • ***Has it** stopped raining?* • ***May we** come in?* • ***Can you** play the piano?*

    11 *Do we go now **or** wait until later?* • *Would you like something hot **or** something cold to drink?*

Wh-questions begin with *wh*-words (question words) and ask for specific information.

    12 ***What's** your name?* • ***How** much does it cost?* • ***When** and **where** do most attacks occur?*

Other *wh*-words include: which, who, whom, whose, why

When we use *what* or *who* as the subject, we usually put the main verb (not *do*) after them.

    13 ***What's making** that noise?* • ***Who used** my computer?* (NOT ~~Who did use my computer?~~)

Note similar uses of *whose* and *which* with nouns: ***Whose** phone is ringing?* • ***Which** team won?*

3 **Find one sentence containing an example of each of the following in the interview on page 44.**

    1 A negative modal: ....

    2 A negative infinitive: ....

    3 A negative gerund: ....

    4 A *wh*-word used as subject: ....

Negative questions and question tags

Negative questions

Negative yes/no questions usually begin with negative forms of *be, do, have* or a modal (1).
In negative *wh*-questions, we put the negative forms after the *wh*-words (2).

1 ***Aren't*** *those books mine?* • ***Doesn't*** *he speak any English?* • ***Didn't*** *she get married last year?* •
Hasn't *the lecture finished yet?* • ***Haven't*** *we seen that film?* • ***Can't*** *you open the window?*

2 *Everyone was invited to the party.* • *Why* ***didn't*** *you go?* (NOT ~~Why you didn't go?~~) • *There are only
ten players on the field.* • *Who* ***isn't*** *here yet?* (NOT ~~Who isn't he here yet?~~)

When we answer negative yes/no questions, we use *Yes* to say the positive is true and *No* to say the
negative is true.

3 ***Aren't*** *they French?* ***Yes.*** (= They are French.) ***No.*** (= They aren't French.)

We put negative adverbs such as *never* and emphatic *not* after the subject (not the auxiliary) in
negative questions.

4 *Have you* ***never*** *eaten meat?* • *Did he* ***not*** *understand the text?* (NOT ~~Did not he understand
the text?~~)

We can use negative yes/no questions to ask for confirmation (5) or to express surprise (6).

5 ***Isn't*** *July 4th a big American holiday?* • ***Haven't*** *we already paid for the tickets?*

6 ***Doesn't*** *she like any music at all?* • ***Haven't*** *you ever seen snow?*

Questions beginning with *Why don't you …?* or *Why not …?* are used for offers or suggestions.

7 ***Why don't you*** *come with us?* • ***Why not*** *have the party on Saturday instead of Friday?*

There is no subject after *Why not …?* (NOT ~~Why not you have the party on Saturday?~~)

Question tags

Question tags (or tag questions) are short forms of questions added after statements.
We usually use a positive statement + negative tag (8) or a negative statement + positive tag (9).

8 *We're late,* ***aren't we?*** • *Mark really loves her,* ***doesn't he?*** • *She lost it,* ***didn't she?***

9 *I can't win,* ***can I?*** • *They don't like it,* ***do they?*** • *You haven't studied at all,* ***have you?***

The full forms (*are we not?, does he not?*) are very formal.

In question tags, we use a pronoun that matches the subject of the sentence and a verb that matches
the main verb auxiliary (if there is one) or *be* (as a main verb), or we use a form of *do*.

10 *You* ***haven't*** *talked to Mary since she went on holiday,* ***have you?*** (NOT ~~didn't she?~~) • *He* ***was*** *guilty,*
wasn't he? • *The evidence* ***showed*** *he was guilty,* ***didn't it?*** (NOT ~~wasn't he?~~)

Note that we use a positive tag with *they* after *no one* or *nobody*: *Nobody likes it, do they?*

We use modals in tags after imperatives for requests or proposals.

11 *Don't say anything,* ***will you?*** • *Pass me that knife,* ***could you?*** • *Let's leave,* ***shall we?***

We can use a positive tag after a positive sentence when we want to confirm information, often after
repeating what a previous speaker said. A negative tag after a negative sentence is very rare.

12 *That's your new car,* ***is it?*** • *So, the students are planning a protest,* ***are they?***

---

4 Find one example of each of the following in the interview on page 44.

1 a negative question: ....

2 a sentence with a question tag: ....

Negative words 48 Subject-verb agreement 4 *Wh*-words 45

5 Using a dictionary if necessary, complete the sentences with these words.

isn't	*doesn't*	*no*	*nondescript*	*non-refundable*	*non-stick*
aren't	*won't*	*not*	*non-event*	*non-resident*	*non-stop*

1 There usually .... any problems cleaning a pan if it's the .... kind.
2 When someone .... living permanently in a country, he or she is a
....
3 If something is expected to be big or dramatic, but it's ...., it can be described as
a ....
4 .... means the money won't be returned, ... it?
5 The word .... is used for something which has .... special or
unusual features.
6 If your journey is ...., you .... be able to visit any of the places
along the way.

6 Complete the questions with these words.

What	*Where*	*Whose*	*are*	*do*	*isn't*
When	*Who*	*Why*	*did*	*don't*	*were*

1 I have twenty names and only nineteen students. .... here today?
2 We have an extra room in our place. .... you stay with us?
3 Everyone was looking for Mr Kidd. .... you tell them he was?
4 There must be hundreds of people working there. .... they all do?
5 My parents worked in Saudi Arabia too. .... they there?
6 Some things were left in class yesterday. .... books .... these?

7 Editing. Correct the mistakes in the use of negatives and questions in this text.

In our group, we had to write down questions before a discussion of the topic: 'What kind of pet is
best?' That was difficult because some of us didn't ever had a pet, so we didn't really could say much
about this topic. I asked Michel, 'What you think is the best pet?' He answered, 'I not care about pets.'
Then he said, 'Why we have pets? We not need them for anything, don't we? And some people think
dogs not clean, so they not good pets.' I asked him, 'Aren't some pets cleaner than dogs? For example,
no one thinks a cat makes more mess than a dog, does he?' He didn't answered. Then Paola explained
that she could have not a cat in her house because cats made her mother sneeze a lot. So she suggested that an important question was: 'Why do some people can't have pets?' I wrote down three other
questions from our group: 'Do some pets more expensive to keep than others?' 'How will be trained
the pet?' 'Who is take care of the pet?'

Negative words

No, none, nobody, no one and *nothing*

Although we normally use negative verbs (*wasn't, haven't*) to express negative concepts (1), we can also use positive verbs with negative words such as *no, none, nobody, no one* and *nothing* (2). We can use these negative words as subjects with positive verbs (3).

    1 *There **wasn't** anything to eat in the hotel room, so we **haven't** had breakfast yet.*
    2 *There was **nothing** to eat in the hotel room, so **none** of us has had breakfast yet.*
    3 ***No one** complained. • **Nobody** told us.* (NOT ~~Not anybody told us.~~/~~Nobody didn't tell us.~~)

We use *no* before nouns and *none* instead of nouns.

    4 *Didn't you bring any money? ~ I have **no** money./I have **none**.* (NOT ~~I have none money.~~)
We don't normally use double negatives. (NOT ~~I don't have no money.~~/~~I don't have none.~~)

We use *none of* before pronouns and determiners (*the, those, our*, etc.).

    5 ***None of them** understood it. • **None of our** friends will come. • **None of the** lights is working.*
In informal situations, *none* is sometimes used with plural verbs: ***None** of them **are** working.*

We can use *no* with both singular and plural nouns or a gerund to emphasize the negative. We can use this structure instead of a negative verb (6) or as a shorthand for 'is/are not allowed' in formal situations (7).

    6 *One class doesn't have a teacher.* → *One class has **no** teacher.*
       Cameras aren't permitted inside the court. → ***No** cameras are permitted inside the court.*
    7 ***No** dogs. **No** skateboards. • **No** talking during the examination. • **No** parking.*
We use *Don't* + verb rather than *No* + gerund in informal situations: *Don't park there.*

We can use *no* or *not/n't any* with comparative adjectives (8) and adverbs (9).

    8 *These seats are **no better** than the others./These seats are**n't any better** than the others.*
    9 *We should leave **no later** than 8.30./We should**n't** leave **any later** than 8.30.*

We use *not* rather than *no* in reduced negatives (10), before the indefinite article *a/an* (11) and before quantifiers such as *all* or *a lot* (12).

    10 *Do you want to keep these boxes **or not**? **If not**, I'll just throw them out.*
    11 ***Not a** single drop of blood was spilt. • A whale is a mammal, **not a** fish.*
    12 ***Not all** Americans are rich. • There is **not a lot** to be gained by being rude to people.*

Inversion after negative words and phrases

We use inversion after negative adverbs such as *never* or *nowhere* when they are placed in front position for emphasis. We put the subject after an auxiliary verb (*be, do, have*) or a modal.

    13 *I have never heard such nonsense.* → *Never **have I** heard such nonsense.*
       They couldn't find a bottle-opener anywhere. → *Nowhere **could they** find a bottle-opener.*

We also use inversion after negative phrases with *no* (14) and *not* (15) in front position.

    14 *The children weren't in danger at any time.* → *At no time **were the children** in danger.*
       You shouldn't go under any circumstances. → *Under no circumstances **should you** go.*
    15 *I didn't realize what she meant until later.* → *Not until later **did I** realize what she meant.*
       Mark is not only single, but he is also rich. → *Not only **is Mark** single, but he is also rich.*

Inversion is typically used in formal or literary English, but we can also use it in informal replies, after *neither, nor* and *no way*.

    16 *I don't understand. ~ Neither **do I**. • We didn't like the film. ~ Nor **did most people**. • I think Mr Atkins should let us leave early. ~ No way **will he** agree to that.*

8 Choose an ending (a–d) for each beginning (1–4) and add *no*, *none* or *not*.

1 I wrote to several people, (...)
2 We needed some glue, (...)
3 .... food is allowed in that room, (...)
4 There's .... much money left (...)

a so you must .... eat in there.
b and we have .... traveller's cheques.
c but .... of them has replied yet.
d but there was .... in the house.

9 Using a dictionary if necessary, complete the sentences with these words.

carefree   indifferent   infrequent   doesn't   no   not
careless   infallible   invisible   never   no one   nothing

If something is (1) ...., it (2) .... happen very often.
When you are (3) ...., you have (4) .... to worry about, but the word
(5) .... isn't the same. It means (6) .... paying enough attention to
detail.
An object is (7) .... if (8) .... can see it.
If people or things are (9) ...., they (10) .... make mistakes or go
wrong.
When people are (11) .... to something, they have (12) .... interest in it.

10 Rewrite these sentences in a more informal style.

Example: Nowhere else do they make this bread.   *They don't make this bread anywhere else.*

1 Never has there been a better chance to make money on the stock market.
....

2 Not until the next morning did we notice that she had not come home.
....

3 At no time did anyone warn us about polluted water.
....

4 The janitor will say, 'No smoking in here,' will he not?
....

11 Complete this text with these words and phrases.

no idea   not only   nor   did I   had I   were they
no sooner   not until   nothing   did we   I had   they were

Have you ever arrived at work thinking something was wrong? It recently happened to me. On
Saturday morning, when I arrived at the City Concert Hall, there were a lot of musicians waiting
outside. (1) .... (2) .... opened the front door than the musicians
started to come in and complain. (3) .... (4) .... unhappy that their
next concert had been cancelled, but (5) .... also very angry that they hadn't been
paid for weeks. I tried to explain that I only looked after the Concert Hall and (6) ....
(7) .... to do with money or music. They said that a lot of tickets had been sold,
but they had (8) .... where the money had gone. (9) ....
(10) ...., I kept telling them. (11) .... two days later
(12) .... all find out that the concert organizer had run off with all the money.

Question words

What or *which*?

We can use *what* and *which* before nouns or as pronouns (1). We use *what* when we think there is an unlimited number of possible answers (2) and *which* when we think there is a limited number (3).

1 **What bus/which bus** should I take? • **What/Which** do you want?
2 **What** are you doing? • **What**'s her home phone number? • **What** would you like to drink?
3 *There are three numbers listed here.* **Which** *is her home phone number?* • *We have both red wine and white wine.* **Which** *would you prefer?*

We use *which* (not *what*) before *one* or *ones* (4). We use *which of* (not *what of*) before determiners (*the, this, my*, etc.) (5) and pronouns (6) when we ask about things and people in a limited set.

4 *There are a lot of cups of tea here.* **Which ones** *already have sugar?* **Which one** *is mine?*
5 **Which of** *these books haven't you read?* (NOT ~~What of these books haven't you read?~~)
6 *Edberg had four sons.* **Which (one) of** *them was the famous artist?* • **Which of** *you is first?*
We can use *who* to ask a general question: *Who is first?* (NOT ~~Who of you is first?~~)

---

12 Choose a question (a–f) to follow each statement (1–6) and add *What* or *Which*.

1 I'm one of the girls in that old photo. (....)   a .... was your score?
2 'Flunk the test' is an American phrase. (....)   b .... one did you get wrong?
3 He gave us our exam results. (....)   c .... are you waiting for?
4 I'd like to leave soon. (....)   d .... is you?
5 I got 19 out of 20 correct. (....)   e .... of them have you read?
6 I haven't read all his books. (....)   f .... does it mean?

Question words with prepositions and adverbs

We can use *wh*-questions to ask about the objects of prepositions. We usually put the preposition at the end of a *wh*-question (7). In formal uses, the preposition is sometimes put at the beginning (8).

7 *He's going to fill the hole with something.* → **What** *is he going to fill the hole* **with**?
   You gave your old computer to someone. → **Who** *did you give your old computer* **to**?
8 **With what** *is he going to fill the hole?* • **To whom** *did you give your old computer?*
We must use *whom* (not *who*) after a preposition. (NOT ~~To who did you give your old computer?~~)

In some *wh*-questions (*What ... for?, What/Who ...like?*), the preposition is always at the end.

9 **What** *are you doing that* **for**? • **Who** *does she look* **like**? (NOT ~~Like whom does she look?~~)

There are some prepositions which we use at the beginning (not the end) of *wh*-questions.

10 **During which** *period were the French in control?* • **Since when** *have these records been kept?*
Other prepositions used like this include: above, after, before, below

We usually put adverbs after *wh*-words (11), but we can use some adverbs before *wh*-words (12).

11 **How often** *do you exercise?* • **What else** *did he say?* • **When exactly** *did he leave Cyprus?*
12 **Precisely where** *did you last see the keys?* • **Exactly when** *did he leave Cyprus?*

Wh-words with *ever* (such as *wherever, whoever*) are used to express surprise or disbelief.

13 **Wherever** *did you find that?* • **However** *did she do it?* • **Whoever** *told you such nonsense?*
We don't use *whichever* in this way: **Whatever** *do you mean?* (NOT ~~Whichever do you mean?~~)

Adverbs 118 Determiners 83 *One, ones* 104 Pronouns 97 Prepositions 125

13 Complete these quiz questions with these words and try to choose correct answers.

by	for	how	often	where	who	with
during	from (×2)	of	what (×2)	which (×2)	whom	

1 . . . . century did the French Revolution begin? (. .)
(A) 17th (B) 18th (C) 19th

2 . . . . does an annual meeting take place? (. .)
(A) every week (B) every month (C) every year

3 Cider is a type of drink. is it made . . . . ? (. .)
(A) apples (B) grapes (C) oranges

4 . . . . did Paul McCartney write many of the Beatles' hit songs? (. .)
(A) Mick Jagger (B) Elton John (C) John Lennon

5 . . . . these countries is not in South America? (. .)
(A) Bolivia (B) Nicaragua (C) Paraguay

6 Mel Gibson is a well-known actor. is he . . . . ?(. .)
(A) Australia (B) Canada (C) Scotland

7 'War and Peace' is the title of a famous book. was it written
. . . . ? (. .)
(A) Charles Dickens (B) William Shakespeare (C) Leo Tolstoy

8 . . . . is a whisk used . . . . ? (. .)
(A) beating cattle, horses, etc. (B) playing cellos, violins, etc. (C) stirring eggs, cream, etc.

14 Complete this dialogue (from an American crime thriller) with these words and phrases.

how ever	what … about	where	where … from	who
how long	whatever	where exactly	which … in	who else

The phone woke me up. I automatically reached over and picked it up.

'Good morning, darling. I guess you're not coming to get me, are you?'

'What? (1) . . . . is this?

'It's me. Charles. (2) . . . . were you expecting?'

'Sorry. I'm still asleep. Aren't you in New York?'

'(3) . . . . are you talking . . . . ? (4) . . . . gave you that idea?'

'You're not? Oh, no, I can't think straight. (5) . . . . are you?'

'I'm at the airport. I just got back from Glasgow.'

'Oh, goodness. (6) . . . . have you been waiting? I'm so sorry.'

'It's okay. Don't panic. I'm just about to pick up my bag.'

'I'm up. I'll be there. (7) . . . . are you? (8) . . . . terminal are you
. . . . ?'

'It's okay. I'll catch the train into town. Can you meet me at the station?'

'Yes. It'll be quicker that way. I'll see you in about forty-five minutes.'

'Okay. Bye.'

I started to put the phone down, but there was something wet and sticky on it. Was it blood?

(9) . . . . had it come . . . . ? There was more of it on the sheet.

(10) . . . . did it get there?

Other question types

Questions inside questions

We can put a yes/no question asking what people think (1) or say (2) after the *wh*-word (*what, who*) inside a *wh*-question.

1 *Do you think something is wrong?* → *What **do you think** is wrong?*
  (NOT ~~What you think is wrong?~~)
2 *Did he say someone was waiting outside?* → *Who **did he say** was waiting outside?*

When we put a yes/no question inside a *wh*-question, we use question word order in the yes/no question, not in the *wh*-question.

3 *Does he believe the fighting will end?* → *When **does he believe** the fighting will end?*
  (NOT ~~When does he believe will the fighting end?~~)

Statements used as questions

We can use a statement as a yes/no question to ask for confirmation of something (4) or to repeat what was just said, usually to express surprise (5). We can use a *wh*-word in a statement to ask for clarification or to get more information about part of what was just said (6).

4 *Monday **is** a holiday?* • *Mr. Jones **was** your teacher too?* • *David **doesn't** know about this?*
5 *Paul won first prize.* ~ ***He won first prize?*** • *I had a ticket, but didn't go.* ~ ***You didn't go?***
6 *She zapped it.* ~ *She **did what to** it?* • *I met Popeye.* ~ *You met **who?*** (NOT ~~Did you meet who?~~)

Rhetorical questions

Rhetorical questions have the form of a question, but can be used to assert something (7). We can use rhetorical questions to establish a topic (8), or to highlight a previous question (9) before giving an answer.

7 *Mike isn't here yet.* ~ ***Who cares?*** (= I don't care.) ***Isn't he always late?*** (= He is always late.)
8 ***Do you remember the oil crisis?** We were sure then that cars would have to become smaller.*
9 *What do you think of it?* ~ ***What do I think of it?** I think it's just too expensive.*

Reduced questions

In informal situations, yes/no questions are sometimes used without *Are you?* or *Do/Did you?* (10) and *wh*-questions can be reduced to the *wh*-word alone (11) or short phrases (12).

10 *Feeling okay?* • *Tired?* • *Going out?* • *Need some help?* • *Like it?* • *Have fun last night?*
11 *We must buy that piano.* ~ ***How?*** ~ *I'll find the money.* ~ ***Where?*** ~ *I know someone.* ~ ***Who?***
12 *You have to do it.* ~ ***Why me?*** • *Your plan won't work.* ~ ***Why not?*** • *Bring a knife.* ~ ***What for?***

We also use the phrases *How about?* (13) and *What about?* (14) without verbs before nouns and gerunds to make suggestions or to draw attention to something.

13 ***How about** a cup of tea?* • ***How about** watching TV?* (NOT ~~How about shall we watch TV?~~)
14 ***What about** your homework?* • ***What about** playing 'Go'?* (NOT ~~What about we play 'Go'?~~)

Indirect questions

We use indirect questions when we report what was asked. We don't use question word order or a question mark in indirect questions (15). We begin indirect yes/no questions with *if* or *whether* (16).

15 *Why did you start the programme?* → *I asked her **why** she (had) started the programme.*
   What do you mean? → *I asked her **what** she meant.* (NOT ~~I asked her what did she mean?~~)
16 *Do you teach karate?* → *I asked **if** they taught karate.* (NOT ~~I asked did they teach karate?~~)
   Is it an umbrella or a weapon? → *I asked **whether** it was an umbrella or a weapon.*

Gerunds 139   Indirect questions 154   Question word order 45

15 Rewrite these statements as questions beginning with *What, When, Where* and *Who*.

Example: They think something is wrong. ..*What do they think is wrong?*..............

1 You believe someone is responsible for the current conflict.

....

2 Her father thought she might have gone somewhere.

....

3 The weather forecaster said the rain should stop at some time.

....

4 You imagine their new house is going to look like something.

....

16 Choose a question (a–e) to follow each beginning (1–5) and add these words.

did   didn't   do   does   how   which   who   why

1 Will it be sunny tomorrow? (...)
2 Mary, you have to crawl through the tunnel. (...)
3 I understood nothing he said. (...)
4 I don't know how I'll pass the exam. (...)
5 He says there is a problem with the contract. (...)

a .... he? With .... part?
b .... about studying?
c .... knows?
d You ....? Neither .... I!
e .... I have to? .... me?

17 This dialogue takes place in a police station between Mrs Adams and Detective Grimshaw. Complete it with these words.

he did   he's   he was   I do   you're   you don't
did he   is he   was he   do I   are you   don't you

'Can we leave now or (1) .... going to start paying us for all the time we're spending here?'

'Your son isn't going anywhere, Mrs Adams. (2) .... in deep trouble this time.'

'(3) .... really? Maybe you're the one who's in trouble, detective. My son has done nothing. This is police harassment.'

'I asked your son what (4) .... doing in John Mansfield's house last night and what do you think he said?'

'What (5) .... think? I think (6) .... making all this up because (7) .... have a clue. You're just trying to blame my Tommy for something he didn't do. He worked for Mr Mansfield. That's all.'

'Listen. I didn't tell your son that Mansfield was killed with a knife. He told me. He wasn't just helping us make this up, (8) ....?'

'Oh, (9) .... make you think he was going to confess? I don't know what you think (10) .... One thing (11) .... know for sure is that he was at home with me all last night. Why (12) .... just leave him alone and go find the real killer?'

Tests

A Choose the word or phrase that best completes each sentence.

1 What do you think _____ me?
   a told   b they told   c didn't tell   d did he tell

2 Why not _____ the meeting for Monday morning?
   a schedule   b scheduling   c you schedule   d do you schedule

3 They explained that she couldn't take the course, _____ ?
   a could she   b couldn't she   c did she   d didn't they

4 _____ real work was done in the office while the boss was away.
   a Not a   b Not any   c No   d None

5 Good morning, gentlemen. _____ of you is first in line?
   a Which   b Whose   c Who   d Whom

B Identify the one underlined expression (A, B, C or D) that must be changed in order to correct these sentences.

1 My neighbour used to say, 'How about <u>helping</u> me carry this?' or 'Give me a hand with this, <u>would</u>
                                    A   B
   you?', but at no time he <u>asked</u> me if I ever <u>needed</u> help with anything.
                              C   D

2 I'm <u>not trying</u> to work more, but quite often I <u>have no</u> time for lunch or I <u>don't have</u> much of an
        A   B   C
   appetite, and so I <u>take no longer</u> a whole hour for my lunch break.
                        D

3 I told Sarah that <u>it wasn't</u> my party. I explained that it was my brother's party, so none of my
                      A
   friends <u>had been invited</u>. I guess she <u>didn't believe</u> me because her first question was,
            B   C
   'Why <u>you didn't</u> invite me to the party?'
         D

4 'Did you see those students cheating during the exam?' ~ 'No, but <u>didn't you tell</u> the teacher?'
                                                                      A
   'I decided <u>not to tell</u> her because I didn't really think it was my business and no one wants to be a
               B
   tell tale, <u>does he</u>? Don't say anything about this to anyone, <u>will you</u>?'
               C   D

5 <u>Not</u> many people realize that a spider is <u>no</u> insect because insects <u>don't</u> have eight legs and <u>none</u> of
    A   B   C   D
   them make webs.

C Fill in the missing words in this dialogue.

'Isn't window-shopping fun? Look at these lovely vases. (1) _____ they beautiful?'

'They're okay.'

'Let's buy one!'

'With (2) _____ ?'

'Oh, come on, just one.'

'No, I don't think so. They're (3) _____ nicer than the ones we already have at home.'

'Oh, you're such a spoilsport!'

'No, (4) _____ . I'm simply trying to avoid spending money that we haven't got!'

'(5) _____ we buy anything at all?'

'No. But you can enjoy looking. That, after all, is what window-shopping means.'

D Complete each sentence in such a way that it is as similar as possible in meaning to the sentence above it.

1 The room wasn't only cold, it was also very damp.
   Not _____

2 Your sister said she gave the money to someone.
   Who _____ ?

3 Andreas thinks that something has been stolen.
   What _____ ?

4 She suggested that I take the train instead of driving.
   She said, 'Why _____ ?'

5 'What's his name and where does he live?'
   They asked me _____

E Complete this text with these words and appropriate answers to the questionnaire.

did   how   never   no   nothing   what   where   which   who   why

Your parents have sent you a ticket to fly to New York where they are planning to celebrate their wedding anniversary. (1) .... much is happening at work, you've (2) .... been to New York and you've had (3) .... holiday trips for more than a year, so you've quickly packed a couple of large suitcases and headed to the airport. You are now sitting on board British Airways flight BA 21, non-stop from London to New York, waiting to take off. The flight attendant hands you a questionnaire. You decide to complete it.

(4) _____ is your flight number?	_____
(5) _____ are you taking this flight?	Business _____ or Leisure _____
(6) _____ paid for your flight?	Myself _____ or Somebody else _____
(7) _____ you check in bags for this flight?	_____
(8) At _____ airport did you board this flight?	_____
(9) _____ will you leave this flight?	_____
(10) _____ many flights have you made in the last 12 months?	_____

5 The passive

Passive verbs, or passives, are formed with *be* plus the past participle of a transitive verb (*My car **was stolen***). We use passive verbs to say what happens to the subject (*Two men **were arrested***) in contrast to active verbs which are used to say what the subject does (*The police **arrested** two men*).

1 Read through this news report and find two more examples of the same verb (*find* and *move*) being used as both an active and a passive verb.

FOR AS LONG AS people can remember, small towns like Stone Creek and Pineville in northern Alabama have been hit by storms every spring. They are as predictable as the apple blossoms that are always shaken loose from the trees and blown along the country roads. Some trees may be knocked over or the roof of a building might be slightly damaged, but usually the effects of the storms are more inconvenient than deadly. This year was different.

Last night, a powerful storm roared into the area, sending devastating tornadoes spinning through the small farming communities. It destroyed farms, schools and churches and buried people in the ruins of their own homes. It transformed the landscape. Herds of cattle that had been moved into barns for safety are nowhere to be seen, nor are the barns. Other buildings where tractors and equipment were being stored seem to have been completely blown away.

The scenes of devastation this morning are described by one rescue worker as 'like the end of the world'. Since first light, rescue crews have been moving through the countryside, looking for survivors. Small teams have had to be flown in to some areas by helicopter because the roads have been blocked by dozens of fallen trees. In other areas, rescuers don't know what they will find as they search through the debris. 'We're guessing that there are some people who may have been pinned down under their own ceilings,' says Greg Hayden, a firefighter from Atlanta. 'Sometimes we can't tell the houses from the stables or the garages. It's a mess. Dozens of people and animals could have been buried in there.'

One by one, the miracles and the tragedies are coming to light. Jim Clinton, having been warned of the approaching storm on his radio, drove his wife and daughter to his local church. He thought it would be safer there than staying in his small house. Two of the church walls collapsed, but after being trapped inside for four hours, the Clintons were found alive by rescuers this morning. Not far away, an old couple had retreated to the basement of their home as the storm approached. Tragically, they were both killed when part of a wall crashed through the floor on top of them. The names of all victims are being withheld until their families can be notified.

At least 38 people have died and many more are missing. About 100 people have been seriously injured and more than 1,000 have been left homeless. The search for the missing may last for days, but the effects of this one storm are going to be felt for many years. 'It's like someone dropped a bomb,' said one shocked woman as she searched through the remains of what used to be her home. ●

2 Complete this summary using appropriate forms of verbs from the news report.

At least 38 people have died, about 100 (1) .... seriously ....,
and more than 1,000 (2) .... homeless in northern Alabama after the area
(3) .... by a powerful storm last night. Farms, schools and churches
(4) .... and some people (5) .... in the ruins of their own homes.
Fallen trees (6) .... roads in some areas, so rescue teams (7) .... by
helicopter. The effects of this storm (8) .... for years.

pinned down

Active and passive

buried دفن
ruin = *damages* تخريب
herds قطيع
barns حظيرة

We use an active verb to say what the subject does (1) and a passive verb to say what happens to the subject (2).

   1 *After the accident, someone **called** the police and they **arrested** the drunk driver.*
   2 *After the accident, the police **were called** and the drunk driver **was arrested**.*

We use the object of an active verb as the subject of a passive verb (3). We can't create passives from intransitive verbs (4).

   3 *We clear **the table** and wash **the dishes**.* → ***The table** is cleared and **the dishes** are washed.*
   4 *We swam every day. • Rick came later.* (NOT ~~Rick was come later.~~)

The passive verb has two parts. We use a form of the verb *be* plus a past participle.

   5 *You have to rewrite the first paragraph.* → *The first paragraph has to **be rewritten**.*

We can use a *by*-phrase after the passive verb to say who or what causes the action.

   6 *My car was repaired **by Andrew**. • Some roads are blocked **by fallen trees**.*

3 **Passive tenses: Complete this table with one example of each type of passive from the news report on page 56.**

Present simple passive: *am/is/are* + past participle
ACTIVE: *You place an order one day and they deliver your groceries the next.*
PASSIVE: *An order **is placed** one day and your groceries **are delivered** the next.*
1 ....

Present continuous passive: *am/is/are + being* + past participle
ACTIVE: *They are building a new school and creating two new roads for access.*
PASSIVE: *A new school **is being built** and two new roads **are being created** for access.*
2 ....

Present perfect passive: *have/has* + *been* + past participle
ACTIVE: *I've prepared the turkey and peeled the potatoes.*
PASSIVE: *The turkey **has been prepared** and the potatoes **have been peeled**.*
3 ....

Past simple passive: *was/were* + past participle

stranded: عالق، محاصر

ACTIVE: *Air Canada cancelled our flight and stranded us in Vancouver.*
PASSIVE: *Our flight **was cancelled** and we **were stranded** in Vancouver.*
4 ....

Past continuous passive: *was/were + being* + past participle
ACTIVE: *They were cleaning the floor and washing the windows earlier today.*
PASSIVE: *The floor **was being cleaned** and the windows **were being washed** earlier today.*
5 ....

Past perfect passive: *had* + *been* + past participle
ACTIVE: *Everyone had warned me about the weather before I went to Scotland.*
PASSIVE: *I **had been warned** about the weather before I went to Scotland.*
6 ....

Passives with *by*-phrases 64   Past participles 220   Transitive and intransitive verbs 6   The uses of the passive 62

Passives with modals, infinitives and gerunds

p. expelled, ...b
expel (handwritten note)

Modal passives

We form simple modal passives with a modal (*can, may, will*, etc.) + *be* + a past participle (1).
We use *could, might, would* + *be* + a past participle when we need to use a past tense (2).

  1 *The police will arrest violent demonstrators. So, if you are violent, you **will be arrested**.*
     *You **can be kept** in custody for 24 hours and you **may be questioned** about your activities.*
  2 *'The police can't stop us!' The demonstrators claimed that they **couldn't be stopped**.*
     *They boasted that although they **might be arrested**, they **wouldn't be silenced**.*

We form modal perfect passives with a modal + *have been* + past participle.

  3 *Tony didn't study for the test. His answers **must have been copied** from someone else.*
     *If he had been caught cheating, he **would have been expelled** from school.*

We can form modal continuous passives with a modal + *be being* + past participle (4). We rarely use these passives. Instead, we use an active or a continuous passive without a modal (5).

  4 *I see that men are working on the roof today. I think it **may be being repaired** at last.*
  5 *Perhaps they're repairing it at last. • I think it's being repaired at last.*

We form phrasal modal passives with the present (6) or past (7) of a phrasal modal such as *be going to* or *have to* + *be* + past participle. We can use two phrasal modals together (8).

  6 *Someone has to tell Chris to stop interrupting.* → *Chris **has to be told** to stop interrupting.*
     Are you going to need this extra paper? → *Is this extra paper **going to be needed**?*
  7 *I had to find a place for all the boxes.* → *A place **had to be found** for all the boxes.*
     Someone was probably going to steal them. → *They **were** probably **going to be stolen**.*
  8 *We're going to have to sell my old car.* → *My old car **is going to have to be sold**.*

Passive infinitives and gerunds

We use *to be* + past participle for the passive infinitive (9) and *to have been* + past participle for the perfect passive infinitive (10).

   9 *He's trying to finish the work soon. He expects most of it **to be finished** before the weekend.*
  10 *They have chosen Emily Watson to play the part. She's really excited **to have been chosen**.*

We use *being* + past participle for the passive gerund (11) and *having been* + past participle for the perfect passive gerund (12).

  11 *He was asking about a lot of personal things. I didn't like **being asked** about my private life.*
  12 *I think they've promoted Tom, but he didn't mention **having been promoted** when we talked.*

We put *not* before passive infinitives (13) and passive gerunds (14) to form negatives.

  13 *They didn't invite us. It was strange **not to be invited**.* (NOT … *to be not invited.*)
  14 *No one had informed me about that. I resented **not having been informed**.*

4 Using information from the news report on page 56, complete these sentences with *be*, *to be*, *being* or *been* and decide what type of passive each one is.

1 After .... trapped for hours, they were found alive. (...)
2 Herds of cattle are nowhere .... seen. (...)
3 Small teams have had to .... flown in to some areas. (...)
4 Other buildings seem to have .... blown away. (...)
5 If the wind returns, more trees may .... knocked over. (...)
6 Dozens of people could have .... buried in there. (...)

a Simple modal passive
b Modal perfect passive
c Passive gerund
d Phrasal modal passive
e Passive infinitive
f Perfect passive infinitive

Infinitives and gerunds 140 Modals and phrasal modals 29

5 Complete this news report with these verbs in the passive.

block   close   destroy   expect   flood   injure   knock   leave   report   rescue

Many homes on the island of Jamaica (1) were destroyed by hurricane Lester yesterday.
Today, high winds (2) .... to bring more rain and problems for the island's residents.
Some parts of the island (3) have been blocked without electricity last night and many roads
(4) .... by fallen trees that (5) .... down during the storm. The area
around Savanna-La-Mar on the south coast (6) .... and some residents have had
(7) .... from the roofs of their houses. Most businesses and schools in Kingston
(8) .... today as people emerge from their battered homes to survey the damage. More
than 100 people (9) ...., but no deaths (10) ....

6 Complete each sentence with a passive so that it has a similar meaning to the one above.

1 You can't see the house from the street.
The house ....

2 'They won't correct your papers before Friday.'
He said our papers ....

3 Someone must have taken the towels out of the dryer.
The towels ....

4 Nobody's going to steal your books from this room.
Your books ....

5 People were telling me what to do all the time and I didn't enjoy it.
I didn't enjoy ....

7 Choose one passive verb phrase for each space in these sentences (from a report on the use of DNA testing by the police).

is also called   has also been used   can be used
is believed   have been shown   may have been convicted
was released   had been sentenced   would never have been solved

DNA is the chemical in the cells of plants and animals which carries inherited characteristics, or
genetic information. DNA testing (1) .... to identify each person as a
unique individual on the basis of that genetic information. It (2) ....
'genetic fingerprinting'. The results of DNA testing are now being accepted as evidence in cases where
it (3) .... that the wrong person (4) ....
of a crime.
In recent years, more than seventy people (5) .... to be innocent
through DNA testing. Many of those people (6) .... to life in prison.
In one case, a man (7) .... after nineteen years in prison. DNA testing
(8) .... in some murder cases that (9) ....
without it.

Passive verbs

Verbs with and without objects

We create passives from verbs which can have objects (transitive verbs) (1), not from verbs which don't have objects (intransitive verbs) (2).

   1 *He repaired the bike. Then he painted it.* → *The bike **was repaired**. Then it **was painted**.*

   2 *Nothing happened.* • *We arrived early.* (NOT ~~We were arrived early.~~)

We usually create passives from verbs which describe actions (3), not states (4).

   3 *They scored a goal in the last five minutes.* → *A goal **was scored** in the last five minutes.*

   4 *My sister has two sons.* • *That belongs to me.* (NOT ~~That is belonged to me.~~)

There are a few verbs that we usually use in the passive.

   5 *Her parents **were married** in 1983 and she **was born** two years later.*

We create passives from transitive phrasal verbs (6), not from intransitive phrasal verbs (7).

   6 *She locked her house up. They broke into it.* → *Her house **was locked up**. It **was broken into**.*

   7 *Friends came over later.* • *My cold went away.* (NOT ~~My cold was gone away.~~)

Verbs with two objects

We can create two passive structures when we use those verbs which can have an indirect object (*Maria*) and a direct object (*first prize*).

   8 *They awarded Maria first prize.* → ***Maria was awarded** first prize.*

   9 *They awarded first prize to Maria.* → ***First prize was awarded** to Maria.*

Other verbs like this include: give, hand, lend, pass, sell, send, show, teach, throw, write

The passive structure we choose depends on which person or thing we want to talk about.

  10 *No one taught us English.* → *English **wasn't taught** there.* OR *We **weren't taught** English.*

In the passive, we put the indirect object as subject or after the preposition *to*, not after the verb.

  11 *He handed Cecilia a note.* → ***Cecilia** was handed a note.* OR *A note was handed **to Cecilia**.*
     (NOT ~~A note was handed Cecilia.~~)

When a verb with two objects is used in only one active structure, we can only create one passive. If we can put the indirect object after the active verb, we can use it as subject of the passive.

  12 *The judge fined him £250.* (NOT ~~The judge fined £250 to him.~~) → *He **was fined** £250.*
     (NOT ~~£250 was fined to him.~~)

If we can't put the indirect object after the active verb, we can't use it as subject of the passive.

  13 *Then we explained our solutions to him.* → *Then our solutions **were explained** to him.*
     (NOT ~~We explained him our solutions.~~) (NOT ~~He was explained our solutions.~~)

Other verbs used like this include: demonstrate, describe, mention, present, report, suggest

We can use a direct object as subject of a passive, but not another noun that classifies it.

  14 *Many people considered John Nash a genius.* → *John Nash **was considered** a genius.*

  15 *They elected Clinton President twice.* → *Clinton **was elected** President twice.*
     (NOT ~~President was elected Clinton twice.~~)

8 Rewrite each sentence with the verbs in the passive, where possible.

1 Someone saw Erin outside the theatre as she was waiting to go in. She had a new hairstyle.

....

2 Karen feels sad because they didn't promote her and she has to carry on as if nothing happened.

....

3 He throws the ball to Evans. Evans tries to go past Jennings, but Jennings stops him. It's a foul.

....

9 Using a dictionary if necessary, choose an adjective for each space and choose a, b or both as correct sentences.

illegible	*inaudible*	*knowledgeable*	*reusable*
impossible	*inexplicable*	✓*returnable*	*unspeakable*

Example: It says here that your deposit isn't ... returnable .... .
a It won't be given back. ✓   b You won't be given back. ...

1 He doesn't think it's .... to sell ice to Eskimos.
   a He thinks they can be sold ice. ...   b He thinks ice can be sold them. ...

2 His sudden disappearance remains .... We have no idea what happened.
   a We can't be explained. ...   b It can't be explained. ...

3 They think Ted Green is more .... about orchids than anyone else.
   a An expert is considered Ted Green. ...   b Ted Green is considered an expert. ...

4 She couldn't read us the note because of his .... handwriting.
   a We couldn't be read. ...   b It couldn't be read. ...

5 His first two or three sentences were .... , but he soon got more confident.
   a He spoke up. ...   b He was spoken up. ...

6 None of us will ever understand the .... suffering of the refugees.
   a We can never be described. ...   b It can never be described. ...

7 You can have one of these .... envelopes to send Marta the magazine.
   a Marta can be sent the magazine. ...   b The magazine can be sent to Marta. ...

10 Editing. Correct the mistakes in this text.

The Christmas I remember best from my childhood ~~was~~ happened when I was about five, just after my younger sister born. Lots of people were come to our house with presents for us. I gave the job of taking the gifts and saying 'Thank you'. As each guest was arrived, I handed boxes or bags which filled with things that wrapped in Christmas paper. I told which ones were for me and which ones had to be place in a pile for my new sister. So many presents brought for us. I will never forget the experience of given so much. It really was a very special Christmas.

The uses of the passive

11 Write the numbers of appropriate examples in the spaces on this and the opposite page.

Focusing on what is done and who is affected

We use passives when we describe a process by talking about what is done, not who does it ▢ , and when we report events, but we don't know, or it's not important, who performed the actions ▢ .

    1 *Wine **is made** from grapes.* • *Oranges **are grown** in Spain.* • *Oil **has to be imported**.*
    2 *My bag **was stolen**.* • *Some trees **have been cut** down.* • *I think the old road **has been repaired**.*

We use passives to talk about the subject as the person or thing affected by the action ▢ , often when that subject is the topic of two or more sentences ▢ . We can use passives for several actions that affect the same subject in a single sentence ▢ .

    3 *Two old people **were attacked** in the park.* • *A tourist **was robbed**.* • *I **wasn't** badly **injured**.*
    4 *After registration, courses **cannot be added**, **dropped** or **changed** without permission.*
    5 *The house is still for sale. It **was built** in 1928. It **was** completely **renovated** in 2002.*
The same subject can be used with different tenses: *It **was built** in 1928 and **is being renovated**.*

In informal situations, we use indefinite pronouns such as *someone* and generic pronouns such as *they* or *you* plus active verbs more than passives.

    6 ***Someone** stole my bag.* • ***They** make wine from grapes.* • ***You** should wash fresh fruit.*
We can also use *one*, but it is very formal: ***One** should always wash fresh fruit.*

Impersonal style

We often use passives when general information is presented in an impersonal way (not intended for a particular person). For example, passives are often used in rules and warning notices ▢ , in descriptions of procedures, especially in research reports ▢ , and other types of formal written reports where personal reference (*I, we*) is typically avoided ▢ .

    7 *Twenty students **were given** a test in which they **were asked** to answer 100 questions.*
    8 *In the past year, two new computers **were purchased** and some old furniture **was replaced**.*
    9 *Parking **is prohibited**.* • *Cars **will be towed** away.* • *Trespassers **will be prosecuted**.*

We can use passives when we want to avoid personal commands ▢ and to avoid implying that we are only talking about ourselves or our personal actions ▢ .

    10 I can't do all this work in one day. → *All this work **can't be done** in one day.*
    11 You must remove your shoes before entering. → *Shoes **must be removed** before entering.*

12 Rewrite these library rules using active verbs with *you* as subject.

Reference books can only be consulted in the library. Special permission must be obtained to use them outside the library. All books should be returned on time or a fine will have to be paid. If the fine is not paid, borrowing rights will be lost. Library books may not be borrowed for others or given to others. If a book is lost, the cost of replacement must be paid.

....
....
....
....
....
....

Reporting in the passive

We can use reporting verbs in the passive when we don't know, or don't want to mention, the speaker of statements and questions ▢ or of orders and requests in infinitives ▢.
  12 *We **were instructed** to wait here.* • *I **was asked** to work late on several occasions.*
  13 *I **was told** that everyone had passed.* • *Some students **were asked** if they were communists.*

We can use reporting verbs in the passive after empty subject *it* to distance ourselves from the reported information ▢. We can use this structure with verbs such as *claim* or *imply* when we are not sure if the information is reliable ▢.
  14 ***It is often said** that children can learn foreign languages more easily than adults.*
  15 ***It was claimed** that Sandy had stolen something.* ***It was** also **implied** that he was lazy.*
Note that these passive reporting verbs are followed by a *that*-clause. (NOT ~~It was reported a problem.~~)
Other verbs used in this structure include: allege, assert, hint, report, state, suggest, suspect

We can use empty subject *it* before a reporting verb such as *mention* in the passive.
  16 *Someone mentioned (to me) that he was Irish.* → ***It was mentioned** (to me) that he was Irish.*
      (NOT ~~Someone mentioned me that he was Irish.~~) (NOT ~~I was mentioned that he was Irish.~~)

We can use a present passive reporting verb plus an infinitive as a way of distancing ourselves from the truth of a current report ▢. We can use a past passive reporting verb plus a perfect infinitive for a report of something in the past ▢.
  17 *'The rebels are near the capital.'* → *The rebels **are reported to be** near the capital.*
  18 *'She inherited a lot of money.'* → *She **was rumoured to have inherited** a lot of money.*

We can use a passive reporting verb between *There* and *to be* to report the existence of something.
  19 *'There are lots of problems'* → ***There are said to be** lots of problems.* (NOT ~~There said to be~~ …)
  20 ***There were reported to be** thousands of refugees in camps all along the border.*
Note that *tell* is not used in this way. (NOT ~~There were told to be thousands of refugees~~ …)

---

13 Complete these sentences, using appropriate forms of these verbs in combination.

not mention / receive   report / die   ✓request / keep   say / be   tell / not use

Example: Dog owners *are requested to keep* their dogs under control in the park.
1 There .... more sheep than people in some parts of Scotland.
2 The students .... their computers yesterday because of a virus.
3 Mr Harman's first wife .... in a boating accident two years ago.
4 It .... earlier, but six more applications .... last week.

---

14 Rewrite these sentences with verbs in the passive, where possible.

People have claimed that they cannot use tasks successfully with beginner level students. I designed the following study so that I could investigate that claim. I created two groups of students, each with different proficiency levels. I gave them a task in which I showed them a set of pictures and I asked them to tell a story. I recorded them as they spoke and then I examined their stories.

....
....
....
....

Passives with *by*-phrases and ergatives

Passives with *by*-phrases

The agent is the person or thing that does or causes the action. In active sentences, the agent is the subject (1). In passive sentences, we don't usually mention the agent. We can include the agent in a *by*-phrase after the verb when the meaning is not complete without it (2) or for emphasis and contrast (3). We don't usually include pronouns or nouns with general meaning such as *people* in a *by*-phrase (4).

1 ***Shakespeare*** *wrote Hamlet.* ***Many famous actors*** *have played the title role.*
2 *Hamlet was written* ***by Shakespeare****.* (NOT *Hamlet was written.*)
  The title role has been played ***by many famous actors****.* (NOT *The title role has been played.*)
3 *Was the Mona Lisa painted* ***by Michelangelo*** *or* ***(by) Leonardo da Vinci****?*
4 ***We/People*** *store equipment in the basement.* → *Equipment is stored in the basement.*

We can use a *by*-phrase for information about causes (5) and the method of 'doing' something (6).

5 *The girl was bitten* ***by a snake****.* • *Flu is caused* ***by a virus*** *and can't be cured* ***by antibiotics****.*
6 *The temperature can be controlled* ***by adjusting*** *the thermostat.*

We use a *by*-phrase for the agent of an action and a *with*-phrase for the thing used to perform that action (7). After verbs such as *cover* or *decorate* used in the passive in descriptions, we typically use a *with*-phrase rather than a *by*-phrase (8).

7 *The rescue was* ***filmed by a man*** <u>with a video camera</u>. • *The box* ***was locked*** <u>with a gold key</u>.
8 *The Christmas tree* ***was covered*** <u>with ornaments</u> *and* ***decorated*** <u>with lights</u>.
  (NOT *The tree was decorated by lights.*)
Other verbs used in the passive plus *with* include: align, associate, crowd, fill

15 Complete these sentences (from an article about Shakespeare) with appropriate forms of the verbs, plus *by* or *with* where necessary.

The Globe

consider   establish   experience   fill   perform   not write

1 Shakespeare was born in 1564 and .... many to be the greatest English writer.
2 His early reputation .... writing and appearing in his own plays.
3 His plays .... interesting characters and memorable speeches.
4 Today, at the new Globe Theatre, the plays .... in conditions similar to those which .... audiences in Shakespeare's time.
5 Some people have claimed that many of the plays .... Shakespeare.

Ergatives

Ergatives are transitive verbs that are used without an object (9). We use ergatives to say that an action simply happens, without an agent. We sometimes use ergatives instead of passives (10).

9 *The park* ***closes*** *at six.* • *The door suddenly* ***opened****.*
10 *The park is closed (by the guard) at six.* • *The door was suddenly opened.*

We can use ergatives when we want to describe natural processes and changes (11) or to describe actions, but not mention a cause (12).

11 *The snow* ***is melting****.* • *This material won't* ***shrink****.* • *The river* ***has dried up*** *this summer.*
12 *Exchange rates* ***stabilized*** *yesterday.* • *I don't know how it happened, but the string* ***broke****.*
We don't use reflexive pronouns with ergatives. (NOT *The string broke itself.*)
Other verbs used like this include: burst, crack, crash, grow, increase, shake, start

By or with 132   Reflexive pronouns 100   Transitive verbs 6

Passives with *get*

We can use *get* + past participle (1) instead of *be* + past participle (2) as a passive, usually in informal situations.

    1 *I'll **get paid** on Friday.* • *My books **got damaged** when the basement **got flooded** last year.*
    2 *I'll **be paid** on Friday.* • *My books **were damaged** when the basement **was flooded** last year.*

We use auxiliary *do* in passives with *get* when we form questions or negatives.

    3 *Why **does** Susan **get asked** to go to all the parties? We **don't get invited** to any of them!*

We often use passives with *get* for unexpected events (4) and difficult or bad experiences (5).

    4 *Professor Brown **got stuck** in traffic so her lecture **got moved** till later in the afternoon.*
    5 ***Did** anyone **get injured**? Some people **got hurt**. They were lucky they **didn't get killed**.*
Others like this include: *get arrested, get broken, get caught, get divorced, get smashed*

16 Choose an ending (a–d) for each beginning (1–4) and add these verbs.

get beaten up   *reacted*   *were reported*   *were stolen*
get caught   *were defeated*   *were smashed*   *were treated*

1 After their team .... 2–0 by a local rival on Wednesday night, (...)

2 Several shop windows .... (...)

3 'Did any of the thieves .... ?' asked one shop owner in frustration. (...)

4 Some people .... in hospital for minor cuts and bruises, (...)

a but no serious injuries ...., according to the police.

b 'Of course not,' he explained. 'Because nobody wants to .... by those hooligans.'

c and items such as televisions, radios and cameras ....

d angry football fans .... violently.

17 Add appropriate forms of these verbs to the text. Then in the space below, write those expressions (if any) that are used in the text to identify the agents of these verbs.

carry   *crash*   *explode*   *hand*   *injure*   *knock*   *open*   *run*   *shake*   *stop*   ✓*tell*

When I was in Ireland, people often .... *told* .... me that I was lucky. I remember one time, years ago, when I was sitting with friends in the Emerald Arms, Belfast. The door suddenly (1) .... and a voice called out, 'Bomb! Get out!' Conversations (2) .... instantly as everyone and everything suddenly moved. Glasses and bottles (3) .... to the floor. As I started to get up from my seat, I (4) .... down. I struggled to my feet and then I (5) .... along by the surging crowd towards the back door. I was pushed out of the door backwards by the force of the people behind me. Then I just (6) .... like everyone else until I reached a crowd at the end of the street. As I stood there waiting, an old woman told me that there was blood on my cheek. We waited, but no bomb (7) ...., no walls (8) .... and no windows shattered into a thousand pieces. I wiped the blood from my cheek with a piece of cloth that (9) .... to me by the old woman. I thanked her. 'It's just a scratch,' she said. 'You're lucky you didn't (10) .... seriously ....'

Agents: (Example) ... *People,* ....

....

Tests

A Choose the word or phrase which best completes each sentence.

1 We were told to put it where it was usually _____ .

a belonged   b fit   c had   d stored

2 It wasn't the first time they had been _____ how it worked.

a taught   b reported   c explained   d described

3 DNA tests _____ accepted in court cases.

a are known   b were used   c have been   d will have

4 Something _____ happened or they would be here by now.

a must   b must be   c must have   d must have been

5 There _____ to be serious flaws in the design.

a claimed   b reported   c were said   d were told

B Identify the one underlined expression (A, B, C or D) that must be changed in order to correct these sentences.

1 When he said they weren't going to <u>get engaged</u> because they were <u>getting married</u> right away, I
    A   B

assumed he wasn't already <u>got married</u>, but I didn't know he had just <u>got divorced</u> that day.
                          C   D

2 No one <u>died</u>, but four people <u>were injured</u> and had <u>to be taken</u> to hospital after a small plane
        A   B   C

<u>was crashed</u> near Dublin last night.
    D

3 The main door <u>couldn't be opened</u>. It <u>had been locked by a special key</u> that the caretaker
                A   B

<u>didn't have</u>. He <u>had been given</u> a large set of keys, but none of them fitted the main door.
    C   D

4 The sign said parking <u>was prohibited</u>, but my car <u>wasn't left</u> there more than five minutes while I
                        A   B

ran to pick up the shoes <u>were repaired</u> at Mendems, but I <u>was given</u> a parking ticket anyway.
                        C   D

5 A new company has <u>taken</u> over the office which <u>located</u> next to yours and it's going to be
                    A   B

<u>redecorated</u> after it's been <u>cleaned up</u> a bit.
    C   D

C Complete this text with appropriate passive forms of these verb phrases plus *by*, if necessary.

believe   bite   consider   can cure   experience   recommend   may say

A hangover is the unpleasant physical feeling which (1) _____ the day after drinking
too much alcohol. The expression 'a hair of the dog that bit you' refers to another drink of alcohol
that you might have to help you recover from a hangover. In the past, it (2) _____
that, if you (3) _____ a mad dog, you (4) _____ placing a hair from
that dog on the wound. This treatment (5) _____ widely _____
doctors up to the middle of the eighteenth century, but it (6) _____ no longer
_____ effective. The same (7) _____ about trying to use more
alcohol as a cure for a hangover.

D Complete each sentence in such a way that it is as similar as possible in meaning to the sentence above it.

1 'They didn't build Rome in a day.'
  There's a saying that Rome _____ .

2 They have collected the tests and checked the answers.
  The tests _____ .

3 A bee sting is more likely to cause death these days than a snake bite.
  Death _____ .

4 It was reported that there were serious problems with the new design.
  There _____ .

5 No one gave us instructions or showed us what to do.
  We _____ .

E Choose one verb phrase from each pair to fill each space in the text.

a *are feeding*   c *are being caused*   e *being hit*   g *brought*
b *are being fed*   d *have caused*   f *having hit*   h *was brought*

i *died*   k *frightened*   m *have driven*   o *to take*
j *was died*   l *was frightened*   n *have been driven* p *to be taken*

Thailand has a problem with unemployed elephants which (1) _____ on to the
streets by the country's economic crisis and a loss of traditional employment. Many of them
(2) _____ by tourists who like (3) _____ photographs of them.
Major traffic problems (4) _____ by homeless elephants wandering the streets.
Traffic (5) _____ to a standstill one day by a raging bull elephant which
(6) _____ by the sounds of motorcycles and cars. Another elephant
(7) _____ after (8) _____ by a car in Bangkok last month.

6 Articles and nouns

Nouns are either proper, with a capital letter (*Shakespeare*), or common, without a capital letter (*poet*). Some common nouns are countable and can be singular (*woman, poet*) or plural (*women, poets*). Other common nouns are uncountable and are not used in the plural (*poetry, weather*).

With nouns, we can use an indefinite article (***a** poet, **an** old woman*), a definite article (***the** weather, **the** women*), or no article (*We're studying _ poetry written by _ women*).

1 Read these statements and choose what you think is the best answer.

1 A person is more likely to die in a car accident than an aircraft accident.	True / False
2 It is safer to fly in a newer plane than in an older plane.	True / False
3 A smaller plane is much safer than a larger plane.	True / False
4 The chance of being killed in a major airline crash is close to one in	8 / 18 / 80 million.
5 Airplane accidents rarely occur during the take-off and landing.	True / False
6 The more stops in a flight, the more dangerous it will be.	True / False
7 The likelihood of surviving an aircraft accident is about	8 / 18 / 80 per cent.
8 Natural materials are safer than synthetic materials if there is a fire.	True / False

2 Read through this text and find:

1 another use of the indefinite article *an*
2 a proper noun with the definite article

Flying in modern jets is one of the safest forms of transportation. It has been estimated that travelling by air is twenty-five times safer than travelling by car. This
5 means that you are much more likely to get killed driving to or from the airport than during the flight.

The safest planes are the large modern jets of the major commercial airlines of Europe and
10 the United States. One study showed that the chance of being killed in a commercial airline crash was only one in eight million. Smaller planes, commuter planes and older planes are far more likely to be involved in accidents.
15 Most airplane accidents occur during the take-off and landing parts of a flight. It follows that a non-stop flight will be safer than a flight with one or more stops. The duration of the flight doesn't seem to be a factor.

20 It is estimated that eighty per cent of the people involved in an aircraft accident survive. You can increase your chances of survival by knowing what to do before an accident occurs. Keep your seat belt fastened at all times.
25 Identify the nearest emergency exit and count the number of seats between you and the exit. You may have to feel your way to the exit in the dark. Learn how to open the emergency door in case you are the first person to reach it. Wear
30 clothes made from natural fibres such as cotton and wool rather than synthetic materials which may burn or melt on the skin. Think about carrying a smoke hood with you on the plane. If there is a fire, the hood can help
35 protect you against smoke and toxic gases. Above all, don't panic.

Types of articles and nouns

Articles

We use the definite article *the* with singular and plural nouns.

  1 **The** names of **the** authors of **the** books on **the** top shelf begin with **the** letter 'A'.

We use the indefinite article *a/an* with singular nouns. Choosing *a* or *an* depends on the first sound, not letter, of the next word. We use *a* before consonant sounds (2) and *an* before vowel sounds (3).

  2 *Have **a** banana! • Is this **a** one-way street? • I need **a** holiday. • Write **a** 'U', then **a** 'P'.*
  3 *Have **an** apple! • Is this **an** old Rolls Royce? • He has **an** honest face. • Write **an** 'N', then **an** 'O'.*

We sometimes use nouns without articles.

  4 *Do you take milk or sugar? • I like fish, but not chips. • Girls are quicker than boys.*

The articles *a/an* and *the* are types of determiners. (See page 83.) We can use other determiners (*this, those, my, your,* etc.) instead of articles, but not with them.

  5 **These** books belong on **that** shelf. • *Nora wiped **her** cheek.* (NOT ~~Nora wiped her the cheek.~~)

Nouns

We begin proper nouns with capital letters and use them as the names of people, places, organizations, days, months and special occasions. Most of them have no article (6). But we use some proper nouns with the definite article in the plural (7) and some in the singular (8).

  6 *Elvis Presley, Shakespeare, Denmark, Rome, NATO, Microsoft, Monday, July, Christmas*
  7 **the** Robertsons, **the** Arabs, **the** Alps, **the** Netherlands, **the** United Nations, **the** Middle Ages
  8 **the** Queen, **the** United Kingdom, **the** BBC, **the** Eiffel Tower, **the** White House, **the** Gulf War

We use common nouns to categorize or label people and things. They are countable or uncountable. We can use countable common nouns in the singular, with *a/an* and *each* (9), or in the plural, with numbers and *many* (10).

  9 *Do you have a black **pen** or a **pencil**? • Each **child** should have a **book**.*
  10 *We don't sell **pens** or **pencils**. • There are twenty **children**. • How many **books** will you need?*

We usually use uncountable common nouns when we talk about an abstract concept, an activity, a substance or a material. Uncountable nouns are not used with *a/an* or in the plural. We can use uncountable nouns with no article (11) and *much* (12).

  11 *Her poem is about **flying**, **freedom** and bad **luck**.* (NOT ... ~~a bad luck.~~)
  12 *They have **food** and **clothing**, but they don't have much **water**.* (NOT ... ~~waters.~~)
Uncountable nouns are also called non-count nouns or mass nouns.

3 **Complete this table with appropriate examples from the text about flying on page 68.**

	Indefinite article	Definite article	No article
Proper nouns	*a Rolls-Royce* *an Audi*	*the United Kingdom* *the United States*	*Shakespeare* (1) ....
Common nouns Countable: singular	*an accident* (2)	*the shelf* (3)	*(by) bus* (4) ....
Countable: plural		*the books* (5)	*children* (6) ....
Uncountable		*the food* (7)	*clothing* (8) ....

Articles: *a/an* or *the*

4 **Write the numbers of appropriate examples in the spaces.**

A/an or *the*

We usually use *a/an* to classify people or things when we mention them first ___. We use *the* to identify people or things when we think they are already known ___.
  1 *We read **a** story about **a** man, **a** young Irish girl and **a** priceless diamond ring.*
  2 *Do you remember **the** story about **the** man who tried to steal **the** ring from **the** Irish girl?*

A/an: classifying

When we classify something, we are saying that it is a member of a category. We use *a/an* when we classify the kind of thing we're talking about ___ or when we want to talk about any example of the kind of thing we're talking about ___.
  3 *What's that? ~ It's **a** mouse. • His first film was **a** comedy.* (NOT *His first film was comedy.*)
  4 *Do you have **a** ruler? • I'm looking for **a** knife.* (NOT *I'm looking for knife.*)

We use *a/an* when we classify people by the work they do ___ or the kind of beliefs they have ___.
  5 *I'm **a** socialist, not **a** communist. • Isn't your friend Voltra **a** vegetarian?*
  6 *Sheila's **an** architect. • Stanley talks like **an** engineer. • I'm **a** student.* (NOT *I'm student.*)

We can use *a/an* when we classify things in definitions ___, in descriptions of particular features ___ and with a proper noun for one example of the type of thing mentioned ___.
  7 *That painting is **a** Picasso. • Have you driven **a** Mercedes? • Is your watch **a** Calvin Klein?*
  8 *The professor had **a** big nose, **a** small mouth and **an** enormous moustache.*
  9 *Is **a** tomato **a** fruit or **a** vegetable? • **A** dolphin isn't **a** fish, it's **a** mammal.*

The: identifying

When we identify something, we are treating it as already known. We use *the* when we assume that people are familiar with the same ordinary things as we are in our daily lives ___ and in the physical world outside ___.
  10 *Please don't mention **the** sun, **the** sky, **the** earth, **the** weather or **the** environment today.*
  11 *Where's **the** phone? I left it beside **the** radio on **the** table in **the** corner near **the** window.*

We use *the* when we identify people by their jobs ___ or their unique roles in society ___. We also use *the* with professional organizations ___.
  12 *Will you wait for **the** plumber? ~ I can't. • I have to go to **the** dentist. • Ask **the** caretaker.*
  13 *He's thinking about joining **the** police or **the** army. • His brother works for **the** government.*
  14 *Would you recognize **the** Pope, **the** Emperor of Japan, **the** Dalai Lama or **the** Queen?*

We can use *the* when we want to talk about something as a general concept and we're not referring to a specific example. We do this with inventions and musical instruments ___ and with people, things and animals in generalizations ___.
  15 ***The** horse was a symbol of freedom to **the** Apache. • **The** customer isn't always right.*
    (= any customer)
  16 *What was life like before **the** computer? • Can anyone here play **the** piano or **the** organ?*

We use *the* when we identify things or parts of things with descriptive phrases after the noun, especially prepositional phrases with *of* ___ and relative clauses ___. We also put *the* before superlative adjectives and emphasizing adjectives such as *main* or *first* ___.
  17 ***The** best part was being **the** first person to get in. That was **the** main reason for going early.*
  18 *Can I see **the** book that you bought? • **The** person who called yesterday said you owed him £20.*
  19 *It's **the** middle of June already and I haven't finished painting **the** front of my house.*

A/an, one, the or no article 72 Emphasizing adjectives 111 Superlative adjectives 120

5 Complete these descriptions with *a*, *an*, *the* or no article (–).

..The.. Channel Islands are .a. group of .–. islands in (1) .... English Channel near (2) ....
north-western coast of (3) .... France. They have belonged to (4) .... Britain since (5) ....
Normans arrived in (6) .... 11th century, although they are not part of (7) .... United Kingdom.

Charlie Chaplin was (8) .... English film actor. He was also (9) .... director. He did most of his
work in (10) .... USA. Many people consider him (11) .... greatest comic actor of (12) ....
silent cinema. He appeared in many films as (13) .... poor man with (14) .... small round hat,
(15) .... small moustache and (16) .... trousers and (17) .... shoes that were too big for him,
causing him to walk in (18) .... funny way.

6 Choose an answer (a–f) for each question (1–6) and add *a* or *the*.

1 How often have you done this? (...)
2 What exactly is an olive? (...)
3 Where's your dictionary? (...)
4 Why is it so bright outside tonight? (...)
5 What kind of career does Sally want? (...)
6 What does Mrs Reynolds' son do? (...)

a It's on .... bottom shelf of my bookcase.
b I think he's in .... navy.
c She'd like to be .... journalist.
d I'm sure it's .... fruit.
e It must be .... moon.
f Yesterday was actually .... first time.

7 Complete this news item with *a*, *an*, *the* or no article (–).

There's (1) .... giant tortoise in (2) .... Galapagos Islands nicknamed (3) .... Lonesome
George who has never found (4) .... mate. Recent studies by scientists suggest that (5) ....
lonely tortoise, now living on (6) .... Pinto Island, actually belongs to (7) .... species from
(8) .... island of (9) .... Espanola. (10) .... scientists plan to bring (11) .... female from
Espanola to see if (12) .... George will become interested in mating.

8 Editing. Correct the mistakes in the use of articles in this text.

I remember /really embarrassing moment when I was starting to learn the English. My teacher's name
was Trevor Jones. He was from Cardiff in the Wales. He was always making the jokes. One day he
wrote words 'English Gramer' on blackboard. He asked us if that was correct. Immediately I offered
to answer question. I told him the E should be changed to the A. Trevor said that was good answer
and he changed letter. Then he asked me if I was happy with new spelling. With the absolute confidence, I said that it was now correct. Suddenly, the other students started laughing. I looked around
in the confusion. My friend whispered that it needed second M. 'Oh, it should have the M too!' I
shouted out and Trevor nodded with the smile. It was correct. But I still remember terrible feeling of
the embarrassment from that moment.

A/an or one, a/an or no article, the or no article

A/an or one

We can use *a/an* or *one* before a noun to talk about a single thing or person.

   1 *In some places, there are graves that are used again after **one/a** year and **one/a** day.*

We use *one* to emphasize the number (*only one* or *just one*) (2) or to talk about a particular but unspecified occasion, usually in narrative (3).

   2 *We only have room for **one** passenger. • He tried to balance on **one** leg, but he fell over.*

   3 ***One** day there was a terrible storm. • **One** time we almost had an accident.*

We use *one* in exact numbers, especially in phrases with larger numbers (4). We use *a/an* in approximate amounts and fractions (5).

   4 *Our first car cost **one** thousand, **one** hundred and twenty pounds. • Add **one** cup of flour.*

   5 *That trip cost almost **a** hundred pounds. • It took about **a** day and **a** half to complete.*

A/an or no article

We use *a/an* when we are thinking of something as a single unit (6). We use no article when something is not a single unit or it is uncountable (7).

   6 *Would you like **a** coffee? • We have started **a** new research project. • Look! I caught **a** fish!*

   7 *Do you prefer coffee or tea? • He's doing research on fish or shellfish.* (NOT ~~He's doing a research~~ …)

We use *a/an* before a noun to talk about a single example or instance of a more general thing (8) and no article when we are talking about the general concept (9).

   8 *We bought **a** cheap wine. • I have **a** terrible fear of heights. • The old man had **a** good life.*

   9 *I hate cheap wine. • Fear of death can affect anyone. • Life is beautiful, so enjoy it!*

The or no article

We use *the* for a specific meaning (10) and no article for a general meaning (11) before plural nouns such as *dogs* and uncountable nouns such as *money*.

  10 ***The dogs** next door are friendly. • The children have already spent **the money** we gave them.*

  11 *My sister is afraid of **dogs**. • Michelle's boyfriend is always talking about **money**.*

We use *the* with nouns such as *history* or *poetry* when they are followed by *of*-phrases (12) and no article in other contexts (13).

  12 ***The poetry** of Philip Larkin is unusual. • We studied **the history** of Scotland.*

  13 ***Poetry** isn't their favourite subject. • He taught us Scottish **history**.* (NOT ~~He taught us the Scottish history.~~)

We can use *the* with nouns to talk about a specific time (14) or place (15) and no article with those same nouns after the prepositions *in* or *at* when we're talking more generally (16).

  14 *That was **the Christmas** before you were born. • Did you hear that noise during **the night**?*

  15 *After you pass **the school**, you'll see **the church**. • **The prison** is a big red building.*

  16 *Most people would rather be in **school** or in **church** than in **prison**. • I can never study at **night**.*

Other prepositional phrases like this include: at Christmas, at university, in town, in winter

We use no article in many prepositional phrases referring to general concepts, as in *going by bus*, where there isn't a particular bus being classified or identified (17). We also use no article when we talk about sports (18).

  17 *They came by bus. • Let's go to bed. • Send it by email.* (NOT ~~Send it by the email.~~)

  18 *Anwar loves cricket. • Tennis is her favourite sport. • I don't play golf.* (NOT ~~I don't play the golf.~~)

9 Complete this text with *a/an*, *one* or no article (–).

..One.. time I went out on ...a... blind date with (1) .... man who had just started working in Cathy's office. That was (2) .... big mistake! We went to (3) .... cocktail bar. There was only (4) .... free table, in the darkest corner of the bar. He asked if I'd like (5) .... screwdriver. Well, I know there's (6) .... tool called (7) .... screwdriver, but I'd never heard of (8) .... drink called that. He explained that it was made with (9) .... vodka and (10) .... orange juice. I said I'd rather have (11) .... glass of (12) .... white wine. He said he had (13) .... very special white wine from France in his flat and I would really like it. He gulped back his drink and asked if I was ready for another drink before we left. I said I could only stay for (14) .... drink. When he went to the bathroom, I quickly grabbed my coat and left. Maybe it was called (15) .... 'blind' date, but I could see very clearly where it was going. I had to make (16) .... quick exit.

10 Using a dictionary if necessary, complete these definitions with *a*, *an*, *the* or no article (–).

...A... Christmas tree is (1) .... evergreen or artificial tree decorated with (2) .... lights and (3) .... coloured ornaments in (4) .... people's homes at (5) .... Christmas.
..An... Easter egg is (6) .... egg made of (7) .... chocolate or (8) .... hen's egg with (9) .... painted shell, given as (10) .... present to (11) .... children at (12) .... Easter.
...–.... Passover is (13) .... Jewish religious festival in (14) .... memory of (15) .... freeing of (16) .... Jews from (17) .... slavery in (18) .... Egypt.
...–.... Ramadan is (19) .... ninth month of (20) .... Muslim year, when (21) .... Muslims do not eat or drink anything between (22) .... sunrise and (23) .... sunset.
...–.... Thanksgiving (Day) is (24) .... public holiday in (25) .... USA, on (26) .... fourth Thursday in (27) .... November, and in (28) .... Canada, on (29) .... second Monday in (30) .... October.

11 Complete this news report with *a*, *an*, *one*, *the* or no article (–).

John Millar, who lives near (1) .... Stirling in (2) .... central Scotland, thought he had found (3) .... bargain when he bought (4) .... Volkswagen for just (5) .... thousand, (6) .... hundred and sixty-five pounds at (7) .... auction in (8) .... April this year. Everything was fine for about (9) .... month, then (10) .... day, (11) .... car just stopped. John took it to (12) .... local garage where (13) .... mechanic thought there was (14) .... problem with (15) .... petrol supply. He was really surprised when he discovered (16) .... source of (17) .... problem. He had to remove (18) .... large, tightly-sealed plastic bag from (19) .... petrol tank. Inside (20) .... bag was (21) .... wad of (22) .... hundred pound notes. It amounted to fifteen thousand pounds. Suddenly, (23) .... Volkswagen was (24) .... even bigger bargain than John had imagined. But John is (25) .... honest Scot and he reported his discovery to (26) .... police. They are now trying to find (27) .... car's previous owner because they want to know where (28) .... money came from and why it was hidden. John is waiting patiently and hoping that it will eventually be his. When that happens, he won't have to worry about (29) .... money for (30) .... petrol for quite some time.

Nouns: countable and uncountable

12 Write the numbers of appropriate examples in the spaces.

Countable nouns

Countable nouns can be singular or plural and are normally used to refer to people, creatures and objects ___ or actions and events ___, which can be thought of as separate individual things.

 1 *actor, bird, car, child, dog, ladder, man, monkey, mountain, telephone, etc.*
 2 *arrival, crash, goal, lesson, mistake, party, punch, problem, riot, theft, etc.*

Uncountable nouns

Uncountable nouns are used with singular verbs, but not to refer to individual things. They are not typically used with *a/an*. We use uncountable nouns to talk about substances and materials ___, abstract ideas, qualities and states ___, or activities ___.

 3 *camping, chess, jogging, photography, research, shopping, tennis, training, work, etc.*
 4 *anger, bravery, education, evidence, freedom, honesty, ignorance, love, poverty, safety, etc.*
 5 *alcohol, chocolate, cotton, fur, ink, meat, paint, petrol, rice, salt, shampoo, soil, wool, etc.*

There are some uncountable nouns in English such as *advice* or *information* which may have countable equivalents in other languages.

 6 *advice, applause, assistance, cash, equipment, evidence, furniture, health, homework, information, laughter, leisure, luck, machinery, money, permission, pollution, progress, rubbish, traffic, violence, etc.* (NOT ~~an advice, a homework, equipments, informations~~)

Countable and uncountable uses

Some nouns can be countable or uncountable. It depends whether we're using the noun to refer to a single thing ___ or to a substance or general idea ___.

 7 *She owns **a business**. • I saw **a chicken**. • There's **a hair** in my tea. • Did you hear **a noise**?*
 8 ***Business** is booming. • Do you eat **chicken**? • He has long **hair**. • There's too much **noise**.*

We can also use nouns such as *piece* or *drop* in phrases which are countable ___ when we want to talk about separate units or parts of nouns which are uncountable ___.

 9 *Nobody likes having to move **furniture**. • She had **blood** on her sleeve.* (NOT ~~She had a blood on her sleeve.~~)
 10 *There wasn't **a piece of furniture** left in the house. • I could see **drops of blood** on the floor.*

Others like this include: an act of bravery, a bit of cheese, a bottle of water, a carton of milk, a chunk of concrete, items of information, sheets of paper, two slices of bread (NOT ~~two breads~~)

13 Using a dictionary if necessary, complete each definition with one set of nouns (not necessarily in this order) and *a/an* or no article.

bread / piece / soup / toast   breakfast / cereal / fruit / milk / mixture / nuts
country / government / ✓system

Democracy is _a system_ of (1) .... in which everyone in (2) ....
can vote.

A crouton is (3) .... small square .... of (4) .... or
(5) .... fried ...., usually served with (6) ....

Muesli is (7) .... of (8) ...., (9) ...., and
(10) .... dried ...., usually eaten with (11) .... at
(12) ....

Nouns: generic, pair, group, plural and singular (+s)

Generic nouns

We use nouns as generic nouns when we make general statements about any example (*a/an*), the general concept (*the*) or most examples (no article with plural) of the thing we're talking about (1) rather than real or particular examples (2).

  1 ***An orange*** has lots of vitamin C. • ***The telephone*** rules my life. • ***Women*** live longer than ***men***.
  2 *I just ate an orange.* • *Cindy's new telephone is pink.* • *I can see about ten women and two men.*

Pair nouns

We use pair nouns such as *scissors* or *trousers* to refer to things made of two matching parts that we use or wear. We usually use them with plural verbs (3). When we put pair nouns after the phrase *a pair of*, we use a singular verb and a plural pronoun (*them, they*) (4).

  3 *These **scissors** aren't very sharp.* • *White **trousers** don't go very well with black shoes.*
  4 *A good **pair of scissors** is hard to find.* • *There's a nice **pair of trousers** on sale. You should get them because they're really cheap. In fact, you should buy two pairs!* (NOT ~~two trousers~~)
Others include: binoculars, clippers, jeans, pants, pliers, pyjamas, shoes, sunglasses, tights

Group nouns

We can use group nouns to talk about a group of people as a single unit, with singular verbs and pronouns (5), or as several people, with plural verbs and pronouns (6). Group nouns are also called collective nouns.

  5 *The **public is**n't really interested in what the **government is** doing unless **it** increases taxes.*
  6 *The **public are** more likely to complain if **they** have to pay more taxes.*
Others include: audience, band, club, committee, family, jury, majority, parliament, team
In American English, singular verbs are typically used after group nouns.

We can use some proper nouns as group nouns, with plural verbs, for teams and organizations.

  7 *England **are** ready to play France.* • *British Rail **have** announced new plans.*

Plural and singular (+s) nouns

Plural nouns are words with distinct meanings that are not used in the singular.

  8 *He said **thanks** for looking after his **belongings**.* • *Good **manners** are important.*
Others include: clothes, congratulations, groceries, outskirts, remains, surroundings, troops
Plural nouns that do not end with *-s* include: cattle, clergy, people, police, poultry

Singular (+s) nouns are words that end in *-s* and appear to be plural, but are used with singular verbs when we talk about areas of study, activities and disease.

  9 ***Statistics was*** *a difficult course.* • ***Aerobics is*** *hard work.* • ***Rabies has*** *become a deadly disease.*
Others include: athletics, billiards, cards, diabetes, electronics, measles, physics, politics

We also use singular verbs after some phrases with nouns in the plural describing amounts.

  10 *Five miles **is** a long walk.* • *Twenty pounds **is** too much!* • *Two weeks **isn't** enough time.*

14 Using a dictionary if necessary, choose an ending (a–f) for each beginning (1–6) and add these nouns plus *is* or *are*.

binoculars   clergy   fortnight   mathematics   outskirts   press

1 The .... of a town ....   a to see things far away.
2 The .... a general term   b the science of numbers.
3 The .... people   c called a .... in Britain.
4 .... described as   d for newspapers and journalists.
5 .... used   e the parts that are far from the centre.
6 Two weeks .... sometimes   f such as priests and ministers.

Possessive and compound nouns

15 Write the numbers of appropriate examples in the spaces.

Possessive noun or compound noun?

We usually use a possessive noun when something belongs to a particular person or thing ☐ and a compound noun to talk about a common combination of things, not possession ☐.
 1 *Each **student's office** has a computer. • That red thing on a **chicken's head** is called 'a comb'.*
 2 *You have to take these forms to the **student office**. • Do you like **chicken soup**?*

Possessive nouns

We form possessive nouns by adding an apostrophe s (**'s**) to most nouns, or only an apostrophe (**'**) to nouns ending in s.
 3 *one man's story, Lee's birthday, children's books, girls' stories, Burns' poems*
Note that it is possible to write both *Dickens' novels* and *Dickens's novels*.

We use possessive noun phrases to express the idea of 'having' (in a very general sense) which exists between the first noun and the second noun. We usually use them when the first noun refers to people and other living things ☐, groups and organizations ☐, times ☐ and places ☐.
 4 *London's night life, China's economic policy, Europe's currency, the world's population*
 5 *My mother's sister, the Beatles' music, the killer's mistake, a dog's life, birds' nests*
 6 *the company's change of plan, the committee's decision, the BBC's news programmes*
 7 *yesterday's meeting, next week's schedule, a week's pay, Monday's news*

We also use possessive nouns in personification, that is, when something abstract is treated as if it was a person ☐, or when an object is described as 'having' something ☐.
 8 *Death's cold hand, love's passionate embrace, jealousy's dark thoughts*
 9 *the car's previous owner, the computer's faulty design, the newspaper's circulation*

Possessive nouns can sometimes be used without a following noun when that noun is treated as known ☐, or is presented as one of a larger number rather than a particular one ☐.
 10 *It's a film of Hitchcock's. • She's a friend of Margaret's.* (= one of Margaret's friends)
 11 *She's at the doctor's. • He has Alzheimer's. • We stayed at Tom's. • It's bigger than Paul's.*

We can use an *of*-phrase after a noun to express 'having', especially when one thing is part of another ☐, when describing actions, ideas or processes ☐, or when a long phrase is used for the possessor ☐.
 12 *the development of industry, the concerns of students, the withdrawal of NATO forces*
 13 *the arm of the chair, pages of a book, the roof of the building, the cost of repairs*
 14 *What was the name of that girl in Amsterdam? • He's the son of the woman we met in Bonn.*

Compound nouns

Compound nouns consist of two (or more) words used to refer to people or things more specifically in terms of what they are for ☐, what they are made of ☐, what work they do ☐, what kind they are ☐, or where and when they happen or are used ☐. Hyphens are sometimes used in compound nouns ☐.
 15 *bus driver, car mechanic, history teacher, production manager, airline safety inspector*
 16 *application form, can opener, fire extinguisher, swimming pool, emergency exit door*
 17 *detective story, horror movie, junk food, women priests, health food magazine*
 18 *chicken soup, feather pillows, glass bottle, paper plates, vegetable curry filling*
 19 *birthday party, morning sickness, street lights, winter coat, dining room table*
 20 *a house-husband, a get-together, a do-it-yourself store, a live-and-let-live approach*

Of-phrases 132 Possessive pronouns 97 Possessives with relative clauses 178

16 Choose one expression from each pair for each space in this verse from a greetings card.

1 (Life's troubles / Troubles of life)
.... can sometimes leave us with a frown,

2 (each day's worries / worries of each day)
And the .... can get us down;

3 (morning special of news / morning's special news)
But this .... is here

4 (world's problems / worlds of the problems)
To make all the .... disappear;

5 (love's woman / woman's love)
Because of one ...., we can say

6 (Mother Day / Mother's Day)
Thanks and best wishes to you on this ....!

17 Part A. Write these noun phrases in the appropriate spaces in the text.

application forms	*consumer groups*	*credit rating*	*money matters*
bottom line	*credit card offers*	*give-aways*	*sense of responsibility*
buy-now-pay-later world	*credit cards*	*high-risk borrowers*	*T-shirts*
college student	✓ *credit card users*	*interest rates*	

Part B. Find two possessive noun phrases with incorrect forms in this text and write correct versions here:

.... ; ....

Is your child starting school soon? Does he or she have a credit card yet? This isn't as strange as it sounds. According to Cathy Yuen, director of College Marketing Services in Los Angeles, ~credit card users~ are getting younger and younger. You may be surprised to learn that teenagers have become one of the most important (1)........................ . In the USA, those teens spend over $150 billion a year and an increasing amount of that spending is done with (2)........................ . For credit card companies, it has become crucial to establish a credit relationship with consumers as early as possible. That first credit card is the one that people are likely to keep using for the longest time. As a result, the typical (3)........................ receives over forty (4)........................ every year. Some lenders are now sending credit card (5)........................ to high school students with offers of (6)........................ such as free (7)........................ . Younger teens used to have to wait until they were eighteen to sign a contract to get a card, but now their parents are co-signing. Credit card companies lose less money with teenagers than with adults, mainly because of parents willingness to help pay off their childrens credit card debt. Yuen says that, in terms of the (8)........................, teens are not (9)........................ . There is also an advantage to getting an early start in the world of credit. If you establish a good (10)........................ early on, you can get better (11)........................ when you want to borrow money later for a car or a house. Teenagers may not be famous for their (12)........................ when it comes to (13)........................, but in this (14)........................, they are learning at an early age how to get what they want by using plastic.

Articles and nouns in discourse

New, old and restated information

We use articles and nouns in different ways to help readers and listeners interpret information in discourse. We introduce new information with *a/an* and repeat old information with *the*.

1 *A gunman tried to use **a** female employee as **a** hostage after **a** failed attempt to rob **a** bank this morning. **The** hostage was released unharmed and **the** gunman surrendered.*

2 *There was once **a** king of **a** far-away country who had **a** beautiful daughter. **The** king had searched **the** whole country to find a young prince to marry his daughter.*

3 *We read **a** report in **a** medical journal about **a** new treatment for asthma. **The** report said that **the** treatment had been effective, but was still experimental.*

We can use *the* plus a more general noun when old information is restated.

4 *After police surrounded the bank, **the woman** was released and **the situation** ended peacefully.*

5 ***The** beautiful **girl** was known throughout **the land** as '**the** lonely **princess**'.*

6 *Soon after the report was released, **the news** of **the breakthrough** brought a barrage of phone calls from asthma sufferers.*

Writers sometimes begin stories by presenting introductory information with *the* as if it is old information and the narrative has already begun.

7 ***The boy** with fair hair lowered himself down the last few feet of rock and began to pick his way toward **the lagoon**.*

Associated and condensed information

We can express associated information with *the* and a different noun. In most cases, the connection is between two nouns, based on common knowledge (a house usually has a kitchen).

8 *We were thinking of buying **a house** in Wimbledon, but **the kitchen** was too small.*

9 *Luckily there was **a taxi** available and **the driver** spoke English.*

10 *She's written **a new book**. I can't remember **the title**. **The cover** is red with gold letters.*

In some cases, the connection is between a verb and a noun.

11 *I really liked it, but didn't **buy** it because **the price** was too high.*

12 *He **asked** me about you. There was something odd about **the tone** of **the question**.*

13 *We were **driving** through heavy rain when **the windscreen wipers** stopped working.*

14 *I **worked** there for a while, but **the pay** was terrible.*

We can also repeat information in a condensed way with *the* plus a compound noun. We can combine elements of information from one or more sentences to form the compound noun.

15 ***The curve** that indicates **supply** can **shift** in response to many factors that can't be measured. However, **the supply curve shift** can be measured.*

16 *You have to fill out a **form** to **apply** for a **credit card**. **The credit card application form** actually represents a contract.*

18 Add these nouns, plus *a/an* or *the*, to these sentences.

bicycle   board   film   job   owner   pay   price   restaurant   shop   teacher

1 Suzy got .... part-time .... in .... Italian
.... , but .... was really low.

2 I found .... old .... in a repair shop. .... said it had
been his son's.

3 In class, ... always writes things on ....

4 According to Allied Cinemas, it will cost you more to see .... this summer.
.... increase will take effect on June 1st.

A/an or the 70   Compound nouns 76

19 Write appropriate articles (*a*, *the* or no article (–)) in this introduction to a short story.

Inside ..the.. station cafe it was warm and light. (1) .... wood of (2) .... tables shone from wiping and there were (3) .... baskets of (4) .... pretzels in glazed paper sacks. (5) .... chairs were carved, but (6) .... seats were worn and comfortable. There was (7) .... carved wooden clock on (8) .... wall and (9) .... bar at (10) .... far end of (11) .... room. Outside (12) .... window it was snowing.

20 Choose an ending (a–j) for each beginning (1–10) and add *a*, *one*, *the* or no article (–).

1 There was .... dog looking lost outside (...)
2 She's spending .... Christmas in hospital. (...)
3 I can't understand .... finance report (...)
4 There was only .... toilet roll left (...)
5 There's .... girl pounding the grand piano. (...)
6 We're going to buy .... new lawnmower. (...)
7 .... young boy had gone missing. (...)
8 She has .... terrible cough. (...)
9 He spent his teenage years indoors, worrying about .... pimples (...)
10 As I told you, ... my computer keeps crashing. (...)

a She's really banging the instrument.
b Youth is really wasted on the young!
c They needed people to help with the search.
d so Mary stopped to help .... poor animal.
e I'll get rid of the thing and get .... new one.
f because the language is too technical.
g so the stuff was treated like .... gold.
h The old machine was always breaking down.
i The problem won't go away without .... medical treatment.
j It isn't .... happiest time of her life, I'm sure.

21 The following parts of a description of a car crash are not in the correct order. Write the numbers in the best order to describe how the crash happened.

4 ... - ... - ... - ... - ... - ... - ... - ... - ...

1 There was a small white van behind the tour bus.
2 I saw a tour bus coming down the main road towards me.
3 The bus signalled that it was turning left into the side street,
✓4 When I was waiting to cross King street,
5 There was also a Mercedes waiting to come out of a side street and turn right.
6 but it couldn't complete the turn because of the Mercedes.
7 and it crashed right into the Mercedes.
8 But the white van had already started to pass the bus
9 So the Mercedes started to come out and turn right.

Tests

A   Choose the word or phrase that best completes each sentence.

1 A demonstration is an act of showing by giving proof or _____ evidence.

   a a   b an   c the   d –

2 What's in this book? Look at the _____ page.

   a content   b contents   c content's   d contents'

3 Dessert is any sweet food eaten at _____ end of a meal.

   a a   b an   c the   d –

4 She worked here for a while then _____ afternoon she just quit and left.

   a an   b one   c the   d –

5 The police have a new _____ in their search for the bank robbers.

   a assistance   b clue   c progress   d information

B   Identify the one underlined expression (A, B, C or D) that must be changed in order to correct the sentence.

1 Two <u>metres</u> <u>are</u> about <u>the size</u> of most <u>doorways</u>.
   　　　A　　B　　　　　C　　　　　　　D

2 I take <u>the bus</u> to <u>the university</u> and meet Tom at <u>the sports complex</u> so we can play <u>the tennis</u>.
   　　　　A　　　　　B　　　　　　　　　　　　　C　　　　　　　　　　　　　　D

3 In <u>one class</u> we had to do <u>a research</u> on <u>the language</u> used in <u>business</u>.
   　　　A　　　　　　　　　　　B　　　　　C　　　　　　　　　D

4 He took one pair of <u>shoes</u>, two <u>shirts</u> and two <u>trousers</u>, but he forgot to take <u>socks</u>.
   　　　　　　　　　A　　　　　　B　　　　　　C　　　　　　　　　　　　　　D

5 <u>Teenagers</u> with <u>credit cards</u> like to buy <u>CD's</u> and <u>clothing</u>.
   　　A　　　　　　　B　　　　　　　　　　C　　　　D

C   Complete this first paragraph of a novel with a, an, the or no article (–).

In my grandmother's dining room there was (1) _____ glass-fronted cabinet and in (2) _____ cabinet a piece of skin. It was (3) _____ small piece only, but thick and leathery, with strands of (4) _____ coarse, reddish hair. It was stuck to (5) _____ card with (6) _____ rusty pin. On (7) _____ card was some writing in (8) _____ faded black ink, but I was too young then to read.

D Rewrite these headlines as sentences with appropriate articles and other necessary changes.

Masked Man Robs Woman Outside Post Office

1 Yesterday, _____

Bank of England Raising Interest Rates by $1\frac{1}{2}$ %

2 In business news, _____

Murder of Priest in Kent Shocks Community

3 Yesterday's news of _____

New Account of Scottish History by English Writer Criticized

4 Reviewers have criticized _____

E Write the correct forms, with articles, of these noun combinations in the spaces below.

authors / report	*earth / health*	*group / latest report*
century / middle	✓ *environmental disaster / threat*	*organization / Sims*
challenges / urgency	*destruction / environment*	*population / world*

The Earthguard Institute has issued a report warning of <u>the threat of environmental disaster</u>

by (1) _____ unless we do something soon.

'(2) _____ facing us requires action now,' said Dennis Sims, one

of (3) _____ .

(4) _____ is a watchdog group that regularly issues reports

on (5) _____ and its people. According to

(6) _____ , rising temperatures, falling water supplies

and shrinking forests are problems that will only get worse as

(7) _____ increases to 9 billion by 2050.

'People's optimism about the future is blinding them to the potential for worldwide disaster,'

Sims warned. 'We must try to reduce global warming by replacing coal and oil with

renewable energy sources such as wind and solar power. If we continue

(8) _____ , our grandchildren will inherit a wasteland.'

7 Determiners and quantifiers

Determiners are words such as articles (*a/an, the*), demonstratives (*this, that, these, those*) and possessives (*my, your, her, his, its, our, their*) which we can use with a noun to help identify who or what the noun refers to (***That*** man with ***the*** beard is ***my*** uncle).

Quantifiers are words and phrases which we use when we talk about quantities that are countable (*a few, many, twenty*) or uncountable (*a little, much*). We can use quantifiers before nouns (*I ate **a few** biscuits and drank **some** milk*), instead of nouns (*Did you want **any**? There wasn't **much** left.*) and with *of*-phrases (*I left **most** of the biscuits for you. I couldn't eat **all** of them.*)

1 Read through this story and find:

1 another example of *all* with a determiner
2 *all* without a determiner

A My grandfather always drove the car and my grandmother sat beside him. I sat in the back seat, my eyes just below the level of the window, seeing the world through their voices.

5 B My grandfather had learned to drive in the country where there were few people or vehicles on the road. My grandmother sometimes mentioned that there were a lot of other cars on the road now and he should take a little more 10 care. In reply to this, my grandfather liked to say, 'All cars have brakes.' He would slow down to turn a corner and we would hear the sound of screeching tyres behind us, followed by the loud blast of a car horn. 'George, you have to signal 15 sooner,' she would suggest. 'Oh, what's all the fuss about?' he'd ask. She'd say, 'That car could have hit us,' and he'd reply, 'Oh, all cars have brakes.'

C Both of my grandparents had grown up on farms 20 in this area, but during their lifetimes the whole area had changed a lot. They said it was strange that there were no farms now. In place of those old farms were lots of new houses, new streets and a big new shopping centre. There were still a 25 few old houses with large gardens and my grandparents lived in one of them.

D The advantage of all these changes, my grand-mother tried to point out, was the convenience of 30 shopping. Everything was close now, even a new supermarket. My grandfather enjoyed the advantages, but he complained about some of the problems that came, he said, from 'too many people in too little space trying to do too much 35 at once!' But he really liked the new coffee house that sold fresh pastries. We seemed to end up there each Saturday.

E It was on our return from one of those Saturday trips that we had our accident. We had eaten some 40 strawberry tarts and my grandfather was telling me how lucky I was that I didn't have to get up every morning and pick strawberries on the farm as he had to. We reached our driveway and turned in. Perhaps his thoughts were back on the farm. 45 Perhaps he didn't expect anyone to be there. He just kept driving up our driveway and straight into the back of another car. There was a terrible crunching sound and we jolted to a stop. A woman appeared beside his window. 'Are you 50 okay?' she asked. 'Of course not! What are you doing in my driveway?' he demanded. 'I was hoping to persuade you to sell your house. Couldn't you stop?' she asked. 'You were in the way!' he almost shouted. 'Well, all cars have brakes, you know,' she said in a very matter-of-fact way.

2 Choose one of the following as the final sentence of each of the paragraphs (A–E) above.

1 There was always someone trying to get them to sell it. (...)
2 As my grandmother turned to see if I was okay, her worried look changed to a smile. (...)
3 He always winked and said it was a special treat for me. (...)
4 I think they sometimes forgot I was there. (...)
5 The circumstances would change, but this answer seemed to cover every situation. (...)

Determiners

Articles

The articles (*a/an, the*) are the most common determiners. (See page 70.)

   1 *I'm sure I read **an** essay or **a** story by Theroux, but I can't remember **the** title.*

Demonstratives

The demonstratives (or demonstrative determiners) have different forms before singular nouns (*this, that*) and plural nouns (*these, those*).

   2 *I love **this** chair. • **That** car was speeding. • **These** people were here first. • I forgot **those** papers.*
We can use the same words as pronouns: *Here are the files. **Those** are older. **These** are new.*

We use *this/these* when we are talking about things close to the speaker or closely connected to here and now. We use *that/those* for things we are treating as further away from here and now. We make this distinction when we talk about times and events (3), places (4) and people (5).

   3 *I'm free **this** afternoon. • I'm busy **these** days. • **That** party was great! • I hated **those** meetings.*
   4 ***This** classroom is better than **that** awful place we had before with **those** tiny windows.*
   5 *Look at **these** people in **this** photo – they're crazy. • Do you remember **that** weird teacher we had?*

We can also use demonstratives to make a contrast between what has already happened (*that/those*) (6) and what is going to happen (*this/these*) (7).

   6 *We discussed the economy last week. In **that** class, we were concerned with money.*
   7 *In **this** class, we will shift our focus to politics and the use of power.*

We can use *that/those* to add an element of 'distance' when we express negative feelings.

   8 ***Those** idiots in Parliament do nothing but talk. • I never liked **that** old grey carpet.*

Possessives

The possessives (or possessive determiners) are *my, your, his, her, its, our* and *their*. We use possessive determiners before nouns (*my seat*), unlike possessive pronouns such as *mine*, which are used instead of nouns and noun phrases.

   9 *Are these **our** seats? ~ I think 12A is **your** seat and 12B is **my** seat.* (NOT ~~mine seat~~)
Note that the possessive determiner *its* is different from *it's* (= it is or it has).

We use possessive determiners to express a personal connection to things we own (10), a part of a thing or a person (11), a feeling or thought (12), a family member or friend (13) or an event (14).

  10 *I don't know where I left **my** bag. Can I borrow **your** dictionary for a minute?*
  11 *The guard put **his** hand on **my** shoulder. The guard dog just stood there, wagging **its** tail.*
  12 *Tasha tried not to show **her** disappointment. She just thanked the teacher for **his** advice.*
  13 ***My** wife has invited **her** parents and a couple of **their** friends to **our** son's birthday party.*
  14 *When is **your** birthday? • In **our** last conversation, he told me about **his** holiday in Spain.*

We usually use *the* rather than a possessive in a prepositional phrase when we're talking about part of the body of someone already identified. The part is treated as a place, not as a possession.

  15 *One man was shot **in the** leg. • Robin leaned forward and kissed me **on the** cheek.*
Note that we say *He kissed **my** cheek.* (NOT ~~He kissed the cheek.~~)

3 **Find examples of these determiners with nouns in the story on page 82.**

   1 four different demonstratives   ....
   2 four different possessives   ....

Quantifiers

Quantifiers and nouns

Quantifiers are words such as *both*, *most*, *several* and *two* and phrases such as *a little* and *a lot* which we use when we are talking about numbers (*How many?*) or amounts (*How much?*). We can use quantifiers before nouns, like determiners (1), or instead of nouns, like pronouns (2).

1 *There were **two** pies left.* • *Can I have **a little** sugar, please?* • *We've had **several** complaints.*
2 *'Let's get **both**,' she said.* • *I don't need **a lot**.* • ***Most** were about the loud music.*

We use some quantifiers (*a few, many*) only with plural nouns (3), some (*each, every*) only with singular countable nouns (4) and some (*a little, much*) only with uncountable nouns (5).

3 *There are **many** occasions when seat belts save lives, yet **a few** drivers still won't wear them.*
4 ***Each** person has to take a card. **Every** card has a different number.* (NOT *Every cards* ...)
5 *I think the soup needs **a little** salt.* • *I hope there isn't too **much** traffic.* (NOT *too much cars*)

We can use the quantifiers *all*, *every* and *no* with numbers before nouns.

6 ***All eleven** players were tired.* • *We get a bill **every three** months.* • ***No two** people are the same.*

4 **Write these quantifiers in appropriate places in the chart.**

✓*all*   *a few*   *a little*   *both*   *each*   *every*   *many*   *much*   *one*   *several*   *ten*

1 all, ... are used before uncountable nouns (*money*).
2 .... are used before singular countable nouns (*book*).
3 all, ... are used before plural nouns (*books*).

Quantifiers with *of*-phrases

We can use quantifiers with *of* before determiners (7) and pronouns (8).

7 ***Two of the** students were late.* • *Take **any of these** chairs.* • ***Some of my** friends got ill.*
8 ***Two of them** were absent.* • *You can't take **any of those**.* • ***Some of us** felt really tired.*
In these structures, there must be a determiner before the noun and *of* before a pronoun.
(NOT *Two of students*; *Take any these chairs*; *Some my friends*; *Two them*; *Some us*)

We can also use quantifiers plus *of* before proper nouns as place names.

9 ***Most of** Europe will have sunny weather tomorrow.* (NOT *Most Europe*; *Most of the Europe*)

We usually put *of* between a quantifier and a determiner, but we can omit *of* after *all*, *both*, *half*.

10 ***All of these** books are old.* • ***Both of his** sons play rugby.* • *I spent **half of the** morning in bed.* •
***All these** books are old.* • ***Both his** sons play rugby.* • *I spent **half the** morning in bed.*

We can use *every one* (not *every*) and *none* before *of*-phrases (11) or as pronouns (12).

11 ***Every one** of my friends had a mobile phone, but **none** of them called me.*
12 *Is there no sugar? ~ There's **none**.* • *Did you check **every** container? ~ I checked **every one**.*

5 **Find four quantifiers with *of*-phrases in the story on page 82 and write them in the spaces.**

....

Countable/uncountable nouns 74   Determiners 83

6 Complete each paragraph with one set of words (not in the order listed).

a / both / each / half   his / my / these / those   his / much / some / the   a little / most / some / thirty
a few / our / that / this

A I got (1) .... earrings, the small ones I'm wearing, from (2) ....
   grandmother. I really didn't like (3) .... green earrings that Andy brought back from
   (4) .... trip to Sri Lanka.

B Look at (5) .... photograph here in the newspaper. Doesn't it remind you of
   (6) .... strange woman who came to teach (7) .... French class for
   (8) .... weeks last year?

C Peter wasn't paying (9) .... attention to the lecture when Angela leaned over and
   tapped him on (10) .... shoulder. As he turned, she pointed to (11) ....
   notepad and whispered, 'Can I borrow (12) .... paper?'

D Although there are (13) .... mountain peaks that receive over (14) ....
   inches of rain annually, (15) .... of Arizona has a warm, dry climate with only
   (16) .... rain in winter.

E When two horses in (17) .... race finish together at exactly the same time, it's called
   a dead heat. It means that (18) .... of them win and (19) .... of them
   receives (20) .... the prize money.

7 Using a dictionary if necessary, complete these sentences with the quantifiers and the other words.

a few   every   most   lottery   maximum   quota
any   many   much   majority   minority   unanimous

1 A .... is the smaller part of a group, sometimes consisting of only
   .... people.

2 The .... weight allowed per passenger is a restriction on how ....
   luggage each passenger is permitted to put on board an aircraft.

3 A .... system is one that sets a limit on how .... people are
   permitted to do something.

4 A .... choice is one that .... person agrees with.

5 In a .... , people can usually choose .... number that they think
   will win.

6 A .... decision is one that is based on what .... people want.

8 Editing. Correct the mistakes in the use of determiners and quantifiers in this text.

I read a newspaper article about some ~~of~~ Spanish boys who got lost while they were hiking in

Scotland. One of boys fell and twisted the ankle badly so he couldn't move. Most them stayed with

injured boy while two the older boys left to find help. However, this two boys didn't know where to

go and, after walking round in big circle for a few hour, ended up back with his friends. Luckily, each

boys had brought some water and food with him, so all them managed to survive a cold wet night

out of doors. They were rescued the next day.

Some and *any*, *no* and *none*

9   Write the numbers of appropriate examples in the spaces.

Some and *any*

We use *some* and *any* with plural and uncountable nouns ☐ or as pronouns ☐ to talk about an indefinite number or amount. We can also use *some* and *any* with *of*-phrases when we are talking about something specific ☐.

1   ***Some*** *students don't get* ***any*** *homework.* • *I wish I had* ***some*** *money.* • *Do you have* ***any*** *matches?*
2   *I love seashells. I was hoping to find* ***some*** *on the beach, but I didn't see* ***any***.
3   ***Some of*** *the new teachers have already arrived. Have you met* ***any of*** *them yet?*

We use *some* in positive sentences ☐ and in questions or offers expecting positive answers ☐.

4   *Did you get* ***some*** *new furniture?* • *Can I borrow* ***some*** *paper?* • *Would you like* ***some*** *tea?*
5   ***Some*** *trees stay green all year.* • *We have* ***some*** *friends in Rome.* • *Let's get* ***some*** *blueberries.*

We use *any* in sentences with a negative element ☐. We also use *any* in questions when no specific answer is expected ☐, in *if*-clauses ☐ and when we mean 'it doesn't matter which one' ☐.

6   *Do Mr and Mrs Young have* ***any*** *children?* • *Is there* ***any*** *food left?* • *Are there* ***any*** *questions?*
7   *Ani can't eat* ***any*** *milk products.* • *We never have* ***any*** *free time.* • *He denied* ***any*** *wrongdoing.*
8   ***Any*** *piece of paper will do.* • ***Any*** *doctor knows that.* • *Call* ***any*** *time after eight.*
9   *If there are* ***any*** *problems, give me a call.* • *I asked her if she had* ***any*** *money.*

We can use *some* when we want to talk in a vague way about a large amount or number ☐, an approximate number or percentage ☐ or a person, place, or thing whose identity is unknown ☐.

10   *It will take* ***some*** *time to recover.* • *They have known about the problem for* ***some*** *years now.*
11   *He now lives in* ***some*** *village in Wales.* • *There was* ***some*** *woman here asking about you.*
12   *That was* ***some*** *twenty years ago.* • ***Some*** *fifty percent of working women don't want children.*

No and *none*

We can use *no* and *none* to emphasize 'not any' ☐. We use *no* rather than *not any* before subject nouns ☐.

13   *There* ***aren't any*** *farms left in that area.* → *There are* ***no*** *farms left.* • *There are* ***none*** *left.*
14   ***No*** *explanation was given.* • ***No*** *dogs are allowed.* (NOT ~~Not any dogs are allowed.~~)

We use *no* before singular and plural nouns ☐. We use *none* as a pronoun and with *of*-phrases ☐.

15   *I had six phone messages, but* ***none*** *from Mr Blake.* ***None of*** *them seemed very urgent.*
16   *When my parents were young, they had* ***no*** *television and* ***no*** *video games so they read books.*

10   Choose an ending (a–f) for each beginning (1–6) and add *any*, *some* or *no*.

1   I don't know what Brian does with all his money. (...)
2   I hope you'll be careful when you're using the paint. (...)
3   Do you mind having black coffee today? (...)
4   You have to pick a number between one and ten. (...)
5   I think we'll probably need paper plates and napkins. (...)
6   The concert was good, but I couldn't stay to the end. (...)

a   I'll bring ....
b   I'm afraid there's .... milk.
c   He never has ....
d   So I missed .... of it.
e   Choose .... of them.
f   Don't spill ....

11 Rewrite these sentences, adding *some* and *any*. Make any other necessary changes.

Example: Have you had news from your family in Prague? I heard that areas were badly flooded.

*Have you had **any** news from your family in Prague? I heard that **some** areas were badly flooded.*

1 There was woman here yesterday asking if we had old clothes, but I told her we had not them.

....

2 Information in that newspaper article was incorrect. There isn't wolf or bears in Scotland.

....

3 I've managed to find dry paper to start a fire, but I can't light it. Don't you have match?

....

4 I'm sure I made mistake when I was typing. If you find mistake, please correct them.

....

12 Complete these sentences (from an article on student life) with *any* (x4), *no* (x3) or *some* (x3).

Did you know that (1) .... thirty percent of students have to leave university, not because they can't cope with their studies, but because they simply can't afford it?

In one survey, researchers found that students cited '(2) .... money' more often than (3) .... other reason such as 'courses too difficult' for ending their studies.

During interviews with the researchers, (4) .... of these former students said that they had tried to do part-time jobs after classes, but they had discovered that they didn't have (5) .... time or they had (6) .... energy left for study when they finished their jobs at night.

When the researchers asked these students if they had received financial support from their parents, (7) .... said they had, but the majority said they hadn't received (8) ....

Most of those interviewed said they had (9) .... plans to return to university (10) .... time soon.

13 Using a dictionary if necessary, complete these sentences with the quantifiers and adjectives.

any   some (x2)   *no* (x2)   *none* (x2)   *dead   empty   extinct   scoreless   uninhabited*

1 I went to get those .... boxes from the back of the bookshop, but someone else had taken the whole stack. There were .... left.

2 Morgan Island is .... now. At one time there were .... twenty fishing families who lived on the rocky island during the summer months, but nowadays there are ....

3 There may still be .... red squirrels in the forests of Scotland, but there aren't .... left in England. They are certainly .... in the southern parts of England.

4 The last England–Sweden game had a lot of great football, but .... goals, ending in a .... draw.

5 Latin is considered a .... language in the sense that there is .... population of speakers who learn it as their first language.

All and *both*, *half* and *whole*

All and *both*

We use *all* before plural nouns and uncountable nouns to make very general statements (1) and *all (of)* before determiners plus nouns to make more specific statements (2).

1 **All** *cars have brakes.* • **All** *students must wear uniforms.* • **All** *information is confidential.*
2 **All (of)** *these cars are for sale.* • **All (of)** *the information you asked for is on our web site.*

We use *all of* (not *all*) before pronouns (3). We use *everyone/everything* rather than *all* by itself (4).

3 *Did you write down their phone numbers?* ~ *No, not* **all of them.** (NOT ~~all them~~)
4 *Everyone laughed at his jokes.* • *Everything was a mess.* (NOT ~~All was a mess.~~)

We use *both* instead of *all* or *both of* instead of *all of* when we talk about two things or people.

5 *Use* **both** *hands to hold it.* • **Both (of)** *my brothers are older than me.* • **Both of** *them live in London.*

We can use *all* and *both* for emphasis after subjects and pronoun objects (6) or after auxiliary verbs and *be* (7).

6 *The men* **all** *agreed to wait.* • *Tim explained it* **all.** • *We* **both** *need a holiday.* • *I like them* **both.**
7 *We had* **all** *heard about the two Williams sisters. They were* **both** *very talented.*

Half and *whole*

We use *half* before determiners (8) or between determiners and nouns (9) to talk about measured amounts. We sometimes use *half (of)* when we are talking about approximately half (10).

8 *A pint is more than* **half** *a litre.* • *We'll be there in* **half** *an hour.* (NOT ~~half of an hour~~)
9 *Get a* **half** *litre if you can.* • *A* **half** *hour should be long enough.* (NOT ~~a half of hour~~)
10 *I've only answered* **half (of)** *the questions.* • *I lost* **half (of)** *my money.* • *Take* **half (of)** *this pie.*
We use *half of* before pronouns: *I can't eat* **half of** *it.* (NOT ~~I can't eat half it.~~)

We use *whole* between a determiner and a singular noun (11) and *the whole of* before determiners, pronouns and proper nouns for places (12) to emphasize a full or complete amount.

11 *The* **whole** *area had changed.* • *I can't eat a* **whole** *pie!* • *The woman told us her* **whole** *life story.*
12 *I spent* **the whole of** *this past weekend in bed.* • *The strike is affecting* **the whole of** *France.*

---

14 **Choose an answer (a–d) for each question (1–4) and add *all*, *both*, *half* or *whole*.**

1 How much longer will the rain last? (...)
2 How much is sixteen ounces? (...)
3 How much are those two books? (...)
4 How much money did he lose? (...)

a You can have .... of them for £5.
b It might go on like this for the .... week.
c .... of it, so he's penniless now.
d I think it's almost .... a kilo.

---

15 **Write one of these quantifiers in each space. Add *of* where necessary.**

all (×2)   *both* (×2)   *half*   *no*   *none*   *one* (×2)   *whole*

Nowadays, (1) .... young girls can play football if they want to. When I was young,
I really wanted to play football, but (2) .... girls were allowed to in my school. In fact,
(3) .... the girls was allowed to play any ' boys' sports'. It was just (4) ....
the rules. I learned about the game from my father and my uncle. (5) .... them had
been football players and they often watched games on TV. I knew that (6) .... teams in
a match started with eleven players and (7) .... them had special positions. I learned
that that there was a break after forty-five minutes, when (8) .... the game was over and
that 'full time' meant the (9) .... game was finished. It was fun to watch, but I would
rather have been (10) .... the players.

Countable/uncountable nouns 74 Determiners 83 *Everyone/everything* 98 Fractions 93

Each and *every*, *either* and *neither*

Each and *every*

We use *each* and *every* before singular countable nouns. We use *each* when we're talking about two or more people or things separately (1). We use *every* when we're talking about three or more people or things together (2).

    1 ***Each*** *day is better than the last.* • *He came in with a cup in **each** hand.* (NOT … ~~in every hand.~~)
    2 ***Every*** *window was broken.* • *The Browns go to Benidorm **every** year.* (NOT … ~~every years.~~)

We use *each of* (not *every of*) before determiners with plural nouns (3) and plural pronouns (4). We can put *each* (not *every*) in different positions (5).

    3 ***Each of*** *her toenails was a different colour.* (NOT ~~Each her toenails~~ …)
    4 ***Each of*** *you must work alone.* • *Give a pen to **each of** them.* (NOT … ~~every (of) them.~~)
    5 *We **each** got one piece.* • *We were **each** given one piece.* • *We were given one piece **each**.*

We use *every* (not *each*) when we want to emphasize 'as many/much as possible' (6), when we talk about something happening at regular intervals (7) and after *almost* and *nearly* (8).

    6 *He had **every** opportunity to complete the work.* • *We wish you **every** success in your new job.*
    7 *There's a bus **every** ten minutes.* • *Take two tablets **every** four hours.* (NOT … ~~each four hours.~~)
    8 *His team lost almost **every** game.* • *We run nearly **every** day.* (NOT ~~We run nearly each day.~~)

Either and *neither*

We use *either* before singular nouns (9) and *either of* before determiners plus plural nouns or pronouns (10) to talk about 'one or the other' of two people or things.

    9 ***Either*** *parent can sign the form.* • *Left or right? ~ You can go **either** way.* (NOT … ~~either ways.~~)
   10 ***Either of*** *the parents can sign.* • *Coke or Pepsi? ~ I'd be happy with **either of** them, thanks.*

We use *neither/neither of* instead of *either/either of* when we mean 'not one and not the other' of two people or things. We use singular verbs after subjects beginning with *neither of* in formal situations (11). Plural verbs are sometimes used in informal situations (12).

   11 ***Neither*** *parent has signed it.* • ***Neither of*** *the boxes was big enough.* • ***Neither of*** *us likes coffee.*
   12 *I'm sorry, but **neither of** my kids are up yet. ~ So, do **neither of** them want to go with us?*

16 Using a dictionary if necessary, complete the sentences with these words.

| choice | doubles | either | neither (×2) | quarterly |
| couple | each (×2) | every | pair | twins |

1 Behind the nun came four young white-faced boys, dressed in grey uniforms, walking in pairs,
    .... holding hands.

2 Simon Weston and Joe Barnes were actually .... who had been adopted by
    different families when they were born and .... of them knew about the other
    until they were almost forty years old.

3 The .... was between a boat trip or a bus tour round the island and
    .... would have been fine with me, but Shirley wasn't feeling well and didn't want
    to leave the hotel.

4 Jim and Tracy are a young .... who have been together for about three years, but
    .... of them wants to get married.

5 Next year you'll have to send £400 in .... payments, which is £100
    .... three months.

6 In a mixed .... match in tennis, ... team consists of a man and a
    woman.

Many, much and a lot (of), more and most

Many, much and a lot (of)

When we talk about large numbers and amounts in a vague way, we can use *many* before plural nouns (1), *much* before uncountable nouns (2) and *a lot of* before both types of nouns (3).

1 **Many** people believe in life after death. • There are **many** ways to improve your health.
2 How **much** money did you bring? • Please hurry, because there isn't **much** time left.
3 I used to smoke **a lot of** cigarettes when I studied. I drank **a lot of** coffee too. (NOT ~~a lot coffee~~)

We usually use *many/much* in formal situations and *a lot of* or *lots of* in informal situations.
When we talk about a large number or amount in a specific way, we use *many of* before determiners plus plural nouns or plural pronouns (4) and *much of* before determiners plus uncountable nouns or singular pronouns (5). We can use *much of* (not *many of*) with singular countable nouns or proper nouns for places when we mean 'a large part of' (6).

4 **Many of** their customers have complained. **Many of** them have started going to other shops.
5 How **much of** your time is devoted to research? ~ Not **much of** it, I'm afraid.
6 Cats spend **much of** the day asleep. • It will be a dry sunny day over **much of** Britain.

We can use *many* and *much* without nouns.

7 People still use butter in cooking, but **many** say they don't use as **much** as before.

We can also use *a lot* (not *a lot of*) without a noun in informal situations: *We don't need a lot.*

We usually use *many* and *much* in questions and negatives (8). We can use them in positive statements after *as, so* and *too* (9). We can also use the phrases *a good/great deal (of)* instead of *much (of)*, and *a large number (of)* instead of *many (of)*, in positive statements, usually in formal situations (10).

8 How **many** do you want? • How **much** do they cost? • There aren't **many** left. • I don't have **much** cash.
9 Take **as much** time as you need. • I have **so much** work to do! • You bought **too many** things.
10 It requires **a great deal of** money and **a large number of** dedicated people to run a school.

We can use *many* (not *much*) after determiners (11) or before *a/an* (12) in formal situations.

11 I'm just one of **her many** admirers. • He explained **the many** rules and regulations they had.
12 He had spent **many an** uncomfortable night in cheap hotel rooms with thin walls.

We can use *much* (not *many*) as an adverb after negative verbs or before comparatives.

13 I didn't sleep **much** last night because I was so worried. • I'm feeling **much** better now.

We can use *a lot* as an adverb after positive and negative verbs: *The area had changed a lot.*

More and most

We use *more* and *most* instead of *much/many* in comparisons. We use *more* for 'a larger number or amount' (14) and *most* for 'the largest number or amount' (15).

14 **More** children are being educated at home. They are spending **more** time with their parents.
15 **Most** American teenagers say they have **most** fun when they are shopping 'at the mall'.

We also use *more* and *most* before adjectives/adverbs: *more quickly, the most expensive*

We can use *more of* and *most of* before determiners (16), pronouns (17) and proper nouns (18).

16 I've already eaten **more of** the cake than I should. • **Most of** those bananas were rotten.
17 I really liked it, but I can't eat any **more of** it. • I had to throw **most of** them away.
18 I hope to see **more of** Spain during my next trip. • **Most of** Venice is under water.

We can use other quantifiers before *more* (not *most*) with the meaning 'additional'.

19 I don't need **much more** time, just **two more** hours. • Is there **any more** tea? • There's **no more**.

Countable/uncountable nouns 74 Determiners 83 *More/most* with adjectives/adverbs 120

17 Rewrite these sentences, adding *many* and *much*. Make any other necessary changes.

Example: There wasn't food left, but we weren't very hungry so we didn't need.

*There wasn't **much** food left, but we weren't very hungry so we didn't need **much**.*

1 There hasn't been discussion of the new road, but older village residents are against it.

....

2 Did you ask how these postcards cost? How them are you going to buy?

....

3 I'll be later today because I have so different places to go to and there's so traffic in town.

....

4 I asked my classmates if they did homework and said they didn't do unless there was a test.

....

18 Add *many*, *many of*, *much* or *much of* to these sentences from an article on British pubs.

1 Pubs are important in the social life of .... British people.
2 .... village pubs are very old and are the centre of village life.
3 For .... the year they rely on local customers.
4 In the summer they get .... their customers from nearby towns or cities.
5 .... old pubs are quite small and don't have .... room inside.
6 In recent years, ... them have added garden areas, with tables outside.

19 Choose an ending (a–f) for each beginning (1–6) and add *more*, *more of*, *most* or *most of*.

1 Saudi Arabia is very hot (...)
2 I liked those pens so much (...)
3 I earn a lot .... than you (...)
4 I can eat .... types of fruit, (...)
5 As .... you know, (...)
6 The pie is really good, (...)

a so I have .... to spend.
b I am not very good at making speeches.
c but I don't like .... vegetables.
d and .... it is desert.
e but I can't eat any .... it.
f that I bought two .... them.

20 Complete this weather forecast with *many* (x2), *more* (x3) and *much* (x2).

There's not (1) .... sunshine in the forecast for this weekend and (2) ....
areas will see (3) .... rain than usual for this time of the year. Saturday will start with
some bright spells and scattered showers, (4) .... of them heavy, giving way to
(5) .... persistent rain later in the afternoon. Southwest winds will bring
(6) .... unsettled weather and rain to (7) .... of England and Wales
on Sunday.

(A) few and (a) little, fewer/fewest and less/least

A few and a little

When we talk about small numbers and amounts in a vague way, we can use *a few* before plural nouns (1) and *a little* before uncountable nouns (2). We can also use *a few* and *a little* without nouns (3).

1 *There may be **a few** minutes left at the end.* • *I brought **a few** pieces of paper.*
2 *There may be **a little** time left at the end.* • *If you add **a little** salt, the soup will taste better.*
3 *Do you want milk? ~ Just **a little**.* • *Did you see any stars? ~ There were **a few**.*
(NOT ~~There was a few.~~)

When we talk about a small number or amount in a specific way, we use *a few of* before determiners or plural pronouns (4) and *a little of* before determiners or singular pronouns (5).

4 *I've seen **a few of** those cartoons that Gary Larson draws. Mary has **a few of** them on her wall.*
5 *I use **a little of** this moisturizing cream when my skin feels dry. You only need **a little of** it.*

We can use *a little* as an adverb after verbs or before participle adjectives and comparatives.

6 *I only slept **a little**.* • *We were **a little** annoyed at first.* • *My mother is feeling **a little** better now.*

Few and little

We use *few* (not *a few*) and *little* (not *a little*) when we are talking about 'not many or much', usually in formal situations (7). We often use *not (very) many* (instead of *few*) and *not (very) much* (instead of *little*) to emphasize a negative view of the quantity (8).

7 *The refugees have **few** possessions and **little** hope of returning home soon.* (NOT ~~a little hope~~)
8 *They **don't** have (very) **many** possessions. They **don't** have (very) **much** hope.*

We also use *few* and *little* between determiners and nouns when we want to emphasize that the small quantity is the complete number or amount, usually in formal situations.

9 *I quickly packed **my few** belongings and spent **the little** money I had on a one-way ticket home.*

Fewer/fewest and less/least

We use *fewer* and *less* instead of *few/little* in comparisons. We use *fewer* (for 'a smaller number of') before plural nouns and *less* (for 'a smaller amount of') before uncountable nouns.

10 *I've been trying to eat **fewer** snacks and **less** junk food as part of my diet.*

In informal situations, *less* is also used with plural nouns: *There were less questions than last time.*

We can use *fewer of* and *less of* before determiners (11) and pronouns (12).

11 *There are **fewer of** those small shops now.* • *I'd like to spend **less of my** time in meetings.*
12 *The swans are back, but there are **fewer of them** this year.* • *Sugar isn't good for you. Eat **less of it**!*

We use *the fewest* (13) and *the least* (14) when we talk about the smallest number or amount.

13 *Ali made **the fewest** mistakes. Nick is the most cheerful and seems to have **the fewest** worries.*
14 *You complain that you make **the least** money here, but that's because you do **the least** work.*

We also use *least* and *less* before adjectives/adverbs: *less quickly, the least expensive.*

---

21 Choose an ending (a–e) for each beginning (1–5) and add *a few*, *few*, *a little* or *little*, plus *of* where necessary.

1 We had very .... problems living here (....)
2 The teacher seemed .... disappointed (....)
3 The home-made soup was very salty (....)
4 We shared the .... pieces of fruit (....)
5 It's been .... warmer recently (....)

a and the .... water that was left.
b so I only ate .... it.
c and we've had .... sunny days too.
d until our car was stolen .... days ago.
e that only .... us had done the work.

Comparatives, *least/less* 120   Countable/uncountable 74   Determiners 83

Multipliers, fractions and percentages

Multipliers

Multipliers are words and phrases such as *once, twice* or *three times* that we use before determiners when we are talking about how often something happens (1) or how much more something is (2). We can also use multipliers plus *as ... as* with *many* or *much*, adjectives and adverbs (3).

   1 *I play tennis **once a** week.* • *I see my sister about **four times a** year.* • *We eat **three times a** day.*
   2 *He sold it for **twice the** original price.* • *Those tomatoes are **two or three times the** average size.*
   3 *We have **twice as many** saucers as cups left.* • *She's paid **three times as much as** I am.* • *He can run **twice as fast as** me.* • *Some of the essays were **twice as long as** mine.*

Fractions and percentages

We can use fractions (*a quarter, two-thirds*) with *of* before determiners and pronouns.

   4 *It takes **a quarter of** an hour.* • *I only used **two-thirds of** the oil, so there's **a third of** it left.*
We can use *half* without *of* before determiners: *Half (of) my answers were wrong.*

We use percentages (*5%, five per cent*) before nouns, or with *of* before determiners and pronouns.

   5 *There was a **10%** increase.* • *They take **thirty per cent** of my pay. I get **seventy per cent** of it.*
Percent is sometimes written as one word, especially in American English.

Fractions and percentages with singular or uncountable nouns have singular verbs. With plural nouns, they have plural verbs.

   6 ***Two-thirds** of the report **is** written.* • *About **twenty per cent** of the students **are** Asian.*

22 **Using a dictionary if necessary, complete the sentences with these words and phrases. Add *of*, *as*, *a* and *the* where necessary.**

✓*eighth*   *four times*   *once*   *quarter*   *twenty per cent*   *twice*   *two-fifths*

Example: A furlong is ..... an eighth of a ..... mile.
   1 The money was divided equally among the four brothers, so each received
      .... it.
   2 .... year we have our annual family gathering at my grandparents' house.
   3 A centimeter is about .... inch, or 0.394 inches to be exact.
   4 A litre bottle holds almost .... much as a pint.
   5 Did you know that at least .... adult population can't read?
   6 At £200,000, the selling price is almost .... price (£51,000) that Dan and
      Ginny Swisher paid for their house just six years ago.

23 **Add these words and phrases to this text.**

a few   *fewer*   *fewest*   *fifty per cent*   *little*

Although the world's population is still increasing, the rate of growth has slowed down from 64% thirty years ago to about 48% today. There is (1) .... chance that population growth will level off before 2050 at the earliest, but there are (2) .... indications that the growth rate will probably keep declining. Women in the wealthiest countries continue to have the (3) .... children. However, partly because of better education and employment opportunities, many women in poorer countries are choosing to have (4) .... babies. In some places, the birth rate is now (5) .... lower than just thirty years ago.

Tests

A Choose the word or phrase which best completes each sentence.

1 When Mary said to the dog, 'Stop wagging your tail', _____ tail started wagging faster.

a your   b hers   c its   d their

2 The new job provided money for expensive toys, but not very _____ time to play with them.

a little   b few   c much   d a lot

3 They said on the news that _____ of Scotland was covered in snow.

a each   b half   c whole   d any

4 Cars were parked on _____ side of the street.

a all   b both   c each   d every

5 She liked to say that she was just one of his _____ happy customers.

a all   b lots of   c many   d some

B Identify the one underlined expression (A, B, C or D) that must be changed in order to correct the sentence.

1 <u>All their neighbours</u> <u>each</u> gave <u>a little money</u> and <u>some their friends</u> helped too.
     A   B   C   D

2 <u>A third of them</u> had blue triangles and <u>two-thirds</u> had green squares or circles, but I didn't like
     A   B

<u>either colours</u> or <u>any of the designs</u>.
    C   D

3 We spent <u>a great deal of time</u> looking through <u>a large number of books</u> to help him find
           A   B

<u>a few information</u> about Bermuda, but he knew <u>most of it</u> already.
   C   D

4 I talked to the students and <u>all</u> think that <u>both</u> Mike and I have <u>lots of</u> money, but we really don't
                 A   B   C

have very <u>much</u>.
    D

5 Claire and Charles said that they'd seen <u>most of the Europe</u> on their trip and <u>they both</u>
                            A   B

mentioned that <u>every city centre</u> was starting to look the same, with only <u>a few exceptions</u>.
          C   D

C Choose the best word from each pair to complete this text.

all / both	*any / some*	*many / a lot of*	✓ *my / mine*
a few / a little	*either / neither*	*that / the*	

When we were young, _____my_____ sister and I spent (1) _____ time together on our own. Our parents (2) _____ worked and they always seemed to be busy with (3) _____ big project. One of them was usually there when we came home from school, but sometimes (4) _____ of them could make it home before dark and they would ask our neighbour, Mrs Green, to check if we were okay. I remember one time when we were playing basketball. My sister got annoyed and threw the ball at me. I turned my back and it bounced off and hit her straight in (5) _____ face. As her nose started to bleed, Mrs Green arrived and let out a terrible shriek. We all got a fright, but there was only (6) _____ blood. It wasn't serious. We decided not to tell our parents about it.

D Complete each sentence in such a way that it is as similar as possible in meaning to the sentence above it.

1 There aren't a lot of people who are willing to help others.
   Not many _____

2 We've written fifty per cent of the report already.
   Half _____

3 We weren't given any explanation for the delay.
   No _____

4 We all want to live forever.
   All _____

E Complete this text with these words plus *of* where necessary.

a great deal	*few*	*many*	*most*	*twelve times*
a third	*fewest*	*more*	*ninety per cent*	*two-thirds*

I read several studies about dating. In one American study, the researchers asked a large number of college students about arranging a date. They focused on dates arranged by women (see Table 1). (1) _____ the students preferred hints. In a hint, for example, the woman mentions that she has noticed something about the man or seen him somewhere. If he talks to her, she can pay (2) _____ attention to him and act as if he is very interesting. Then maybe she can say that she'd like to talk to him again. These types of hints were preferred by about (3) _____ the students.

About a third of the women said they wanted to wait for the man to ask. But only three per cent of the men wanted that. This means that almost (4) _____ as many women as men think that this is a good idea. Such a large difference suggests that a lot of women are waiting and hoping for something that very (5) _____ men will do. This may be one of the (6) _____ reasons why students think it is hard to get a date.

Another reason may be their different opinions about asking directly. 'Asking directly' was chosen by the (7) _____ women. More men, almost (8) _____ them, liked this approach. In fact, in another study I read, (9) _____ college men said that if they were asked directly, they would say 'Yes'. An example of asking directly was: 'I have some tickets for a concert. Would you like to go with me?' In my opinion, this example may not provide reliable evidence about dating. The man may want to go to the concert and say, 'Yes', but he may not like the woman. Is this a date? I don't think so. I believe that we need (10) _____ these studies to find out if men and women define 'date' in the same way.

Table 1

If a woman is interested in going on a date with a man, the best thing for her to do is …	Men agree	Women agree
… ask him directly	30%	2%
… give him a hint	67%	63%
… wait for him to ask her	3%	35%

8 Pronouns, substitution and ellipsis

Pronouns are forms such as *it, someone, these, they, them, theirs, themselves* and *each other* that we use instead of nouns and noun phrases. (*There was a five-pound note on the floor of the cafeteria.* **Someone** *must have dropped* **it**. *The boys looked at* **each other**.)

Substitution is the use of forms such as *one, ones, so* and *do so* instead of noun phrases, verb phrases and clauses. (*'Is it a real* **one**?' *asked Barney. 'I think* **so**,' *said Max*.)

Ellipsis is the process of leaving out words and phrases instead of repeating them. (*Max looked round quickly, then __ reached down, __ grabbed the money and __ hurried out of the room.*)

1 Read through these short texts and find:

1 another example of *it*
2 a sentence with *she* and an example of ellipsis

A I was born in 1939. The other big event of that year was the outbreak of the Second World War, but for the moment that did not affect me. Sydney in those days had all of
5 its present attractions and few of the drawbacks. You can see it glittering in the background of the few photographs in which my father and I are together. Stocky was the word for me.

10 B In the 1940s, a couple of American scientists tried to raise a chimpanzee named Viki in their own home, treating her as a human child. They spent five years trying to get Viki to say English words by shaping her mouth
15 as she made sounds.

C They always say that boys are better at maths than girls. When we actually look at the test results, we find that girls generally do better than boys during the primary school years, but
20 the advantage shifts to boys in high school. That shift occurs when students are given more freedom to select the subjects they will study and girls tend not to go for more maths.

D You know the feeling. You meet someone
25 for the first time, and it's as if you've known each other all your lives. Everything goes smoothly. You know just what she means; she knows just what you mean. You laugh at the same time. Your sentences and hers have
30 a perfect rhythm. You feel terrific. You're doing everything right.

E She took his right hand and placed it against hers, palms touching. He didn't get the point at first. Then he realized that she was comparing
35 the size of their hands. The difference made her laugh.
'What's funny?'
She told him his hand was funny.
'Why mine? Why not yours?' he said. 'If the
40 difference is great, maybe you're the funny one, not me.'
'You're the funny one,' Lu Wan said.
She matched left hands now and fell sideways to the bed laughing. Maybe she thought they were
45 two different species.

2 Choose one of the following as the final sentence of each of the texts A–E above.

1 And you think she's terrific too. (...)
2 They are more likely to choose something else. (...)
3 One of them was exotic and it wasn't her. (...)
4 Handsome was the word for him. (...)
5 Despite their efforts, she never did speak. (...)

Personal, generic and possessive pronouns

Personal pronouns: *I, me, they, them,* etc.

The personal pronouns used as subject pronouns before verbs are *I, you, he, she, it, we, they.*
Those used as object pronouns after verbs and prepositions are *me, you, him, her, it, us, them.*

    1 ***We** like **her**. • **She** loves **him**. • **He** hates **you**. • **You** told **them** about me. • I hope **they**'ll listen to **us**.*

When we use a personal pronoun without a verb in a short response, we use the object form (2).
We usually use the object form of the pronoun after *as* and *than* in comparisons (3).

    2 *I'm feeling hungry. ~ **Me** too. • Who was making all that noise? ~ **Them**, not **us**.*
    3 *We don't have as much as **them**. • Both of my brothers are older than **me**.*

Subject pronouns are sometimes used, but they sound very formal: *They are older than I.*

We usually use *it* for an animal. We can use *he* and *she* when we think of the animal as having human qualities or a special personality, for example, when it's a pet or a character in a story.

    4 *Pooh is a friendly bear. **He** enjoys eating, singing and playing with his friends.*

We use the combination *he or she* (rather than *he*) when we are talking about a person who could be male or female (5). We often use a plural noun and *they* instead of *he or she* (6).

    5 *By the age of two, **a child** can understand five times as many words as **he or she** can say.*
    6 *By the age of two, **children** can understand five times as many words as **they** can say.*

Generic pronouns: *you, we, one, they*

The generic pronouns are *you, we, one* and *they*. We use *you* for 'people in general', including the speaker (7). We use *we* (rather than *I*) to make a statement of opinion more general and to include the reader/listener (8). The use of *one* for 'people in general' is very formal and rarely used in modern English (9).

    7 *If **you** are 'self-absorbed', it means that **you** are only concerned about yourself and your own interests.*
    8 *When **we** think of cheese, **we** don't usually think of sheep, but as **we** saw in the last chapter, …*
    9 *If **one** wishes to be a good parent, **one** should never lose **one**'s temper with a young child.*

In informal situations, we can use *they* to talk about 'other people in general' or 'people in authority' (10), instead of using a passive (11).

    10 ***They** say that an apple a day keeps the doctor away. • **They** should keep criminals in prison.*
    11 *It is said that an apple a day keeps the doctor away. • Criminals should be kept in prison.*

Possessive pronouns: *mine, theirs,* etc.

The possessive pronouns are *mine, yours, his, hers, ours* and *theirs*. We use them in place of possessive noun phrases (*Mary's room*) (12) and in answer to questions with *Whose?* (13).

    12 *I couldn't work in Mary's room. **Hers** is even smaller than **yours** or **mine**. •*
        *Mary's parents have a computer too, but I think **theirs** is different from **ours**.*
    13 *Whose bag is this? ~ I thought it was **yours**. It isn't **mine**.* (NOT ~~It isn't the mine.~~)

We use possessive pronouns in *of*-phrases (*of mine*) after noun phrases beginning with determiners or quantifiers (*a, some,* etc.) (14). We can use this structure to talk about non-specific examples (*a painting of his*) rather than specific or unique examples (*his painting*) (15).

    14 *Was Erica a roommate **of yours**? • I went hiking with some friends **of mine**.*
    15 *Sam Piper is a successful artist. I read that a painting **of his** recently sold for over £10,000.*

---

3 **Find examples of these types of pronouns in the texts on page 96.**

    1 two different generic pronouns in one text ....
    2 three different possessive pronouns in one text ....

Demonstrative and indefinite pronouns

Demonstrative pronouns: *this, these, that, those*

The demonstrative pronouns, or demonstratives, are *this, that, these* and *those*. We use *this/these* for things near or closely connected to the speaker (1) and *that/those* for things further away (2).

    1 (Picking up a box and some letters at the post office) ***This*** *is quite heavy.* • ***These*** *look like bills.*
    2 (Pointing to the box and letters across a room) ***That*** *must have books in it.* • ***Those*** *are just bills.*

We can use *this/these* when we introduce people (3) and *that/those* when we identify people (4).

    3 (Introducing people) ***This*** *is Ann Thomas and* ***these*** *are her two sons, Nick and Jason.*
    4 (Identifying people in the distance) ***That's*** *Mrs Parker and* ***those*** *are her two grandchildren.*
We also use demonstratives as determiners before nouns: *that woman, those children.*

We can use demonstratives to make a contrast between what is close in time (*this, these*) (5) and what is further away in time (*that, those*) (6).

    5 *The next question is* ***this****: who will pay for it?* • ***These*** *are the best days of your life, so enjoy them.*
    6 *Jack and Sandy got married? ~ When did* ***that*** *happen?* • ***Those*** *were the happiest days of my childhood.*

Indefinite pronouns: *someone, something,* etc.

Someone and *something* are indefinite pronouns. Others are *anyone/anything, everyone/everything* and *no one/nothing.* We use them to talk about people (7) and things (8) in a very general way, usually because we can't or don't want to identify them more specifically.

    7 ***Someone*** *must have taken my book. Has* ***anyone*** *seen it? ~* ***No one*** *took it. It's over there.*
    8 *The fire destroyed* ***everything****. We couldn't find* ***anything*** *afterwards. There was* ***nothing*** *left.*
We can use *somebody, nobody,* etc. instead of *someone, no one,* etc. with no change in meaning.

After indefinite pronouns as subjects, we usually use singular verbs and plural pronouns.

    9 ***Someone has*** *been calling and saying* ***they*** *have to talk to you about their schedule.* • *If* ***anyone calls****, just take their number and say I'll call* ***them*** *back as soon as possible.*

We usually use *someone/something* in positive sentences or questions expecting positive answers (10). We use *anyone/anything* in sentences with negative elements or in open questions (11) and when we mean 'it doesn't matter who or what' (12).

    10 *I was looking for* ***someone*** *who spoke Arabic.* • *Can I ask you* ***something*** *about the homework?*
    11 *Can you see* ***anyone*** *outside?* • *I didn't say* ***anything****.* (NOT *I didn't say something.*)
    12 *It isn't difficult,* ***anyone*** *can do it.* • *Jerry is really helpful, he'll do* ***anything*** *you ask him to.*

Somewhere, anywhere, etc. are indefinite adverbs that we use to talk about places in a non-specific way.

    13 *Let's go* ***somewhere*** *different for lunch. ~ But there's* ***nowhere*** *within walking distance.* • *I've looked* ***everywhere*** *for my glasses, but I can't find them* ***anywhere****.*

We can put adjectives (14) and *else* (15) after indefinite pronouns and adverbs.

    14 *Do you have* ***anything smaller****?* • *I think he's* ***someone important****.* • *There's* ***nothing new*** *here.*
    15 *Do you want* ***anything else****?* • *It wasn't me, it was* ***someone else****.* • *There's* ***nowhere else*** *nearby.*

4 **Find two sentences containing indefinite pronouns in the texts on page 96.**

....

....

Adjectives after pronouns 112   Demonstrative determiners 83   *Every 89   Some, any, no 86*

5 Add these pronouns to the following sentences.

him   his   that   this   they   it   yours

1 Excuse me, Graham. Is this bag .... ?
2 I think .... should cut government spending rather than raise our taxes again.
3 We read a story about Winnie the Pooh and a friend of .... called Christopher Robin.
4 John volunteered to take Ann and Bill's mail, so I gave .... to ....
5 I know we allowed you to go away for a whole month before and now we're asking you to take only a fortnight, but .... was last year and .... is now. Things have changed.

6 Rewrite these sentences in a more informal style, using *you*, *we* and *they*.

Example: It is said that one cannot teach an old dog new tricks.

They say you can't teach an old dog new tricks. ....

1 A person should not use a phone while he or she is driving.
You know that ....

2 This old factory is going to be demolished so that a new school can be built.
I heard that ....

3 People who are self-indulgent allow themselves to do or have too much of what they like.
If ....

4 One should not criticize when one is not sure of one's facts.
I think that ....

7 Using a dictionary if necessary, complete these definitions with the noun phrases and pronouns.

camouflage   a disguise   a mirage   everything   no one   nothing   something (×3)

1 .... is .... you use to change your appearance so that .... can recognize you.
2 .... is a way of hiding .... by making it look the same as .... around it.
3 .... is an effect caused by hot air on roads or in deserts which makes you think you see .... such as water when .... is there.

8 Editing. Correct the mistakes in this text.

I studied English in my first school, but I don't remember learning ~~something~~ anything there. We had one teacher who always brought music tapes and she played it for we to learn the words. I think they were hers favourite songs, but in our class no really understood the words. She put us in groups to discuss the songs, but every talked about different something in his groups. And no ones were trying to practise his English very much. I only remember the words of one song that went like that: 'You can't always get what your want, but if you try sometimes you get what your need.' That was interesting words and obviously I did learn somethings from that teacher.

Reflexive and reciprocal pronouns

Reflexive pronouns: *myself, themselves*, etc.

The reflexive pronouns, or reflexives, are *myself, yourself, himself, herself, itself, ourselves, yourselves* and *themselves*. We use a reflexive pronoun instead of an object pronoun when the object is the same person or thing as the subject.

    1 *Be careful or **you**'ll hurt **yourself**. • I'm afraid **I** might cut **myself**.* (NOT ~~I'm afraid I might cut me.~~)
      • *Isn't it amazing how **the human body** heals **itself** after an injury?* (NOT … ~~the body heals it~~ …)

Reflexives have no possessive form. We use *my own*, etc. before nouns: *He has his own ideas.*

We can also use reflexives after most prepositions when the object of the preposition is the same as the subject (2). We use object pronouns (not reflexives) after prepositions of place such as *above, below, beside* and *near* and verbs such as *bring* and *take* plus *with* (3).

    2 *Alice never buys anything **for herself**. • Carlos only thinks **about himself**.*
    3 *Amy put the bag down **beside her**. • You should take an umbrella **with you**.* (NOT … ~~with yourself.~~)

We can also use reflexives for emphasis. We can use them after noun phrases and pronouns to emphasize a particular person or thing (4) or after verb phrases to emphasize 'without help' (5).

    4 *This book was signed by the writer **herself**! • You **yourself** said that she was a great writer.*
    5 *I repaired the flat tyre **myself**. • Terrie and Marnie painted the whole house **themselves**.*

We use reflexives after *by* to emphasize 'alone': *She lives by herself. • I'll do it by myself.*

There are some actions such as *shave* and *shower* that we usually describe without reflexives (6), but which we can describe with reflexives for special emphasis if, for example, the action is difficult (7).

    6 *Their father used to get up, shave, shower, get dressed and make breakfast for all of them.*
    7 *But since his accident, he can't shave **himself** or even dress **himself** without their help.*

9 **Choose an ending (a–d) for each beginning (1–4) and add appropriate pronouns.**

1 He got a hammer and some nails (…)	a and take care of …………
2 Remember to eat well, exercise regularly (…)	b and they saw the city below …………
3 Thanks for offering to help, (…)	c and repaired it …………
4 The plane started to descend (…)	d but I can do it …………

Reciprocal pronouns: *each other* and *one another*

We can use the reciprocal pronouns *each other* and *one another* with no difference in meaning.

    8 *The cat and the dog hate **each other/one another**. • They always avoid **one another/each other**.*

We use reciprocal pronouns (9) instead of reflexives (10) when the same action or feeling goes both ways between two or more people or things.

    9 *The candidates described **each other**.* (= Each one described the other one.)
    10 *The candidates described **themselves**.* (= Each one described himself or herself.)

We can use reciprocal pronouns after prepositions (11) and as possessives (12).

    11 *The two girls never argued **with one other**. They were always chatting **to each other**.*
    12 *They even wore **each other's/one another's** clothes sometimes.*

We can use *each* as subject and *the other(s)* as object when the action of the verb goes both ways (13). When the action goes one way, we use *one* as subject and *the other(s)* as object (14).

    13 *I asked the boys if they had broken the window and **each** blamed **the other**.*
    14 *There are two buses at 5.30 and **one** always follows **the other** in case the first one gets full.*

Object pronouns 97 Prepositions of place 129

10 Add the pronouns *it, they, we* and *you* plus appropriate reflexives to this text.

They say that if you want something done right, (1) .... have to do it
(2) .... And we all know that if something is broken, (3) .... certainly
won't fix (4) .... As a result, there are many more DIY ('Do It Yourself') shops in
Britain these days. It seems that (5) .... have all suddenly decided to do our home
repairs (6) .... So, are all the real builders and plumbers out of work now?
Apparently not. They're even busier now, trying to fix the mess left by those who discovered that
(7) .... really couldn't do it (8) .... and had to call for professional help.

**11 Complete these sentences with the prepositions *about, by, for, near, with*, plus
appropriate pronouns.**

1 Erica York was a self-taught mathematician who liked to spend hours .... in the
library.
2 The man seemed very self-centred and only wanted to talk ....
3 People who are self-employed work ...., not a company.
4 I took a small knife ...., hoping I would only have to use it in self-defence.
5 Test your self-restraint by placing something you really like to eat ...., but don't
eat it.

**12 Using a dictionary if necessary, complete these descriptions with one set of words (not
necessarily in this order).**

another / each / one / the other   *another's / each / one / other's*   *each / other / you / yourself*

Mutual respect is a feeling of admiration that people have for (1) ....
(2) .... equally, and self-respect is a feeling of pride in (3) .... and the
belief that what (4) .... do or say is right and good.
An exchange is an arrangement through which two people or groups from different countries visit
(5) .... (6) .... homes or do (7) .... (8) ....
jobs for a short time.
Wrestling is a sport in which two people fight by holding onto (9) ....
(10) .... while (11) .... tries to throw or force (12) .... to the
ground.

**13 Complete these sentences with appropriate forms of the verbs plus a reflexive or
reciprocal pronoun.**

agree with   blame   express   hurt   meet

1 All students are required to give a presentation on their projects and to .... as
clearly as possible.
2 The boy said that his sister had slipped on the wet floor and ....
3 Both drivers said it wasn't their fault. They .... for the accident.
4 My aunt and uncle always seem to have different opinions about things and they almost never
....
5 Before they got married, Gavin and Gwen visited his parents in England and then her parents in
California, so they could .... families.

Empty subject *it*

We use *it* as an empty subject with the verb *be* in expressions of time, distance and weather.
  1 ***It's** eleven o'clock.* • ***It's** two miles to town.* • *Is **it** raining?* (NOT ~~Is raining?~~)

We use *it* as a personal pronoun subject when we are referring to a thing or animal (2).
We use *it* + *be* before an adjective or noun plus a noun clause (3).
  2 *Where's <u>the breadknife</u>? ~ **It's** in the drawer.* • *We saw <u>their new puppy</u>. **It** was really cute.*
  3 ***It's** sad <u>that she's leaving so soon</u>.* • ***It** was just a coincidence <u>that we were both in London</u>.*

We can also use *it* + *be* before an adjective or noun plus a gerund (4) or infinitive (5).
  4 ***It** was nice <u>talking to you</u>.* • ***It's** an advantage<u> having a rich father</u>.*
  5 ***It's** not wise <u>to hike in the mountains by yourself</u>.* • ***It** might be an exaggeration <u>to say he's rich</u>.*

We can use a noun clause (6), gerund (7) or infinitive (8) as subject instead of *it* in formal situations.
We don't use a noun clause, infinitive or gerund instead of *there* (9).
  6 ***It** was obvious <u>that Brazil was going to win</u>.* → *That Brazil was going to win was obvious.*
  7 ***It's** often a problem for Henry <u>being so tall</u>.* → *Being so tall is often a problem for Henry.*
  8 ***It's** a real pleasure <u>to meet you at last</u>.* → *To meet you at last is a real pleasure.*
  9 *There will be someone to meet you at the airport.* (NOT ~~To meet you at the airport will be someone.~~)

After *it*, we usually use a form of the verb *be*, but we can use verbs such as *surprise* and *frighten* plus an object to describe a reaction (10) and verbs such as *seem* and *appear* to express a conclusion (11).
  10 ***It surprised** everyone that Marion won.* • ***It** really **frightened** me to see the horse and rider fall.*
  11 ***It seems** that he was unhappy in London.* • ***It appears** that he has been neglecting his studies.*

We can also use *it* as an empty object after 'liking' (or 'not liking') verbs before a noun clause (12) and after verbs such as *find, make* and *think* before an adjective plus a clause or infinitive (13). After some verbs such as *regard, see* and *view* used to express an opinion, we put *as* after *it* (14).
  12 *I **hate it** when the alarm suddenly goes off.* • *My parents **love it** that we live closer now.*
  13 *I **find it** surprising that you waited so long.* • *The loud music **made it** difficult to talk.* •
      *We **thought it** strange that he was still in his pyjamas.* (NOT ~~We thought strange that he was~~ …)
  14 *They **regard it as** encouraging that both sides are willing to continue negotiations.*

14 Rewrite these sentences in a less formal style beginning with *it*.

1 That Tony never helps with the cleaning really annoys everyone.

   ....

2 Not having a car can be a big disadvantage.

   ....

3 To see potential problems in advance is very important in my job.

   ....

4 Why she left so suddenly was a complete mystery.

   ....

5 To discover that your passport was missing must have been a shock.

   ....

6 That people can eat such unhealthy food and live so long always amazes me.

   ....

  Infinitives and gerunds 139   Noun clauses 161   Personal pronouns 97

Empty subject *there*

We use *there* as an empty subject with the verb *be* before a noun phrase. The noun phrase determines whether the verb is singular or plural. We often include an adverbial, such as a preposition phrase of place (*in Travel magazine*) or time (*on Friday*) after the noun phrase.

1 **There was** an article in Travel magazine about Munich. • **There are** two meetings on Friday.

In informal situations, *there's* is often used with plural nouns: *Don't forget there's two meetings.*

We use *there* + *be* to say (2) or ask if (3) people and things are present or exist (or not).

2 **There was** an old man in the waiting room. • **There are** no snakes in Ireland.

3 **Are there** any questions? • **Is there** a bathroom upstairs? (NOT ~~Is a bathroom upstairs?~~)

We don't use *it* to say or ask if things are present or exist. (NOT ~~Is it a bathroom upstairs?~~)

We can use *there* (not *it*) + *be* with quantifiers to present information about amounts and quantities.

4 **There's** a lot of crime now in the city centre. • **There wasn't** much room inside his car.
   (NOT ~~A lot of crime is now in the city centre.~~ • ~~It wasn't much room inside his car.~~)

When we express an opinion about things being present or existing, we can put modals and/or adverbs such as *certainly* or *probably* between *there* and *be* (5). We can also put *seem* or *appear* between *there* and *to be* (6).

5 **There should be** a guard rail here. • **There certainly are** problems. • **There will probably be** a fight.

6 **There seem to be** a lot of unanswered questions. • **There didn't appear to be** anyone in charge.

We can also use *there* + *be* with adjectives such as *likely* and *sure* plus *to be* and a noun phrase to show how certain we are about the information being reported.

7 **There isn't likely to be** peace for many years. • **There are sure to be** protests about the decision.

We can use the passive forms of verbs such as *report, say* and *think* between *there* and *to be* to report information, but we don't usually use a passive after *there*.

8 **There were thought to be** some problems in the original design and indeed a number of flaws were found. (NOT … ~~and indeed there were found a number of flaws.~~)

After *there* + *be*, we usually introduce new information with *a/an* or indefinite pronouns (9), but we can use *the* or demonstratives when we treat information as familiar or given (10).

9 **Is there a problem?** ~ Yes, I think **there's something** wrong because **there's a long queue.**

10 I think we should go early. **There's the problem** of parking and when we go later **there's** always **that long queue** to get into the car park.

15 Correct the mistakes in the use of *there* and *it* in these sentences.

Example: I'm sure ~~it~~ there will be someone to help you with your luggage.

1 It was such a nice day in the valley that it was a surprise to hear there was snowing in the mountains.

2 It isn't much time left to prepare for the meeting if it's first thing tomorrow morning

3 There certain to be questions about Ireland in the history test.

4 It was said to be hundreds of people stranded by the floods.

5 A lot of fat and sugar is in pies and cakes.

6 Everyone found very amusing that I'd started taking karate lessons.

7 They viewed it offensive that he just slumped in the chair and put his feet up on the coffee table.

8 It really wasn't surprising that there were found no survivors in the wreckage of the plane.

Substitution: *one* and *ones*

We can use *one* and *ones* instead of repeating countable nouns (1). We use *one* instead of a singular noun (*banana*) or a noun phrase (*a small ripe banana*) (2). We use *ones* instead of a plural noun (*bananas*), but not instead of a plural noun phrase (*these small bananas*) (3).

1 *We bought bananas at the local market. Would you like* **one**? ~ *Oh, I love the small* **ones**.
2 *I'm not sure if there's a small* **one** *that's ripe.* ~ *Oh, yes, there's* **one** *in this bunch.*
3 *I've never seen these small* **ones** *in the supermarket.* (NOT *I've never seen ones* …)

Instead of repeating plural noun phrases (4) or uncountable nouns (5), we use *some* or *any*.

4 *I love these small bananas, but I've never seen* **any** *in the supermarket. I must get* **some**.
5 *I'm going to buy more fruit. Do you need* **any**? *I'll get* **some** *for the picnic.* (NOT *some ones*)

We use *one* to talk about an object in general (6) and *it* for a specific example of an object (7).

6 *Do you have a French dictionary? I'm looking for* **one**. (= not a specific French dictionary)
7 *Do you have the French dictionary? I'm looking for* **it**. (= a specific French dictionary)

We don't usually use *a/an* with *one* (8) or quantifiers with *ones* (9) unless we include an adjective.

8 *I need a pen, preferably* **a red one**. *Do you have* **one**? (NOT *Do you have a one?*)
9 *Most of the tomatoes were still green, but I picked out* **three ripe ones**. (NOT *three ones*)
We can use *each/every* with *one*: *I examined each/every one.*

We don't usually use *the* with *one* or *ones* unless there is an adjective before them (10), or a descriptive phrase or clause after them (11).

10 *We bought a new table, so you can have* **the old one**. (NOT … *you can have the one.*)
11 *Do you mean* **the one in the kitchen** *or* **the one that used to have the computer on it**?

We usually use demonstrative pronouns or possessive pronouns (rather than determiners with *one* or *ones*) (12) unless we include an adjective (13).

12 *I put our books in two piles.* **These** *are* **mine** *and* **those** *are* **yours**. (NOT … *those ones are your ones.*)
13 *Computers have changed a lot.* **My new one** *is so much faster than* **that other one** *I used to have.*
In informal situations, *my one, your one,* etc. and *that one, this one,* etc. are sometimes used.

16 Choose an ending (a–d) for each beginning (1–4) and add these words:

any   it   one   ones (×2)   *some   them*

1 Sharon: I need six large brown envelopes. (. . .)
2 Rachel: We have a lot of small . . . . , (. . .)
3 Ask Jack, he had . . . . earlier, (. . .)
4 Sharon: I got . . . . from him, (. . .)

a but . . . . wasn't large enough.
b but he may have used . . . . already.
c but no large . . . . , I'm afraid.
d Do you have . . . . ?

17 Editing. Correct the mistakes in this text.

My mother told me this story about her first fridge. After my parents got married, they rented a flat.
     One
She said it was a very small ˅ with an oven, but no fridge, so they started looking for it in the

newspaper. She said that fridges weren't as common then and some ones were really expensive. But

she kept looking for it. She eventually found a second-hand that wasn't too expensive and the man

said he would deliver it for free, so she bought right away. She was really happy. She waited a week,

then two weeks, but she never saw the man or the fridge again. Later, she heard about some other

people who had gone to see that man and his fridge and every had fallen for the same trick.

Substitution: *so* and *do so*

We can use *so* instead of repeating a clause after some verbs expressing opinions or expectations.
  1 *The rain will stop soon. ~ I hope* ***so****.* (= I hope the rain will stop soon.) (NOT ~~I hope it.~~)
Other verbs used in this way include: *be afraid, believe, expect, guess, think*
We don't use *so* after *be sure* and *know*: *It's getting late. ~ I know.* (NOT ~~I know so.~~)

To express the negative, we use *so* after the negative forms of *believe, expect* and *think* (2). We use *not* after the positive forms of *be afraid, guess* and *hope* (3).
  2 *Perhaps it will be nice and sunny. ~ I don't think* ***so****.* (NOT ~~I don't think./I don't think it.~~)
  3 *The weather may actually get worse. ~ I hope* ***not****.* (NOT ~~I don't hope so./I don't hope it.~~)

We also use *so* after *say* and *tell* (someone) instead of repeating what was said.
  4 *Jones was fired. They said* ***so*** *on the news.* (= They said that Jones was fired on the news.)
    I thought it was a mistake to fire him and I told them ***so****.* (NOT *… ~~I told them it.~~*)

We can use *if so* instead of repeating a clause in a conditional sentence.
  5 *Landa says you took her book.* ***If so****, you must return it.* (= If you took her book, …)

We can use *so* after *less* and *more* instead of repeating an adjective (6) or an adverb (7).
  6 *He used to be really serious. He's* ***less so*** *now.* (= He's less serious now.)
  7 *They're working hard, even* ***more so*** *than usual.* (= even harder than usual)

We can use different forms of *do* plus *so* instead of repeating the same verb and object.
  8 *They asked me to revise the first paragraph and I* ***did so****.* (= I revised the first paragraph.)
    • *Anne Elliot refused Wentworth's offer of marriage, then regretted* ***doing so****.*

We usually use *do so* in formal situations. In informal situations, we can use *do it* or *do that* (9). When we repeat the verb with a different subject, we use *do it* (not *do so*) (10).
  9 *Jump across the stream. Come on. Just* ***do it****! ~ Oh, no. It's too far. I can't* ***do that****.*
  10 *Brandon forgot to take the rubbish out and I can't* ***do it****. Can you* ***do it****?* (NOT ~~Can you do so?~~)

---

18 Complete these sentences with *so* or *it* plus appropriate forms of *do* where necessary.

  1 Adam likes to drive fast, even more .... since he got that new sports car.
  2 Did we miss the bus? ~ I'm afraid .... Will there be another one? ~ I certainly
     hope .... !
  3 Can you complete the work today? ~ I don't think .... I'm sure I can't
     .... before Friday.
  4 WARNING. Dangerous currents. Anyone who swims here .... at their own risk.
  5 One of my friends has asked me to go snowboarding, but I've never .... before.
  6 Many teenagers want to earn money in part-time jobs and are encouraged .... by
     their parents.

---

19 Complete this dialogue with *one, ones, so* or – (= nothing).

  'Would you like to hear a joke? Have you heard the (1) .... about the five flies?'
  'I don't think (2) .... ?'
  'Okay. If there are five flies on the table and I kill one, how many will be left?'
  'I'm not sure (3) .... Will there be four (4) .... left?'
  'Wrong! There'll only be the dead (5) .... ?'
  'What about the other (6) .... ?'
  'Well, they'll fly away, of course!'
  'Ha! I should have known (7) .... ?'

Ellipsis

20 Write the numbers of appropriate examples in the spaces.

Leaving words out

Ellipsis means leaving words out. Instead of repeating a noun phrase (*the guard*), we can use a pronoun or we can leave the pronoun out 1 . Instead of repeating a verb phrase (*take*), we can use a substitution form or leave the substitution form out 2 .

1 *The guard looked over and <u>he</u> smiled./The guard looked over and _ smiled.*
2 *She could take the money, but she won't <u>do it</u>./She could take the money, but she won't _ _ .*

We usually use ellipsis instead of repeating words before nouns in phrases joined by *and, but, or*.

3 *You'll need a pen **or** _ pencil. • Ashley's aunt **and** _ uncle own property in France **and** _ Italy.*
We can also use ellipsis after a comma in a list: *I'm afraid of bees, _ wasps and _ spiders.*

Leaving out subjects and objects

After *and, but, or* in compound sentences, we usually leave out a repeated subject ⬚ , a repeated subject and auxiliary ⬚ or a repeated subject and verb ⬚ .

4 *She was shouting **and** _ _ throwing things. • Should we bring our bags **or** _ _ leave them here?*
5 *We sat **and** _ talked. • He came, **but** _ left early. • They ran **or** _ walked the rest of the way.*
6 *He looked okay, **but** _ _ tired. • I enjoy films, _ _ going to the theatre, **and** _ _ walks in the park.*

We can also leave out repeated subjects in later clauses after *then* and *yet* ⬚ . We don't usually leave out subjects (and auxiliaries) after subordinating conjunctions ⬚ .

7 *We tidied up **before** <u>we</u> left. • He's tired **because** <u>he's</u> ill.* (NOT ~~He's tired because ill.~~)
8 *The bird looked up, **then** _ suddenly flew away. • Nella liked England, **yet** _ longed for Italy.*

We usually leave out repeated objects ⬚ or preposition phrases ⬚ from the first clause. We use an object pronoun rather than leave out the object from second or later clauses ⬚ .

9 *We gave food _ _ and water to everyone. • I lived _ _ _ _ _ and studied in Rome for a year.*
10 *She makes _ and sells jewellery. • We usually boil _ _ or poach some eggs for breakfast.*
11 *She makes jewellery and sells it.* (NOT ~~She makes jewellery and sells.~~)

Leaving out verb phrases

After an auxiliary verb in the second or later clause, we usually leave out a repeated verb phrase ⬚ . We can leave out repeated adjectives and preposition phrases after *be* as a linking verb ⬚ .

12 *We thought they would be late, but they **weren't** _. • I'm afraid he's in love and she **isn't** _ _.*
13 *I've seen the film, but Mike **hasn't** _ _ _. • The boys weren't feeling cold, but I **was** _ _. •*
     *We would help you if we **could** _ _. • Sarah will eat broccoli, but Jessica **won't** _ _.*

We can also leave out a repeated verb phrase after infinitive *to* ⬚ or *not to* ⬚ . After verbs such as *agree* and *want*, we can also leave out *to* ⬚ .

14 *She'll leave unless he begs her not to _. • Some boys kept talking after I told them not to _.*
15 *I don't smoke now, but I used to _. • We haven't applied for a grant, but we plan to _ soon.*
16 *They asked us to do this and you agreed (to) _ _. • You can stay here if you want (to) _.*
After a negative, we include *to*: *He'd like me to stay, but I don't want to.* (NOT ... ~~but I don't want.~~)

In formal situations, a repeated verb can be left out of a second clause when both clauses have the same structure ⬚ . We usually repeat the verb when the subject is a pronoun ⬚ .

17 *The girls go first and the boys _ after them. • Alex chose Oxford and Alison _ Cambridge.*
18 *We go first and they go after us.* (NOT ~~We go first and they after us.~~)

We can leave out repeated words after question words when we ask ⬚ or report questions ⬚ .

19 *I have to leave now. ~ Why _? • It will cost a lot of money to repair the damage. ~ How much _?*
20 *Dr Foster has said he's planning to go on holiday, but he hasn't told us where _ or when _ yet.*

Auxiliary verbs 17 Compound sentences 12 Subordinating conjunctions 12 Substitution 105

21 Complete these definitions using the nouns plus *they*, *them* or – (= nothing).

litter   pollution   rubbish   waste

(1) .... : small pieces of paper or containers that people leave, (2) ....
drop or (3) .... throw away in a public place.
(4) .... : the act of using things in a careless way, causing (5) .... to be
lost or (6) .... destroyed (7) .... unnecessarily.
(8) .... : the substances that make air, water or soil dirty and (9) ....
make (10) .... unsuitable for people to use.
(11) .... : things that people throw away because (12) .... no longer
want or (13) .... need (14) ....

22 Choose the best ending for each beginning and write it in the space, leaving out appropriate words.

✓ *we are hoping to leave soon*	*she didn't want to come with us*	*he didn't help us move it*
we can go by train	*she's working in Boston*	*no one was caught*
I sat in the back	*she wouldn't tell us what she found*	*the others hadn't been there*

Example: We're packing our bags and hoping to leave soon ....
1 We can go to Edinburgh by bus or ....
2 Elizabeth is working in New York or ....
3 I didn't think anyone would be caught and ....
4 Lucy found something, but ....
5 We had already been to Athens, but ....
6 Chris could have helped us move the table, but ....
7 My grandparents sat in front and ....
8 I invited Malia to come with us, but ....

23 Create the shortest possible version of this text by drawing a line through the repeated words that could be left out of each sentence.

He put the money on the table and ~~he~~ sat down. He sat in his hot clothes and he felt heavy. The woman looked over at him and she smiled. Her smile said she was in charge and she could take his money if she wanted to take his money. Of course she could take his money, he thought, but obviously she didn't want to take his money yet. The smile lingered for a moment or two longer, then it disappeared and it was replaced by a dark stare.

'I asked you to pay me a thousand and you agreed to pay me a thousand. This is only five hundred.'

'You'll get your thousand. I'll give you half of your thousand now and I'll give you the other half of your thousand later when I get the orchid.'

'I could get the orchid and I could find someone else who'd want to buy it.'

'You won't find someone else who'd want to buy it. Nobody else is even looking for this orchid.'

The dark stare wanted to stay, but it was slowly replaced by half a smile. It said she would give me half of the smile now and the other half of the smile later.

Tests

A Choose the word or phrase that best completes each sentence.

1 _____ a phone in here?

   a Is   b Is it   c Is it's   d Is there

2 Billy's shoes look really dirty. Didn't he bring clean _____?

   a one   b ones   c any   d some

3 You can't carry all those boxes. I'll get someone else to _____ for you.

   a do   b do it   c do so   d do these

4 He came with his parents and two friends of _____.

   a them   b their   c theirs   d themselves

5 I asked Meg earlier if she thought it would rain and she said, 'I _____.'

   a hope   b hope it   c hope not   d don't hope so

B Identify the one underlined expression (A, B, C or D) that must be changed in order to correct the sentence.

1 She didn't bring a jacket or <u>anything</u> like that with <u>herself</u>, so I gave her <u>one</u> of <u>mine</u>.
                      A   B   C   D

2 There were two men arguing with <u>each other</u> in the car park when suddenly <u>one</u> punched <u>other</u>
                               A   B   C

   and knocked <u>him</u> to the ground.
                D

3 After fresh tea is made, <u>she puts</u> milk in the tea cup, then <u>pours</u> the tea and <u>adds</u> a little sugar
                            A   B   C

   before <u>she tastes</u>.
              D

4 The couple who <u>bought the old pub</u> in Torbrex <u>regarded as an opportunity</u> to <u>make money</u> and
                    A   B   C

   <u>enjoy themselves</u> too.
       D

5 I'm not sure why <u>it was necessary</u> to evacuate the whole airport, but <u>there was discovered a knife</u> in
                   A   B

   someone's bag after <u>they had gone</u> through an electronic security check <u>without being stopped</u>.
                       C   D

C Complete this text by writing two of these words in each space.

do (×2)   else   it   myself   someone   something   them

I'm not sure exactly why I became a regular blood donor. Perhaps it was because a few years ago I started feeling a need to do something positive instead of just feeling helpless in a world full of disasters. It's sort of the same feeling I would have if I saw someone drowning. It wouldn't make any difference whether I knew them or not. I would have to (1) _____ to help. If I didn't think I could save (2) _____ , I would try to find (3) _____ who could (4) _____ . It's the same thing for me when I give blood or when I can get other people to come with me and give blood. It's just a good thing to do.

D Complete each sentence in such a way that it is as similar as possible in meaning to the sentence above it.

1 Having wealthy parents should have been useful, but they didn't actually support her.
It _____

2 He doesn't like her and she doesn't like him.
They _____

3 Someone will be at the airport to meet you, I'm sure.
I'm sure there _____

4 To go swimming out in the ocean by yourself would not be a good idea.
It _____

5 Thousands of people were said to be affected by the rail strike.
There _____

E Complete this text with these words.

anyone   anywhere   him   himself   it   me   myself   one   ours   she   that

My mum and I got a guard dog because (1) _____ sometimes has to go away on business trips and didn't want to leave (2) _____ at home by (3) _____ . We called (4) _____ Rufus. When Rufus was about four months old, he started barking if (5) _____ came near the cottage, especially the postman. When friends of (6) _____ came to visit, Rufus would go to the front door and growl even before we knew they were outside. We didn't train him to do (7) _____ , he just seemed to train (8) _____ to be our watchdog. However, when he was about seven months old, he started growling at people in the street and barking ferociously if (9) _____ of them came near our car in a car park. It has become really embarrassing and now we can't take him (10) _____ with us. We like (11) _____ that he's protective, but we are now afraid that he might become really dangerous and even attack someone. We're not sure what to do.

9 Adjectives and adverbs

Adjectives are single words (*exciting, new, thorough*) and compounds (*hard-working, well-organized*) that modify nouns. We can use them before nouns (*The **new** teacher has **exciting** ideas*) or after linking verbs such as *be* and *seem* (*She's **hard-working** and her classes seem **thorough** and **well-organized***).

Adverbs are words (*always, really, thoroughly, totally*) that modify verbs, adjectives, other adverbs and sentences (*She **always** does everything **really thoroughly** and seems **totally** dedicated to her job*).

1 Read through this magazine article and find:

1 another example of an adverb modifying an adjective
2 a set of three adjectives before a noun

THE ANCIENT CHINESE ART of Feng Shui has been adopted by modern designers as a way of creating environments which feel comfortable and harmonious. Originally developed
5 as a means of planning the perfect agricultural system in harmony with the forces of nature, Feng Shui has been used for centuries to improve the physical surroundings in which people live and to maintain balance in their lives.
10 Those principles of Feng Shui that are beneficial in the organization of outdoor environments can also be used in the design of areas inside the house such as the bedroom, which is considered to be the most important room in the house.
15 Finding the best position for the bed is very important. The main rule of bed positioning is never to have the foot of the bed directly facing the door. That is what is known as the 'death position'. Traditionally, the dead were laid out with their feet
20 pointing towards the door to give them better access to heaven. (It also made it easier for the living to carry them out.)
Ideally, you should position the bed diagonally opposite the door, with the head against a wall, not a

25 window. Avoid putting the bed directly under a horizontal beam that seems to cut across the sleeper. Such a position is believed to cause headaches and even illness.
Small tables on both sides (not just one side) at
30 the head of the bed help maintain balance, but it is best to avoid cluttering the room with a lot of furniture. Let air flow easily through the space. Those large heavy wooden wardrobes, often with boxes or suitcases stored on top, are a really bad idea.
35 As they tower over the bed, they can make the sleeper feel vulnerable and cause a restless sleep. Do not position tables or other furniture with pointed edges facing the sleeper as their negative energy will cause health problems.
40 The bedroom should be kept as a relaxing space and should not be used for work or as an office. There should be a feeling of lightness, not seriousness, in the air. Blue curtains and bedcovers are more soothing than brown ones. Soft natural
45 materials are recommended. With Feng Shui in your bedroom, you can create a peaceful sanctuary from the stresses of contemporary living.

2 Using adjectives and adverbs from the Feng Shui text, complete this summary.

You can use Feng Shui to make your bedroom a sanctuary. Finding the (1) .... position for the bed is (2) .... (3) .... It should be (4) .... opposite the door, not (5) .... under a (6) .... beam, and with the head against a wall. You can have (7) .... tables on both sides of the head of the bed, but avoid (8) .... wardrobes or furniture with (9) .... edges facing the sleeper. (10) .... curtains and bedcovers made from (11) .... (12) .... materials are also recommended.

Adjectives: emphasizing, describing, classifying

Emphasizing adjectives

Emphasizing adjectives are restrictive or intensifying. We use restrictive adjectives when we talk about something as special or unique (1). We use intensifying adjectives to reinforce the meaning of the noun (2). We usually put restrictive before intensifying (3).

1 *Safety is my **chief** concern.* • *Our **main** problems are financial.* • *Try to give a **specific** reason.*
2 *I haven't played before, I'm an **absolute** beginner.* • *The meeting was a **complete** waste of time.*
3 *The boy was the **only real** hero in the story.* • *Maria got 100%, which was the **first perfect** score.*

3 **Find the two emphasizing adjectives in the text on page 110 and add them to these lists of examples. (One is in the first paragraph and the other is in the third paragraph.)**

Restrictive	Intensifying
chief, exact, first, major, only, principal, sole, specific, ...	*absolute, complete, entire, extreme, real, sheer, total, utter, ...*

Describing adjectives

When we use more than one adjective to describe someone or something, we usually put them in the order presented in the table below, with age (*old*) before colour (*green*), etc. Note that this is the normal order, but it is not the only possible order.

4 *I loved that **old green** sofa with the **lovely round** seats and the **big soft** cushions.*

We can often use describing adjectives with different meanings depending on the context.

5 *The Smiths live in a **modest** home near Canterbury.* (= 'not very large or expensive')
*Jill is a very **modest** young woman.* (= 'shy' or 'not willing to talk about her own abilities')

4 **Find one example of each type of describing adjective in the text on page 110 and add it to the correct list below.**

Opinion	Size	Physical quality	Age or Time	Shape	Colour
excellent, lovely, ugly,	*big, huge, long, tiny,*	*dry, hard, hot, light,*	*new, old, recent, young,*	*circular, round, spiky, square,*	*green, pink, red, yellow,*
. . . .	. . . .	. . . .	. . . .	. . . .	. . . .

Classifying adjectives

When we use more than one adjective to classify someone or something, we usually put them in the order presented in the table below, with material (*nylon*) before purpose (*running*) etc. Note that this is the normal order, but it is not the only possible order.

6 *I hate **nylon running** shorts.* • *It's **southern French** style.* • *We found a **Victorian medical** text.*

5 **Find one example of each type of classifying adjective in the text on page 110 and add it to the correct list below.**

Location	Origin or Source	Material	Type	Purpose
distant, indoor, southern, west,	*African, French, Muslim, Victorian,*	*leather, metal, nylon, plastic,*	*economic, medical, scientific,*	*camping, running, swimming,*
. . . .	. . . .	. . . .	. . . .	. . . .

Position of adjectives 112   Adjectives with infinitives 144   Adjectives with noun clauses 166

Adjectives: position and punctuation

Position

We usually use adjectives before nouns (1) or after linking verbs such as *be* and *seem* (2).
  1 *I had an **amusing** experience.* • *They faced **enormous** challenges.* • *He has a **kind**, **honest** face.*
  2 *Don't be **silly**.* • *She became **ill**.* • *They felt **angry**.* • *It got **cold**.* • *He seemed **anxious** and **upset**.*
Note that adjectives are called 'attributive' before nouns and 'predicative' after linking verbs.

When we use more than one adjective before a noun, there is a typical order. We usually put emphasizing adjectives before describing adjectives (3) and both of these before classifying adjectives (4).
  3 *The weather has been our **principal recent** concern.* • *Her necklace had **real red** rubies in it.*
  4 *Kenya was the **sole African** representative.* • *The **recent economic** news isn't encouraging.*

Some adjectives are typically used after a linking verb, not before a noun.
  5 *The old man is **asleep**. The girl seemed **glad**.* (NOT ~~the asleep man~~ • ~~the glad girl~~)
Others include: afraid, alike, alive, alone, ashamed, awake, ill, well

In some expressions, we put the adjective after the noun (6) or after an indefinite pronoun (7).
  6 *six feet **tall**, two metres **deep**, two years **old**, notary **public**, the time **available***
  7 *someone **nice**, anything **unusual**, everything **necessary**, nothing **new*** (NOT ~~new nothing~~)

6 **In the text on page 110, find two examples of a describing adjective and a classifying adjective used together.**

………..………………….   …………………..…………….

Punctuation

There is usually no punctuation between two or more different types of adjectives before a noun (8). We normally put a comma between describing adjectives in a set of two or more of the same type, especially those representing opinions where the order could easily be changed (9).
  8 *Anderson works in a **lovely old Victorian** building. His office has **big black leather** chairs.*
  9 *She likes **wild, vivid, flashy** designs.* • *He was just a **normal, quiet, rather shy** teenager.*

We put *and* between two colours (10) or between two classifying adjectives of the same type (11).
  10 *I lost my **blue and white** scarf.* • *He wore a **red and black** cap.* (NOT ~~a small and black cap~~)
  11 *She likes **Greek and Lebanese** food.* • *We discussed **financial and educational** topics.*
We put *and* between adjectives after linking verbs: *It's small and black.* (NOT ~~It's small black.~~)

We normally put a comma between the first two adjectives and the word *and* between the last two adjectives in a set of three colours (12) or three classifying adjectives of the same type (13).
  12 *The flag had **black, green and yellow** stripes. The tulips were **yellow, orange and red**.*
  13 *In recent years, the island has experienced **social, political and economic** problems.*

7 **Add commas or the word *and* where necessary to these sentences.**

1 The flags of Britain and the USA both have red white blue designs.

2 He described the wonderful friendly outgoing people who worked in the little Italian cafe.

3 You immediately notice the large plastic vases with pink purple flowers on every table.

4 There are many industrial agricultural applications of the new chemical compounds.

5 What are the cultural religious historic origins of these current regional conflicts?

Adjective order before nouns 111 Indefinite pronouns 98 Linking verbs 10

8 **Most of these sentences have adjectives in the wrong position. Write correct versions.**

Examples: I was looking for a plastic little spoon.

I was looking for a little plastic spoon.

There are excellent indoor facilities here.

✓

1 The German entire team played well. ....

2 The wine made a red small stain. ....

3 There's new nothing in the Christian main values. ....

4 You'll need hiking leather comfortable boots. ....

5 It has a pointed long stem with tiny pink flowers. ....

6 The windows are in circular wooden huge frames. ....

7 They are the northern industrial major nations. ....

8 I love those marvellous new Italian designs. ....

9 They found a rocking beautiful antique chair. ....

10 Her alone mother was in the chaos total. ....

11 The old public swimming pool is closed. ....

12 We like economic recent American policies. ....

9 **Using a dictionary if necessary, add one set of adjectives in the best order to each definition.**

northern / sharp / cool / thin   *prickly / juicy / large / tropical / yellow*
similar / white / rare / large / black   *bluish-grey / great / hard / shiny white / small*

panda: a (1) .... (2) .... (3) .... and (4) ....
animal (5) .... to a bear.

pearl: a (6) .... (7) .... (8) .... or (9) ....
ball that forms inside some oysters and is of (10) .... value as a jewel.

pine: a tree that produces cones and has (11) .... (12) .... leaves
throughout the year. Pines grow in (13) .... (14) .... regions.

pineapple: a (15) .... (16) .... fruit with (17) ....
(18) .... flesh and a (19) .... skin.

10 **Complete this text with these sets of adjectives in the best order. Add *and* or punctuation if necessary.**

English older   *Italian Greek*   *big plastic square*   *great little outdoor*
European southern   *Spanish cheap*   *carefree crazy happy*   *sour twisted*

Some people like to talk a lot about food and restaurants they go to. I have a friend called Lee who

lectures on (1) .... history at the university. He gets very excited when he

describes a (2) .... cafe in Rome and 'all the (3) .... people'

who work there. I also remember listening to an (4) .... woman, who is a

professor of (5) .... literature, complaining about how Spanish dishes are served

in some places with (6) .... wine from (7) .... boxes. When she

speaks about it, her mouth becomes (8) ...., as if she were reliving the terrible

experience.

Participle adjectives, compound adjectives and adjectives as nouns

Participle adjectives

We use adjectives derived from present participles (*surprising*) to describe the source or cause of an action or feeling (1). We use adjectives derived from past participles (*surprised*) to describe the one(s) affected by the action or feeling (2).

1 *The news was **surprising**. • The teacher drew a very **confusing** diagram on the board.*
2 *My parents were **surprised**. • The **confused** students said that they couldn't understand it.*

We can treat people and other living things as the source of a feeling (*He's boring*) or the ones affected by it (*I'm bored*) (3). We treat non-living things as the source only (*It's boring*) (4).

3 *Darwin was a **fascinating** person. • I was **disappointed**. • Why is the dog getting so **excited**?*
4 *Mars is a **fascinating** planet. • The news was **disappointing**.* (NOT *~~The news was disappointed.~~*)

11 **Choose an ending (a–d) for each beginning (1–4) and add participle adjectives from these verbs.**

astonish   exhaust   irritate   worry

1 I think it's very .... (...)   a are revealed in a new book.
2 Mrs Barnett seemed .... (...)   b after they had walked ten miles.
3 They were really .... (...)   c that she might not have enough money.
4 The .... tricks of magicians (...) d when students come in late.

Compound adjectives

Compound adjectives can consist of an adjective, adverb or noun and either a present participle or a past participle (5). Compounds with present participles are often based on active verbs (6). Compounds with past participles are often based on passive verbs (7).

5 *I'm in **slow-moving** traffic. • Was it a **well-planned** trip?* (NOT *... ~~a planned-well trip?~~*)
6 *'Modern Maids' is the name of a **house-cleaning** service.* (= a service which <u>cleans</u> houses)
7 *I'd really like a **home-cooked** meal for a change.* (= a meal which <u>is cooked</u> at home)
Others include: energy-saving, life-threatening, low-paid, urgently-needed, well-trained

There are some compound adjectives which consist of combinations of adjectives and nouns (8) or adverbs and adjectives (9).

8 *He likes **fast-food** restaurants. • Let's try to get **front-row** seats. • Do you have a **full-time** job?*
9 *Abortion is a **highly-sensitive** issue. • There are a lot of **politically-independent** voters.*

Adjectives as nouns

We can use some adjectives after *the* as nouns to talk about specific groups of people in society. These noun phrases are plural, without *-s*.

10 ***The rich** aren't happier than **the poor**. • **The disadvantaged** should be cared for by **the wealthy**.*
Note that we can also say *poor people* or *a poor person*. (NOT *~~the poors~~* or *~~a poor~~*)

We can also use *the* before adjectives describing nationality (*Italians, French*) to talk about the people, their governments, their national teams, etc. These noun phrases are plural, but we don't add *-s* to words ending in *-ch, -sh, -se, -ss*.

11 ***The Italians** are here and **the French** have also agreed to send a peace-keeping force. •*
*The United Nations proposal has support from **the Spanish, the Japanese** and **the Swiss**.*

We use some adjectives after *the* to talk about an abstract idea. These noun phrases are singular.

12 ***The unknown** isn't the same as **the impossible**. • In sports, **the unpredictable** often happens.*

Active and passive verbs 57 Past participles 220

12 Add these adjectives to the text.

amazed   amazing   annoyed   annoying   bored   boring   interested   interesting

Monday was a school holiday and, unfortunately, it rained all day, so the children kept telling me
they were (1) .... and there was nothing (2) .... to do at home. I was
trying to write up some of my reports, but they kept interrupting me every five minutes and just
became very (3) .... I'm (4) .... that their teachers can keep them busy
and (5) .... in their lessons every day. After only one morning with them, I was
extremely (6) .... because of the constant noise and squabbling. I was ready to throw
them out in the rain. Instead, I decided to take them to the cinema. It's really (7) ....
to see how calm they can become in a dark cinema. The film seemed rather (8) .... ,
but at least it kept them quiet.

13 Make appropriate compound adjectives from each pair of words and add them to the sentences.

distance / long	*end / never*	✓ *grow / fast*	*keep / peace*
educate / well	*funny / look*	*home / make*	*wash / white*

Example: Ghana had to increase food imports to meet the needs of a ....*fast-growing*.. population.
1 Mrs Baxter offered us scones with cream and her .... jam.
2 Please don't use this phone to make any .... calls.
3 Soldiers have to learn to talk rather than fight when they are sent on .... missions.
4 The president's wife seemed to have a .... supply of new shoes and handbags.
5 We have to invest more in schools and teachers if we want to have a .... population.
6 That .... piece of cloth at the end of each sleeve is called a frill.
7 We rented a small cottage in Devon, with a red-tiled roof and .... walls.

14 Editing. Correct the mistakes in this text.

Sometimes I wonder what people in other countries think about us. We are no longer among the rich

and powerfuls of Europe. In a very short period, we seem to have turned into the poor and weaks.

The situation is appalled. You cannot walk down a street in our cities without seeing a homeless. The

unemployeds stand around on our street corners. The old and sick receives no help. Why are we no

longer shocking that this is going on? Is it like this everywhere? Does the Japanese and the Canadian

have the same problems? I doubt it. The unthinkable have happened here and we must do something

about it soon.

Position of adverbs; adverbs of place, time, frequency, expectation, focus

Position of adverbs

We usually put adverbs immediately before the adjectives and adverbs they modify.
  1 *It's **nearly** complete. • Is it **politically** correct? • She did it **fairly** easily. • He spoke **very** quietly.*

When we use adverbs to modify verbs and sentences, we can put them in front or end position of the clause or sentence (2). We can also put adverbs in mid position after *be* or an auxiliary verb (3) and before the main verb (4).
  2 ***Usually** I have a piece of toast and orange juice in the morning. I might have a snack **later**.*
  3 *Some people are **always** hungry when they wake up. • I've **never** wanted to eat breakfast in bed.*
  4 *I **really** prefer to wait a while before eating. • I **sometimes** drink coffee.*
Note that we don't put adverbs between a verb and its object. (NOT *I drink sometimes coffee.*)

Adverbs of place and time: *nearby, tomorrow,* etc.

We use adverbs of place such as *nearby* and *upstairs* to add information on location or direction (5), usually in end position, and before adverbs of time such as *recently* and *tomorrow* (6).
  5 *He waited **nearby** while she took the money and went **upstairs**. • I slipped and fell **backwards**.*
  6 *You must leave **here immediately**. • I'll be **there tomorrow**. • I haven't been **abroad recently**.*

Adverbs of frequency: *annually, usually,* etc.

We usually put adverbs of definite frequency such as *annually, daily* and *twice* in end position (7) and adverbs of indefinite frequency such as *ever, often* and *usually* in mid position (8).
  7 *The contract is renewed **annually**. • Rooms are cleaned **daily**. • I've seen that film **twice**.*
  8 *We **often** have to work late. • It **usually** rains in the evening. • Doesn't he **ever** study?*

Expectation adverbs: *already, still,* etc.

We use expectation adverbs to express a connection between events and expectations. We use *already* to indicate that an event is earlier than expected, usually in mid or end position.
  9 *His plane has **already** arrived. • Mrs Black had left **already**.* (NOT *Already Mrs Black had left.*)

We use *still* to say that something is going on longer than expected, usually in mid position.
  10 *We are **still** waiting. • I **still** bite my nails when I'm nervous. • Ford **still** avoids crowds.*

We use *no longer* and *not … any longer/more* when an event was expected to continue, but did not. We usually put them in mid or end position (11). When we put *no longer* in front position (12), we must use inversion (the auxiliary verb before the subject).
  11 *It **no longer** works. • We could **not** stay there **any longer**. • She does**n't** live here **any more**.*
  12 ***No longer** do the fishing boats come in large groups to Loch Fyne for the herring season.*

We use *yet* (meaning 'up to now') to show that an event is or was expected. We usually put *yet* at the end of questions, negatives and expressions of uncertainty.
  13 *Have you read it **yet**? • Classes haven't started **yet**. • I'm not sure if he's finished **yet**.*

Focus adverbs: *even, just, only*

We use the focus adverbs *even, just* and *only* to draw attention to one part of the sentence.
  14 *She was **only** joking. • He can't **even** swim. • Her research isn't **just** about English.*

We can change the focus and the meaning when we change the position of these adverbs.
  15 *Mark **only** works here on Fridays.* (= only Fridays, not other days)
     ***Only** Mark works here on Fridays.* (= only Mark, not other people)

Adjectives 111 Auxiliary verbs 17 Inversion 216 Negatives and questions 45

15 Rewrite these sentences with the adverbs in more appropriate positions.

1 We thought we had started early our hike, but already other people had left the campsite.

   ....

2 The workers get paid usually weekly, but they haven't been yet paid for last week.

   ....

3 Still the students hadn't completed all their work when they had to leave yesterday here.

   ....

4 Alice lived recently here, but she doesn't here any more live.

   ....

5 We used to hear hardly ever them, but they've become lately noisy really.

   ....

16 Add these adverbs to this text.

always   ever   no longer   only   outside   recently   sometimes   today   twice   yet

Actress and model Viviane Tavenard is (1) .... the centre of attention wherever she
goes and her appearance in a London boutique this morning was no exception.
But her big smile isn't (2) .... for the crowd of photographers waiting
(3) .... (4) ....
She's enjoying her life these days and is (5) .... concerned about old romances or bad
reviews.
Tavenard has won the Best Actress award (6) .... , but that hasn't stopped her from
working on new and (7) .... unusual films.
'This is an excellent time,' she said (8) .... in an interview with Celebrity Life
magazine. 'I think that my life is the best it's (9) .... been.'
The good news for all you Viviane Tavenard fans is that you may not have seen her best work
(10) ....

17 Using a dictionary if necessary, rewrite each of the sentences with one of these adverbs instead of *just*, plus any other necessary changes.

almost   exactly   now   only (×2)   ✓simply   very recently

Example: They just weren't paying attention.   They simply weren't paying attention. ....
1 The couple had just got married.   ....
2 The baby looks just like her mother.   ....
3 He isn't just an athlete, he's a scholar too!   ....
4 Wait for us, we're just coming.   ....
5 Lunch is just about ready.   ....
6 Wear this silly hat. It's just for fun.   ....

Adverbs: degree, manner, viewpoint, comment

Degree adverbs: *really, very*, etc.

We use degree adverbs to say to what extent something is done or felt. We use some degree adverbs such as *really* or *completely* in mid position or end position in sentences.

    1 *He **totally** forgot.* • *She **really** hates fish.* • *We failed **completely.*** • *Prices increased **moderately.***

We usually use some degree adverbs such as *pretty, quite* or *rather* before adjectives and adverbs (2). We can also use the phrases *a bit* and *a little* as degree adverbs before adjectives and adverbs (3), but we don't use them with adjectives before nouns.

    2 *They're **pretty** good.* • *It's **quite** tasty.* • *Isn't it **rather** cold in here?* • *We listened **very** carefully.*
    3 *She's feeling **a little** tired.* • *The music is **a bit** loud.* (NOT ~~It's a bit loud music.~~)
We don't use *very* before verbs: *I'm not enjoying it **very much**.* (NOT ~~I'm not very enjoying it.~~)

We can use *more/less* and *most/least* as degree adverbs in comparatives and superlatives.

    4 *Going by train can be **more** convenient than flying in Europe and it's usually **less** expensive.*

We also use *too* before adjectives and adverbs and *enough* after them.

    5 *It's **too** difficult.* • *He spoke **too** quietly.* • *Is this box big **enough**?* • *You didn't leave early **enough.***

Manner adverbs: *carefully, quickly*, etc.

We use manner adverbs to say how something is done. We usually put them in end position.

    6 *I'll read it **carefully**.* • *He writes **clearly**.* • *They searched the room **quickly** and **thoroughly.***
Note that we put manner before time: *She works **hard** now.* (NOT ~~She works now hard.~~)

Manner adverbs are sometimes used, especially in novels, to describe how something was said.

    7 *'I have a torch, just follow me,' she said **nervously.***
       *'I would follow you to the end of the world,' he whispered **hoarsely** in reply.*
Others include: angrily, anxiously, cheerfully, gloomily, impatiently, passionately, seriously

Viewpoint adverbs: *commercially, socially*, etc.

We use viewpoint adverbs to describe the perspective or point of view being considered. We usually put them in end position (8), or in front position with a comma (9).

    8 *It did well **commercially**.* • *They're working **individually**.* • *It was not done **scientifically.***
    9 ***Financially**, the project makes sense. **Psychologically** and **socially**, it's a terrible idea.*

Comment adverbs: *probably, surprisingly*, etc.

We use comment adverbs to include a comment or opinion about what is being said or written. We can use some of them such as *probably* in mid position, but we usually put comment adverbs such as *surprisingly* or *of course* in front or end position with commas.

    10 *It was **probably** a misunderstanding.* • ***Surprisingly**, he failed.* • *I'll refund the cost, **of course.***

We can use comment adverbs such as *definitely* and *obviously* to say how sure we are (11) and others such as *fortunately* and *seriously* to say how we feel (12).

    11 *I'll **definitely** call you tonight.* • ***Obviously**, someone forgot to lock the door.*
    12 ***Fortunately**, no one was injured in the crash.* • *We're **seriously** thinking about moving to the country.*
Others include: actually, apparently, certainly, frankly, honestly, no doubt, presumably, sadly

18 Rewrite each sentence with one pair of adverbs added in appropriate positions.

carefully / tomorrow   completely / yesterday   enough / really   too / very much

1 I forgot my brother's birthday.

....

2 The piano is large and our doorway isn't wide.

....

3 We enjoyed the trip, but it was expensive.

....

4 I'll read the report.

....

19 Choose an ending (a–f) for each beginning (1–6) and add these adverbs.

angrily	*casually*	*enough*	*extremely*	*of course*	*traditionally*
carelessly	*completely*	*even*	*individually*	*only*	*very*

1 ...., marriages were arranged, (...)
2 There was .... one ticket left (...)
3 He did the test so ...., (...)
4 ...., each player is good, (...)
5 Although he was dressed ...., (...)
6 Because he was .... annoyed, (...)

a and everyone wanted it, ...
b he wasn't .... relaxed.
c but that's .... changed now.
d he started complaining ....
e but they don't play well .... as a team.
f he didn't .... finish part of it.

20 Add these adverbs to this text.

actually	*certainly*	*nervously*	*probably*	*still*	*uncontrollably*
apparently	*completely*	*of course*	*seriously*	*very*	*unfortunately*

'You've seen the ghost?' I asked.

'More than once,' the old man replied. '(1) ...., I have a photograph. Want to see it?'

This is absurd, I thought, but asked, 'You took a photo of the ghost?'

'No, not me. It's a photo of Lady Barnett from an old newspaper report of her death. She's wearing a long white gown, almost (2) .... the same one she wears when she appears at night.'

He said all this (3) .... (4) .... as if it was solid evidence for the truth of his ghostly tale. 'She was rich and, (5) .... for her, she was murdered for her money. It all happened about ten years ago. The police thought it was her husband who did it. He disappeared soon after. They found him later, locked in a small basement room. His hair had turned (6) .... white and his eyes were wide open. He was dead, (7) ....

He was clutching the key to Lady Barnett's safe deposit box in the bank. I think her ghost had (8) .... found him and had scared him to death.'

'Oh, my god! And she-she-she's still here?' I found myself stuttering (9) ....

'Oh, yes. I think she (10) .... walks through the house in search of his mistress. She only appears when there's a new woman in the house. (11) .... her husband was in love with another woman and he just wanted Lady Barnett's money so he could run away with her.'

'What happened to the mistress?' I asked rather (12) ...., looking round the dark room.

'Nobody knows,' he answered. 'But if I was her, I would stay far away from this house.'

Equatives, comparatives and superlatives

Equatives

Equatives are marked by *as … as* or *not as … as*. We use adjectives and adverbs in equatives to say that a person (1), thing (2), or action (3) is similar (or not) to another in some way.

1 *She's **as** tall **as** her father. • I'm **as** hungry **as** a horse. • He's **not as** young **as** he looks.*
2 *The van was **as** big **as** a house. • His new book is **not as** interesting **as** his other one.*
3 *I came **as** soon **as** possible. • Write **as** fast **as** you can. • It didn't do **as** well **as** we had hoped.*
   (NOT ~~She's as tall her father. Write fast as you can. It didn't do well we had hoped.~~)

We can use focus adverbs such as *just* and *only* before equatives (4). We sometimes use *not so … as* for the negative (5).

4 *Our plan is **just as** good **as** theirs. • You're **only as** old **as** you feel. • He's **not even as** tall **as** her.*
5 *This year's harvest wasn't **so** bad **as** last year's. • He's **not so** arrogant **as** he used to be.*

Note the use of equatives with a singular noun: *He's **not as good a teacher as** Mrs Marshall.*
(NOT ~~He's not as good teacher as Mrs Marshall. He's not as a good teacher as her.~~)

Comparatives

We change adjectives and adverbs to say that a person (6), a thing (7) or an action (8) has more or less of a quality *than* another. We put *more* or *less* before long forms and add *-er* to short forms.

6 *She's **more** intelligent **than** him. She's also **more** interesting. • He's slow**er than** a snail.*
7 *Some ideas are **less** practical **than** others. • His flat is small**er** and cheap**er than** ours.*
8 *I should practise **more** often. • She always finishes her work **faster** than me.*

Subject pronouns are sometimes used after *than* (*faster than I*), but they sound very formal.

We can treat adjectives such as *friendly* or *quiet* as either long forms (9) or short forms (10).

9 *Our neighbours have become **more friendly** recently. • The boys seem **more quiet** than usual.*
10 *Everyone was **friendlier** this time. • My new office is **quieter** than the old one.*

Others include: clever, common, crazy, likely, lonely, narrow, simple, untidy, yellow

We use special forms for the comparative of *good/well* and *bad/badly* (11). We use *further* (from *far*) for distance and when we mean 'additional' (12). *Farther* is only used for distance.

11 *I thought the weather would be **better** in July, but it actually got **worse**.*
12 *How much **further/farther** do we have to walk? • We hope to get **further** details of the plan soon.*

We can use comparative forms, repeated with *and*, to emphasize that something is increasing or decreasing (13). We use *the* + comparative … *the* + comparative to say that one development is connected to another (14).

13 *We meet **more and more frequently**. • It's **less and less common**. • Alice got **taller and taller**.*
14 ***The sooner** we leave, **the faster** we'll get there. • **The older** I get, **the crazier** everything seems.*

Superlatives

We can use adjectives and adverbs to say that people (15) or things and actions (16) have the most or least of a quality. We put *the most* or *the least* before long forms and add *-est* to short forms.

15 *He's **the most likely** to succeed. • It's **the least dangerous**. • She's one of **the cleverest** students.*
16 *Where's **the most beautiful** beach in the world? • That's **the simplest** question of all. •
   The least popular subject is algebra. • I was sure my golf ball had landed **nearest** to the hole.*

Note the special forms for *good/well* (*best*), *bad/badly* (*worst*) and *far* (*farthest/furthest*).

After superlatives we use *in* or *on*, not *of*, before singular words for groups (17) or places (18).

17 *Alan is **the youngest** student **in** the class. • I'm **the tallest in** my family.*
18 *He's **the best** player **in** the world. • I think we stayed in **the worst** hotel **on** the island.*
   (NOT ~~He's the best player of the world.~~)

     Adjectives 111 Adverbs 116–8 Focus adverbs 116 Subject pronouns 97

21 Write the most appropriate forms of adjectives and adverbs from one set in each sentence.

bad / skilled / well   early / new / well-behaved   easy / short / well-known
beautiful / different /quick   fast / old / tall   good / likely / long

1 The .... you wait, the .... you are to miss the ....
   bargains in the sale.
2 Our .... son is .... than his dad, but our other two haven't grown
   as ....
3 The .... group of students is .... than that other group who stayed
   here ....
4 His .... book is .... and .... to read than all the
   others.
5 There are several .... ways to get to the .... beach on the other side
   of the island, but the .... way is by boat.
6 I can't play as .... as most of the others, but I'm not the .... player
   or the .... of all those who want to participate.

22 Complete this first paragraph of an essay about 'fast food' with these adjectives and adverbs.

better   puzzled   as quickly as   more easily   the best
faster   smaller   less beneficial   more wasteful   the most important

When did we decide that 'more convenient' is (1) .... way to choose between two
different things to eat? Why do people now want food (2) .... possible, in containers
that are (3) .... thrown away? How did '(4) .... is (5) ....,'
become our slogan? Don't we see that this is (6) .... and much (7) ....
than making our own food? Is it because we want food to have a much (8) .... place
in our lives? But isn't food one of (9) .... things? Am I the only one who is
(10) .... by this?

23 Editing. Correct the mistakes in this text.

best

In one experiment, students were asked to look at photographs of people and choose the ~~good~~ words

and phrases to describe them. The students didn't know that the researchers had chosen the

photographs to represent two groups. In Group A, they put the good-looking of all the people whose

photographs were used. For Group B, they chose people who (they decided) were not attractive as

those in Group A. According to the students, the people in Group A were warm, kind, exciting and

sensitive than those in Group B. Also, Group A would find high-paid jobs, have successful marriages

and lead happy lives than Group B. The women in Group A were considered to have appealing

personalities and to be socially skilled than the Group B women, but also to be vain, materialistic,

snobbish and likely to get divorced than them. Interestingly, the students decided that Group A

would be bad parents than Group B.

Tests

A Choose the word or phrase that best completes each sentence.

1 I'm _____ a swimmer as my sister.

   a better   b good as   c not as good   d so good

2 Is St Paul's the oldest cathedral _____ Britain?

   a from   b in   c of   d to

3 When we heard the good news, we were _____.

   a delight   b delighted   c delighting   d delightful

4 I'm waiting up here with Tony, but Sandra has _____ gone.

   a already   b downstairs   c once   d yet

5 I left the book on the table. _____, someone else has borrowed it.

   a Perfectly   b Personally   c Presumably   d Properly

B Identify the one underlined expression (A, B, C or D) that must be changed in order to correct the sentence.

1 I stared into the <u>long</u> <u>rectangular</u> <u>black</u> hole, six <u>deep</u> feet, and shuddered.
               A   B   C   D

2 After the <u>first real</u> attack started, some <u>afraid</u> soldiers didn't want to fight <u>any more</u> so they <u>just</u>
             A   B   C   D
  surrendered.

3 I get up <u>early</u>, shower <u>first</u>, then I drink <u>usually</u> some tea and get dressed as <u>fast</u> as I can.
           A   B   C   D

4 We all <u>very</u> agree that some tests are not difficult <u>enough</u> and others are <u>just</u> <u>too</u> hard.
        A   B   C D

5 The <u>Dutch</u> are playing the <u>Italian</u> first, and then the <u>Spanish</u> and the <u>Portuguese</u> play.
      A   B   C   D

C Add one pair of adjectives/adverbs to each sentence in this text.

already / never   black / round   easier / eventually   further / just   longer / reading
short / suddenly

1 I know I'm _____ in my forties, but I _____ imagined that I would need glasses.

2 I _____ kept trying to read the newspaper by holding it _____ away.

3 I really had to decide whether to get _____ arms or a pair of _____ glasses.

4 _____, I chose the _____ solution.

5 _____, with my new glasses, those _____ wiggly lines at the top of the page turned into words.

6 And the _____ spots that seemed to dance on the floor became ants.

D **Complete each sentence in such a way that it is as similar as possible in meaning to the sentence above it.**

1 We all thought they organized the event well and we were all excited by it.
   Everyone thought the event _____.

2 You will get there quicker if you leave here earlier.
   The earlier _____.

3 Mark is a good cook, but David is a better cook.
   Mark is not as _____.

4 Do you have any scarves? I'm looking for one that's woollen, green and fairly long.
   I'm looking for a _____ scarf.

E **Choose the most appropriate word from each pair for each space.**

acute / acutely	*colour / coloured*	*far / further*	*just / only*	*pleased / pleasing*
certain / certainly	*early / earlier*	*Japan / Japanese*	*now / yet*	*young / youngest*

One evening in the spring of 1936, when I was a boy of fourteen, my father took me to a dance performance in Kyoto. I remember only two things about it. The first is that he and I were the (1) _____ Westerners in the audience; we had come from our home in the Netherlands only a few weeks (2) _____, so I had not (3) _____ adjusted to the cultural isolation and still felt it (4) _____. The second is how (5) _____ I was, after months of intensive study of the Japanese language, to find that I could now understand fragments of the conversations I overheard. As for the (6) _____ (7) _____ women dancing on the stage before me, I remember nothing of them except a vague impression of brightly (8) _____ kimono. I (9) _____ had no way of knowing that in a time and place as (10) _____ away as New York City nearly fifty years in the future, one among them would become my good friend and would dictate her extraordinary memoirs to me.

10 Prepositions

Prepositions are single words such as *at, from, in, of* and *on* or phrases such as *in front of, next to* and *out of*. We can use prepositions with noun phrases when we describe people (*a group **of** Italian students*) and things (*the train **from** London*) or when we provide additional information about an action or situation such as the time or place.
(*Their train arrives **at** 4.30 **in** the afternoon. I told them that, if I'm not **on** the platform, they should just walk **out of** the station and wait **in front of** the news-stand **next to** the main entrance and I'll meet them there.*)

1 **Read through this report on working students and find another four phrases with prepositions describing time.**

Contrary to popular belief, students do work

According to one National Union of Students survey, four out of ten students attending universities in the UK had a job during term-time. With more tuition fees and other additional costs, it
5 seems reasonable to assume that this figure is increasing. The students we talked to confirmed that this is the case.

For many of the students we interviewed, the idea of a part-time job on top of their full-time studies is
10 no longer an option, but a necessity. At the same time, some of them said universities offer little help regarding employment or simply advise students against having a job. They expect students to be working on their degrees and nothing else. One
15 medical student reported: 'When I told my director of studies that I had a job in the Christmas break, he frowned. He clearly didn't think it was a good idea.'

Most students are employed in part-time or temporary jobs and, as a result of this, have no job
20 security and don't qualify for sick leave or holiday pay. Many students are hired in place of regular workers, but are generally paid less than them. Some students don't actually work for pay, but do jobs in exchange for lower rent and/or meals. These are
25 usually caretaker jobs.

With the exception of those able to find work inside their universities and colleges, the majority of students have jobs at night or during the weekend. One student reported that, apart from working, her
30 weekends were spent sleeping: 'I work as a security guard until 3 a.m. on Friday and Saturday nights, so I end up sleeping all day Saturday and Sunday.' Another student said she works 22 hours a week in addition to her 20 weekly hours of lectures:
35 'I wouldn't say it has had any effect academically, but it means that I can't go out much.'

According to the NUS employment study, more than 10 per cent of students had missed lectures or failed to submit work because of job commitments.
40 For those with term-time jobs, 30 per cent had missed lectures, while 20 per cent had not handed in assignments. It seems almost inevitable that, due to financial pressures, the university experience will change. Increased costs in education together with
45 pressures to succeed in a competitive world are defining the circumstances in which today's students struggle to complete their degrees. Student life really does involve a lot more work these days.

2 **Complete this summary with appropriate prepositions from the report.**

Although universities often advise them (1) .... having a job, at least four
(2) .... ten students now work (3) .... term-time. Some students do
jobs (4) .... lower rent, but most of them work (5) .... part-time jobs,
(6) .... less pay (7) .... regular workers and usually (8) ....
night or (9) .... the weekend. Students (10) .... term-time jobs are a
lot more likely to miss lectures and assignments, (11) .... a National Union
(12) .... Students study.

Prepositions and prepositional phrases

Simple prepositions

Simple prepositions are single words such as *at, in, of, to* and *with*, which have a wide range of possible meanings (1). There are others, such as *behind, during* and *past*, which have a more limited range of meanings (2). There are also a few words derived from present participles, such as *following* and *including*, which can be used as simple prepositions (3).

    1 ***At** Easter I went **with** a friend **of** mine **to** a special ceremony **in** Westminster Abbey.*
Others include: as, by, for, from, off, on

    2 ***During** the ceremony, we had to sit **behind** a huge pillar. We couldn't see anything **past** it.*
Others include: above, across, against, before, between, inside, over, through, until, without

    3 ***Following** the ceremony, we went to lunch. **Including** lunch, the whole trip took three hours.*
Others include: considering, excluding, facing, regarding

Complex prepositions

Complex prepositions are phrases which consist of two words such as *next to* and *instead of* (4), or more than two words such as *as well as* and *in front of* (5). They all end with a simple preposition.

    4 *Come and sit **next to** me. • Could I have coffee **instead of** tea?* (NOT … ~~coffee instead tea?~~)
Others include: according to, apart from, because of, due to, out of, together with

    5 *There were two or three men **as well as** a group of girls **in front of** me waiting to buy tickets.*
Others include: as a result of, in addition to, in place of, on top of, with regard to

Prepositional phrases

Prepositional phrases consist of prepositions plus objects. The objects are noun phrases (6) and can include object pronouns (7) and gerunds (8).

    6 *The boy cut the rope **with a penknife**. • I gave the keys **to the woman** who works **in your office.***

    7 ***Apart from us**, it was empty. • Let's keep this **between you** and me.* (NOT … ~~between you and I.~~)

    8 *Some people left **without paying**. • **Besides swimming**, I also like hockey and basketball.*

We normally put a preposition immediately before its object, but in questions (9) and relative clauses (10), we often put the preposition at the end. In formal uses, the preposition is sometimes put at the beginning of the question or before the relative pronoun (11).

    9 *He cut it with something.* → ***What** did he cut it **with?***

    10 *Jan is the woman. I gave the keys to her.* → *Jan is the woman **(that/who)** I gave the keys **to.***

    11 ***With what** did he cut it? • Jan is the woman **to whom** I gave the keys.* (NOT ~~to who~~)

Some prepositions are only used at the beginning, not the end, of questions and relative clauses.

    12 ***After** which war was the Treaty of Versailles signed?* (NOT ~~Which war was it signed after?~~)
Others include: above, because of, before, below, besides, during

3 Using information from the report on page 124, complete these sentences and decide how each preposition is being used.

a with an object pronoun   c at the beginning of a relative clause
b with a gerund   d at the end of a relative clause

1 The students .... confirmed that this is correct. (…)
2 Students need jobs, but some .... said universities don't help with employment. (…)
3 One student said that, ..., she spent her weekends sleeping. (…)
4 Higher costs are defining the circumstances .... students try to finish their degrees. (…)

Prepositions of time: *at*, *in*, *on*, etc.

We use *at* with an exact point in time.

  1 *The morning session begins **at** 8.30 and ends **at** noon.* • ***At** that time I was still a student.*

We also use *at* before names of mealtimes or general words for holidays (2) and when we talk about a person's age as a point in time (3).

  2 *I'll see you **at** breakfast.* • *What does your family do **at** Christmas?* (NOT ~~at Christmas Day~~)

  3 *Both my parents left school **at** 16.* • ***At** your age, I was already married and had a baby.*

We use *in* with a period of time.

  4 *We usually listen to music **in** the evening.* • *They did all the repairs **in** one day.*

Note that *in the night* ('during a specific night') is different from *at night* ('during any night').

We also use *in* before the names of months, seasons or years (5), and before phrases identifying centuries and historical periods (6).

  5 *Summer time begins **in** March.* • *It's very dry here **in** summer.* • *Dickens died **in** 1870.*

  6 *The house was built **in** the 19th century.* • *Jazz first became popular **in** the 1920s.*

We can also use *in* for a period of time before something happens or is completed.

  7 *I'll be back **in** an hour.* • *They said they'd finish the work **in** two or three days.*

We use *on* with a specific day, or part of a specific day, and dates.

  8 *I'll see you **on** Sunday.* • *The meeting is **on** Monday morning.* • *The exam is **on** May 30th.*

In informal uses, especially in American English, *on* is often left out: *I'll see you Sunday.*

We also use *on* with special days or occasions.

  9 *I'll be there **on** your birthday.* • *What do you do **on** Christmas Day?* (NOT ~~on Christmas~~)

We don't usually use *at*, *in* or *on* before time expressions beginning with *each*, *every*, *last*, *next*.

  10 *We had meetings every day last week.* • *I'm leaving next Friday.* (NOT ~~on next Friday~~)

We can use *from* and *to* for starting and end points in time (11). We can also use *past* ('later than') with a point in time (12).

  11 *The class meets **from** 2.30 **to** 4.30.* • *We lived in Athens **from** 1998 **to** 2002.*

  12 *What time is it? ~ It's **past** eight o'clock. Actually, it's already twenty **past** eight.*

---

4 Complete each sentence with one pair of words or phrases plus *at*, *in* or *on* where necessary.

Christmas Day / the past	*her birthday / next Saturday*	*six / the morning*
four o'clock / Friday afternoon	✓*midnight / New Year's Eve*	*sixty-five / 2005*
the fourth of July / 1776	*night / winter*	*September / every year*

Example: We all held hands and sang together ..*at midnight on New Year's Eve.*.................................

1 I hated the early shift at the factory because I had to start work ....

2 We're going to have a big party for Rachel ....

3 They harvest the grapes ....

4 Because it was so cold in the bedroom, I often didn't sleep very well ....

5 It wasn't as common for people to get a holiday from work ....

6 I can't leave work early because I have a meeting ....

7 Although he didn't think of himself as old, Frank Jones had to retire ....

8 The American Declaration of Independence was signed ....

At, in, on (place) 128   From, to, past (movement and place) 130

Prepositions of time: *during*, *for*, *since*, etc.

During, for, since

We can use *during* or *in* when something happens at some point(s) within a specific period of time (1). We usually use *during* (not *in*) when we're talking about the whole period of time (2).
1 *We'll be on holiday **during/in** July.* • *The old road is sometimes closed **during/in** winter.*
2 *We need fewer workers **during** long weekends.* • *There were no classes **during** the whole of May.*

We can use *during* (not *for*) to say when something happens and *for* (not *during*) to say how long something lasts.
3 ***During** April, I'm hoping to go to New York **for** a few days.* (NOT ~~during a few days~~)

When we're talking about a period of time up to the present, we can use *for* to say how long it has been (4) and *since* to say when it started (5).
4 *We've been waiting **for** hours.* • *I've been a student here **for** two years.* (NOT ~~since two years~~)
5 *We've been waiting **since** eight o'clock.* • *I've been a student here **since** 2004.*
We usually use a perfect tense, not the present simple, with *since*. (NOT ~~I'm here since 2004.~~)

Before, by, until

We usually use *before* very generally for something happening earlier than a certain time (6). We use *by* more precisely when we mean 'at/on or before' a specific time (7). We use *until* for a period of time up to a specific point in time (8). We can use *not … until* when we mean 'not earlier than' (9).
6 Jill: *Didn't Rob say he would be here **before** six?* (= at some time earlier than six)
7 Bev: *I think he said he hoped to be here **by** six.* (= at or before, but not later, than six)
8 Jill: *I guess we should wait for him **until** six-fifteen.* (= during the period up to six-fifteen)
9 Bev: *I bet he won't get here **until** six-thirty.* (= not earlier than six-thirty)
In informal uses, *till* is sometimes used instead of *until*: *He won't get here till six-thirty.*

We don't usually use two prepositions together, but the combinations *since before* ('from a point in time earlier than') and *until after* ('up to a point in time later than') are sometimes used.
10 *They've lived here **since before** the war.* • *Don't say 'Happy New Year' **until after** midnight.*

5 **Using a dictionary if necessary, complete these definitions with the nouns and prepositions.**

curfew   deadline   expiry date   after   at   by   during   in (×2)   *until*

(1) .... : the end of a period of time (2) .... which something can be used.
(3) .... : a point (4) .... time (5) .... which something must be done or completed.
(6) .... : a law prohibiting people from going outside (7) .... a particular time (8) .... night (9) .... a particular time (10) .... the morning.

6 **Correct the mistakes in these sentences.**

1 I've been waiting since an hour to have a minute with the boss till his next meeting.

2 My sister works as a teacher in Athens since after 2003.

3 Your application form must be received in this office until 9 a.m. in the first of March.

4 I have appointments in every morning this week, but I can see you on next Monday morning.

Prepositions of place: *at*, *in*, *on*

At, *in* and *on* for location

When something is *at* a place, it is close to it, but not touching it (1). We can also use *at* when we talk about a point on a scale or a journey (2).

   1 *We'll meet you **at** the bus stop.* • *I think I heard someone **at** the door.*
   2 *Bake the pie in the oven **at** 170°.* • *I'm sure we stopped **at** York during our trip north.*

When something is *in* a place, it is inside it (3). We can also use *in* when we talk about a place as a general area such as a region or a country (4).

   3 *The money was **in** a box **in** a drawer **in** the desk **in** my office.* • *What's **in** the envelope?*
   4 *Lily is going to spend a week **in** Tuscany this summer.* ~ *Is that **in** France or Italy?*
Note that we say: *Who is the small boy **in** the picture?* (NOT ~~on the picture~~)

When something is *on* a place, it is in contact with a surface (5). We can also use *on* when we talk about a place in relation to a line such as a road or a river (6).

   5 *I left the keys **on** the table.* • *She reached over and put her hand **on** his.*
   6 *You'll pass Stratford **on** the way to Birmingham. It's just a small town **on** the river Avon.*

Verbs and nouns with *at*, *in* and *on*

After verbs such as *shout* and *smile*, we use *at* before an object that is the target of the action.
   7 *Why is that man shouting **at** us?* • *She smiled **at** me.* (NOT ~~She smiled me.~~)
Others include: bark, glance, laugh, look, scream, stare, swear, yell

After verbs such as *believe* and *include*, we use *in* before objects that describe ideas and things as if they were places.
   8 *I don't believe **in** life after death.* • *The tip is included **in** the bill.* (NOT ~~It's included the bill.~~)
Others include: indulge, interfere, invest, join, meddle, result, specialize, wallow

After verbs such as *comment* and *concentrate*, we use *on* before an object.
   9 *We can't comment **on** the test results yet.* • *I can't concentrate **on** my work.* (NOT ~~I can't concentrate my work.~~)
Others include: depend, focus, insist, lecture, plan, rely, remark, report

After nouns such as *ban* and *restriction*, we use *on* before another noun.
   10 *Isn't there a ban **on** pesticides?* • *They have restrictions **on** the amount of money you can send.*
Others include: attack, constraint, effect, emphasis, imposition, limit, perspective, sanctions

---

7   **Choose an ending (a–d) for each beginning (1–4) and add *at*, *in* or *on*.**

1 There are restrictions .... travel (....)
2 Jan kept staring .... the goldfish (....)
3 They believe .... negotiating quietly (....)
4 He was concentrating .... the task (....)

a rather than shouting .... each other.
b of counting the money .... his wallet.
c as it swam round .... its small glass bowl.
d .... some parts of the country.

8   **Add *at*, *in* or *on* where necessary to these sentences.**

Example: Craft shops _{in} many small villages rely _{on} tour buses to bring them customers.

1 The meeting focused economic problems developing countries South-East Asia.

2 You can either stand the bar or sit a table most pubs Britain.

3 We were depending my brother to meet us the exit door after the concert.

4 The children were laughing something they had seen a cartoon.

Prepositions of place: *above, below, between*, etc.

Above and *over*

We use *above* and *over* to say that one thing is in a higher position than another (1).

> 1 *There's a full moon **above/over** the mountain.* • *He has a small scar **above/over** his left eye.*

We can use *above* (not *over*) when one thing is at a higher level or point on a scale than another (2). We can use *over* (not *above*) when one thing covers another in some way (3). More figuratively, *above* can be used with the sense of 'better than' and *over* with the sense of 'more than' (4).

> 2 *It's always colder **above** the snowline.* • *Her name is **above** mine on the waiting list.*
> 3 *There are thick clouds **over** most of Scotland.* • *I had to wear a scarf **over** my head.*
> 4 *His work is **above** average.* • *Are you **over** 21?* (NOT *Are you above 21?*)

Below and *under*

We use *below* and *under* to say that one thing is in a lower position than another (5).

> 5 *Their flat is **below/under** ours.* • *I keep the bleach **below/under** the sink in the kitchen.*

We use *below* (not *under*) when one thing is at a lower level or point on a scale than another (6). We use *under* (not *below*) when one thing is covered by another in some way (7). More figuratively, *under* can be used with the sense of 'less than' (8).

> 6 *Most of New Orleans is **below** sea level.* • *I'm sure the temperature is **below** zero tonight.*
> 7 *The puppy likes to hide **under** the sofa.* • *Do you always wear a vest **under** your shirt?*
> 8 *If you're **under** 21, you can't get into the club.* • *The total cost of the trip was **under** £50.*

We can use *underneath* to emphasize 'covered by': *I keep my money underneath my mattress.*

Between and *among*

We can talk about a place *between* two or more separate people or things (9) or *among* more than two people or things together as a group (10).

> 9 *Find Luxembourg on the map. It's **between** Belgium, France and Germany.*
> 10 *Find Luxembourg on the map. It's **among** the countries of Western Europe.*

More figuratively, *between* (not *among*) can be used to talk about how things are connected (11) and *among* (not *between*) can be used with the sense of 'included in' (12).

> 11 *In the study, they investigated the relationship **between** education, diet and health.*
> 12 ***Among** the advantages of private schools are small classes and more individual attention.*

9 **Using a dictionary if necessary, complete these sentences using an adjective or a noun plus one of the prepositions.**

overalls	overflow	overlap	above	below	over
overcoat	overhead	overpopulation	among	between	under

1 I'm wearing a woollen pullover and a jacket .... this ...., but I still feel cold.

2 High birth rates combined with better health care for children are starting to create serious problems with .... some of the world's poorest nations.

3 There does seem to be quite an .... the subject areas of maths and physics.

4 The work is really dirty so you'd better wear .... your clean clothes.

5 The number of young children starting school this year is well .... normal and we don't have enough room for them all, so we're having to use temporary buildings for the ....

6 A number of people who live near or .... those massive .... power lines say that they have suffered health problems because of them.

Prepositions of movement and place: *from*, *across*, *along*, etc.

From, to, towards

We use *from* for the origin or starting point and *to* for the goal or end point of movement (1). More figuratively, *from* and *to* can be used for the starting and end points of changes (2).

1 *We flew straight **from** London **to** San Francisco.* • *I can walk **from** my flat **to** work.*
2 *He translated the book **from** Russian **to** English.* • *It went **from** quite cool **to** very hot in an hour.*

We can use *towards* ('in the direction of') to focus on the direction of movement (3). More figuratively, *towards* can be used to talk about the direction of development or change (4).

3 *I suddenly saw a car coming **towards** me.* • *If you get lost, try to walk **towards** the south.*
4 *The trend is **towards** much larger farms.* • *This agreement is an important step **towards** peace.*

Note that *toward* is also used, especially in American English: *It's a step toward peace.*

Into and *onto*

We can use *into* when we focus on movement to a place inside something (5) and *onto* (or *on to*) for movement to a surface of some kind (6).

5 *We took a bus **into** the city centre.* • *The waiter poured some wine **into** each glass.*
6 *Let's move the small books **onto** the top shelf.* • *Paint was dripping from his brush **onto** the floor.*

Across, over, through

We can use *across*, *over* and *through* for movement from one side of something to the other.

7 *The early explorers had to get **across/over/through** the Rocky Mountains to reach the coast.*

We usually use *across* for movement to the other side of a surface or area (8), *over* for movement to the other side of something that is viewed as high or as a line (9) and *through* for movement that enters and leaves something (10).

8 *We spent a month travelling **across** America.* • *She pushed a note **across** the table to him.*
9 *The gate was locked so I climbed **over** the wall.* • *It was a good shot, but it went **over** the bar.*
10 *You have to go **through** the kitchen to get to the bathroom.* • *The Thames flows **through** London.*

We can use *across* and *over* for place ('on the other side of'): *There's a cafe **across/over** the street.*

Along and *past*

We can use *along* for movement in one direction or to describe the position of something which is somewhere in that direction (11). We can use *past* for movement beyond a specific point or to describe the position of something beyond a specific point (12).

11 *I like walking **along** country lanes.* • *There's a cafe **along** the street.*
12 *We drove **past** Stratford, but didn't stop there.* • *There's a cafe just **past** the church.*

Off and *out of*

We can use *off* for movement away from a surface or to describe the position of something in relation to a surface (13). We use *out of* for movement from the inside of something or to describe the position of something which is no longer inside (14).

13 *Could you take that box **off** the table?* • *The platform was about two feet **off** the ground.*
14 *I lifted the kitten **out of** the box. As soon as it was **out of** the box, it started crying.*

Note that we don't use *out* (without *of*) as a preposition. (NOT ~~It was out the box.~~)

More figuratively, *off* can be used with the sense of 'not connected to' (15) and *out of* with the sense of 'no longer having' (16).

15 *This part of your essay is completely **off** the main topic.* • *Skye is an island **off** the west coast.*
16 *We're **out of** milk, so I have to go to the shop.* • *A lot of people are **out of** work now.*

From, to, past (time) 126   Over 129

10 Complete these directions with the following prepositions:

across   along   from   out of   past   to (×2)   towards

Tony (talking on the phone): Hi, Angie, it's me again. I'm sorry to bother you, but I'm in the post office and I can't remember how to get (1) .... the Red Lion (2) .... here.

Angie: That's okay. The Red Lion is on King Street, so when you're (3) .... the post office, you should turn right and walk (4) .... the cathedral. Go (5) .... Port Street and turn left when you reach Baker Street. Walk (6) .... Baker Street (7) .... King Street and turn right. The Red Lion will be on your right just (8) .... the library.

11 Using a dictionary if necessary, add one pair of prepositions to each sentence.

along / towards   out of / from   through / to

1 When you go via a particular place, you go .... that place on your way .... another place.
2 When you're going up or down a road, you're going .... it .... one end of it.
3 When you're asked to wait outside a room, you have to be .... the room, but you mustn't move too far .... it.

12 Add these prepositions to the following paragraphs from the beginning of a novel.

along   from   into   on   over   through   towards (×2)

She stands up in the garden where she has been working and looks into the distance. She has sensed a shift in the weather. There is another gust of wind, a buckle of noise in the air, and the tall cypresses sway. She turns and moves uphill (1) .... the house, climbing (2) .... a low wall, feeling the first drops of rain (3) .... her bare arms. She crosses the loggia and quickly enters the house.

   In the kitchen she doesn't pause but goes (4) .... it and climbs the stairs which are in darkness and then continues (5) .... the long hall, at the end of which is a wedge of light (6) .... an open door.

   She turns (7) .... the room which is another garden – this one made up of trees and bowers painted over its walls and ceiling. The man lies on the bed, his body exposed to the breeze, and he turns his head slowly (8) .... her as she enters.

Prepositions used for connections: *of, with, by*

Of and *with*

We use *of* and *with* when we talk about people and things being connected. We can put *of* between two noun phrases to show that the first belongs to or is part of the second (1). We can put *with* between two noun phrases when the second is a particular feature of the first (2).

1   *The roof **of** their house is bright red. • The sleeves **of** this shirt are too long.*
2   *Theirs is the house **with** the bright red roof. • I'm looking for a white shirt **with** short sleeves.*

We can use *of* to say how people are related (3) and *with* to say that people or things are together (4).

3   *Is Briony the daughter **of** Alice Hawthorn? ~ Yes, she's a good friend **of** mine.*
4   *I think Lee went shopping **with** her friends. • Would you like some wine **with** your meal?*

We use *of* after some adjectives (5) and *with* after others (6).

5   *Millie is **afraid of** dogs. • The report was **full of** mistakes.* (NOT ~~It was full with mistakes.~~) •
    *Are you **aware of** the risks involved? • I was **fond of** my old car, but it had too many problems.*
6   *We were **faced with** a difficult choice. • I wasn't **familiar with** that computer programme. •*
    *There are side effects **associated with** most medicines. • He wasn't **satisfied with** my work.*

With and *by*

We can use *with* plus a determiner and noun for the specific thing used to perform an action (7). We usually use *by* plus a noun (no determiner) or gerund when we want to describe the action in a more general way (8).

7   *I paid **with** my credit card. • The thief broke the lock **with** a knife.* (NOT ~~by a knife~~)
8   *I paid **by** credit card. • He opened the door **by** breaking the lock.* (NOT ~~by break the lock~~)
Other *by*-phrases used with a general meaning include: *by air, by bus, by email, by phone*

13 Complete each sentence with one pair of words or phrases (not necessarily in this order) plus *by, of* or *with* where necessary.

a cheque / the yellow lampshade	*the door / a screwdriver*	*the match / scoring*
American history / reading	*her / taxi*	*ours / some friends*
✓ *any problems / the way*		

Example: We weren't aware of ...... any problems ...... until we started getting complaints from people who clearly weren't satisfied ...... with the way ...... their new computers were working.

1   He tried to remove the old broken handle ....
2   I'm becoming more familiar .... about the Civil War.
3   We went out to dinner ....
4   Robertson celebrated his return to the Scottish team .... the best goal .... against England yesterday.
5   They don't allow dogs on the buses so Betty always goes .... whenever she wants to take her dog ....
6   I wanted to buy that lamp .... but I didn't have enough cash and they wouldn't let me pay for it ....

By (time) 127   *By* and *with* after passives 64   Determiners 83   *Of* and possessive nouns 76

Prepositions used for exceptions: *except (for)*, *besides*, *without*, etc.

Except *(for)*, *besides*, *apart from*

We can use *except* or *except for* ('not including') with someone or something not included in a general statement, usually after a quantifier such as *every* (1). We usually use *except for* (not *except*) with information added to a specific statement that makes it not completely true (2).

    1 *It's open every day **except (for)** Sunday. • Everyone liked the film **except** me.* (NOT ~~except I~~)
    2 *She says she's stopped smoking **except for** an occasional cigarette at a party.*

We can use *except* (not *except for*) before preposition phrases (3) and clauses (4).

    3 *I work here all day **except** on Friday. • It will be sunny everywhere **except** in the north.*
    4 *I've never heard their baby cry **except** when it gets tired.*

In negative sentences, we can use *besides* with the same meaning as *except (for)* (5). In other sentences, *besides* usually means 'in addition to' (6).

    5 *I didn't know anyone in London **besides/except (for)** my uncle Henry.*
    6 ***Besides** football, what other sports do you like? • I've talked to a lot of people **besides** Henry.*

We can use *apart from* instead of both *except (for)* ('not including') and *besides* ('in addition to').

    7 *It's open every day **apart from** Sunday. • **Apart from** football, what other sports do you like?*
Note that *aside from* is used like *apart from*, especially in American English.

Without and *minus*

We use *except (for)* with something not included in a general statement. We use *without* for something not included in the wider senses of 'not having' (8) or 'not doing' something (9). We can use *minus* when we want to emphasize that something has been removed (10).

    8 *I prefer tea **without** milk, don't you? • Romeo chose death rather than life **without** Juliet.*
    9 *Bill changed his travel plans **without** any explanation. Then he left **without** saying goodbye.*
    10 *They eventually published the report, **without/minus** several important sections.*

14 Using a dictionary if necessary, complete each sentence with a noun and a preposition.

bread	fruit	meal	pizza		besides	except for	with
fish	ice cream	omelettes	rice		except (×2)	minus	without (×2)

1 We don't usually eat much .... when we have Indian food.
2 My grandfather liked to say that you can't make .... breaking eggs.
3 I first learned how to cook salmon and now I cook a lot of other .... that.
4 They usually drink wine with their evening .... during Lent.
5 My children don't eat a lot of .... bananas at breakfast sometimes.
6 Would you like some .... your strawberries?
7 We won't be able to make .... flour.
8 It was obvious that someone had already decided it was time to start eating because on the table
    was our .... , ... one very large slice.

Phrasal verbs

Words such as *in* or *on* which are used as prepositions before noun phrases (1) can also be used as particles after verbs (2). We can also use other words such as *away, back* or *out* as particles (3). These verb + particle combinations (*sleep in, go out*) are called two-word verbs or phrasal verbs.

    1 *I usually drink coffee **in the morning**.* • *He said he left the keys **on the table**.*
    2 *I **slept in** this morning and missed my bus.* • *He **put on** his boots and overcoat.*
    3 *I tried to catch the dog, but it **ran away**.* • *When will she **come back**?* • *Did you **go out** last night?*

Other phrasal verbs include: fall over, get through, go ahead, sit down, stand up, take off

Some phrasal verbs are used without an object (4) and others are used with an object. When the object is a noun phrase, we can usually put it before (5) or after the particle (6). When the object is a pronoun, we put it before the particle (7).

    4 *It's time to **get up**.* • *I wish these flies would **go away**.* • ***Watch out!*** (NOT ~~Watch out that!~~)
    5 *Don't **turn on** the light. You'll **wake up** the baby.* • *He **took off** his shoes.*
    6 *Don't **turn** the light **on**. You'll **wake** the baby **up**.* • *He **took** his shoes **off**.*
    7 *Don't **turn** it **on**. You'll **wake** him **up**.* • *He **took** them **off**.* (NOT ~~He took off them.~~)

After a phrasal verb we can also use a gerund (8) or a clause (9). We don't usually put clauses or very long phrases between the verb and the particle.

    8 *Have you **given up** smoking?* • *They told us to **carry on** working.* (NOT *… ~~to carry on work.~~*)
    9 *Andy **pointed out** that we didn't have enough time.* • *You should **read over** what you've written.* (NOT ~~You should read what you've written over.~~)

We can use phrasal verbs with prepositions. These combinations of verb + particle + preposition are sometimes called three-word verbs. We put pronouns after the prepositions.

    10 *This book is valuable and you should **hold on to** it.* (NOT ~~hold on it hold it on to~~) • *Go ahead and I'll **catch up with** you later.* (NOT ~~I'll catch up you I'll catch you up~~)

Others include: face up to, get round to, go along with, look forward to, watch out for

We often use phrasal verbs such as *put off* or *leave out* in informal situations (11) rather than other verbs with similar meanings such as *postpone* or *omit* which may sound more formal (12).

    11 *Let's **put** the meeting **off** till next week.* • *Don't **leave out** the author's name.*
    12 *We should **postpone** the meeting until next week.* • *You must not **omit** the author's name.*

15 Using a dictionary if necessary, rewrite these sentences in a more informal style, using appropriate forms of these phrasal verbs.

cut back on	fill in	give up	go in	send back
do away with	find out	go along with	go up	take off

1 You should complete this form and return it with your payment.
    You have to ....

2 My father has abandoned his attempt to get the university to abolish tuition fees.
    My dad ....

3 It was necessary to reduce our spending after we discovered that our rent was increasing.
    We had to ....

4 Please observe local customs at the temple and remove your shoes before entering.
    Please ....

Gerunds 139 Verbs and objects 6

16 Complete this text with appropriate phrasal verbs using these verbs and particles.

bend	breathe (×2)	go	lift	push	raise	stand
away	back		down	in	out	up (×3)

When you have to spend a lot of time sitting at a desk, it is important to take short breaks and stretch your neck and back. You can use this exercise to help you stretch.

(1) .... your chair .... to the side and stand up, making sure there is some space in front of you. (2) .... straight, with your arms hanging loosely by your side.

Breathe in deeply as you (3) .... your arms .... over your head. Pause a moment.

Then (4) .... slowly as you swing your arms forward, letting them fall as you

(5) .... your whole body .... until your hands are near your feet. Pause a moment.

Then, (6) .... as you (7) .... your body .... very slowly, beginning with your hips, then your upper body, followed by your head and arms.

Repeat the exercise at least once before you (8) .... to your desk again.

17 Choose A or B or both as appropriate sentences to use each time in creating this dialogue.

   Ani: What's the meaning of 'reimburse'?

1 Raz: (A) Let's look up it in the dictionary. (B) Let's look it up in the dictionary.

2 Ani: (A) Hand over the dictionary and I'll do it. (B) Hand it over the dictionary and I'll do it.

3 Raz: (A) I left behind it at home this morning. (B) I left it behind at home this morning.

4   (A) I think I put down beside my computer. (B) I think I put it down beside my computer.
    Okay, so we can't use a dictionary. What's the context?

   Ani: It says, 'They reimbursed his tuition fees.'

5 Raz: (A) Maybe it means they worked out what his tuition was.
    (B) Maybe it means they worked what his tuition was out.

6 Ani: (A) But then it says he paid off some debts. (B) But then it says he paid off some.

7 Raz: (A) Maybe it means to pay back money to someone.
    (B) Maybe it means to pay money back to someone.

8 Ani: (A) So, they gave back him the money for his tuition.
    (B) So, they gave him back the money for his tuition.

   Raz: Sounds good to me.

Tests

A Choose the word or phrase that best completes each sentence.

1 I know I don't look like everyone else, but I don't like it when people stare _____ me.

   a at   b on   c to   d – (no preposition)

2 Please don't call me until _____ eight o'clock on Saturday morning.

   a after   b at   c by   d to

3 I _____ waiting here for you since 8.30.

   a am   b was   c have been   d will be

4 The United Nations is drawing up an economic plan aimed at _____ East Timor with a stronger economy based on coffee.

   a provide   b provides   c to provide   d providing

5 If you borrow something from someone, make sure you give _____ .

   a them back to it   b back it to them   c it back to them   d it to them back

B Identify the one underlined expression (A, B, C or D) that must be changed in order to correct the sentence.

1 <u>According to</u> a recent report, more students are choosing to work <u>in</u> part-time jobs <u>instead</u> using
      A   B   C
their weekends to study <u>during</u> term-time.
                      D

2 <u>For</u> a whole week Loretta came <u>to</u> class <u>on</u> every day <u>with</u> her hair a different colour.
   A   B   C   D

3 <u>Between</u> 1850 and 1900, coal production <u>off</u> the US rose <u>from</u> 14 million tons <u>to</u> 100 million.
   A   B   C   D

4 The ball went <u>between</u> the legs of another player, <u>past</u> me <u>towards</u> the goal, and rolled <u>through</u> the
               A   B   C   D
goal line.

5 The children were laughing <u>at</u> a cartoon <u>in</u> which a cat <u>on</u> a wobbly ladder kept trying to get a
                         A   B   C
small bird <u>out</u> its cage.
          D

C Choose one preposition from each pair for each space in the text.

at	*away*	*during*	*from*	*off*	*to*
in	*up*	*for*	*of*	*out of*	*towards*

Does the new 'global economy' simply mean that well-paid jobs will be taken
(1) _____ (2) _____ people in rich countries and changed
(3) _____ low-paid jobs for people (4) _____ poorer countries? Is this
a bad thing? Perhaps. It may actually mean that some poor people who have been
(5) _____ work (6) _____ a long time can start to have a better life and
other people will have to work a bit harder to maintain their comfortable lifestyle.

D **Complete each sentence in such a way that it is as similar as possible in meaning to the sentence above it.**

1 This building will be closed for renovation from the beginning to the end of August.
   During _____

2 What else did you do in addition to shopping when you were in Rome?
   Besides _____

3 Haven't you eaten anything else today besides the apple I gave you earlier?
   Apart _____

4 We won't be able to do much unless we get more financial support.
   Without _____

E **Complete this text using these prepositions.**

across   along   at   by   into   of   past   towards   under   with

Whenever I see a newspaper lying on the ground beside a door, I think of Fred. A few years ago,
Fred had to travel to a meeting and his flight was delayed for several hours because of bad weather.
(1) _____ the time he got to his hotel it was (2) _____ midnight. Once
in his room, he felt really tired so he just undressed and got into bed. (3) _____ some
point during the night, he had to get up and go to the bathroom. He wasn't really awake and it was
very dark, but he could see a light (4) _____ the bathroom door, so he walked
(5) _____ the light. He opened the bathroom door and went in. The bright light
blinded him for a moment. As the door closed behind him, he vaguely wondered why there was a
doormat on the bathroom floor. Facing him was another door (6) _____ a number on
it. It was number 325. That was strange. Then he realized he wasn't in the bathroom. He was in the
corridor. He turned to go back (7) _____ his room, but the door was locked. And he
was naked. He heard voices coming from the far end of the corridor. What was he going to do? Then
he noticed a newspaper on the floor beside the door (8) _____ number 325. He
quickly grabbed the newspaper and held it in front of him as a man and a woman in dark uniforms
came (9) _____ the corridor towards him. The man said, 'Good morning, sir. Having a
bit of trouble?' They were security guards. Fred explained his embarrassing situation and they
unlocked the door for him. He thanked them as if they had just saved his life. After they left, he
opened his door, made sure it wouldn't close again, stepped (10) _____ the corridor
and put the newspaper back on the floor outside number 325. Someone else might need that
newspaper.

11 Infinitives and gerunds

We use the base form of the verb to create infinitives. We can use the base form after *to* (*I didn't really want **to read** when I was younger*) or without *to* in the bare infinitive (*I thought it was torture when the teacher made us **read** aloud in class*).

We add *-ing* to the base form of the verb to create gerunds (*Now I enjoy **reading** more than anything else*). Gerunds have the same form as the present participles of verbs, but they are used as nouns (***Reading** is the key to knowledge*).

1 **Read through this article from an advice column in a magazine and find two more examples of the same verb (*avoid* and *smoke*) being used as both an infinitive and a gerund.**

> **My best friend smokes a lot. I tell her she should quit, but she says she can't. What can I do to help her?**
>
> Quitting is hard but not impossible – as long as
> 5 your friend really wants to kick the habit. 'She has a good chance of stopping successfully if she thinks about quitting as a three-part process: she has to deal with her social habit, her psychological dependence and then her
> 10 physical addiction,' says Lowell Kleinman, MD, a doctor who has helped hundreds of people to stop smoking for good.
>
> Let's start with the habit: when does your friend smoke – on her way to college, after a
> 15 meal, when she's with friends? Help her break the pattern. 'Try going a different way to college, eating at a different place and avoiding social situations that will make her want to smoke,' says Dr Kleinman.
> 20 As for psychological dependence: does your friend smoke when she's bored or stressed? Nicotine can have a calming effect, which is why many people continue smoking even though
> they know it's bad for their heart, lungs, skin
> 25 and teeth. Encourage her to avoid stressful situations and to find healthier ways of coping with stress – doing yoga, keeping a journal or just talking to you.
>
> Finally, physical addiction: when your friend
> 30 doesn't have a cigarette at regular intervals, does she experience withdrawal symptoms – restlessness, anxiety, irritability and strong cigarette cravings? If so, her body is addicted. And traditional techniques, like going cold
> 35 turkey or cutting back gradually, often aren't successful in beating an addiction. Instead, Dr Kleinman recommends Nicotine Replacement Therapy (NRT) – the patch, gum or an inhaler – which helps wean your body off nicotine by
> 40 supplying decreasing doses. The inhaler is available only by prescription, but the patch and gum can be purchased over the counter.
>
> You can also point out that there are real advantages to becoming a non-smoker. She'll
> 45 not only have better health, but also fresher breath, clearer skin and whiter teeth.

2 **Find four phrases in the article above that match the definitions listed here.**

1 ....: the unpleasant state that drug addicts experience when they suddenly stop taking a drug; also a way of treating addicts that makes them experience this state.

2 ....: performing a system of exercises for your body and for controlling your breathing, used by people who want to become fitter or more relaxed.

3 ....: to stop doing something harmful that you have done for a long time.

4 ....: without needing a prescription (written permission from a doctor).

Simple infinitives and gerunds

Infinitives

We usually use infinitives (*to* + verb) and negative infinitives (*not to* + verb) after verbs, adjectives or nouns (1). We can also use them after indefinite pronouns and *wh-*words (2).

   1 *We agreed **to meet** on Friday.* • *I'm happy **to be** here.* • *You made a promise **not to tell** anyone.*

   2 *I was looking for someone **to help** me.* • *I wasn't sure about what **to do** and what **not to do** here.*

We can also use infinitives to express purpose (= in order to): *He only did it to get attention.*

We can use infinitives in clauses with objects, prepositional phrases and adverbs. We don't usually put adverbs between *to* and the verb ('a split infinitive') unless it is for emphasis.

   3 *We're planning **to take the children to the zoo later**.* • *I want **to (really) understand** Islam.*

We usually leave out the second *to* when we join two infinitives with *and*, or with *or* (4). We can use *to* or *not to* alone instead of repeating a verb or clause (5).

   4 *Brian just wants to **sit and _ watch** videos all day.* • *Do they intend **to buy** a flat **or _ rent** one?*

   5 *Would you like to play? ~ I'd **love to _**.* • *I was hoping to go with you, but I've **decided not to _**.*

We don't leave out *be*: *Was Michael happy? ~ He seemed to be.* (NOT ~~He seemed to.~~)

Bare infinitives

We use bare infinitives (base form of the verb) after modals (6), after perception verbs such as *hear* and *see* with objects (7) and after the verbs *let* and *make* with objects (8).

   6 *I can't **stay** long.* • *What will we **do** if they tell us we must **pay** more?* (NOT *… ~~we must to pay more?~~*)

   7 *I didn't **hear** Tom **come** in.* • *I've never **seen** anyone **eat** as much as your friend can.*

   8 *Please **make** her **stop**!* • *They won't **let** us **leave**.* (NOT ~~They won't let us to leave.~~)

After the verb *help*, we can use an infinitive with or without *to*: *Annie helped me (to) clean up.*

Gerunds

We can use gerunds (verb + *-ing*) and negative gerunds (*not* + verb + *-ing*) after verbs and prepositions (9). We can also use gerunds as subjects (10).

   9 *I don't mind **waiting**.* • *Paul enjoys **not having** a job.* • *She watches TV **instead of working**.*

  10 ***Studying** makes me sleepy.* • *My doctor says that **swimming** is the best kind of exercise.*

Gerunds are also called '*-ing* forms'. They are often used after *No* in signs: *No Parking.*

We can use gerunds in clauses with objects, prepositional phrases and adverbs (11). Before gerunds, we can use nouns (*Tom*) or object pronouns (*them*), but possessive nouns and determiners (*Tom's, their*) can also be used, typically in formal situations (12).

  11 *He denied **taking the money**.* • *They recommend **washing silk shirts gently in cold water**.*

  12 *I can't recall **Tom/Tom's** visiting us.* • *We listened to **them/their arguing** all night.*

Gerund or present participle?

We use gerunds like nouns, which can be subjects or objects (13). We usually use present participles as verbs with different forms of *be* (14). We use present participles, not gerunds, in reduced versions of relative clauses or adverbial clauses (15).

  13 ***Talking** and action are two quite different things.* • *Have they finished **(the) cleaning** yet?*

  14 *We **were talking** about money.* • *I **have been cleaning** my room all morning.*

  15 *The man (who is) **talking** to Liz is her dad.* • *While (I'm) **cleaning**, I listen to music.*

---

3 Look at the four definitions listed in 2 at the bottom of page 138 and find one example of:

  1 an infinitive after a verb ....
  2 a bare infinitive after a verb ....

  3 a gerund after an infinitive ....
  4 a gerund after a preposition ....

Complex infinitives and gerunds

Complex infinitives

Instead of the simple infinitive (1), we can use the perfect infinitive (*to have* + past participle) when we want to be clear that we're talking about an earlier time or a completed action (2).

   1 *Ali seems **to be** ill a lot.* • *I'm hoping **to read** the guidebook before we get to Berlin.*
   2 *Ali seems **to have been** ill a lot.* • *I'm hoping **to have read** the guidebook before we get to Berlin.*

We can use the perfect infinitive after *would* plus *like, hate, love* or *prefer* when we talk about earlier events (3). We can also use the simple infinitive after *would have liked*, etc. with a similar meaning (4). We sometimes use the perfect forms of both verbs in informal situations (5).

   3 *I would like **to have been** there.* • *You would hate **to have seen** all the destruction.*
   4 *I would have liked **to be** there.* • *You would have hated **to see** all the destruction.*
   5 *I would have liked **to have been** there.* • *You would have hated **to have seen** it.*

We can use the continuous infinitive (*to be* + present participle) for an action in progress (6) and the perfect continuous infinitive (*to have been* + present participle) for an action in progress at an earlier time (7).

   6 *The children will pretend **to be sleeping**.* • *The girl seemed **to be waiting** for someone.*
   7 *They'll pretend **to have been sleeping**.* • *She seemed **to have been waiting** there for hours.*

We can use the passive infinitive (*to be* + past participle) for present or future actions happening to the subject (8) and the perfect passive infinitive (*to have been* + past participle) for earlier actions (9).

   8 *My computer is supposed **to be repaired** today.* • *The workers want **to be paid** in cash.*
   9 *It was supposed **to have been repaired** last week.* • *They were hoping **to have been paid** already.*

Complex gerunds

Instead of the simple gerund (10), we can use the perfect gerund (*having* + past participle) when we want to be clear that the action was in the past (11).

  10 *Kirsten regretted **telling** us about the money.* • *We thanked them for **supporting** us.*
  11 *She regretted **having told** us about the money.* • *We thanked them for **having supported** us.*

We can use the passive gerund (*being* + past participle) for an action which happens to the subject (12) and the perfect passive gerund (*having been* + past participle) to emphasize that the action happened in the past (13).

  12 *In her book, Annie O'Neill wrote about **being punished** as a child for speaking Irish.*
  13 *She still has nightmares from **having been locked up** in a small dark cupboard for hours.*

---

4 **Complete these sentences with *to be, being, to have* or *having*.**

Example: I didn't mind ......*being*...... the youngest in a family of ten, but I knew I really wanted ......*to have*...... a large living space all to myself when I got older.

1 I'm supposed .... studying today, but I'm too tired from not .... slept at all last night.

2 You wouldn't like .... been living here during the war, with bombs falling and people .... killed every day.

3 The original tower is believed .... been constructed in 1810. It has always had structural problems from not .... been built on more solid ground.

4 The cleaners want .... finished their work in this room before they leave today because there are another two rooms on the second floor that have .... done tomorrow.

Simple infinitives and gerunds 139 Past participles 220 Passives 58

5 Infinitives and gerunds. Complete this table with appropriate examples of verbs from the completed sentences in 4 at the bottom of page 140.

Simple infinitive: *to* + base form of the verb – *to play*: ......to have......

1 Perfect infinitive: *to have* + past participle – *to have played*:
....

2 Continuous infinitive: *to be* + present participle – *to be playing*:
....

3 Perfect continuous infinitive: *to have been* + present participle – *to have been playing*:
....

4 Passive infinitive: *to be* + past participle – *to be played*:
....

5 Perfect passive infinitive: *to have been* + past participle – *to have been played*:
....

Simple gerund: base form of the verb + *-ing* - *playing*: ......being......

6 Perfect gerund: *having* + past participle – *having played*:
....

7 Passive gerund: *being* + past participle – *being played*:
....

8 Perfect passive gerund: *having been* + past participle – *having been played*:
....

6 Complete each sentence, using an infinitive or a gerund, in such a way that it is as similar as possible in meaning to the sentence above it.

1 You were supposed to do your homework before you went out.
Your homework ....

2 She had taken the time to help me and I wanted to thank her for that.
I wanted ....

3 They hadn't been told about the changes and complained about it.
They complained about ....

7 Complete this text with these infinitives and gerunds.

to be burning	*being held*	*to have visited*	*to have been based*
to be using	*meeting*	*not to have seen*	*to have been built*
	travelling		*to have been doing*

Did Marco Polo tell the truth when he wrote about (1) .... to China and
(2) .... the emperor Kublai Khan? Or did the 13th-century Italian explorer just
make up stories about places he would like (3) .... and things he would like
(4) .... instead of (5) .... captive in prison? According to some
experts, his stories appear (6) .... on things he had heard about rather than things he
had seen himself. In his account, the Chinese were said (7) .... paper money and
(8) .... 'large black stones' (coal) for heat long before Europeans. However, the Great
Wall is known (9) .... before his travels, yet he appears (10) .... it.

Verbs with infinitives and gerunds

Verbs used with infinitives only

We use infinitives, not gerunds, after verbs such as *hope* and *offer* (1). After verbs such as *invite* and *tell*, we must include a noun or object pronoun to identify the subject before the infinitive (2). After verbs such as *ask* and *want*, we can include the subject of the infinitive or leave it out if it's the same as the subject of the verb (3).

1 I'm **hoping to get** a day off soon. • We **offered to pay** for the damage. (NOT *offered paying*)
2 They **told me not to wait** for them. • David **invited us to go** with him. (NOT *invited to go*)
3 I **asked Sam to stay**. I **wanted him to wait**, but he **wanted to leave** right away.

Verbs used with gerunds only

After verbs such as *avoid* and *enjoy*, we use gerunds, not infinitives (4). After verbs such as *imagine* and *mind*, we can include a noun or object pronoun before the gerund (5). We put gerunds after verbs with prepositions such as *concentrate on* and after phrasal verbs such as *give up* (6).

4 **Avoid eating** cakes and sweets. • We **enjoy travelling** by train. (NOT *enjoy to travel*)
5 I **imagined Jenny walking** on a sunny beach. • Would you **mind us waiting** outside?
6 He should **concentrate on studying**, not **singing**. • Have you **given up exercising** already?

Verbs used with infinitives or gerunds

After *begin*, *continue*, *intend* and *start*, we can usually use either infinitives or gerunds with little difference in meaning.

7 Josh **started to drink/drinking** the soup, but it was very spicy. He **began to cough/coughing**.
We use infinitives after present participles: *Is it starting to rain?* (NOT *Is it starting raining?*)

After *hate*, *like*, *love* and *prefer*, we can usually use infinitives or gerunds with little difference in meaning (8). When we are talking about an activity in general (not performed by the subject), we use a gerund (9). After *would hate/like/love/prefer* we use infinitives (10).

8 Katy **loves to play/playing** the piano. • Don't you **prefer to study/studying** at home?
9 I **hate wrestling** because it's so violent. It shouldn't be on TV. I don't **like boxing** either.
10 **Would** you **like to come** with us? • I'd **love to see** you tonight. (NOT *I'd love seeing you tonight.*)
Note the use of *would rather* + bare infinitive: *I'd rather stay here.* (NOT *I'd rather to stay here.*)

After *advise*, *allow*, *encourage* and *permit*, we can use a noun or object pronoun as subject of the infinitive. When there is no subject, we use the gerund for an activity in general.

11 They don't **allow us to smoke.** • They don't **allow smoking.** (NOT *They don't allow us smoking.*)

After *feel*, *hear*, *see* and *watch*, we can use a noun or object pronoun as subject with a bare infinitive for a single or completed action and with a gerund for a repeated or continuous action.

12 When I rang the doorbell, I **heard** a dog **bark**. • Did you **hear** that dog **barking** last night?
When there is no subject, we use a gerund: *I also heard shouting.* (NOT *I also heard shout.*)

After *forget*, *regret*, *remember* and *stop*, we use infinitives for actions which will happen later (13) and gerunds for actions which have already happened (14).

13 **Remember to take** an umbrella. (when you go out later) • I **regret to say** this. (I'm going to say it)
14 Don't you **remember taking** it? (when you left earlier) • I **regret saying** that. (I said it earlier)

After *need*, we often use an infinitive, but we can use a gerund with the same meaning as the passive infinitive (15). We can use *mean* with an infinitive (= intend) or *mean* with a gerund (= result in) (16). We can use *try* with an infinitive (= make an effort) or *try* with a gerund (= experiment with) (17).

15 I **need to do** some laundry. • These towels **need washing**. (= These towels **need to be washed**.)
16 I **meant to ask** you about your new job. Will it **mean spending** more time away from home?
17 I must **try to get** to work on time tomorrow. I think I'll **try setting** my alarm a bit earlier.

Simple infinitives and gerunds 139 Reporting verbs with infinitives and gerunds 152 *Need 38*

8 **Add one pair of verbs to each sentence in this table, with the first verb in an appropriate form and the second verb as an infinitive or a gerund.**

enjoy / take   hope / visit   imagine / make   invite / stay   love / be   want / spend

1 **Verb + infinitive.** I .... Japan next summer.
   Others include: agree, aim, apply, decide, demand, fail, offer, plan, refuse, vote

2 **Verb + noun/object pronoun + infinitive.** My friend Ryoko has .... me
   .... with her.
   Others include: command, convince, force, instruct, order, persuade, remind, tell, tempt, urge

3 **Verb (+ noun/object pronoun) + infinitive.** She .... me .... a whole month there.
   Others include: ask, beg, expect, wish

4 **Verb + gerund.** She says she'll .... me to all her favourite places.
   Others include: admit, avoid, consider, deny, finish, give up, mention, practise, recommend, suggest

5 **Verb (+ noun/object pronoun) + gerund.** I can .... her .... plans already.
   Others include: celebrate, detest, dislike, involve, keep, mind, miss, prevent, recall, resent

6 **Verb + infinitive or gerund.** I would .... able to go sooner.
   Others include: begin, continue, forget, hate, like, learn, mean, regret, remember, try

9 **Add appropriate forms of the verbs from each set to each sentence.**

allow / take   avoid / try / drive   force / stop / play   forget / send   mean / tidy   prefer / not talk

1 My teachers would never .... students .... the exams home.
2 Don't .... me a postcard when you go to Japan.
3 I'm sorry about the mess. I .... up before you came back.
4 Most people .... about how much money they have or earn.
5 We usually .... through the centre of town during rush hour.
6 Bad weather .... us .... tennis earlier today.

10 **Editing. Correct the mistakes in the use of infinitives and gerunds in this text.**

I have never forgotten ~~work~~ *working* as a hotel maid one summer when I was a teenager. My aunt was an assistant manager at the hotel and she encouraged me take the summer job. She had been a maid at one time and she advised me remember clean the bathrooms really well. Nobody likes clean bathrooms, but I didn't mind do it as part of my summer job. That's when I was first starting learn English. Some of the visitors were really nice and I could practise speak English with them. I enjoyed try improve my English and it helped me when I went to college later. I also learned that I didn't want work as a hotel maid forever, but I don't regret do it for one summer. I decided study harder at school so I could go to college and try get a better job.

Adjectives with infinitives and gerunds

Adjectives used with infinitives only

We can use infinitives, not gerunds, after some adjectives when we talk about being certain (*sure*) or willing (*eager*) to do something (1) and about our feelings or reactions (*glad, delighted*) (2).

1 *The children are **sure to get up** early tomorrow. They're **eager to go** to the beach.*
2 *I'm **glad to meet** you. • I was **delighted to hear** the good news about your scholarship.*

Other adjectives used like this include: disappointed, happy, pleased, sad, sorry, surprised

After some adjectives, we can use *for* with a noun phrase or pronoun to identify the subject of the infinitive (3). We can use *of* (not *for*) when we are evaluating someone's action (4).

3 *It was **good for the children to visit** their grandparents.* (The children had a good experience.)
4 *It was **good of the children to visit** their grandparents.* (The children acted in a good way.)

Other adjectives used like this include: bad, nice, silly, stupid, wrong

We often use infinitives after *too* + an adjective, or an adjective + *enough*.

5 *Is the tea still **too hot** (for you) **to drink**? • The small bags are **light enough** (for us) **to carry**.*

Adjectives used with infinitives or gerunds

After empty subject *it* + *be* and adjectives such as *nice* and *difficult*, we can use an infinitive (6) or a gerund (7), with little difference in meaning. When we make the object of the infinitive our topic as the subject of the sentence, we use an infinitive after these adjectives (8).

6 *It was really **nice to talk** to Mrs Anderson. • Was it very **difficult to learn** Arabic?*
7 *It was really **nice talking** to Mrs Anderson. • Was it very **difficult learning** Arabic?*
8 ***Mrs Anderson** was really **nice to talk** to. • Was **Arabic** very **difficult to learn**?*

Other adjectives used like this include: easy, exciting, great, hard, impossible, interesting

We can use gerunds as subjects before *be* plus adjectives such as *important* and *necessary* (9). After empty subject *it* + *be* and these adjectives, we use infinitives (10).

9 ***Listening** carefully is **important**, but **writing** everything down isn't **necessary**.*
10 *It's **important to listen** carefully, but it isn't **necessary to write** everything down.*

Other adjectives used like this include: crucial, essential, unnecessary, vital

After an adjective such as *anxious*, we can use an infinitive or a preposition plus a gerund with different meanings (11). After many adjectives, we can only use a preposition and gerund (12).

11 *I was **anxious to leave**.* (I was eager) *• I was **anxious about leaving**.* (I was worried)
12 *Bill is **famous for inventing** microwave popcorn.* (NOT ~~He's famous to invent it.~~) *• Isn't Lucia **capable of doing** it by herself?* (NOT ~~Isn't Lucia capable to do it by herself?~~)

11 Complete each sentence, using an infinitive or gerund, in such a way that it is as similar as possible in meaning to the sentence above it.

1 Planning ahead is essential in my kind of job.
It's ....

2 Jessica didn't see any of her friends at the shopping centre and she was disappointed.
Jessica was disappointed ....

3 Christopher was so good to come to our rescue when our car broke down.
It was so good ....

4 It isn't easy driving those huge buses along narrow winding roads.
Those huge buses ....

Adjectives 111 Empty subject *it* 102 Simple infinitives and gerunds 139 *Too/enough* 118

Nouns and pronouns with infinitives and gerunds

Nouns and pronouns used with infinitives only

We can use infinitives after nouns with meanings similar to those verbs taking infinitives listed in Exercise 8 on page 143 (e.g. *agree – agreement*) (1). We can use these nouns as subjects with *be* before an infinitive, or after empty subject *it* + *be* before an infinitive (2). In these structures we can also use nouns such as *ambition* and *goal* with infinitives to talk about future actions (3).

1 *We **agreed to share** the cost.* • *We had an **agreement to share** the cost.*
2 *The **agreement was to share** the cost.* • *It was our **agreement to share** the cost.*
3 *Our **goal is to save** £500 by next summer.* • *It's his **ambition to become** an astronomer.*

Other nouns used like this include: aim, decision, desire, expectation, hope, offer, plan, wish

We can use infinitives after general nouns for people and things such as *person* or *place* (4), or after indefinite pronouns and adverbs such as *someone* and *nowhere* (5). We do this when we talk about what we can or want to do with those people and things. After nouns and indefinite pronouns, we can use *for* with a noun phrase or object pronoun to identify the subject of the infinitive (6).

4 *Bob's the **person to ask** about graphics.* • *Iceland is a great **place to visit**.* • *I brought **a book to read**.*
5 *He needs **someone to love**.* • *Is there **anything to eat**?* • *They have **nowhere to go** at night.*
6 *It's **time for the kids to go** to bed.* • *There's **nothing for us to do**.* • *I brought **a book for you to read**.*

Nouns and pronouns used with infinitives or gerunds

We don't usually use gerunds directly after nouns, except after a few phrases such as *have a problem* and *it's no use* (7). After nouns such as *interest* and *talent*, we can use a preposition plus a gerund (8). We often use a structure with *the* + noun (*the cost*) and *of* + gerund (*of living*) (9).

7 *Did you have **a problem finding** the place?* • *It was **no use complaining** because no one cared.*
8 *Julia had a **talent for acting**.* • *I had no **interest in studying**.* (NOT *I had no interest to study.*)
9 ***The cost of living** in London is very high.* • ***The thought of eating** eggs makes me feel queasy.* • *He stressed **the importance of being** on time.* • *I don't like **the idea of (you) going** alone.*

After nouns such as *attempt* and *intention* we can use infinitives or prepositions plus gerunds with little difference in meaning (10). When we talk about the use or purpose of something, we can use a noun or indefinite pronoun with an infinitive (11) or *for* with a gerund (12). There's no difference in meaning.

10 *His **attempt to break/at breaking** the record failed.* • *I have **no intention to leave/of leaving**.*
11 *They have a **machine to clean** carpets.* • *I need to find **something to remove** stains.*
12 *They have a **machine for cleaning** carpets.* • *I need to find **something for removing** stains.*

12 Add one combination of noun/pronoun plus a verb as an infinitive or gerund in each space.

cost / rent	information / reserve	plan / take	someone / ask
idea / study	place / stay	problem / keep	task / call

Leila was both excited and nervous about the (1) .... of .... in Edinburgh during the summer. Her (2) .... was .... only two courses at the university because she didn't want to have a (3) .... up with the lectures and assignments. She had heard that the most convenient (4) .... was in the student halls of residence, but they hadn't sent her any (5) .... about .... a room there. So, her next (6) .... was .... and find (7) .... about the kind of accommodation they had and the (8) .... of .... one of their rooms during the summer months.

Tests

A Choose the word or phrase that best completes each sentence.

1 You know they don't allow _____ in here.

  a eat and drink   b you eat and drink   c to eat and drink   d eating and drinking

2 He never _____ doing that.

  a agreed   b concentrated   c mentioned   d persuaded

3 Flights kept _____ because of bad weather.

  a delaying   b being delayed   c having delayed   d having been delayed

4 In my dream, Brad Pitt offered me a ride on his motorbike and I told him I'd rather

  _____ .

  a walk   b walking   c walked   d to walk

5 Mrs Jacobson reminded us of the importance _____ our passports in a safe place.

  a keep   b keeping   c to keep   d of keeping

B Identify the one underlined expression (A, B, C or D) that must be changed in order to correct the sentences.

1 I really do regret not <u>to learn</u> <u>to play</u> the piano when I had so many opportunities <u>to learn</u> and
          A   B   C

  <u>practise</u> in school.
  D

2 When I asked the students <u>to help me move</u> the chairs, some girls <u>volunteered to carry</u> one each
                            A   B

  for me and some boys <u>offered to take</u> the others, but Mark <u>refused me to help</u> at all.
                        C   D

3 When we're <u>ready to leave</u> the house, my mother always <u>tells us wait</u> while she checks in the
             A   B

  kitchen because she's <u>afraid to go</u> out <u>without making</u> sure everything is turned off.
                     C   D

4 I will never forget <u>to visit</u> Egypt as a child. It was so exciting <u>to stand</u> beside the pyramids. When it
                 A   B

  was time for us <u>to go</u> home, my parents say I cried and begged them <u>not to leave</u>.
            C   D

5 It really is better <u>to ask</u> for help instead of <u>pretending to know</u> how <u>to do</u> something when you are
             A   B   C

  probably not capable <u>to do</u> it at all.
              D

C Add these pairs of verbs to this text, with the first verb in an appropriate tense and the second verb as an infinitive or gerund.

allow / go   *assume / be*   *hear / sneeze*   *remember / tell*   *smell / burn*

I had just arrived at the International Adventure Camp in Florida. They had spent the afternoon assigning us to our cabins and telling us all the rules. The evening meal was pizza. Now it was after ten o'clock and we were all (1) _____ in bed asleep. I was still awake, stretched out on the uncomfortable camp bed, when I (2) _____ someone _____ outside the cabin window. Just once, then silence. I (3) _____ the camp leader _____ us that we weren't (4) _____ outside after dark. Someone was breaking that rule. Then I thought I could (5) _____ a cigarette _____ . There was another rule against that.

D Complete each sentence, using an infinitive or gerund, in such a way that it is as similar as possible in meaning to the sentence above it.

1 It's sometimes hard finding a place to park.
A place to park _____

2 Is keeping all these old files really necessary?
Is it really necessary _____

3 He shouldn't buy a new car now.
It would be a mistake for _____

4 Amy was bitten by a dog when she was very young and she still remembers it.
Amy still remembers _____

5 The boy said that he hadn't done anything wrong.
The boy denied _____

E Add one of these verbs as an infinitive or gerund in each space in this text.

go   look   put   start   regain
do   keep   lose   stop   try

If it's so hard to lose weight, why do people keep (1) _____? Because they want
(2) _____ better is the usual answer. The problem is that going on a diet is likely
(3) _____ more harm than good, according to health experts. There is a strong
tendency (4) _____ all the weight lost within one year of (5) _____ the
diet. Only 3 per cent of those who take off weight have been found (6) _____ it off
for at least three years. Moreover, the 'yo-yo' pattern of (7) _____ a diet,
(8) _____ some weight and then (9) _____ it back on may be more
harmful to an individual than not (10) _____ on a diet in the first place.

12 Reporting

We can report what someone says by repeating the original words of the speaker (*He said, 'I'm sorry.'*). This is called direct speech. When we don't need or want to repeat the actual words of the speaker, we can use indirect speech (*He said that he was sorry*) or a summary report (*He apologized*).

1 **Read through this story and find another two sentences containing the verb *say* used with:**

1 direct speech
2 indirect speech

A On Sunday afternoons my grandmother used to take me with her to visit Mr Calum Mackenzie. My grandmother and Mrs Mackenzie, his wife, had been good friends
5 and had gone to church together every Sunday. When Mrs Mackenzie died, my grandmother was one of the women who helped Mr Mackenzie and she still liked to visit him, even on the coldest winter days.
10 B Mr Mackenzie was, as my grandmother put it, 'a man of few words'. This probably wasn't obvious to everyone because, when we arrived, he would always call out, 'Well, hello there!' and give us a big smile like a friendly
15 neighbour ready to stop and chat. But I never saw him talking to any of the neighbours. I remember one time my grandmother commented that maybe he didn't speak much because he didn't hear as well as
20 he used to. Mr Mackenzie turned in his chair. 'Maybe I don't hear anything worth talking about,' he grumbled.
C My grandmother would tell him about everything that had been going on in the
25 church as she walked round the house picking things up and putting them away. The news would be served with the tea and cakes we always had on Sundays with him. From the outside, it would have sounded as if we were

30 all having a lively conversation, punctuated by the sound of teaspoons clinking on saucers.
D When we cleared the tea things away and my grandmother disappeared into the kitchen, a silence would fall over the living room. I would
35 sit quietly with Mr Mackenzie and stare into the glowing embers of the open fire. He would cut up chunks of black tobacco and put them in his pipe and light it. He'd puff away with his eyes almost closed as the sweet smell filled the
40 warm room.
E In my English class we had read a story about the poets Wordsworth and Coleridge. One time Wordsworth went to visit Coleridge at his cottage. He walked in, greeted his friend, and
45 sat down. He didn't say another word for three hours. Nor did Coleridge. Then Wordsworth got up and, as he was leaving, thanked Coleridge for a perfect evening. The teacher asked us what we thought about the story and those
50 who had opinions mostly said that it was a strange story or impossible or that poets must be weird people. I didn't say anything.
F When we eventually got ready to leave, my grandmother would give Mr Mackenzie advice
55 about eating and his health. He would just nod and say, 'Thanks for coming round,' in a voice that told us he had had a perfect afternoon.

2 **Choose one of the following as the final sentence of each of the paragraphs (A–F) above.**

1 But it was really only my grandmother who was talking. (...)
2 We could easily spend an hour like that. (...)
3 He didn't say much, but he obviously wasn't deaf. (...)
4 It always felt so much colder when we left. (...)
5 She said we were going 'just to see how Calum is doing'. (...)
6 It didn't seem strange to me and I knew it wasn't impossible. (...)

Direct speech

We usually put direct speech in quotation marks after a reporting verb such as *reply* or *say*.

    1 *Mark said,* **'I need you here.'** *Dorothy replied,* **'I can't come before next weekend.'**

Quotation marks (or inverted commas) are double in American English: *He said, "I need you."*

We can also put the reporting verb with its subject after direct speech (2) or in the middle of two parts of direct speech (3).

    2 **'That's too late,'** *he said.* **'Well, that's just too bad,'** *she told him and put the phone down.*

    3 **'Hi,'** *he began.* **'It's me again. I was wondering,'** *he continued,* **'if we could start over.'**

After direct speech, the reporting verb is sometimes put before its subject in the reporting clause (4), but not when the subject is a pronoun (5).

    4 **'We will never give up,'** **shouted one of the demonstrators** *as he was dragged away.*

    5 **'Where's Tim?'** **he asks** *impatiently.* **'Not here yet,'** **she replies.** (NOT ~~replies she~~)

Direct speech is sometimes reported in brackets (6), or after a colon (7), without a reporting verb. We can also use direct speech to report thoughts and reactions as if they had been spoken (8).

    6 *Blythe Danner didn't want her daughter to be an actress (***'I thought she was too bright'***).*

    7 *Gwyneth Paltrow never had any doubts:* **'I always knew what I wanted to do.'**

    8 *I suddenly realized* **'I hate him!'** *Then I thought* **'Oh, no!'** *when I remembered that kiss.*

We use quotation marks when we want to report exactly a specific word, phrase or title (9). We put double quotation marks around direct speech that is quoted within another piece of direct speech (10).

    9 *There was a sign with* **'No Entry'** *printed in big red letters.* • *Have you read* **'War and Peace'**?

    10 *She said, 'I heard someone whisper* **"Jan"** *and I turned, but no one was there.'*

In American English, single quotation marks are used around direct speech quoted within direct speech: *"I heard someone whisper 'Jan' and I turned, but no one was there."*

---

3 Find an example of each of the following in the story on page 148:

1 A reporting verb (not *say*) before direct speech: ....

2 A reporting verb after direct speech: ....

4 Using examples 1–3 above as a guide, complete these punctuation rules with the words 'comma' or 'quotation mark'.

After the reporting verb, before direct speech, we put the (1) .... before the (2) .... After direct speech, before the reporting verb plus subject, we put the (3) .... before the (4) .... When the reporting verb plus subject is in the middle of two parts of direct speech, we use a (5) .... to close the first part and a (6) .... to open the second part.

5 Add appropriate punctuation to this text.

Susanna Mrs Alder called out I'd like you to come and meet Michael a girl appeared in the doorway how do you do she said nice to meet you he mumbled please don't call him Michelle or Mikey or any other silly names warned Mrs Alder as she swept out of the room have you read Harry Potter Susanna suddenly said what one he asked oh no you little Mickey Mouse she said as she came into the room you must say which one not what one if you're going to survive here

Indirect speech

We use indirect speech (or reported speech) to report the meaning of what was said, not the exact words. We put indirect speech in a noun clause beginning with *that* (1) or a *wh*-word (*what, where, when,* etc.) (2). In informal uses, we often omit *that*.

1 'It's a strange story.' → *They said **(that) it was a strange story.***
2 'What do you think about the story?' → *The teacher asked us **what we thought about the story.***

Words for places, times and people in indirect speech

In indirect speech, we change those words that refer to the speaker's situation (*I, my, this*) to words that reflect the different point of view of the person reporting (*she, her, that*).

3 '**I** don't like **my** hair in **this** style.' → *She said **she** didn't like **her** hair in **that** style.*

We usually change words that refer to the place of speaking (4) and the time of speaking (5) to reflect the point of view of the person reporting.

4 'Wordsworth lived **here**, but not in **this** particular cottage.' → *The tour guide explained that Wordsworth had lived **there**, but not in **that** particular cottage.*
5 'It rained **yesterday** and most of **last week**.' → *The workman pointed out that it had rained **the day before** and most of **the previous week**.*

Note also: 'now' → then, 'tomorrow' → *the next day,* 'two days ago' → *two days earlier.*

We also change pronouns to reflect the different point of view of the person reporting.

6 '**We** fixed it **ourselves**.' → *The boys claimed that **they** had fixed it **themselves**.*
7 Tom said to Ann, '**I**'ll give **you my book**.' → *Tom said that **he** would give **her his book**.*
8 Sandra said to me, '**I**'ll give **you my book**.' → *Sandra said that **she** would give **me her book**.*

Tense in indirect speech

After a reporting verb in the past simple, we usually change present simple to past simple (9) and present perfect to past perfect (10).

9 'It **is** late and I **have** a headache.' → *She complained that it **was** late and she **had** a headache.*
10 'I**'ve** heard that they **have** been arguing.' → *He said he**'d** heard that they **had** been arguing.*

We can report a past simple as a past simple or change it to a past perfect to emphasize that the event was earlier in the past.

11 'I **didn't see** Mark.' → *He said he **didn't see** Mark.* (OR *He said he **hadn't seen** Mark.*)

We can use the present simple after reporting verbs in the present simple for current (12), future (13) or permanent (14) situations. After a reporting verb in the past, we sometimes use a verb in the present for a situation that has not changed (15).

12 'Business **is** good and profits **are** up.' → *Delco reports that business **is** good and profits **are** up.*
13 'It **is** going to be very cold.' → *The forecast says that it **is** going to be very cold.*
14 'My parents **live** in Monaco.' → *She likes to tell everyone that her parents **live** in Monaco.*
15 'I **love** you.' → *He said he **loves** me.*

Modals in indirect speech

We usually change the modals *can* (→ *could*), *may* (→ *might*) and *will* (→ *would*) in indirect speech.

16 'You **can** go.' → *He said we **could** go.* • 'I'll wait.' → *She said that she **would** wait.*

We don't change *could, might, ought to* or *should* from direct to indirect speech.

We change *shall* to *would* in predictions (16) and to *should* in offers or suggestions (17).

17 'I **shall** do it right away.' → *I remember she said that she **would** do it right away.*
18 '**Shall** I close the door?' → *The new student asked if he **should** close the door.*

We can use *must* or *had to* when we report that something was necessary.

19 'You **must** do more.' → *He said we **must** do more.* OR *He said we **had to** do more.*

Modals 29 Noun clauses 161 Reporting verbs 152 Tenses 17

6 Complete each sentence in such a way that it is as similar as possible in meaning to the sentence above it.

1 'I left my jacket here yesterday.'
  He said that ....

2 'Carlin's new book is the funniest thing I've ever read.'
  The reviewer wrote that ....

3 'We won't eat it now, but we may have it for lunch tomorrow.'
  She said that ....

4 'You should take as much water as you can carry.'
  He advised us that ....

5 'I must get something to eat or I'll faint.'
  You told me that ....

6 'Demand for new computers in the UK is declining.'
  CompCo is reporting that ....

7 'Shall I get rid of these old boxes in the cupboard?'
  She asked if ....

7 Complete this text with these verbs.

are	*is*	*has*	*live*	*can*	*can't*	*will*
were	*was*	*had*	*lived*	*could*	*won't*	*would*

When she died at the age of 122, Jeanne Calment was the oldest person on record. This amazing woman, from Arles in France, had not exactly lived what might be described as 'a healthy lifestyle'. Family and friends reported that she (1) .... fond of cheese, wine and chocolate. She had also smoked cigarettes until she was 117. We asked several experts how a person, especially a cigarette-smoker, (2) .... live so long. They offered more than one answer. 'The average life expectancy (3) .... now about 80 for women and 75 for men,' observed Dr Elizabeth Jones, director of the Centre for Studies on Ageing. She says that there (4) .... been a steady rise in the maximum age of death throughout Europe during the past century and a major reason for this is improved medical care. Another researcher, Dr Michael Glass, says, 'There (5) .... no theoretical reasons why we (6) .... have a life span of 200 years.' Better medical care (7) .... be the only factor, according to Dr Glass. He explained that genetic engineering (8) .... soon allow us to repair or replace damaged cells, the real cause of ageing. He believes that we (9) .... be able to stop the ageing process. Other researchers have noted that attitude is also an important factor in longer life. Dr John Park is the author of 'Living Beyond 100'. 'Those who (10) .... to a ripe old age,' he says, 'are those who (11) .... cope with stress and other difficulties in life.' He wrote in his best-selling book that people who (12) .... past 100 (13) .... almost always optimistic and (14) .... a great attitude to life.

Reporting verbs

Reporting verbs with *that*-clauses

We use verbs such as *mention* or *say* as reporting verbs before *that*-clauses with indirect speech.
  1 'I've been ill.' → She **mentioned that** she'd been ill. • 'It's cold.' → Kara **said that** it was cold.

After reporting verbs such as *tell* and *assure*, we must include an object (the hearer) before a *that*-clause.
  2 'She has gone home.' → He **told me that** she had gone home. (NOT ~~He told that she had gone home.~~)
  3 'You will be paid.' → I **assured them that** they would be paid. (NOT ~~I assured that they~~ ...)
Other verbs used like this include: convince, inform, notify, persuade, remind, warn

After a reporting verb such as *say*, we can use *to* + object before a *that*-clause (4). After a reporting verb such as *agree*, we use *with* + object before a *that*-clause (5).
  4 'I'm not ready.' → He **said (to me) that** he wasn't ready. (NOT ~~He said me that he wasn't ready.~~)
Other verbs used like this include: admit, confess, mention, propose, report
  5 'You're right. There is a mistake.' → He **agreed (with me) that** there was a mistake.
    (NOT ~~He agreed me that there was a mistake.~~)
Other verbs used like this include: argue, check, confirm, disagree

Reporting verbs with infinitives and gerunds

After reporting verbs such as *invite* and *encourage*, we include an object before an infinitive.
  6 'You can go with me.' → He **invited us to go** with him. (NOT ~~He invited us that we could go.~~)
  7 'You shouldn't quit.' → She **encouraged me not to quit**. (NOT ~~She encouraged not to quit.~~)
Other verbs used like this include: ask, expect, order, remind, urge, warn

After a reporting verb such as *offer*, we don't include an object before an infinitive.
  8 'I'll help you later.' → He **offered to help** us later. (NOT ~~He offered us to help us later.~~)
Other verbs used like this include: apply, decide, decline, demand, refuse, volunteer

After a reporting verb such as *promise*, we can use an infinitive or a *that*-clause.
  9 'I'll fix it.' → He **promised to fix** it. OR He **promised that he would fix** it.
Other verbs used like this include: agree, claim, hope, propose, threaten, vow

After reporting verbs such as *deny* and *suggest*, we can use a gerund or a *that*-clause.
  10 'I didn't take it.' → She **denied taking it**. OR She **denied that she had taken it**.
  11 'You should leave.' → He **suggested leaving**. OR He **suggested that they should leave**.
    (NOT ~~He suggested them leaving. He suggested them to leave. He suggested to leave.~~)
Other verbs used like this include: admit, mention, propose, recommend, report

Reporting verbs in summary reports

We can use some reporting verbs to summarize what was said (12). Some verbs, such as *speak*, *talk* and *thank*, are only used in summary reports, not with direct or indirect speech (13).
  12 'Don't come back – or else!' → They **threatened** us. • 'It was me. I did it.' → He **confessed**.
  13 He **talked** to Kevin about the problem. • She **spoke** briefly to reporters. • I **thanked** them.
    (NOT ~~He talked to me, 'Hi, how are you?' • She spoke to us that she liked it.~~)

We can use reporting verbs such as *boast* or *lie* with *about* to create a summary report.
  14 'I beat everyone. I'm the best!' → He **boasted about** his win. • He **lied about** how he did it.
Other verbs used like this include: complain, explain, inquire, joke, protest, speak, write

Indirect speech 150 Infinitives and gerunds 139 Reporting in the passive 63 *That*-clauses 161

8 **Complete each sentence in such a way that it is as similar as possible in meaning to the sentence above it.**

1 'Mr Brody, there's something wrong with the lights.'
I mentioned ....

2 'Julia, you and your friends have to tidy up after the party.'
I reminded ....

3 'Don't touch any of the wires.'
He warned ....

4 'I didn't do anything wrong.'
He denied ....

9 **Complete this text with appropriate forms of these reporting verbs.**

ask   beg   claim   explain   mention   shout   talk   tell   think   wonder

I was in the Arctic last summer to photograph foxes, but I had been having no luck. I was on my
way home one day when I saw a construction engineer called Malcolm Davidson waving and
(1) .... to me as I drove by. We had met the previous weekend and he
(2) .... some areas further north where I might find foxes. I (3) ....
why he was trying to stop me there. I pulled over and got out to (4) .... to him. He
(5) .... if I was still looking for foxes.
   We walked over to what was left of some old rusted cars by the side of the road. I looked down and
saw three little foxes asleep beside a broken car door. He (6) .... me that he would
have to catch them all and move them away from there. It was his next construction site, he
(7) .... 'I'm afraid that when we (8) .... that we are "developing" or
"improving" an area, we don't always make things better for wild animals.'
   'Let me get my camera and take some photos before you do anything,' I (9) .... him.
I ran to get my camera. I do hope they'll survive, I (10) .... to myself.
   That afternoon I used up all the film I had while the young foxes played among the old cars.

10 Editing. Correct the mistakes in this text.

The word 'biker' is used for people who ride motorcycles. They sometimes ride around in gangs.

Some people say ~~me~~ that bikers are dangerous criminals, but I can't agree them that all bikers are like

that. One time I had a flat tyre on the motorway and two bikers in black leather jackets stopped and

offered me to help. I explained them that I can't get the wheel off. One of them told that it was 'no

problem' and assured that it wouldn't take long. He even suggested me to stand behind the car for

safety and warned me watch out for broken glass on the ground. They fixed it really quickly and

joked the small wheels on my little car. I spoke them thanks. They refused take any money when I

offered pay them. They were like angels. Actually, it said on their jackets that they were 'Hell's Angels'.

Reporting statements and questions

Reporting statements

In formal uses, we usually include *that* after reporting verbs when we report a statement (1), but in informal uses we often omit *that* (2).

  1 *The prime minister said **that** she would consider it.* • *The police report **that** crime is down.*
  2 *She said _ she'd think about it.* • *I told him _ I was leaving.* • *He agreed _ it was a good idea.*

We usually include *that* after verbs that describe the speaker's intention (*complain, deny,* etc.) (3), the manner of speaking (4), phrasal verbs (5) and when we include other information between the reporting verb and the *that*-clause (6).

  3 *They **complained that** they had been left out.* • *He **denied that** he was responsible.*
  4 *She **whispered that** she had to go.* • *The poor man **shouted that** he was innocent.*
  5 *One student **pointed out that** the date was wrong.* • *She **called out that** dinner was ready.*
  6 *He said in last week's meeting **that** we were wrong.* • *We agree with the critics **that** it's old.*

We can use nouns such as *announcement* and *response* before a *that*-clause containing indirect speech to report statements. After these nouns, we usually include *that*.

  7 *'Classes are cancelled.'* → *Did you hear the **announcement that** classes were cancelled?*
  8 *'I worked hard.'* → *His **response that** he worked hard isn't true.* (NOT *His response he worked* …)
Other nouns used like this include: argument, claim, comment, explanation, report, statement

We can also report statements by using a noun with *be* and a *that*-clause containing indirect speech.
  9 *'It'll cost a lot.'* → *Her only **comment was that** it would cost a lot.*

Reporting questions

We begin reported questions (or indirect questions) with *wh*-words (10), *if* or *whether* (11).
  10 *'Who is she?'* → *He asked **who** she was.* • *'What does she do?'* → *He asked **what** she did.*
  11 *'Is she a doctor or a nurse?'* → *He wanted to know **if/whether** she was a doctor or a nurse.*

We form indirect questions with the subject before the verb and no question mark (12). We don't change the word order when a *wh*-word is the subject of the question (13).
  12 *'Where are the keys?'* → *I asked **where** the keys **were**.* (NOT *I asked where were the keys?*)
  13 *'Who has the keys?'* → *I asked **who had** the keys.* (NOT *I asked who the keys had.*)

We can report some *wh*-questions with *should* (about the right thing to do) by using an infinitive.
  14 *'When should I come and what should I do?'* → *I asked them **when to come** and **what to do**.*
Note that w*hy* is not used in this way: *I asked them why I should do it.* (NOT … *why to do it.*)

We begin indirect yes/no questions with *if* or *whether*.
  15 *'Are you a nurse?'* → *I asked **if/whether** she was a nurse.* (NOT *I asked if was she a nurse?*)

We use *whether* (not *if*) after a preposition (16), before an infinitive (17) and after the verb *question* (18). *Whether or not* can be used as a phrase, but not *if or not* (19).

  16 *'Is it okay to use a dictionary?'* → *Someone inquired **about whether** it was okay to use a dictionary.* (NOT *Someone inquired about if it was okay to use a dictionary.*)
  17 *'Should I wait for him?'* → *She's wondering **whether to wait** for him.* (NOT … *if to wait for him.*)
  18 *'Are they really terrorists?'* → *The reporter **questioned whether** they were really terrorists.*
  19 *'Did he win or not?'* → *I asked **whether or not** he won.* (OR *I asked **whether/if** he won **or not**.*)

Indirect speech 150 Questions 45 *That*-clauses 161 *Whether* and *if* 192

11 Complete each sentence using indirect speech in such a way that it is as similar as possible in meaning to the sentence above it.

1 'I'm not guilty!' called out one of the defendants.
   One ....

2 It really surprised us when she said she'd been adopted.
   Her statement ....

3 The students' argument is that the cost of tuition has increased too much and I agree.
   I agree ....

4 He claimed, 'I'm not a thief!', but no one believed him.
   No one believed his ....

12 Choose an ending (a–d) for each beginning (1–4) and add the words *that*, *where*, *whether* or *who*.

1 Some of them were arguing about (...)   a .... isn't here.
2 The teacher is trying to find out (...)   b .... the weather was going to be bad.
3 I asked another student (...)   c .... to leave or stay there for another day.
4 We heard one report (...)   d .... to find the library.

13 Rewrite these sentences after correcting the mistakes.

1 One of the visitors asked about if will there be a fridge in the hotel room?
   ....

2 He asked me why to do that and I pointed out it was part of my job.
   ....

3 She asked me what do next and my response that she gets some more chairs.
   ....

4 Her explanation no one asked her if or not she has a degree was incredible.
   ....

14 Change these statements and questions to indirect speech and add them to the text.

'There is a "moster" under my bed.'   'Why aren't you sleeping?'   'Have you seen the monster?'
'I haven't, but I know it has big teeth.'   'What is a "moster"?'   'Where did it come from?'

One time when I was babysitting for some friends, their five year-old daughter got out of bed and
came into the living room. I asked her (1) ....
She climbed on to the sofa beside me and whispered (2) ....
.... I started to ask her (3) ...., then I
realized that she meant 'monster'. I asked her (4) ....
She said (5) ....
I asked her (6) .... She didn't know, but it had
really big eyes and sharp teeth. We eventually both fell asleep on the sofa and, luckily for us, the
monster stayed in the bedroom.

Reporting orders, requests, advice and opinions

Reporting orders and requests

We usually report orders using *tell* with an object and an infinitive.

    1 'Don't touch it.' → He **told us not to** touch it. • 'Be quiet!' → She **told everyone to** be quiet.
Other less common verbs used to report orders include: command, direct, instruct, order

We can also report orders in a *that*-clause with the modals *have to* or *must* (2). After verbs such as *demand* and *insist*, a subjunctive is sometimes used in more formal situations (3).

    2 'Stop arguing!' → Their mother told them that they **had to/must** stop arguing.
    3 'Do it yourself!' → He insisted that I **had to do** it myself. OR He insisted that I **do** it myself.

We usually report requests using *ask* with an object and an infinitive (4). When we report requests by speakers about their own actions, we don't include an object before the infinitive (5).

    4 'Please don't smoke.' → I **asked him not to** smoke. • 'Come in.' → He **asked me to** come in.
    5 'May I leave?' → She **asked to** leave. • 'Can I go?' → He **asked to** go. (NOT ~~He asked me to go.~~)
Other verbs used to report requests include: beg, plead with, request

We can also report requests in an *if*-clause with the modals *could* or *would*.

    6 'Please help me.' → The old man asked (us) if we **could/would** help him.

Reporting advice

We can report advice by using verbs such as *recommend* or *suggest* followed by a *that*-clause with *should* (7) or a subjunctive in more formal uses (8). We can also use a gerund for the suggested action when we don't want to mention who will perform the action (9).

    7 'You should go by train.' → He recommended that we **should go** by train.
    8 'You should take the express train.' → He suggested that we **take** the express train.
    9 'You should drive.' → He recommended **driving**. (NOT ~~He recommended us driving.~~)

We can use the verb *advise* with an object and an infinitive (10) or with a *that*-clause or a gerund (11).

    10 'Wait a few days.' → She advised **him to wait** a few days. (NOT ~~She suggested him to wait.~~)
    11 She advised (him) that he **(should) wait** a few days. • She advised **waiting** a few days.

We can use different reporting verbs such as *remind* and *warn* with *that*-clauses to introduce different kinds of reported advice.

    12 'A taxi will be much faster.' → She **reminded** him that a taxi **would** be much faster.
    13 'You must be careful.' → She **warned** them that they **must/had to** be careful.
We can also report a warning by using an infinitive: She warned them **to be** careful.

Reporting opinions

We use 'thinking' verbs with *that*-clauses to report opinions.

    14 'Oh, it's nice!' → She **thought** that it was nice. • 'I'll win.' → He **believes** that he'll win.
Other verbs used like this include: expect, feel, imagine, reckon, suppose, suspect

We can use the verbs *say* and *tell* in the continuous to report general opinions in informal situations.

    15 The students **were saying** that the test was unfair. • Teachers **are telling** us there's a problem.

We can also report opinions and feelings with nouns (16) and adjectives (17) before *that*-clauses.

    16 'Girls mature earlier than boys.' → It is her **view that** girls mature earlier than boys.
Other nouns used like this include: belief, conclusion, diagnosis, hypothesis, opinion, theory
    17 'It's a mistake.' → I was **sure** that it was a mistake. OR She is **certain** that it is a mistake.
Other adjectives used like this include: aware, convinced, doubtful, positive, sorry, worried

        Infinitives and gerunds 139   Modals 29   Subjunctive in *that*-clauses 167   *That*-clauses 161

15 Complete each sentence in such a way that it is as similar as possible in meaning to the sentence above it.

1 Professor to her students: 'Please do not eat or drink during lectures.'
The professor asked ....

2 Guard to the prisoner: 'Stand up when the judge comes in.'
The guard ordered ....

3 Worker to his boss: 'Can I leave early on Friday?'
The worker asked ....

4 Scott's mother to Scott : 'You should apply to several universities.'
Scott's mother recommended ....

16 Change each piece of advice to an appropriate reported form and add it to the text.

'Place your napkin in your lap.'   *'Don't put a lot of food on your plate all at once.'*
'Don't rest your elbows on the table.'   *'Don't take more food until it is offered.'*
'Chew your food with your mouth closed.'   *'Ask somebody.'*
'Don't talk with your mouth full.'   *'Please pass the salt.'*

My friend Karen Currie and I were huddled beside the small heater in her room, eating slices of
pizza from a cardboard PizzaLand container. She was telling me about an old book she had been
reading, called 'Table Manners for Young Ladies'. It instructed the reader, when she is sitting at
the table before the meal, (1) .... and
(2) ....
It told her, while she is eating, (3) .... and
(4) .... Certain things were bad manners
and the book advised her (5) .... and
(6) .... It also said that, when she needed
something, such as salt, she (7) ....
(8) .... rather than reach across the
table for it.
'Ah, the good old days,' she sighed as she reached into the box for another slice.

17 Complete each sentence with an adjective or noun and a *that*-clause based on one of the direct speech sentences.

aware	*diagnosis*	*'I lost my temper.'*	*'Take the early flight to Glasgow.'*
positive	*belief*	*'Dogs aren't allowed here.'*	*'You will all pass the exam.'*
sorry	*recommendation*	*'You have an ear infection.'*	*'A perfect life can be achieved.'*

1 It was our travel agent's ....

2 Idealism is the ....

3 My doctor's .... was

....

4 Sarah has quietened down and she's very ....

5 Our teacher was ....

6 The visitor obviously wasn't ....

Tests

A **Choose the word or phrase that best completes each sentence.**

1 They recommended that the windows _____ opened.

   a had to   b not be   c ought not to   d should not

2 He _____ to take part.

   a advised not them   b invited not them   c offered them not   d ordered them not

3 She _____ that she liked cold coffee.

   a described   b replied   c spoke   d talked

4 The teachers were talking about a trip to see castles and the students were wondering

   _____ .

   a why to go.   b where they go?   c when it was.   d what were they?

5 Her father _____ that Ellen had been to Prague before.

   a mentioned   b persuaded   c reminded   d told

B **Identify the one underlined expression (A, B, C or D) that must be changed in order to correct the sentence.**

1 We thought <u>flying would be</u> faster, but when Thomas suggested <u>she go</u> by train Marla realized <u>she</u>
         A   B

   <u>had</u> enough time and <u>she will be</u> able to see all the small towns along the way.
    C   D

2 Because I suspected that our bill <u>was too high,</u> I asked our waiter if he <u>would check it</u> again and he
                                 A   B

   <u>agreed me</u> there <u>had been</u> a mistake.
     C   D

3 Jessica was complaining to the coach <u>that she felt tired</u> and told him <u>she had to rest</u>, but he
                                        A   B

   <u>encouraged not to quit</u> and <u>said she didn't have</u> much farther to go.
           C   D

4 One student inquired about <u>if it was</u> okay to ask <u>what was going</u> to be in the test and the teacher's
                                    A   B

   only comment <u>was that</u> he had already told them <u>what would be tested</u>.
             C   D

5 We've <u>invited Josh to come</u> and he's <u>offered us to bring</u> extra food, but Linda <u>has warned us</u> that he
          A   B   C

   sometimes <u>promises to do things</u> then forgets completely.
             D

C **Complete this text with appropriate forms of the verbs.**

ask   explain   point out   reply   not say   not speak   talk   tell

In her best-selling book 'You Just Don't Understand', Deborah Tannen recalled a joke that her father liked to (1) _____ people. In the joke, a woman went to court to get a divorce from her husband. When the judge (2) _____ her why she wanted a divorce, she (3) _____ that her husband (4) _____ anything to her in two years. The judge turned to the husband and asked him why he (5) _____ to his wife in two years. The husband (6) _____, 'I didn't want to interrupt her.' Tannen (7) _____ that the joke was based on an old-fashioned stereotype of women: that they (8) _____ all the time. Her research had shown that it was, in fact, a false stereotype.

D Complete each sentence using indirect speech in such a way that it is as similar as possible in meaning to the sentence above it.

1 'I will buy the flowers myself.'
   Mrs Dalloway said _____

2 'Henry, did you leave your keys in the door?'
   She asked _____

3 An announcement was made that the strike was over.
   There was _____

4 'I shall return tomorrow.'
   His only comment _____

5 It surprised us that he said, 'I won't do it.'
   His statement that _____

6 I remember one time when my aunt said to me, 'Don't talk with your mouth full.'
   I remember one time when my aunt told _____

7 They said, 'You can stay at our house.'
   They invited _____

E Rewrite one of these sentences as indirect speech or a summary report in each space.

'Do you know where Rob is?'   'I'm sorry.'
'I'll be there by eight o'clock.'   'I think he went out about half an hour ago.'
'I forgot that I promised to take my mother into town this morning.'

I was sitting in my living room, surrounded by my luggage, waiting for Rob to come and drive me to the airport. It was already twenty past eight and there was still no sign of him. He had said
(1) _____. I had
already tried to call him at home. His younger sister answered, so I asked her
(2) _____. She sounded
sleepy, but said (3) _____.
Normally it would only take about five minutes to drive from his place to mine, so something had gone wrong. Suddenly the phone rang. It was Rob. He
(4) _____ for being late
and explained (5) _____.
It wasn't the first time his forgetfulness had made me nervous and his mother had made me take second place in his plans.

13 Noun clauses

A noun clause (or nominal clause) is a clause we can use like a noun or noun phrase as the object of a verb. We can introduce noun clauses with *that* (*I'm hoping **that the weather is going to be nice this weekend***), a *wh*-word (*Do you know **what the forecast is**?*) and *if* or *whether* (*I was wondering **if/whether we might be able to have a picnic on Sunday***).

1 Read through this magazine article and find:

1 another sentence containing two noun clauses beginning with *that*
2 a sentence containing a noun clause beginning with *if* or *whether*

ACCORDING TO ONE OLD SONG, love and marriage go together like a horse and carriage. These days, however, a long-lasting marriage may be almost as hard to find as a horse
5 and carriage on our busy streets. Statistically, it is now more likely that a marriage will end in divorce than continue in a loving relationship. It makes you wonder if getting married is worth the effort.

Is it simply the case that marriage has become a
10 gamble with less than a 50% chance of success? Not really, say researchers at the Newport Institute, who have discovered that there are clear clues to what makes a successful marriage. The Newport researchers have been conducting a study of
15 married couples for the past ten years. They started with 50 pairs of newly-weds and interviewed them every six months. During that time, 11 of the couples dropped out of the study, 15 couples split up and 24 couples stayed married. The researchers
20 were delighted that so many of their couples stayed together, but they don't think that it was simply a matter of luck.

One clear sign of a happy relationship is the frequent use of 'we' by a couple. This is one
25 indication that the couple speaks with a single voice about their experiences. Another clue is how past experiences are described. The happily married couples tend to focus on their experiences together, even when describing difficulties. As an
30 example, two different couples described holidays in which their suitcases were lost. One couple (still married) reported that it was one of their best memories because they went out and bought some

really different clothing and had a crazy time.
35 Another couple (no longer married) ended up blaming each other for everything going wrong during the holiday.

Researchers have also noticed that individuals in successful marriages tend to talk about their
40 spouses in much more positive ways. They focus on accomplishments. They often mention something new they enjoy doing now because of their partner. They also seem to be willing to change in ways that allow the couple to do things
45 together. In marriages that aren't working, there is more focus on self. One of the individuals typically insists that he or she will not stop doing something despite the fact that it is a source of conflict. Sometimes one of them will say that he or she
50 actually prefers it that the other has separate interests.

When the researchers asked couples what advice they would give to younger people thinking about getting married, they got some revealing answers.
55 Among those who eventually got divorced, the man would often give a response that was quite different from the woman's. It was obvious that these individuals had really different views about marriage. Among those who remained married, the
60 answers were more similar and often referred to the ideas of friendship, support and 'being on the same team'. On the basis of their study, the researchers have concluded that a modern marriage may begin with passionate love, but its survival depends a lot
65 on 'companionate love', a feeling that includes affection, caring and friendship.

2 After reading the magazine article, decide whether these statements are true (T) or false (F).

1 In this article, the author claims that more than half of all marriages end in divorce.   T/F
2 In the Newport study, more than twenty couples were interviewed twice a year for ten years.   T/F
3 After ten years, the researchers found that three-quarters of the couples were still married.   T/F
4 Couples who get divorced frequently speak with a single voice about their experiences.   T/F
5 The researchers reported that happily married couples typically had separate interests.   T/F
6 The researchers concluded that passionate love was the crucial factor in a long-term marriage.   T/F

That-clauses and *wh*-clauses

that-clauses

We can use noun clauses beginning with *that* (*that*-clauses) after verbs used to report thoughts (1) and feelings (2). We also use *that*-clauses to report statements in indirect speech (3).

   1 *People used to believe **that the earth was flat**.* • *I didn't realize **that you were waiting for me**.*
   2 *Do you ever feel **that you might be in danger**?* • *I always worry **that something could go wrong**.*
   3 *He mentioned **that he had seen the report**.* • *She whispered **that she would have to leave early**.*

We can also use *that*-clauses after nouns and adjectives.

   4 *I was faced with the problem **that I had no money**.* • *Were you surprised **that he passed the test**?*

In informal situations, we often use noun clauses without *that*, especially after the verbs *know*, *say* and *think*.

   5 *I knew (that) **you'd finish first**.* • *Dan said (that) **he had a cold**.* • *Do you think (that) **it's OK?***

We usually include *that* in formal uses (6), after nouns (7), and when a phrase (8) or a clause (9) comes between the verb and the *that*-clause.

   6 *A recent government study has concluded **that** drug use among adolescents is declining.*
   7 *A contract is a written agreement **that** you and/or others will do something.*
   8 *They discovered during the investigation **that** some money was missing.*
   9 *Sheila forgot when the meeting was and **that** she was supposed to unlock the door for us.*

We must include *that* (= 'the fact that') when we use a *that*-clause as subject.

  10 ***That Juliet loved him** was never in doubt.* • ***That he said nothing** doesn't surprise me.*

wh-clauses

We can use noun clauses beginning with *wh*-words such as *what, where* and *how* (*wh*-clauses) after verbs used to report thoughts and questions (11). Like indirect questions, *wh*-clauses have the subject before the verb and no question mark (12).

  11 *I wonder **what it means**.* • *They don't know **where he went**.* • *He asked **how often we studied**.*
  12 *I can't understand **what she is saying**.* (NOT ~~I can't understand what is she saying?~~)

We can use *wh*-clauses, but not *that*-clauses, after prepositions.

  13 *He disagreed with **what we said**.* • *I read about **how he did it**.* (NOT ~~I read about that he did it.~~)

We can also begin noun clauses with *if* and *whether* after verbs used to report 'not knowing' or an indirect yes/no question (14). We use *if/whether* when we are not sure (15) about the information expressed in the noun clause and *that* when we are sure (16).

  14 *I can't remember **if/whether I locked the door**.* • *He asked us **if/whether we were students**.*
  15 Was he married? Mary didn't know. → *Mary didn't know **if/whether** he was married.*
  16 He was married. But Mary didn't know. → *Mary didn't know **that** he was married.*

---

3 Find examples of the following in the magazine article on page 160.

  1 A *that*-clause reporting a statement: ....
  2 A *that*-clause after a noun: ....
  3 A *that*-clause after an adjective: ....
  4 A *wh*-clause used to report a question: ....
  5 A *wh*-clause after a preposition: ....

Noun clauses as subjects and objects

Noun clauses as subjects or after empty subject *it*

We can use a noun clause beginning with *that* (= 'the fact that') (1) or a *wh*-word (2) as the subject before a verb, but usually only in formal situations.

    1 **That we won the match** *surprised everyone.* • **That the other team played badly** *really helped us.*

    2 **How the thieves broke in** *is obvious, but* **why they only took one old computer** *is a mystery.*

Instead of putting the noun clause in subject position, we usually use *it* as an empty subject and put the *that*-clause (3) or the *wh*-clause (4) at the end.

    3 *It surprised everyone* **that we won the match.** • *It really helped us* **that the other team played badly.**

    4 *It's obvious* **how the thieves broke in,** *but it's a mystery* **why they only took one old computer.**

We can use *whether* or *if* in a noun clause at the end after *it* as subject (5), but only *whether* in a noun clause in subject position (6).

    5 **It** *doesn't really matter* **whether/if** *you go now or later.*

    6 **Whether** *you go now or later doesn't really matter.* (NOT ~~If you go now or later doesn't matter.~~)

Noun clauses as objects or after empty object *it*

We can use a noun clause as an object after a verb to express facts (7) or ideas (8), and in indirect speech (9).

    7 *We learned* **that pineapples don't grow on trees.** • *No one noticed* **that the keys were missing.**

    8 *She could never anticipate* **what he might want.** • *Ewan suggested* **that we should leave early.**

    9 *He screamed* **that he hated school.** • *She said* **that she felt that everyone was against her.**

After verbs such as *show* and *tell*, we include an indirect object (*you, me*) before a noun clause as direct object.

    10 *I'll show* **you** *how it works.* • *He told* **me** *that he loved me.* (NOT ~~He told that he loved me.~~)

Other verbs used like this include: assure, convince, inform, notify, persuade, remind, warn

After verbs of 'liking' (or 'not liking'), we use *it* as an empty object before a noun clause.

    11 *He doesn't* **like it** *that she still smokes.* • *I* **hate it** *that nobody ever cleans up after the meetings.*

After 'thinking' verbs such as *consider* and *think*, we can use *it* as an empty object plus a noun (12) or adjective (13) before a noun clause. After verbs such as *regard, see* or *view*, we use *it* + *as* before a noun or adjective and a noun clause (14).

    12 *They consider* **it an offence** *when women go out in public without covering their heads.*

    13 *We thought* **it odd** *that no one called us.* (NOT ~~We thought odd that no one called us.~~)

    14 *Many people regard* **it as a really bad idea** *that the police have started carrying guns.*

4 Verbs used with noun clauses. Find one example from 7–14 above to write in each space.

    1 'Feeling' verbs (*fear, sense, worry*): she felt that everyone was against her. (9)

    2 'Learning' verbs (*discover, find, realize*): ....

    3 'Noticing' verbs (*observe, perceive, recognize*): ....

    4 'Predicting' verbs (*expect, forecast, hope*): ....

    5 'Showing' verbs (*demonstrate, indicate, reveal*): ....

    6 'Speaking' verbs (*explain, mention, whisper*): ....

    7 'Suggesting' verbs (*advise, propose, recommend*): ....

    8 'Thinking' verbs (*believe, conclude, imagine*): ....

5 Rewrite these sentences in a less formal style beginning with *it*.

1 That they don't have any money left doesn't surprise me at all.

  ....

2 That children would rather sit watching TV instead of playing outside just astonishes me.

  ....

3 Why the government didn't act immediately to stop the movement of all animals has never been explained.

  ....

4 Whether Nicole's father had been for or against her marriage wasn't clear, but he did participate in the wedding ceremony.

  ....

6 Add one set of words to each paragraph (not necessarily in this order).

it / that / that   *it / that / what*   *that / where / whether*

A He wanted to know (1) .... we were doing, but (2) .... was obvious (3) .... he didn't really seem very interested in our answer.

B Sometimes one of them will say (4) .... he or she actually prefers (5) .... (6) .... the other has separate interests.

C (7) .... Robert's new schedule will be an improvement remains to be seen, but no one liked it (8) .... he just decided (9) .... the changes would be made without consulting anyone.

7 Correct the mistakes in these sentences.

1 Mr Baker complained about the noise was predictable, but we assured it wouldn't happen again.

  ....

2 The headmaster warned during our meeting some teachers wouldn't like their classrooms had suddenly been changed.

  ....

3 They told me about Geoff had said in the meeting, but I thought strange he hadn't mentioned money.

  ....

4 The police regarded suspicious the dead woman's husband had recently taken out a life insurance policy in her name.

  ....

5 The prosecutor showed the jury how could the crime have been committed by Feldman, but he didn't convince that Feldman was guilty.

  ....

Nouns with noun clauses

Noun clauses after nouns

We often use noun clauses after nouns derived from those verbs listed in exercise 4 on page 162 (*conclude – conclusion, indicate – indication*). We usually include *that* after these nouns.

1 *Her **conclusion that** boys are faster is wrong.*
2 *There have been some recent **indications that** the economy is slowing down.*

Others include: belief, discovery, expectation, feeling, observation, proposal, realization

We can also use noun clauses after nouns expressing possibility, often omitting *that* in informal situations (3). After nouns such as *issue* and *question*, we include *of* before a *wh*-clause (4).

3 *There's a **possibility (that)** I'll be in town next week. Is there any **chance (that)** we can meet?*
4 *We considered the **issue of what** we mean by freedom. • It's a **question of how** we can survive.*

Other nouns used with *of* include: consideration, discussion, example, knowledge, matter, problem, review

Parenthetical noun clauses are sometimes used after nouns as a way of providing extra information or as a reminder. They are separated by commas (5), dashes (6) or brackets (7).

5 *His excuse**, that he had fallen asleep on the bus,** was hard to believe.*
6 *One idea – **that Elvis is still alive** – keeps coming up in interviews with fans.*
7 *They were questioning her about her first explanation (**that there had been a burglar**) when she suddenly changed her story completely.*

Noun clauses after nouns plus linking verbs (*be, seem, appear*)

We can use the verb *be* between a noun and the noun clause used to talk about it (8). In informal uses, we often leave out *that* after *be* (9).

8 *One **theory is that** gravity travels at the speed of light. Our **concern is how** we can test the theory.*
9 *Matt's basic **problem was (that)** he had failed two tests. The **truth is (that)** he never studies.*

We can use a noun plus *seem* or *appear* before *to be* and a noun clause (10). We can also use empty subject *it* plus *seem* or *appear* (without *to be*) before a noun clause (11).

10 *The assumption **seemed/appeared to be that** we would all pay more for high-speed service.*
11 ***It seems that** it was too expensive. • **It appears that** they didn't do any real market research.*

The fact that …

We can use *the fact that* (rather than *that*) to introduce a noun clause as subject or object (12). After verbs such as *discuss*, we must use *the fact that* (not *that*) to introduce a noun clause (13).

12 ***The fact that** he was married didn't bother her. She also ignored **the fact that** he had children.*
13 *We discussed **the fact that** he had been absent a lot. (NOT ~~We discussed that he had been absent a lot.~~)*

Other verbs used like this include: conceal, dispute, disregard, hide, overlook, support

We also use *the fact that* (not *that*) after prepositions (14) and phrasal verbs (15). We can use other nouns with more specific meanings such as *idea* or *news* instead of *fact* in these structures (16).

14 *He pointed **to the fact that** Britain is an island. (NOT ~~He pointed to that Britain is an island.~~) • **Despite the fact that** she's small, she's very strong. (NOT ~~Despite that she's small, …~~)*
15 *They **covered up the fact that** people had died. (NOT ~~They covered up that people had died.~~)*
16 *I don't agree with **the idea that** older is wiser. • They played down **the news that** prices had risen.*

Noun clauses with *that* or relative clauses with *that*?

We can use the word *that* after a noun to introduce a noun clause (17) or a relative clause (18). In a relative clause (not a noun clause), *that* is a pronoun and can be replaced by *which* or *who*.

17 *The story **that** he was in a crash isn't true. (NOT ~~The story which he was in a crash …~~)*
18 *The story **that/which** he told us isn't true. • I saw a boy **that/who** looked just like Harry.*

Empty subject *it* 102, 162 Linking verbs 10 Phrasal verbs 134 Relative clauses with *that* 173

8 **Rewrite these sentences as a single sentence using a noun derived from the verb in the sentence above it, plus other appropriate changes.**

Example: I expected that the task would be simple. That was obviously too optimistic.
My *expectation that the task would be simple was obviously too optimistic.*

1 He explained that he had been stuck in traffic for over an hour. It didn't sound right.
His ....

2 They discovered the boy suffered from asthma. It changed their attitude.
Their ....

3 People believe there are aliens from outer space living among us. It's quite widespread.
The ....

9 **Complete this report with these phrases plus *that* where necessary.**

belief	*example of*	*against the idea*	*to the fact*
conclusion was	*in agreement*	*despite the fact*	*with the view*

In our group we discussed the death penalty. Two people agreed (1) .... the death penalty was necessary for serious crimes. They pointed (2) .... it was still used in the USA as punishment for murder and their (3) .... it acted as a deterrent, stopping people from committing crimes. One woman argued (4) .... the death penalty could stop or reduce crime. She said that the USA provided an (5) .... what happens when a society is based on violence. (6) .... they had the death penalty, the USA continued to have the worst and most violent crime rates. It was her (7) .... no government should be allowed to kill its own people, even if they are criminals. The others in our group were generally (8) .... there should not be a death penalty.

10 **Using a dictionary if necessary, complete the following definitions with these nouns plus *that* (= noun clause) or *which* (= relative clause).**

déjà vu   premonition   scepticism   superstition

1 A .... is a feeling .... something is going to happen, often something .... is unpleasant.

2 .... means having doubts .... statements are true or .... something will happen.

3 A .... is a belief .... events happen in a way .... cannot be explained by reason.

4 .... is the sense .... you have already experienced something .... is happening now.

11 Editing. Correct the mistakes in the use of noun clauses in this text.

the idea that

According to one definition, the women's movement is a social and political movement promoting⁄ men and women should have equal rights in society. It tries to raise issues how equality can be accomplished by first getting people to recognize the fact which women don't have equal opportunity. It is based on the belief people's attitudes can be changed and the assumption other peaceful changes can be made through the legal system, in spite of it is largely controlled by men.

Adjectives with noun clauses

We can use *that*-clauses (1) and *wh*-clauses (2) after adjectives. After some adjectives, such as *sorry* and *happy*, we include prepositions before *wh*-clauses, but not before *that*-clauses (3).

  1 *Mark was **surprised that** you asked about him.* • *It isn't **surprising that** the weather was bad.*
  2 *We weren't **certain when** he would arrive.* • *Isn't it **amazing how much** teenagers can eat?*
  3 *I'm **sorry about what** I said.* • *I'm **sorry that** I was late.* (NOT ~~I'm sorry about that I was late.~~) •
     *We're happy **with how** it looks.* • *We're happy **that** it looks OK.* (NOT ~~We're happy how it looks.~~)

We can use empty subject *it* before a linking verb (*be, seem*) and an adjective plus a noun clause (4). In formal situations, the noun clause is sometimes used as subject (5).

  4 ***It's disgraceful that** children can't spell their own names!* • ***It seems odd that** he didn't call.*
  5 ***That children can't spell their own names** is disgraceful!* • ***That he didn't call** seems odd.*

In informal situations, we often use noun clauses without *that* after adjectives.

  6 *I'm **sure** (that) it's a mistake.* • *We're **glad** (that) you're here.* • *He's **lucky** (that) he wasn't hurt.*

We can use adjectives for personal feelings (*afraid, worried*) before noun clauses describing the cause of those feelings (7). We can also use adjectives expressing degree of certainty (*positive, sure*) before noun clauses describing the information we are more or less certain about (8).

  7 *We were **afraid** (that) you wouldn't come.* • *Aren't you **worried** (that) Tess might get injured?*
Other adjectives used like this include: amazed, angry, disappointed, happy, proud, sad
  8 *He was **positive** (that) he had chosen the right answer.* • *I'm not **sure** if I heard him correctly.*
Other adjectives used like this include: certain, confident, convinced, doubtful, unsure

---

12 Rewrite these pairs of sentences as a single sentence containing a noun clause.

Example: He made such a mess. I was angry about it.   <u>I was angry (that) he made such a mess.</u>

1 Our old car might break down. We were afraid of that.
    We ....

2 Karen suddenly decided to quit her job. I was completely surprised by that.
    I ....

3 The test would be easy. Sean was absolutely sure of it.
    Sean ....

---

13 Choose an adjective or an adjective with a preposition for each space. Add *that*, *how*, *what* or *when* where necessary.

aware of   embarrassed by   glad   amazed   surprising   unlikely

Our teacher always encouraged us to try to guess what new words and phrases meant because it was
(1) .... we would always be able to use our dictionaries. It was good advice, but I was
very (2) .... wrong my guesses could be sometimes. For example, I had guessed that
the phrase 'kick the bucket' must mean that you are very happy and you show that you are happy
by kicking a bucket. You just give it a good kick. That made sense to me. So, it was rather
(3) .... I discovered that it meant the same as 'die'. I was really (4) I
hadn't tried to use the phrase. I would be so (5) .... people would think if they had told
me that they had good news and I had said, 'Great! Now you'll kick the bucket!' They would be
totally (6) .... I had said such an inappropriate thing.

The subjunctive or *should* in noun clauses

14 Write the numbers of appropriate examples in the spaces.

We can use the present subjunctive, which has the same form as the base form of the verb, in *that*-clauses ☐ . We put *not* before the verb in the negative subjunctive ☐ . We only use the subjunctive in formal situations. We can use *should* before the base form of the verb instead of the present subjunctive ☐ .

1 *Dr Evans specifically requested that no one **have** access to patients' files unless authorized.*
2 *We have already recommended that young children **not be** left alone in parked cars.*
3 *The doctor requested that no one **should have** access to the files. • We have already recommended that children **shouldn't be** left alone.*

The past subjunctive (*were*) is also used in noun clauses after *wish*: *I wish (that) I were taller.*

We can use the present subjunctive or *should* in *that*-clauses after verbs expressing orders ☐ , rules ☐ or suggestions ☐ .

4 *The committee <u>has suggested</u> that the cost of admission **(should) be** increased.*
5 *The job description <u>stipulates</u> that the applicant **(should) have** a degree in English.*
6 *The judge <u>insisted</u> that the boy **(should) be** punished and that he **(should) pay** for the damage.*

Other verbs used with the subjunctive include: advise, ask, demand, order, propose, require

We can use the subjunctive or *should* in a reported order ☐ , but not in a reported statement ☐ .

7 *'He has to be over eighteen.'* → *They insist that he **(should) be** over eighteen.*
8 *'I AM over eighteen!'* → *He insists that he **is** over eighteen.*

We can also use the subjunctive or *should* in *that*-clauses after nouns expressing orders ☐ , rules or suggestions ☐ and after adjectives expressing what is necessary ☐ .

9 *It is our <u>recommendation</u> that he **(should) not say** anything until the investigation is over.*
10 *Isn't there a <u>rule</u> that safety equipment **(should) be** worn whenever machinery is running?*
11 *They gave <u>instructions</u> that all passengers **(should) have** passports ready for inspection.*
12 *It is <u>essential</u> that no one **(should) feel** excluded. It is <u>vital</u> that every voice **(should) be** heard.*

Other adjectives used like this include: crucial, imperative, important, necessary

15 Choose an ending (a–f) for each beginning (1–6) and add appropriate forms of these words, using the subjunctive or *should* where appropriate.

arrest	give	insist	recommend	spend	suggestion
crucial	have	not disturb	requirement	stipulate	wear

1 The nurse says it's .... (...)
2 The advertisement .... (...)
3 The travel agent .... (...)
4 Someone offered the .... (...)
5 The school had a .... (...)
6 The prisoner .... (...)

a that the winner .... a car as the prize.
b that uniforms .... at all times.
c that the applicant .... two years' experience.
d that the patient ....
e that they .... the wrong person.
f that we .... a week in Paris.

Uses of noun clauses

Complex information in noun clauses

We can use noun clauses in a series to present complex information. We include *that* when we want to avoid ambiguity (e.g., to avoid 'We have seen researchers' in the example below) or we can omit *that* to avoid repeating it too often (e.g. 'people will believe they witnessed …').

1 *We have seen **that** researchers have been able to show **that** people will believe **(that)** they witnessed certain things because of information presented in police questions.*

We can also use several noun clauses in a list for a series of linked ideas (2) or alternatives (3).

2 *Bleck has argued **that** the long human childhood is needed for learning complex skills, **that** it allows children time to grow into many tasks **and that** it is actually beneficial for parents.*

3 *It is clearly not true **that** students learn everything they are taught **or that** they know only what they are taught **or that** they can remember everything they are taught.*

We can include a phrase (4) or clause (5), separated by commas, after *that* in a noun clause. We put the first comma after *that*, not before it. We don't put commas round a *wh*-clause used as a subject after *that* (6).

4 *An important discovery was **that,** <u>in both types of environments</u>, **the children's language developed at the same rate.*** (NOT *An important discovery was, that in both types …*)

5 *Some teachers believe **that,** <u>if students see or hear errors</u>, **they will learn those errors**.*

6 *The idea **that** <u>what you eat</u> **affects your long-term health** shouldn't really be a big surprise.*

The position of noun clauses

We usually put noun clauses at the end of sentences when they are objects, especially when they are long and contain a lot of information.

7 *It's usually assumed **that government officials speaking on important matters of national security are telling the truth**.*

We can use noun clauses in front position as a connection to information already given (8) or to repeat or rephrase old information before presenting new information (9).

8 *Five days after the earthquake, a woman was found alive under the ruins of her house. **That she had survived** was described as a miracle. **How she did it** no one knew.*

9 *Speakers continually design their linguistic messages on the basis of assumptions about what their hearers already know. **What a speaker assumes is true or is known by the hearer** can be described as a presupposition.*

We can use *The fact that* … with a noun clause in front position when we want to present information (including new information) as an established fact.

10 *Jim's early years were spent with his deaf parents. His only contact with spoken language was through television. **The fact that he couldn't speak English by the age of four** is evidence that children need more than simple exposure to language.*

We can use noun clauses in mid position to spell out details of a fact or idea (11). We can show that information is additional (and could be omitted) by putting it in a parenthetical noun clause separated by commas, dashes or brackets (12).

11 *It isn't hard to work out how the widespread assumption **that women talk more than men** came to be one of our social myths.*

12 *The idea behind 'Secret Santas' is for each person in a family or group to buy one present, 'from Santa', for only one other person. This solution (**that you buy one present instead of ten or twenty**) helps to reduce the stress of Christmas as well as the cost.*

Empty subject *it* 102, 162 Parenthetical noun clauses 164 *The fact that* 164

16 Add one set of clauses to each paragraph (not necessarily in this order).

what happened that day / what they're thinking / who their best friends are
if women and men talk equally / people think / the women talked more
that men think / that they hear women / women talk a lot
that men get the impression / that women are less likely than men / that women never tell jokes

A For women, the essence of friendship is talk, telling each other (1) ....
.... and feeling, and (2) .... When asked
(3) ...., most women name other women they regularly
talk to.

B Women can and do tell jokes. However, it is true (4) ....
to tell jokes in large groups, especially groups including men, so it's not surprising
(5) .... (6) ....

C Studies have shown that, (7) .... in a group,
(8) .... (9) ....

D The finding (10) .... (11) ....
.... may be due to the fact (12) .... talking in social
situations where men have little to say.

17 Write one of these clauses in each space in the following sentences (from a magazine article) and add *that* where it is appropriate.

Columbus wasn't the first European   *there was another world*
Columbus reached Iceland   *he could reach China*
Columbus's visit to Iceland gave him the confidence   *there would eventually be a place to land*

Was it from the Vikings in Iceland that Christopher Columbus learned the crucial information
(1) .... further to the west?
Columbus's son described a voyage his father had made to the northern edge of Europe in 1477.
Many scholars now believe (2) .... during that voyage.
Seven years later, in 1484, Columbus proposed to the king of Portugal that, by crossing the Atlantic,
(3) ....
The idea (4) .... to reach America may come as a
surprise to some, but scholars in northern Europe have always suspected
(5) .... to set sail across the Atlantic, knowing that, if he
kept going, (6) .... on the other side.

Tests

A Choose the word or phrase that best completes each sentence.

1 Can you understand _____ ?

   a she is saying   b what is saying   c what she is saying   d what is she saying

2 _____ you wait or come back later is up to you.

   a If   b That   c When   d Whether

3 They will recommend that she _____ soon.

   a leave   b is leaving   c left   d will leave

4 Elizabeth explained during the meeting that it was a _____ of what should have priority.

   a belief   b fact   c possibility   d question

5 The regulations _____ that a lawyer always be present during any interrogations.

   a assure   b require   c seem   d state

B Identify the one underlined expression (A, B, C or D) that must be changed to correct the sentence.

1 <u>Sandra stayed with John</u> wasn't surprising, but it was obvious to everyone that <u>they had decided</u>
        A   B
   <u>they were just friends</u> and that <u>marriage wasn't in their plans</u>.
            C   D

2 He didn't know <u>who</u> it was and couldn't imagine <u>why</u> they did it, but there must have been
                 A   B
   somebody <u>that</u> started the rumour <u>which</u> he was from London and very wealthy.
             C   D

3 I heard <u>about that the director said</u> to them <u>that he didn't think it</u> necessary <u>that he should have</u>
                   A   B   C
   <u>to agree</u> with everything <u>they proposed</u>.
      D   D

4 It <u>became obvious</u> that a lot of British people didn't <u>like</u> that their government <u>considered</u> it
        A   B   C
   <u>essential</u> that they should join the European Community.
      D

5 Martin <u>told me that</u> he wanted to <u>remind that</u> <u>what was important</u> was not the cost, but
           A   B   C
   <u>how well the job was done</u>.
         D

C In the original version of this paragraph there were six conjunctions (five *thats* and one *how*) introducing noun clauses. One example is shown. Add the others in appropriate places.

Categorization plays a crucial role in human cognition, yet we give little thought to this process.
                      that
Indeed, it seems/most of us have a very simple idea of categorization works: we take it for granted
categories have clear boundaries, and all members of a given category must have something in
common. If we consider the purpose of categorization, we see it is not surprising we hold such
a view.

D Complete each sentence with a noun clause in such a way that it is as similar as possible in meaning to the sentence(s) above it.

1 His parents weren't English. He didn't conceal it.

He _____

2 Why anyone would want to jump out of a plane and put their trust in a parachute has always been a big mystery to me.

It _____

3 We expected that no one would be there.

Our _____

4 Her comments had upset Mark's mother. Bridget was sorry about that.

Bridget _____

5 These apples don't look very nice, but they're delicious.

Despite _____

E In each space, write an appropriate form of one of these words or phrases and, where necessary, one of these conjunctions: *that*, *if* or *when*.

argue	*feel*	*notice*	*emotion*	*view*
concede	*know*	*rule out*	*reason to*	*unfair*

Kanzi is an adult bonobo, or pygmy chimp, kept at Georgia State University in Atlanta. He has grown up among humans, and is adept at communicating with symbols. He understands some spoken English, and can respond to phrases such as 'go out of the cage' and 'do you want a banana?'
Jared Taglialatela and Sue Savage-Rumbaugh, who work with Kanzi, (1) _____ he was making gentle noises during his interactions with them. 'We wanted to (2) _____ there was any rhyme or (3) _____ they were produced,' says Taglialatela.

So his team studied 100 hours of videotape showing Kanzi's day-to-day interactions and analyzed the sounds he made at various times. They picked situations in which the bonobo's actions were unambiguous: for example, while he was eating a banana, pointing to the symbol for 'grapes', or responding to a request to go outside the cage.

They identified four sounds Kanzi made in different contexts: banana, grapes, juice and yes. In each context, Kanzi made the same sound. 'We haven't taught him this,' says Taglialatela. 'He's doing it on his own.'

Some will (4) _____ the sounds are simply the result of differences in Kanzi's emotional state. Taglialatela (5) _____ emotions may play a part, but says they are not the whole story. For instance, Kanzi's sound for 'yes' stayed the same across very different emotional states.

Primatologist Frans de Waal of Emory University in Atlanta, Georgia, agrees.
'(6) _____ is involved doesn't (7) _____ he's following rules that have some sort of cognitive component.'

Kanzi is just the latest primate to challenge the (8) _____ animals have no language ability. Language used to be popularly defined as symbolic communication until Washoe, a chimpanzee, stumped everyone by learning to communicate in American Sign Language. 'The linguists then came up with a definition that emphasized syntax much more than symbols,' says de Waal. 'Sometimes we (9) _____ it's a bit (10) _____ they move the goalposts as soon as we get near.'

14 Relative clauses

Relative clauses are usually introduced by relative pronouns such as *that, who* or *which* and are used to provide information about someone or something just mentioned. We can use relative clauses to identify people (*I've just seen the woman **who lives upstairs***), describe things (*She's climbing up a ladder **that wobbles with every gust of wind***) and add comments (*I think she's going to clean her windows, **which seems rather dangerous in the circumstances***). We can sometimes use a relative clause with no relative pronoun (*With every step _ **she takes**, water splashes out of the bucket _ **she's carrying***).

1 Read through this text and find one relative clause in each paragraph.

A The recent discovery of the wreck of an old ship on the ocean floor near the coast of North Carolina has revived interest in the colourful character who was the ship's last captain. The ship is believed to be the 'Queen Anne's Revenge', which sank in 1718. Her captain, who was the most notorious pirate of his day, was called Blackbeard.

B Blackbeard, whose real name was Edward Teach, had been a sailor on British ships in the Caribbean during Queen Anne's War (1702–1713). These ships were often involved in attacks on French and Spanish ships in the region and were allowed to keep a percentage of whatever they captured from these enemies of the queen.

C All this changed in 1713 when the European powers declared peace and the war ended. Teach and hundreds of other sailors had to choose between returning to unemployment in Britain or continuing to do what they knew best, only as pirates. They started as small bands in small boats, attacking and robbing merchant ships, and eventually took control of larger ships which had the speed and power to dominate the trade routes in and near the Caribbean. When they captured a large French ship, which they renamed 'Queen Anne's Revenge', Blackbeard and his crew finally had a true pirate ship, 80 foot long, with three masts and more than three dozen cannons.

D Blackbeard soon learned that a fearsome reputation, a pirate flag and some warning shots from his cannons were all that he needed to stop most ships without a fight. In contemporary accounts, Blackbeard is described as a 'demon from hell', whose huge black beard was twisted into long tails and who carried several guns and swords in belts slung across both shoulders. Sticking out from the sides of his cap were long smouldering fuses that he could use to ignite cannons during an attack.

E Blackbeard's reign of terror lasted until 1718 when he was killed in a sea battle with two British ships which had been sent to put an end to piracy in the region. After his death, Blackbeard became a romantic figure and stories about his daring adventures and tales of secret buried treasure helped to create the popular image of pirates we still have today. ■

2 Complete this description using relative pronouns, or no relative pronoun where appropriate.

Between 1713 and 1718, a pirate, (1) .... real name was Edward Teach, but (2) .... was known as Blackbeard, attacked ships (3) .... sailed in and near the Caribbean. This pirate, (4) .... some described as a 'demon from hell', had a large black beard (5) .... was twisted into long tails. He wore belts across both shoulders in (6) .... he carried guns and swords. His pirate days came to an end in 1718 (7) .... he was killed in a sea battle, but the stories (8) .... spread about his adventures helped to create the romantic image of pirates (9) .... we have today.

Relative clauses and relative pronouns

Relative clauses

We use a relative clause to give more information about a noun phrase in a preceding clause. Instead of repeating the subject noun phrase, we can use a relative pronoun (*who, which*).

1 I have a friend. <u>The friend</u> OR <u>He</u> lives in London. → *I have a friend **who lives in London**.*
2 We found a shop. <u>The shop</u> OR <u>It</u> sold old records. → *We found a shop **which sold old records**.*

When we use a relative pronoun instead of an object noun or pronoun, we put the relative pronoun at the beginning of the relative clause. We don't repeat the noun or pronoun.

3 I loved the card. You sent <u>it</u>. → *I loved the card **that** you sent.* (NOT … ~~the card that you sent it.~~)
4 He's one man. I admire <u>him</u>. → *He's one man **whom** I admire.* (NOT … ~~whom I admire him.~~)

We usually try to put relative clauses immediately after the noun phrases they describe (5), but we can include a preposition phrase between the noun phrase and the relative clause (6).

5 The food came in plastic bags. We had to eat <u>the food</u>. → *The food **that we had to eat** came in plastic bags.* (NOT ~~The food came in plastic bags that we had to eat.~~)
6 *A pirate is <u>a person</u> on a ship **who** attacks and steals from other ships.*

Relative pronouns: *who, whom, which, that*

We use *who* and *whom* when we are talking about people. We can use *who* as the subject of a relative clause (7) and *whom* as the object (8). *Whom* is formal. In informal situations, we can use *who* as the object or, more usually, we leave out the relative pronoun (9).

7 Michael is a teacher. <u>He</u> works in Dublin. → *Michael is a teacher **who** works in Dublin.*
8 The person wasn't Michael. You met <u>him</u>. → *The person **whom** you met wasn't Michael.*
9 *The person **who** you met wasn't Michael./The person _ you met wasn't Michael.*

We can use *whom* after prepositions at the beginning of a relative clause in formal situations. In informal situations, we can put the preposition after the verb and use *who* at the beginning or, more usually, we leave out the relative pronoun.

10 The man is Joe Nash. You should talk <u>to him</u>. → *The man **to whom** you should talk is Joe Nash./ The man **who** you should talk **to** is Joe Nash./The man _ you should talk **to** is Joe Nash.*

We use *which* and *that* for things or animals (11) and after group nouns such as *team* for a group of people we are thinking of as a single unit (12). *Which* is more formal. In informal situations, we sometimes use *that* instead of *who/whom* for people (13).

11 *I found the keys **which/that** were missing. • They own a cat **which/that** doesn't have a tail.*
12 We were in the team. <u>The team</u> won the cup. → *We were in the team **which/that** won the cup.*
13 The woman is a nurse. <u>She</u> lives next door. → *The woman **that** lives next door is a nurse.*

We can use *which* after prepositions at the beginning of a relative clause in formal situations. In informal situations, we put the preposition after the verb and use *that* at the beginning of the relative clause or, more usually, we leave out the relative pronoun.

14 I can't remember the hotel. We stayed <u>in the hotel</u>. → *I can't remember the hotel **in which** we stayed./I can't remember the hotel **(that)** we stayed **in**.* (NOT … ~~the hotel we stayed in it.~~)

3 **Find two relative clauses beginning with *that* which could be used with no relative pronoun in the article on page 172.**

....

Defining and non-defining relative clauses

Defining relative clauses

In a defining relative clause, we include information that identifies or classifies people (1) and things (2). The meaning of the sentence is not complete without the defining relative clause.

1 *Do you remember the woman **who used to work in the bookshop**? She's a teacher now.*
2 *Do you have a thing **that measures temperature**? ~ You mean a thermometer? Sorry, I don't.*

We often use *(that)* at the beginning of a defining relative clause instead of the object (3) or the object of a preposition (4). We usually use *(that)* after noun phrases containing superlatives (5) or quantifiers (6).

3 I brought the dictionary. Maria wanted <u>it</u>. → *I brought the dictionary **(that)** Maria wanted.*
4 The film is 'Twins'. He's talking <u>about it</u>. → *The film **(that)** he's talking **about** is 'Twins'.*
5 *It's the **best** film **(that)** I've seen in years. • He was the **worst** teacher **(that)** I had at school.*
6 *There's **a lot (that)** I don't know about computers. • **Every** person **(that)** we met had a cold.*

We can also begin defining relative clauses with *who*, *whom* and *which*.

7 *I don't know anyone **who/whom** I can trust. • There are two rules **which** you must always obey.*

Non-defining relative clauses

When we want to include essential information, we use a defining relative clause (8). When we are simply adding extra information, we use a non-defining relative clause (9). We usually put a comma before a non-defining clause and a comma after it, unless it is the end of the sentence.

8 *The first caller **who can give the correct answer** will win the prize.*
9 *The first caller, **who was from the London area,** didn't give the correct answer.*

We can also use brackets or dashes: *The second caller **(who sounded Scottish)** got it right.*

We usually use *who*, *whom* or *which* at the beginning of non-defining relative clauses (10). We don't usually begin non-defining relative clauses with *that* or without a relative pronoun (11).

10 *Our new boss, **who seems to be nice,** has said nothing about Mr Bell, **whom he replaced**.*
11 *The Mini, **which some people initially laughed at,** soon became the most popular car.*
   (NOT *The Mini, (that) some people initially laughed at, soon became the most popular car.*)

We can use non-defining relative clauses with *which* to add comments about preceding statements (12). We also use *which* in preposition phrases such as *in which case* at the beginning of non-defining relative clauses used to add comments (13).

12 *They said Catherine had been in prison, **which simply wasn't true.***
13 *There may be a strike, **in which case** the office will remain closed.*

In non-defining relative clauses we can use *of which* and *of whom* after quantifiers such as *some* (14) or superlatives such as *the most famous* (15). We do this when we want to add information about part of something or about an individual from a group already mentioned.

14 *The last lecture, **some of which** I just didn't understand, was about osmosis.*
15 *At the conference, there were several writers, **the most famous of whom** was Paul Theroux.*

We can also put superlatives after the relative pronoun: *… writers, of whom the most famous was …*

---

4 In the article about Blackbeard on page 172, find the four relative clauses beginning with *which*, and decide whether they are defining or non-defining.

Defining: ....

Non-defining: ....

Relative clauses and relative pronouns 173   Quantifiers 84   Superlatives 120

5 Add one set of relative pronouns (not necessarily in this order) to each description. Which one could be left out?

that / which / who (×2) / whom   *that (×2) / which / who (×2)*

Laurel and Hardy were a pair of comedy actors (1) .... made over 100 films from 1926 to 1940. Stan Laurel, (2) .... was born in Britain, and Oliver Hardy, an American, were first successful in silent films and were famous for their slapstick style of comedy. In their films, Laurel often caused the many accidents (3) .... happened to them both, after (4) .... Hardy would get angry and say, 'This is another fine mess (5) .... you've gotten me into.'

A Jekyll and Hyde is a person (6) .... has two personalities, one of (7) .... is bad and the other good. The expression comes from a novel about Dr Jekyll, (8) .... investigates the good and evil parts of human nature and invents a drug (9) .... can separate them. When he takes the drug, he becomes an evil version of himself, (10) .... he calls Mr Hyde.

6 Add one of these clauses to each of the sentences below. Use relative pronouns and make other appropriate changes. Add commas where necessary.

he or she controls a sports game   *most people know him as Mark Twain*
some of them are poisonous   *it uses exaggerated actions, often involving accidents*
it consists of nine islands   *the largest part of it is below the surface of the water*
you rent a room or flat from him   *each competitor takes part in three different sports in it*
✓he has never been married

Example: A bachelor is a man who has never been married.

1 Slapstick is a type of comedy ....

2 A referee is an official ....

3 A triathlon is a sports event ....

4 A landlord is a person ....

5 An iceberg .... is a solid mass of ice floating in the ocean.

6 Snakes .... are long reptiles without legs.

7 Tuvalu .... is a country in the south Pacific.

8 Samuel Clemens .... was a major American writer.

7 Editing. Correct the mistakes in the use of relative clauses in this text.

     that
A strange thing/happened to me once was getting a letter said I had been 'terminated'. The letter, that came from the university, was an official notice of termination (means 'the end') of employment. It was like being fired from my job, which it felt really weird. I didn't have a job at the university that I could be fired from it! I was just a student didn't have a job. When I called the office, they said it was an error had been caused by a new computer. I wasn't the only one had been terminated by that computer. A lot of other people didn't have jobs at the university lost them that day.

Reduced relative clauses

A relative clause formed with a participle and no relative pronoun is called a reduced relative clause. We use present participles (1) and past participles (2).

1 There are two students <u>who are waiting outside</u>. → *There are two students **waiting outside**.*

2 The strawberries <u>which had been dipped in chocolate</u> were really delicious! → *The strawberries **dipped in chocolate** were really delicious!*

We use a present participle in place of an active verb (3) and a past participle in place of a passive verb (4).

3 There were teachers <u>who were shouting</u> and children <u>who were running</u> out of the building. → *There were teachers **shouting** and children **running** out of the building.*

4 Debbie only drinks juice <u>that is made</u> from fresh fruit <u>that is grown</u> organically. → *Debbie only drinks juice **made** from fresh fruit **grown** organically.*

We can use participles instead of verbs referring to the past, present or future.

5 The winner is the person <u>who scored/scores/will score</u> the most points in the game. → *The winner is the person **scoring** the most points in the game.*

6 First prize is for the most points <u>which were scored/are scored/will be scored</u> in the game. → *First prize is for the most points **scored** in the game.*

We can use a participle from a simple passive to describe a general situation (7), a continuous passive to emphasize that a situation is continuing (8) or a perfect passive to emphasize that a situation has continued from an earlier time (9).

7 *We are concerned about people **held** in prison without a trial.* (= who are held)

8 *We are concerned about people **being held** in prison without a trial.* (= who are being held)

9 *We are concerned about people **having been held** in prison for years.* (= who have been held)

Participles can also be used in non-defining relative clauses, usually in written descriptions and narratives.

10 *The old car, **trailing black smoke**, drove off towards town.* (= which was trailing smoke) • *Robert Ball, **nicknamed 'Big Bob'**, was my favourite teacher.* (= who was nicknamed)

We put *not* before the participle in negative reduced relative clauses.

11 *My parents, **not having much money**, never went on holiday.* (= who didn't have) • *I'd prefer shirts **not made with polyester** if you have any.* (= which aren't made)

We can use some adjectives and adjective phrases after nouns in a way that is similar to reduced relative clauses.

12 *There was one seat **available** on the flight.* (= one seat which was available) • *Mercury is a metal, **silver in colour**, often found in liquid form.* (= which is silver in colour)

Others include: necessary, possible, present, ready, responsible, suitable

We don't use a participle instead of a verb that describes a single or sudden action (13) or a verb with a subject that is different from the relative pronoun (14).

13 *There was a sudden bang **that woke me up**.* (NOT ~~There was a sudden bang waking me up.~~)

14 *There are several things **that we need** from the shop.* (NOT ~~There are several things needing …~~) • *This isn't the information **that I was given** before.* (NOT ~~This isn't the information given before.~~)

We usually use an infinitive, not a participle, after a noun preceded by the adjectives *first, second*, etc.

15 *Neil Armstrong was the first person **to walk** on the moon.* (= who walked on the moon) (NOT ~~Neil Armstrong was the first person walking on the moon.~~)

Active and passive 57 Non-defining relative clauses 174 Infinitives 139 Past participles 220

8 Using a dictionary if necessary, complete these definitions with the nouns and appropriate forms of the verbs in reduced relative clauses.

jigsaw   mermaid   cause   have   send   work
memo   shadow   cut   print stand

1 A .... is a written note .... between people .... in the same organization.

2 A .... is an imaginary creature .... the body of a woman but a fish's tail instead of legs.

3 A .... is a picture .... on cardboard or wood and .... into various shapes that have to be fitted together again.

4 A .... is a dark area on a surface .... by an object .... between direct light and that surface.

9 Change each of these clauses to a reduced relative clause and write it in one of the spaces below.

it was standing on the bed.   they are sitting in it
it is based on a true story   they didn't have children
it is parked outside   they went out to concerts and the theatre
it was covered with feathers   they were accused of crimes
it starts at 8 p.m.   they were committed during the war

1 There's a black car .... with two policemen ....

2 I found the puppy .... and .... from one of the pillows that it had ripped open.

3 The film .... is a drama ....

4 Many people .... had to be set free because no witnesses could be found to testify against them.

5 We envied the Andersons. Paul and Marjorie Anderson, ... , were free to spend more of their time ....

10 Make this text shorter by creating reduced relative clauses where possible.

For all you food-lovers ~~who will be~~ sitting at home and who will be looking for something that is interesting on TV this afternoon, there's a fabulous new show which is called 'The Asian Kitchen', which has been created and which has been produced by Mary Sah, which begins at 4.30 this afternoon. Among the dishes which will be featured will be Saucy Tofu, which consists of tofu squares which have been dipped in a special batter, which have been deep-fried and which have been covered in a creamy peanut sauce, and Evil Shrimp, which is made with hot peppers which have been sauteed with other vegetables, and which are served with shrimp which are sizzling in a shallow pool of red curry. It's the most delicious thing on TV today!

Possessives and pronouns with relative clauses

11 Write the numbers of appropriate examples in the spaces.

Possessives with relative clauses

We use *whose* instead of possessive determiners such as *his* before nouns. We usually use *whose* to refer to people ⬚ , but it can also be used after nouns for organizations ⬚ and places ⬚ .

1 *Is he the boy? <u>His</u> bag was stolen.* → *Is he the boy **whose** bag was stolen?* (NOT ~~who his bag~~)

2 *Napa is in a region **whose** wines are famous.* • *Come to Jamaica, **whose** people welcome you.*

3 *Delco is a company **whose** products are everywhere.* • *That's the club **whose** coach was fired.*

We can also use *whose* to talk about things that are part of ⬚ or belong to ⬚ other things.

4 *Draw a circle. <u>Its</u> radius is one inch.* → *Draw a circle **whose** radius is one inch.*

5 *They live in a small town **whose** name I've forgotten.* (NOT ~~a small town which name~~)

Instead of *whose* before a noun, we can use *of which* after a noun when we talk about things ⬚ . In informal uses, we can put *which* or *that* at the beginning and the noun plus *of* at the end ⬚ .

6 *They live in a small town **which/that** I've forgotten the name **of**.*

7 *It's a small town, the name **of which** I've forgotten.* • *Draw a circle, the radius **of which** is one inch.*

In formal uses, *of which* is sometimes before the noun: *Draw a circle, of which the radius is …*

Pronouns with relative clauses

We can use relative clauses after personal pronouns ⬚ and indefinite pronouns ⬚ .

8 *Do you know **anyone who** has a van?* • *There must be **something (that)** we can do about the cold.*

9 *She insists that it's **you who** must apologize.* ~ *But it wasn't **me who** broke the window.*

The use of subject pronouns sounds very formal: *It wasn't **I who** broke the window.*

We can also use the pronoun *those* (not *these*) with *who, which, that* or reduced relative clauses.

10 ***Those who** know him well say he will fight.* • *Ask **those (who) are** waiting outside to come in.* •
*His ideas are similar to **those (which/that)** we've heard before.* (NOT ~~similar to which~~) •
*Organic vegetables are **those (which/that have been)** grown without the use of chemicals.*

We can use quantifiers as pronouns followed by *who* or *that* ⬚ . We can also leave out the relative pronoun or use a reduced relative clause after quantifiers ⬚ .

11 *We saw **some (that)** we liked in Italy.* • *I didn't find **a lot (that was)** written about Jeffreys.*

12 *There aren't **many who** like her.* • *There isn't **much that** he misses.* (NOT ~~much which~~)

---

12 Add these clauses, with appropriate changes, to the sentences below.

his or her parents are dead   *they have completed their questionnaires*
the wood of it is strong and durable   *large flags were hanging from its upper windows*
this person doesn't care about money   *many of his paintings look like large comic strips*

1 An orphan is a child ....
2 Have you ever met anyone .... ?
3 The oak is a kind of tree ....
4 We passed an old palace ....
5 Those .... should hand them in.
6 Roy Lichtenstein, ..., helped establish pop art.

Indefinite pronouns 98   Personal pronouns 97   Possessive determiners 83   Quantifiers 84

Prepositions in relative clauses

We can use prepositions at the beginning or the end of relative clauses. We usually put prepositions at the end in informal situations.

1 This is the room. I work <u>in it</u>. → *This is the room **in which** I work* OR *the room **that** I work **in**.*

When we put prepositions at the end, we usually use *that* (2) or no relative pronoun (3) at the beginning. In formal situations, we can include *which*, *who* and *whom* at the beginning (4).

2 *Cook's was the shop **that** everybody went **to** for shoes.* • *There were bunk beds **that** we slept **in**.*
3 *Your opponent is the person _ you play **against**.* • *The day _ I'd been waiting **for** soon arrived.*
4 *Camden is the area **(which)** I grew up **in**.* • *Is he the boy **(who/whom)** you were telling us **about**?*

We always put the preposition at the end after a phrasal verb in a relative clause.

5 *There are things **(which)** he's had to cut back **on**.* (NOT … ~~things on which he's had to cut back.~~) •
*He is a person **(who/whom)** I've always looked up **to**.* (NOT … ~~a person to whom I've looked up.~~)

When we put prepositions at the beginning of a relative clause, we use *which* (not *that*) (6) or *whom* (not *who*) (7).

6 *A clothes horse is a frame **on which** clothes are hung to dry.* (NOT … ~~a frame on that clothes~~ …)
7 *A lot will be expected from people **to whom** a lot is given.* (NOT … ~~people to who a lot is given.~~)

There are some prepositions which we only use at the beginning (not the end) of relative clauses.

8 *The mid-nineteenth century was a period **during which** many people left Ireland.*
(NOT … ~~a period which many people left Ireland during.~~)
Others used like this include: after, because of, before, below, besides

13 Add these clauses, with appropriate changes, to the sentences below.

you look through it *you must complete something before it*
you look up to him or her *you have promised to be responsible for his or her moral education*

1 A deadline is a point in time ....
2 Your godchild is a child ....
3 A role model is a person ....
4 A telescope is a piece of equipment .... to see things
  that are far away.

14 Editing. Correct the mistakes in the use of relative clauses in this text.

The saying for ~~that~~ ^{which} I had to find the meaning was: 'People who live in glass houses shouldn't throw stones'. My first guess was that it was about a situation which those want to fight should first think about defending themselves from attack. Obviously, a person who the house is made of glass, it's something is easily broken, should be careful. If you throw a stone, the person you threw the stone at him could throw it back and smash your house. However, this saying, the meaning of it I looked up in the Oxford Dictionary of English Idioms, is not really about fighting. It means that you should not criticize others for faults similar to you have yourself. I think this is good advice for anyone is critical of other people.

Relative clauses with *where*, *what*, *whatever*, etc.

Relative clauses with *where*, *when*, *why* and *how*

We can use *where* instead of *in which*, *at which*, etc. after nouns for places (1) and after nouns such as *point* and *stage* (2). More figuratively, we can use *where* after nouns like *situation* (3).

   1 There's a small box. I keep keys <u>in it</u>. → *There's a small box* **where/in which** *I keep keys.*

   2 *We have reached a stage* **where** *we now have more people applying than we have space for.*

   3 *Women are better in situations* **where** *strategy is more important than strength.*

Other nouns used like this include: activity, case, example, experience, society

We can use *when* instead of *at which*, *during which*, etc. after nouns referring to time.

   4 *Do you have a moment* **when** *we can talk?* • *That was a period* **when** *everything was fine.*

We don't use *when* after *each/every time*: *That happens each/every time (that) it rains.*

After the noun *reason*, we can use *why* or no relative pronoun.

   5 *There may be good reasons* **(why)** *he couldn't come.* • *There's no reason* **(why)** *you can't do it.*

We can use *where*, *when*, *why* and *how* in place of a noun and relative pronoun combined.

   6 *That's* **where** *his car was parked.* • *He pointed to* **where** *he used to live.* (= the place where) •
     That's **when** *I start.* • *They were talking about* **when** *they were children.* (= the time when) •
     That's **why** *I'm here!* • *She never told anyone* **why** *she had to leave.* (= the reason why) •
     That's **how** *it's done.* • *We showed him* **how** *we make rice pudding.* (= the way in which)

We don't use *how* after *the way*: *the way (that) we make it.* (NOT ~~the way how we make it.~~)

Relative clauses with *what*

We can use *what*, meaning 'the thing(s) that', at the beginning of relative clauses used as objects (7) or subjects (8).

   7 She gave them <u>the things that</u> she had. → *She gave them* **what** *she had.*

   8 **What** *they're doing seems wrong.* (NOT ~~What they're doing it seems wrong.~~)

We don't use *what* after quantifiers (9) or after nouns or pronouns (10).

   9 *Some people lost* **all (that)** *they had invested.* (NOT ~~They lost all what they had invested.~~)

  10 *We'll buy* **the food and everything (that)** *we need later.* OR *We'll buy* **what** *we need later.*
     (NOT ~~the food what we need; everything what we need~~)

Relative clauses with *whatever*, *whoever*, etc.

We can use *whatever*, meaning 'any thing(s) that' (11), and *whoever*, meaning 'any person(s) that' (12), at the beginning of relative clauses used as objects or subjects. We use *whichever* when we're talking about 'any thing(s) that' from a limited number or set of choices (13).

  11 *If you take the big boxes, I'll take* **whatever** *is left.* • **Whatever** *she did made them happy.*

  12 *We will work with* **whoever** *they send.* • **Whoever** *said those things is mistaken.*

  13 *Write in pen or pencil,* **whichever** *you prefer.* • *I'll go by bus or train,* **whichever** *is cheaper.*

We can use *whatever*, *whoever* and *whichever* to say 'it doesn't matter what, who or which'.

  14 *I'll always love you,* **whatever** *you do.* • *I'm not waiting all day for her,* **whoever** *she is.* •
     He'll be in trouble, **whichever** *he chooses.* • **Whichever** *way they go, we'll catch them.*

We can also use *wherever*, *whenever* and *however* with the meanings 'in or at any place, time or way that ...' (15) and 'it doesn't matter where, when or how ...' (16).

  15 *He always keeps in touch* **wherever** *he is.* • **Whenever** *I see Penny, she asks me about you.*

  16 *Please sit* **wherever** *you like.* • *Call* **whenever** *you can.* • *Just buy it,* **however** *much it costs.*

Relative pronouns 173 Non-defining relative clauses 174 Quantifiers 84 *What or which* 50

15 Complete this email message with *how (x2)*, *what*, *when*, *where* **and** *why*.

Do you have a minute or two this morning (1) .... we can talk? I'm at a point
(2) .... I need to check with you about (3) .... I should organize the
report and (4) .... I should include or leave out. If you agree with (5) ....
I'm planning to organize it, then there's no reason (6) .... we can't have it finished
by Friday.

16 Using a dictionary if necessary, complete these definitions with the following words.

crime	*prison*	*revenge*		*that*	*when*	*which*
motive	*quarantine*			*what*	*where*	*why*

1 .... is a place .... people are kept as punishment for crimes.
2 A .... is an explanation of .... someone acts in a particular way.
3 A .... is an offence for .... you may be punished by law.
4 .... is deliberate punishment or injury .... is inflicted in return for
.... someone has suffered.
5 .... is a period .... an animal or person is kept away from others in
order to prevent the possible spread of disease.

17 Choose an ending (a–e) for each beginning (1–5) and add these words:

however   whatever   whenever   whichever   whoever

1 You can dress (...)   a .... they want to on Sunday morning.
2 We lived on potatoes (...)   b .... we think would enjoy the party.
3 The girls can get up (...)   c and .... else was available.
4 We'll go there (...)   d .... you like because it's really casual.
5 They said we could invite (...)   e on Monday or Tuesday, ... day you're free.

18 Complete this email message with the following words:

how	*what*	*when*	*which*	*why*
that	*whatever*	*where*	*whichever*	

Thanks for your email and the good news about the report. I've tried several times to think about the
report, but then the phone rings and I have to pay attention to (1) .... is going on right
at that moment. I can assure you that this won't happen every time (2) .... we have to
do one of these quarterly reports, but right now I'm in a position (3) .... every problem
in the office seems to land on my desk, (4) .... is partly my own fault, I know. Anyway,
that's not (5) .... you wanted to hear about, I'm sure. I don't think there's a slot in my
schedule this morning (6) .... we can talk. How about late this afternoon around three
or four, (7) .... is best for you. If you already have some idea (8) ....
we should put the report together, then I agree with you that there shouldn't be any reason
(9) .... we can't complete it before the deadline. I'll talk to you later.

Tests

A Choose the word or phrase that best completes each sentence.

1 The house I grew up _____ has been demolished and replaced by an office building.

   a in   b in it   c in that   d in which

2 Fieldwork is practical work _____ outside the school or office.

   a doing   b done   c which do   d that does

3 A letterbox is a narrow opening in a door through _____ mail is delivered.

   a it   b that   c which   d where

4 I didn't recognize the man who she was talking to _____.

   a him   b her   c his wife   d –

5 Could you ask those _____ outside to make less noise?

   a wait   b waiting   c waited   d to wait

B Identify the one underlined expression (A, B, C or D) that must be changed in order to correct the sentence.

1 Her new boyfriend, who's from Denmark, seems nicer than Jordy, who was from Spain, or
                    A   B

  Graham, that had really long hair, and whom nobody really liked.
           C   D

2 A slot is a narrow opening through which something can be put or a channel
                             A

  into which something fits or along something slides or a position for something in a timetable.
         B   C   D

3 I have friends who had a baby a few years ago when we were neighbours in Wimbledon and, every
           A   B

  time when I go back to visit them, their child, whose name is Sam, seems to have grown another
        C   D

  ten centimetres.

4 We had about ten people helping us carry our belongings to a van parked outside when there was a
                  A   B

  sudden crash making us turn round to find the big mirror lying in pieces on the ground.
         C   D

5 Everyone who was on the committee agreed that we should set aside some of the money
         A

  we had collected to pay whoever still had to be paid for their work and then we should put all
        B   C

  which was left into a savings account.
        D

C Complete this text. Use appropriate words to begin the relative clauses.

Genetic engineers, (1) _____ success stories include crops (2) _____
will grow in areas (3) _____ they have never grown before, have produced their first
genetically engineered insect. (4) _____ is being called the 'biotech moth' is a modified
version of a small moth known to attack and destroy cotton plants. This new version will be sterile,
so it will produce no offspring. The Department of Agriculture is planning an experiment in
(5) _____ some 3,600 of these biotech moths will be set free under large screened
cages in a cotton field. The goal is to have a moth-free field in one generation.

D **Complete each of the sentences using a relative clause so that it is as similar as possible in meaning to the sentence above it.**

1 Betty is derived from the name Elizabeth.
Elizabeth is the name _____

2 Her parents were born in India.
India is _____

3 I liked Hemingway's short stories best.
Hemingway is the author _____

4 Her parents will never like me, no matter what I do.
Whatever _____

5 He talked about humanism during the first lecture.
I was at the first lecture, _____

E **Add one of these sentences, changed to an appropriate relative clause, to each space.**

it is called a beanstalk   *they grow very quickly*
he suspects something is wrong   *he then cuts it down*
he steals some things from him   *his mother thinks they are worthless*
it is often told to children   *he is chasing him*
he discovers a giant there   *he sells a cow*

Jack and the Beanstalk is a traditional tale or fairy story
(1) _____ . Jack is a boy (2) _____
for three magic beans (3) _____ , but
(4) _____ into a really tall plant
(5) _____ . Jack climbs up the beanstalk into the clouds
(6) _____ (7) _____ . The
giant, (8) _____ , tries to find Jack and recites the famous lines:

'Fee, fi, fo, fum, I smell the blood of an Englishman.
Be he alive or be he dead, I'll grind his bones to make my bread.'

Jack escapes down the beanstalk, (9) _____ , so that the giant,
(10) _____ , falls to the ground and is killed.

15 Conditionals

Conditional sentences present one event, typically in a clause beginning with *if* (*If I don't leave the house before 7.30*), as a condition for another event, expressed in a main clause (*I usually miss the bus to town*). In real conditionals, the events happen, have happened or are likely to happen (*If I miss the bus, I have to walk all the way to town*). In unreal conditionals, the events have not happened, are not likely to happen or are imaginary (*If I lived in town, I wouldn't have this problem*).

1 **Read through these paragraphs and find two *if*-clauses with verbs in the past simple:**

1 another expressing a real condition
2 one expressing an unreal condition

Anna

She started when she was fourteen. She wanted to be just like the boys. In those days, if she had a cigarette in her hand, she was cool. That's what
5 they all thought back then. But it's easier to start than to stop. She is trying to quit, but it isn't simple. If she has a cup of coffee, she always wants to smoke a cigarette.

Belinda

10 She had always known that she wasn't the fastest or the most talented. Her mother had once told her, 'If you are successful, it will be because of hard work.' And that was how she had approached her tennis. Like going to work. She saw the other
15 kids just hanging around while she ran to tennis practice. She had spent her whole life on tennis courts. Now she had won her first championship. She heard her mother's words, 'If you don't have a struggle, you won't experience the triumph.'

20 Cathy

The teacher was describing a film about a farmer who had turned one of his fields into a baseball park. The farmer had heard a voice telling him, 'If you build it, they will come.' She wanted us to
25 write about that as our topic. I couldn't imagine that happening where I live. I like swimming, but if I put a huge swimming pool in front of my house, people would think I was crazy. Plus, I wouldn't want lots of people coming to my pool. If I went to
30 all that trouble, I would put the pool at the back of my house.

Dave

'If I were you, I would sell it.' That was his sister's advice in response to his request for help. She
35 was putting on her coat and getting ready to leave. If he had wanted to sell his car, he would have done that already. But he didn't have a job, so he couldn't really afford to keep the car. It was his own fault, he knew that. If he had worked harder
40 at school, he would have had some kind of career by now. That obviously wasn't happening. 'If you were in my situation, I would help you out!' he called out to his sister.

Erin

45 When she was younger, she didn't care about anything. She thought she was really tough. If she caught a cold, she didn't stop. Nothing could get her down or make her stay at home. But these days she gets sick really easily, so she has to pay
50 more attention. If she catches a cold, she goes to bed immediately. She doesn't try to be tough because she's not as strong as she used to be.

2 **Choose one of the following as the final sentence of each paragraph (Anna–Erin).**

1 And I would build a high fence round it. (.....................)
2 But she isn't complaining. (.....................)
3 She has had to avoid one so that she can avoid the other. (.....................)
4 But she had already left. (.....................)
5 Now she knew what they meant. (.....................)

Real conditionals

Factual conditionals

We use a factual conditional to express a fixed connection that exists between two events now or always (*if* + present tense + present tense). It is also called the 'zero conditional'.

    1 *If I **wash** the dishes, he **dries** them.* • *If the fruit **feels** soft, it's ready to eat.*

We can also use factual conditionals to express a connection that existed before now (*if* + past tense + past tense).

    2 *If it **rained**, we **went** by bus.* • *If my uncle **caught** fish, he always **gave** us some.*
Note that it is only in factual conditionals that *if* is used with a meaning similar to 'when'.

Predictive conditionals

We use a predictive conditional to express a likely connection between one event (*if* + present tense) and another possible event (*will*). It is also called the 'first conditional'.

    3 *If your friends **don't arrive** by five, we'll **leave** without them.* • *If I **see** Eva, I'll **tell** her.*

The most common modal used in the main clause is *will*, but we also use other modals and phrasal modals such as *can* and *be going to*.

    4 *If we **get** there early, we **can** sit at the front.* • *If he **says** that again, I'm **going to** scream!*

We don't usually put *will* in the *if*-clause unless we are using the full emphatic form to mean 'if you insist' (5) or when it is part of a polite invitation or request (6).

    5 *If you **will** put off doing your homework, then of course you'll get bad marks.*
    6 *If you'll just follow me, I'll take you to your room.* • *If you'll open the door, I'll bring these in.*

---

3 **Find an example of each of the following in the paragraphs on page 184.**

    1 a present tense factual conditional

    . . . .

    2 a past tense factual conditional

    . . . .

    3 a predictive conditional

    . . . .

---

4 **Choose an ending (a–f) for each beginning (1–6). Choose the correct verb.**

    1 If there <u>is/was</u> a lot to do, (. . .)
    2 If the students <u>come/came</u> to us, (. . .)
    3 If the test <u>is/will be</u> difficult, (. . .)
    4 If there <u>is/was</u> a lot to carry, (. . .)
    5 If you <u>don't/didn't</u> want to study, (. . .)
    6 If it <u>is/was</u> cold and wet, (. . .)

    a she won't do well.
    b we can't make you do it.
    c she goes by bus.
    d we can usually help them.
    e we ask the porter to help us.
    f everyone helped.

Unreal conditionals

Hypothetical conditionals

We use a hypothetical conditional to express a distant and unlikely connection between one imaginary event (*if* + past tense) and another imaginary event (*would*). It is also called the 'second conditional'.

    1 *If I got the job, I'd move to London.* • *If you lived closer, we'd visit you more often.*

The past subjunctive (*were*) is also used in a hypothetical conditional: *If I were you, I'd go.*

The most common modal in the main clause is *would*, but we also use other modals such as *could* and *might* .

    2 *If you came in the summer, you could stay with us and you might even get your own room.*

We don't usually put *would* in the *if*-clause unless we are using it to express a desired outcome (3).

    3 *If he would only behave himself, I'd take him with me.* • *If it would stop raining, we'd go.*

Counterfactual conditionals

We use a counterfactual conditional to express an imaginary connection between one event that never happened (*if* + past perfect) and another event that also never happened (*would have* + past participle). It is also called the 'third conditional'.

    4 *He didn't call me. I didn't help him.* → *If he had called me, I would have helped him.*

The most common modal in the main clause is *would have*, but we also use other modals such as *might have* and *could have*.

    5 *If she had asked us, we might have known how to fix it, or we could have tried at least.*

The contracted form *you'd* can be *you had* in the *if*-clause or *you would* in the main clause.

    6 *If you'd seen him, you'd have laughed.* (= If you had seen him, you would have laughed) •
    We'd have been really disappointed if they'd lost. (= We would have … if they had)

---

5 **Find an example of each of the following in the paragraphs on page 184.**

    1 a hypothetical conditional

    ....

    2 a counterfactual conditional

    ....

---

6 **Complete each sentence with an unreal conditional using information from the sentences above it.**

Example: I don't have extra pens. I won't give you one. →
      If I had extra pens, I would give you one.

1 I don't know Jason's phone number. I can't tell him what happened.
    If ....

2 She didn't prepare for the test. She didn't pass.
    If ....

3 You didn't warn us about the bad weather. I didn't bring a raincoat.
    If ....

4 I'm not in your situation. I'll start looking for another job.
    If ....

7 **Choose one of these verbs for each space in this text (about saving money for retirement).**

£31 per month

£552 per month

decided	were	would contribute	would start
started	had started	would cost	would have contributed
wanted	could do	would end up	could have paid

How many times have you heard, 'If I (1) .... you, I
(2) .... saving now for retirement.'? If you (3) ....
to have £100,000 at age 65, you (4) .... it for as little as £31 per month.
The earlier you start, the lower your monthly payments will be and the lower your total payment
(the amount you contribute) will be.

Look at Sandra. She's 24 now. Beginning next year, if she (5) ....
investing £31 every month, she (6) .... only £14,880 in total over forty
years. So, she'd invest less than £15,000 in total and receive £100,000 from her investment.

Now look at David. He's 55. If he (7) .... investing at 30, he
(8) .... only £46 every month and (9) .... £19,320.
But if he (10) .... to start investing now, it (11) ....
£552 every month and he (12) .... paying a total of £66,240. Doesn't it
make sense to start early?

8 **Editing. Correct the mistakes in the use of conditionals in this text.**

My mother keeps trying to give me a big old armchair that used to belong to my grandparents.
                                                                              sat
I remember that, when I was a child, if my grandfather sit in that chair after dinner, he

always fall asleep. He snored too. If his feet are near the fire, his slippers start to smoke and my

grandmother has to rush over and wake him up. I have also noticed recently that if my father sit

in that chair, he immediately go to sleep and start snoring. My mother get really annoyed if that

happen. It's like a chair with a curse. I am worried that if I take the chair, the same thing happen

to me. I don't have this dilemma if my older brother didn't move away two years ago. If he stays,

he is given the chair first and I am not faced with the problem. But it is a really nice-looking chair

and maybe I could make room for it. If I move a small table, the chair fit in my living room next

to the fire. Do I really have a problem if I settle into its comfortable embrace after dinner and give

in to its seductive charms? But who wake me up if my slippers catch fire?

Mixed conditionals

Mixed real conditionals

In factual conditionals, we usually use the same tense in both clauses (1), but we sometimes use a mixture of past and present tenses in the clauses (2).

    1 *If it **snowed** heavily, we **didn't go** to school. • If she **works** late, I **wait** for her.*

    2 *If you **saw** the film, you **know** how it ends. • If they **don't understand** what to do, they probably **weren't listening** earlier.*

Some factual conditionals are used to describe habits in the past with *would* (*'d*). It has the same meaning as *used to*. It makes the sentence look like a hypothetical conditional, but it isn't.

    3 *When we were kids, if it **rained** a lot, we**'d stay** indoors. But if it **was** sunny, we**'d** often **go** down to the lake.*

In predictive conditionals, we usually use the present simple in the *if*-clause (4), but we can also use the past simple (5) or present perfect (6) .

    4 *If we **don't eat** now, we**'ll get** hungry later during the concert.*

    5 *If you **studied** for the test, you **won't have** any problems.*

    6 *If they**'ve finished** already, we**'ll give** them something else to do.*

When we use predictive conditionals to express a preference, we can include *would* with verbs of 'liking' or 'not liking' in the main clause (7). We can also use *would rather* plus the base form of a verb when we express a preference between alternatives which have been suggested (8).

    7 *If it **isn't** too late, we**'d like** to watch the news on TV.*

    8 *If it**'s** OK with you, I**'d rather stay** here. (You suggested going somewhere else.)*

Mixed unreal conditionals

In hypothetical conditionals, instead of connecting an imaginary event to a possible present or future event using *would* (9), we can connect it to a possible past event with *would have* (10).

    9 *If we **were** rich, we **would offer** to help those poor people who are suffering.*

    10 *If we **were** rich, we **would have offered** to help those poor people who were suffering.*

In counterfactual conditionals, instead of connecting an imaginary past event to another past event using *would have* (11), we can connect it to a present event or situation using *would* (12).

    11 *If your parents **hadn't met**, you **wouldn't have been born**.*

    12 *If your parents **hadn't met**, you **wouldn't be sitting** here now.*

9 **Add *he* or *he'd* and the following words to this extract from the poem *The Rum Tum Tugger* by T. S. Eliot.**

chase   have   prefer   rather   wants

The Rum Tum Tugger is a Curious Cat.
If you offer him pheasant, (1) .... would .... have grouse.
If you put him in a house, (2) .... would much .... a flat,
If you put him in a flat, then (3) .... rather .... a house.
If you set him on a mouse, then (4) .... only .... a rat,
If you set him on a rat, then (5) .... rather .... a mouse.
Yes, the Rum Tum Tugger is a Curious Cat.

Real conditionals 185   Unreal conditionals 186   *Would* for habitual actions in the past 33

Order and punctuation in conditionals

We can put the *if*-clause before or after the main clause (1). When we put the *if*-clause first, it's clearer to separate the two clauses with a comma (2).

1 ***If you feel dizzy**, you shouldn't go to work.* • *You shouldn't go to work **if you feel dizzy**.*
2 *If I had some eggs, I could make a cake.* ~ *If I go and get some eggs, will you make one?*

We can also emphasize the fact that the main clause is a consequence of the *if*-clause by putting *then* at the beginning of the main clause.

3 *The bus service is limited. If you hire a car, **then** you'll be able to go wherever you choose.* •
*If the key isn't in the drawer, **then** Cathy must have taken it.*

Note that we don't use *so* in this way. (NOT *If it isn't there, so Cathy must have taken it.*)

When we add an *if*-clause after a main clause as an additional comment, we can use a comma to show that the *if*-clause is separate.

4 *I'd like to get a ticket, if they still have some.* • *Kate always goes to work, even if she feels bad.*

10 Add the word *if* four times to the following description. Put in the missing full stops and commas.

A number of idioms have come from the game of cricket something is described as *not cricket* it

means that it is not fair or honourable someone is *on a sticky wicket* they are in a difficult situation

this is because balls do not bounce very well the ground near the wicket is sticky (wet and muddy) it

is said that someone had *a good innings* it means they had a long life or career.

11 Choose one verb from each pair to complete the clauses below. Add the completed clauses to the sentences (1–8), with appropriate punctuation.

completes	*don't watch*	*isn't*		✓*have paid*	*take*
has completed	*didn't watch*	*wasn't*		*are paying*	*took*
didn't eat	*will stay*	*would arrive*		*wouldn't be*	
hadn't eaten	*would stay*	*would have arrived*		*wouldn't have been*	

Example: if you ..... have paid ..... the men already

if I .... so much at lunch   if Sarah .... all her work already

if it .... going to be a problem   I .... so tired now

if you .... television as a child   we .... in bed until noon

if they .... the test earlier today   it .... by now, I'm sure

Example: ..... If you have paid the men already, ... they probably won't come back to work after lunch.

1 .... they won't get the results until tomorrow.

2 .... I'd like to leave my bike in the hallway tonight.

3 If William sent the letter last week ....

4 If it was a terribly cold day outside ....

5 If the neighbour's dog hadn't started barking at 4 a.m. ....

6 I wouldn't feel so full now ....

7 .... we can let her leave early today.

8 .... you probably won't know why some of these people
from old TV programmes are famous.

Even if 192 *Then and so* 214

The uses of conditionals

12 Write the numbers of appropriate examples in the spaces.

Factual conditionals: *What happens if ... ? What happened if ... ?*

We use factual conditionals to describe typical patterns in the present ☐ or the past ☐ .
1 *What happens if there's a lot of demand? If demand increases, prices usually go up.*
2 *What happened if there was bad weather? If it was really bad, crops failed and people starved.*

We can use factual conditionals to express rules ☐ , habits ☐ and correlations, such as scientific observations ☐ . We can also use them with imperative forms in the main clause when we are explaining how to do something ☐ .
3 *If people earn more, they spend more. • If the paper turns red, the solution is acid.*
4 *If it was a nice Sunday morning, we always walked to church.*
5 *If the ball touches the line, it's in, not out.*
6 *If you need customer service, press 1. If you want to place an order, press 2.*

Predictive conditionals: *What will happen if ... ?*

We use predictive conditionals to describe possibilities.
7 *What will happen if the situation gets worse? If things get worse, we'll leave the country.*

We can use predictive conditionals for plans ☐ and predictions ☐ . We can also use them with questions in the main clause to ask about future events ☐ or to make requests ☐ .
8 *If we have time later, we'll go to the theatre and get tickets for the concert.*
9 *If Williams is mentally ready, she'll win easily.*
10 *If you have a moment, will you check this for me?*
11 *If the camps are closed, where will these people go?*

Hypothetical conditionals: *What would happen if ... ?*

We use hypothetical conditionals to describe imaginary or fictional situations.
12 *What would happen if a volcano erupted underneath the ocean? If a volcano erupted underneath the ocean, there would be a huge tidal wave.*

We can use hypothetical conditionals to talk about completely imaginary situations ☐ , or to describe the potential outcomes of a course of action ☐ . We can also use them when we want to express willingness to do something, despite lack of ability ☐ .
13 *If I were feeling better, I would help you move your boxes.*
14 *If England was a communist country, there wouldn't be a queen.*
15 *If they agreed to make classes smaller, we could give each student more attention.*

Counterfactual conditionals: *What would have happened if ... ?*

We use counterfactual conditionals to imagine past events happening in a different way and having different outcomes.
16 *What would have happened if she hadn't said 'Yes'? • If she had said 'No', I would have been devastated.*

We can use counterfactual conditionals when we express regret ☐ or assign blame ☐ .
17 *If I had told her that I loved her more often, she might not have left me.*
18 *If you had listened to his advice, we wouldn't have lost all our money.*

Factual and predictive conditionals 185   Hypothetical and counterfactual conditionals 186

13 Each of these questions can be answered by one of the example sentences (1–18) on page 190. Decide which type of conditional each answer will be and choose the most appropriate sentence.

Example: Can you remember your childhood? What happened if the weather was nice?
(factual, 4 ....)

1 What do you think will happen if there's a Carrera-Williams final? (.........................)

2 What happens in the economy if real wages rise? (.........................)

3 What would happen if your ideas about class size were adopted? (.........................)

4 Can you remember what the rule is if the ball hits the line? (.........................)

5 What would you have felt if Helen had given a negative answer? (.........................)

6 What do I do if I want to order something? (.........................)

7 What did he actually say would happen if he didn't have the flu? (.........................)

8 What would have happened if I had paid better attention to what your father said?
(.........................)

14 Choose an ending (a–e) for each beginning (1–5) and add these verbs:

don't want   had asked   hadn't forgotten   need   was

1 If you .... for directions, (...)

2 If this .... your car, (...)

3 If I .... to order the book yet, (...)

4 If we .... the bread, (...)

5 If you .... to talk to the operator, (...)

a would you lend it to other people?

b lunch would have been much better.

c we wouldn't have got lost.

d press 3.

e can I just examine one copy?

15 In this extract from his book 'I Can't Accept Not Trying', basketball star Michael Jordan explains his approach to any task as a process of concentrating on taking one step at a time. Put these *if*-clauses back where Michael Jordan put them.

if not   if you tried as hard as you could
if it's complete   if you've done your best
if that's your goal if the only measure of success was becoming a doctor

I think I could have applied that approach to anything I might have chosen to do. It's no different from the person whose ultimate goal is to become a doctor.
(1) .... and you're getting Cs in biology then the first thing you have to do is get Bs in biology and then As. You have to perfect the first step and then move on to chemistry or physics.
Take those small steps. Otherwise you're opening yourself up to all kinds of frustration. Where would your confidence come from (2) ....?
(3) .... and didn't become a doctor, would that mean your whole life was a failure? Of course not.
All those steps are like pieces of a puzzle. They all come together to form a picture.
(4) ...., then you've reached your goal.
(5) ...., don't get down on yourself.
(6) ...., then you will have had some accomplishments along the way.

Only if, even if, unless, whether, if so, etc.

Only if, if only

We use *only if* to emphasize a special condition (1). We sometimes put the word *only* before the verb in the main clause (2). The phrase *if and only if* is a more emphatic version, meaning 'on one condition only' (3).

1 *These can be used **only if** there is an emergency.* • *He'll come **only if** he's ordered to.*
2 *My children will **only** eat a breakfast cereal **if** they've seen it on TV first.*
3 *You broke the law **if and only if** the agreement formed a legal contract.*

We can use *if only* in unreal conditionals when we express wishes (4) or regrets (5).

4 ***If only** I had an extra copy, I'd gladly give it to you.* (I wish I had an extra copy.)
5 ***If only** she had been wearing a seat belt, she could have survived the crash.*

Even if, even though

We use *even if* ('despite the possibility that') to say that a condition may exist, but it won't affect the future or possible situation described in the main clause (6). We use *even though* ('despite the fact that') to talk about the existence of a condition that won't affect the past or present situation in the main clause (7).

6 *We'll have a great time **even if** it rains.* (It may rain, but it won't stop us.) • ***Even if** British History wasn't a required subject, I'd enjoy learning about it.*
7 *We had a great time **even though** it rained.* (It rained, but it didn't stop us.) • ***Even though** Matthew never studies, he passes all the tests.*

Unless

We use *unless* to say 'except under the following circumstances' or 'except if'. It is used to draw attention to the condition as an exception and sometimes means the same as *if … not*.

8 *He won't come **unless** you ask him.* (He won't come if you don't ask him.) • ***Unless** there's a miracle, I'll have to ask for extra time to complete my report.*

Unless is more limited than *if … not*. We don't use *unless* in counterfactual conditionals (9), when there is a negative cause or reason (10) or when we begin the main clause with *then* (11).

9 ***If** we had**n't** worked so hard, we would never have finished the project on time.*
10 ***If** he did**n't** have such a big nose, he'd be handsome.* (NOT ~~Unless he had such a big nose, …~~)
11 ***If** they cannot agree on the terms of the contract, **then** a strike is inevitable.*

Whether (or not)

We can use *whether* instead of *if* when there are options (two or more possibilities) (12). We can use *whether or not* when one of the options is the negative of the other (13). We often put *or not* at the end of the clause, especially when we begin the sentence with *whether* (14).

12 ***Whether** we win or lose, we always enjoy playing.* • *I love soup, **whether** it's hot or cold.*
13 *They are going to send relief supplies **whether or not** the fighting has ended.*
14 ***Whether** it's raining **or not**, they're determined to play golf tomorrow.*
Note that we can also say: *If it's raining or not … .* (NOT ~~If or not it's raining, …~~)

If so, if not, etc.

When we want to refer back to something which has already been mentioned, we can reduce the *if*-clause. There are several ways of doing this.

15 *Some books may have missing pages. **If so**, they can be exchanged.*
16 *Rules really must be enforced. **If not**, they can easily be ignored.* (If the rules aren't enforced …)
17 *I think you should take the job. **If you do**, I'll help you get started.* (If you do take the job …)

Counterfactual conditionals 186   *Even if/though* 204   *Unreal conditionals* 186   *Whether and if* 154, 161

16 Complete each sentence in such a way that it is as similar as possible in meaning to the sentence above it.

1 We'll have to leave without your friend if she doesn't come soon.
Unless ....

2 We're going to start playing if Andy's ready or if he's not ready.
Whether ....

3 If you aren't a registered student, they won't let you take books out of the library.
They'll only ....

4 Our team played really well, but we didn't win the game.
Even ....

17 Complete each sentence with one of these words or phrases (from an article on teaching).

only if   unless   even though   if it isn't   if only   whether or not

1 The style of teaching at universities has hardly changed in the past 1,000 years ....
you count the invention of the blackboard 200 years ago.

2 Too many students leave the system thinking, '.................... I'd taken more practical courses.'

3 Colleges still rely on exams .... it is well-known that exams measure a very small part of a person's abilities.

4 Lectures are still the preferred teaching medium of professors .... they are of any real benefit to most students.

5 The system will change .... forces from the outside make it change.

6 .... a required course, then it has little chance of attracting high enrolment.

18 We can mark a condition without using an *if*-clause. Using a dictionary if necessary, put the conditional expressions from these sentences into one of the three categories below.

1 **Assuming** the information is correct, we have to reconsider our plans.

2 **Given** clear weather and good winds, the flight may arrive early.

3 **Providing (that)/provided (that)** everyone is available, the next meeting will be on Monday.

4 Start slowly; **otherwise**, you won't be able to make it to the end.

5 **Suppose** your computer crashes, how will you get your files out of it?

6 **Supposing** you won the lottery, what would you do?

7 You can keep playing your music **as long as/so long as** no-one complains.

8 **What if** I sent the file by email – could you look at it before tomorrow's meeting?

9 **With** a little help, we could make this school a much better place.

10 **Without** your advice, I wouldn't have known how to do it.

A Simple condition ('if this is the case'): (1) Assuming, ...

B Exclusive condition ('**only if** this is the case'): ....

C Exceptional condition ('**if** this is **not** the case'): ....

Tests

A Choose the word or phrase which best completes each sentence.

1 What's a miracle? Well, popcorn's a miracle if you _____ know how it's made.

a didn't   b don't   c won't   d wouldn't

2 Some of you may have already completed section one. _____, you can go on to section two.

a If so   b If you do   c If you may   d If not

3 In summer, if my dad finished work early, he _____ sometimes take us swimming.

a is   b was   c will   d would

4 If you don't mind, I _____ finish my coffee before we leave.

a would   b would have   c would like   d would rather

5 If they'd _____ Justin more time, he'd have been able to do a better job.

a give   b giving   c given   d gave

B Identify the one underlined expression (A, B, C or D) that must be changed in order to correct the sentence.

1 If I <u>were</u> late, they usually <u>made</u> me <u>stay</u> after school and I <u>had</u> to do extra homework.
    A   B   C   D

2 We <u>must</u> maintain a system of law, and <u>support</u> a police force. If we <u>don't</u>, the criminals <u>would</u>
     A   B   C   D
soon be in charge.

3 I'm not the kind of person who <u>goes</u> around <u>thinking</u> if only I <u>have</u> done this or that. I just <u>feel</u>
                                A   B   C   D
lucky.

4 Things <u>will be</u> better if I <u>will get</u> a job and <u>earn</u> some money so I <u>don't have</u> to live with my
         A   B   C   D
parents.

5 The Czech Republic's top general <u>has warned</u> staff officers <u>they will lose</u> their jobs <u>if only</u> they
                                    A   B   C
<u>don't learn</u> English, according to a story in the Daily Telegraph.
  D

C Complete this paragraph, adapted from a novel, with one suitable word in each space.

I looked at the pie sitting right there in front of me. (1) _____ I throw this pie at him, I thought to myself, he (2) _____ never love me. And then it hit me: he doesn't love me. It hit me with a shimmering clarity: that was all there was to it. It (3) _____ matter (4) _____ he was crazy. It didn't matter if I (5) _____ innocent or guilty. Nothing mattered except that he didn't love me. If I (6) _____ this pie at him, he will never love me. But he doesn't love me anyway. So I can throw the pie (7) _____ I want to. I picked up the pie, thanked God for the linoleum floor, and threw it.

D **Complete each of the sentences in such a way that it is as similar as possible in meaning to the sentence above it.**

1 The party is not likely to happen because no one is willing to help.
  Unless _____

2 She didn't escape injury; she wasn't wearing a crash helmet.
  If only _____

3 I still loved her despite the fact that she could be very difficult.
  Even though _____

4 We're leaving tomorrow if you like the idea or if you don't like the idea.
  Whether _____

5 I arrived late; the traffic was so bad.
  I'm sorry, but if _____

E **Complete this text with the following clauses.**

if he loses	*if anyone asked me*	*if he doesn't really fight*	*unless he's an idiot*
if he wins	*if he does that*	*if that is the result*	*if that happens to him*

Boxing, men and women don't make a good combination. (1) _____, I would say that there are three reasons why a man should never get into a boxing match with a woman. The first is that, (2) _____, people will say that he beat up a woman.
(3) _____, he must be a bully. The second is that,
(4) _____, they will say he was beaten up by a woman.
(5) _____, he must be very weak. The only other possible outcome is a draw.
(6) _____, they will say that he must have been only pretending to fight and not really using his physical strength. (7) _____, he must be a cheat and someone who cannot be trusted. Given these three good reasons, a man,
(8) _____, must realize that he should never get into a boxing match with a woman. A woman already knows that boxing is a stupid, primitive activity. She doesn't need other reasons.

16 Adverbial clauses

Adverbial clauses usually begin with conjunctions such as *although*, *because* or *when*. The conjunction shows the relationship between the adverbial clause and the rest of the sentence. (***Although the sun's shining***, *it's freezing outside this morning. I'm not going out **because it's so cold**.)

We can use adverbial clauses (*I might go out **when it gets warmer***) to provide additional information about an action or situation in a way that is similar to adverbs (*I might go out **later***) and prepositional phrases (*I might go out **in the afternoon***).

1 Read through the following text and find one adverbial clause in each paragraph.

A   After her husband passed away, Emily Armstrong continued to take care of the special garden he had created in front of their small house. She imagined that Harry was 'up there' and looking down from time to time, so she tried to take good care of his proud creation.

B   Before he began his career with the national weather service, Harry had studied geography and art. Although he'd had to give up his artistic ambitions, Harry still managed to find ways to be creative in his spare time. He had designed and created something unique in their front garden.

C   It wasn't a garden in the usual sense. There were no plants. Emily had tried to put in some flowers around the edges, but they always died. Her neighbour, Mrs Blair, said it was probably because there was all that cement in the soil. Harry hadn't known, when he was mixing the cement, sand and water, then pouring it out into the wooden frame, that his concrete map would end up as the only thing in the garden, apart from the weeds that grew in small cracks in the river valleys.

D   When there was a spell of warm summer weather, the weeds would spread out from the cracks, especially in the south around the London area.

Before Emily could get to them, they would almost be in Wales, a wild patch of green in the pale grey expanse of the rest of the country.

E   The busiest time was autumn, when Emily had to go out and sweep the whole country every morning. If it wasn't wet, she could just use a brush to push the leaves down through England and sweep them away in the general direction of France. When it rained a lot, she would stand inside, watching the leaves pile up in a soggy mess over most of Scotland.

F   Even though it wasn't really cold during most of the winter, there would occasionally be freezing days of snow and sleet, after which Harry's concrete map would be transformed into a shining sculpture of pure ice. The rough edges of Britain would change into smooth glistening lines and the country would become an abstract shape, as if it had been carved from a large flat slab of marble by an expert hand. On a cold clear December morning, Emily would look out at the sculpture in her garden with a strong sense that, at that very moment, Harry was also looking down and enjoying the scene. He had used weather to create art from geography.

2 After reading the text above, decide whether these statements are true (T) or false (F).

1 Harry Armstrong had studied art before he worked for the national weather service.	T / F
2 When Harry died, his wife created a concrete map of Britain in their front garden.	T / F
3 While he was mixing the concrete, Harry decided that his map would be the only thing in the garden.	T / F
4 Weeds grew in the cracks because the flowers Emily planted always died.	T / F
5 If the weather was dry, Emily could brush the leaves off the map.	T / F
6 When the weather was freezing in winter, the map looked like an ice sculpture.	T / F

Adverbial clauses and conjunctions

Adverbial clauses

We can use an adverbial clause (*before he left*) as part of a sentence in a way that is similar to an adverb (*earlier*) or a prepositional phrase (*at ten o'clock*).

    1 *I talked to Bill **before he left**. = I talked to Bill **earlier**. = I talked to Bill **at ten o'clock**.*

We usually put an adverbial clause after the main clause in the sentence (2). If we put an adverbial clause before the main clause, we include a comma between them (3).

    2 *You won't pass the test **if you don't study**. • We had to turn on the heating **because it was cold**.*

    3 ***If you don't study,** you won't pass the test. • **Because it was cold**, we had to turn on the heating.*

We sometimes use more than one adverbial clause in a sentence.

    4 *Don't touch the paint **before it has dried** + **because bubbles may form** + **if anything touches it**.*

Conjunctions

We use a subordinating conjunction such as *after* or *while* to connect an adverbial clause to another clause and to show how the meanings of the two clauses are related.

    5 ***After you have a rest,** you'll probably feel better. • I can't listen to music **while I'm studying**.*

Other subordinating conjunctions include: as, as if, as soon as, if, in order to, since, so, so that

When we connect an adverbial clause to another clause, we use a single conjunction (6). We don't use an adverbial clause as a separate sentence (7).

    6 ***Because there were no lights,** I couldn't see anything. It was dark **so I couldn't do any work**.*
      (NOT ~~Because there were no lights, so I couldn't do any work.~~)

    7 *We couldn't use our computers **because there was no electricity this morning**.*
      (NOT ~~We couldn't use our computers. Because there was no electricity this morning.~~)

We can use some words, such as *after*, *before* and *than*, as conjunctions with adverbial clauses or as prepositions with noun phrases (8). After conjunctions, we use subject pronouns (*we, they*) plus verbs (9). After prepositions, we use object pronouns (*us, them*) (10).

    8 *I'll talk to you **after I get out of my next meeting**. = I'll talk to you **after the meeting**.*

    9 *Tony had arrived **before we got there**. • We had more money **than they had**.*

    10 *Tony had arrived **before us**. • We had more money **than them**.*

Some conjunctions we use with adverbial clauses (*because, although, while*) have similar meanings to prepositions used with noun phrases (*because of, despite, during*).

    11 *There were delays **because** the weather was bad. = There were delays **because of** bad weather.*

    12 ***Although** she's old, Agnes still plays tennis. = **Despite** her age, Agnes still plays tennis.*

    13 *He got injured **while** we were playing. = He got injured **during** the game.*

---

3 Find adverbial clauses in the text on page 196 with meanings similar to these phrases.

    1 After her husband's death: ....

    2 Because of the cement: ....

    3 During warm summer weather: ....

    4 Despite the usually mild winter weather: ....

    5 Like a carving: ....

Time clauses with *when, while, as*

We can use *when* at the beginning of an adverbial clause describing a period of time (1) or a point in time (2).

    1 **When I was young,** *we didn't watch TV.* • *Most people don't have cars* **when they're students.**
    2 **When we heard the news,** *we were delighted.* • *I'll check my email* **when I get to work.**

Note that we don't use *will* in the *when*-clause. (NOT *I'll check my email when I will get to work.*)

We also use clauses beginning with *when* to describe something that happens soon after something else in another clause (3) or that interrupts something in another clause (4). We can use *when* like *if* in a factual conditional to talk about 'every time' something happens (5).

    3 *We had just reached the shelter* **when the rain started pouring down.**
    4 *I was sleeping like a baby* **when the alarm went off.**
    5 **When demand increases,** *prices rise.* • *The roof used to leak* **when we had heavy rain.**

We can use a clause with *while* ('during the period that') or *when* to describe a period of time with another clause to describe what happens at some point in that period of time (6). We often use *while* to connect clauses in which two things happen at the same time for the whole period of time (7).

    6 **While / When you were out,** *your mother called.* • *I fell asleep* **while/when I was reading.**
    7 *There was nowhere to park, so I just drove round in the car* **while Tim was in the bank.**

We can use *as* like *when* and *while* for a period of time during which something happens (8). We can use *as* or *just as* (not *while*) to focus on the precise moment that something happens (9). We also use *as* to show a connection between one type of change over time and another (10).

    8 **As / When / While I was getting ready to leave,** *I heard that my flight had been cancelled.*
    9 **As I walked out of the hotel,** *a gust of wind blew my hat off. It happened* **just as I stepped outside.**
    10 **As I get older,** *I care less about what other people think.* (NOT *While I get older, I care less …*)

---

4 Complete each sentence in such a way that it is as similar as possible in meaning to the sentence above it.

1 I watched Maurice drive by in his new car while I was standing at the bus stop in the rain.
When ....

2 You'll know that the fruit is getting ripe when the skin starts to turn yellow.
As ....

3 We shouldn't talk about anything to do with work during lunch.
While ....

4 I was getting out of the shower when the phone rang in the other room.
Just as ....

5 Using information from the text on page 196, draw a circle round the appropriate conjunction(s) in the following sentences. More than one conjunction may be appropriate.

1 When / While Harry started working for the national weather service, he'd given up his artistic ambitions.

2 When / While it was wet during the autumn months, Emily couldn't brush the leaves away.

3 As / While the weather got warmer, weeds would spread out from the cracks.

4 As / When / While Emily looked at the sculpture on a cold clear December morning, she had a sense that Harry was doing the same thing.

Time clauses with *after*, *before*, *until*, *since*, etc.

We use *after* ('at a point later than') in the adverbial clause when the other clause describes something that happens later (1). We use *before* ('at a point earlier than') in the adverbial clause when the other clause describes something that happens at any time earlier (2). We often use *after* with the present simple or present perfect (not *will*) for a completed action (3).

1 *After they left,* we cleaned up and went to bed. • What will you do *after you graduate?*
2 *Before he leaves,* I'll ask him about the money. They had eaten breakfast *before we got up*.
3 I'll help you *after I write / have written my report*. (NOT ~~after I will write my report~~)

We use *until* ('up to the time that') to focus on the end point or outcome of something (4). We use *since* ('from the time that') to talk about a starting point for something in another clause that happens later or that is still true (5).

4 We'll wait *until you're ready*. • Heat the wax *until it melts*. (NOT ~~Heat it before it melts.~~)
5 How long is it *since you've been there?* • I've lived here *since I was ten*. (NOT ~~after I was ten~~)
We use the present perfect or past simple (not present simple) after *since* (NOT ~~since I'm ten~~).

We can use *once* to introduce a clause that describes a starting point for another action or situation. We often use *once* like *after* with the present simple or present perfect in a clause describing something as completed.

6 *Once you've seen Ani,* you won't forget her. • Everyone likes it here *once they get used to it*.

When we want to say that one thing happens very quickly after another, we can use *as soon as* and *immediately* to introduce the clause with the first action (7). Phrases such as *the instant/minute/ moment/second (that)* are used in the same way (8).

7 I came *as soon as I heard the news*. • *Immediately I saw him,* I recognized his face.
8 There are some students who rush out of the room *the minute (that) class ends*.

6 **Using a dictionary if necessary, complete these descriptions with the following words.**

blender   postscript   prediction   skewer   after   before   until   while

1 A .... is a statement about an event .... it happens.
2 A .... is a wooden or metal stick pushed through pieces of meat or vegetables to hold them .... they are cooking.
3 A .... is extra information added .... a letter or story is complete.
4 A .... is a machine for chopping or mixing bits of food .... they become a liquid.

7 **Complete these sentences with *have ('ve) been* or *will ('ll) be*.**

1 Where will the refugees go after the camps .... closed?
2 I'm sorry about the delay, but I .... back as soon as I have checked this.
3 My back still hurts and it will soon be two weeks since I .... at work.
4 I'm sure we .... in London in August before we go to the Edinburgh Festival, so we can visit your new house then.
5 The moment we hear that the airport is open, relief supplies .... loaded on to the waiting aircraft.
6 New students should not register for classes until they .... given their registration numbers.
7 Once you .... here for a few weeks, you won't want to leave.
8 The children .... hungry when they come back from swimming this morning.

Manner clauses with *as*, *as if*, *as though*, etc.

We can use manner clauses beginning with *as* ('in the form or way that') (1) and *just as* ('in exactly the form or way that') (2) when we are describing how something was or how something was done.

   1 *The film depicts life **as it was in 1900**. • Complete each exercise **as I showed you**.*
   2 *I wrote the note **just as you told me to**. • Everything happened **just as my mother had predicted**.*

We use *as if* and *as though* with the same meaning in manner clauses after verbs such as *look, seem, sound, taste*, etc. (3). We can also use *as if/though* after verbs such as *act, behave* and *talk* when we are describing behaviour (4).

   3 *Can I help you? You look **as if you're lost**. • He sounds **as though he might be getting a cold**.*
   4 *She always tries to act **as if she's my boss**. • They talked about it **as though it was worthless**.*
Subjunctive *were* is sometimes used after *as if/though*: *He treats me as if I were a child.*

In informal situations, *like* is sometimes used instead of *as* or *as if*.

   5 *No one will ever love you **like** I do. • It feels **like** winter has suddenly arrived.*
Note that *like* is often used as a preposition: *It feels like winter.* (NOT *It feels as winter.*)

We use *as ... as* ('in the same way that') to say that two actions or situations are similar or different in some way (6). Between the first and second *as* we can put adjectives and adverbs (7) or quantifiers such as *many* and *much* (8).

   6 *Is Max still funny in the same way that he used to be?* → *Is Max still **as funny as he used to be**?*
   7 *The weather isn't **as hot as** it was last year. • We didn't play **as well as** we did against France.*
   8 *Were there **as many** problems **as** you anticipated? • It didn't cost **as much as** he said.*
We sometimes form the negative with *not so ... as*: *Ben is not so naïve as you think.*

8 **Choose the best answer (a–d) for each question (1–4) and add *as* or *as if*.**

   1 Did she seem afraid? (   )
   2 Had she changed much? (   )
   3 Did she fit in well? (   )
   4 Did she write it correctly? (   )

   a No, she was just .... you had described her.
   b Yes, she did it .... she was supposed to.
   c Yes, she looked .... she had seen a ghost.
   d Not really, because she acted .... she was better than us.

9 **Add one of these clauses, introduced by *as though*, *just as* or *as . . . as*, to the following sentences. Make any other necessary changes.**

   ✓everyone has been saying   it really is   the guidebook had described it
   I remembered it   it was made yesterday   they have done
   nothing had happened

Example: Is the new Italian restaurant/good ..... as everyone has been saying ...... ?
                               ^as
   1 No one talked about it. They all behaved ....
   2 I went to see my old school and it hadn't changed. It was still ....
      ....
   3 This tea is terrible. It tastes ....
   4 When you emulate someone successful, you try to do well ....
   5 We found the little church hidden in the forest, ...
   6 If you underestimate the cost of something, you think it isn't much ....
      ....

Reason clauses with *because*, *as*, *since*, etc.

We use *because* at the beginning of a clause to give a reason or explanation for something (1) or to support a statement in an earlier clause (2).

    1 *Because there had been an accident,* we all arrived late. • I didn't eat *because I wasn't hungry*.

    2 He says he didn't drive through a red light, but he's lying, *because I saw him do it*.

We sometimes use *as* or *since* instead of *because* in reason clauses (3). We can use *as* or *while* to talk about time and reason together ('while and because') (4). We can use *since* to talk about a starting point and a reason together ('from that time and because') (5).

    3 *As it was late, we decided to stop working.* • *Since she knew Latin,* I asked her to translate it.

    4 *As / While we're on the subject of money,* I'd like to ask about next year's budget.

    5 *Since his wife left him,* he's been depressed. • *Since it's been snowing,* we've stayed indoors.

We can use *now (that)* like *since* ('from that time and because') to introduce a clause explaining a present situation. We usually use the present simple or present perfect after *now (that)*.

    6 *Now (that) we're married,* we never go out. • I enjoy opera *now (that) I've learned more about it*.

In formal situations, other conjunctions such as *for* (7) and *in that* (8) are sometimes used instead of *because* to add a reason or explanation for a preceding statement.

    7 It would be wise to save some of the money, *for there may be unexpected expenses later*.

    8 We definitely have a problem *in that there are more students than we have room for*.

10 Complete each sentence in such a way that it is as similar as possible in meaning to the pair of sentences above it.

1 All the banks will be closed on Monday. It's a holiday.
    As ....

2 She has had to use crutches. She had an operation on her foot.
    Since ....

3 We're all together today. We should decide on a date for the Christmas party.
    While ....

4 I wonder what he'll do next. He has finished his exams.
    Now that ....

11 Match a sentence from the first group (1–4) with one from the second group (a–d) with a similar meaning and add *as if* or *because*.

Example: I'd love to go out more, but I haven't had much free time lately. (e)

1 It's more expensive to eat in a restaurant, but I don't like to cook. ( )

2 If I wanted to avoid doing something, I pretended to be ill. ( )

3 The cost of meat is higher now, but I don't eat it, so my food bill hasn't increased. ( )

4 No matter what the discussion is about, no one ever pays attention to my suggestions. ( )

a .... I'm a vegetarian, I'm spending less than other people these days.

b I acted .... I wasn't feeling well when I didn't want to do things.

c I spend more money on meals .... I don't make them myself at home.

d They always treat me .... I have nothing useful to say.

e I haven't been to a film or a play in ages ...... because ...... I've been busy at work.

Purpose clauses with *so that*, *in order that*, *in order to*, etc.

We use purpose clauses to describe goals or the intended outcomes of actions. We can use *so that* (1) or *in order that* (2) to introduce purpose clauses, often with modals such as *can* (after a clause with a present tense) or *could* (after a past tense). We usually use *so* without *that* in informal situations (3).

   1 *I'm going early* **so that I can find a good seat.** • *I'll take my umbrella* **so that I won't get wet.**
   2 *Her father had worked hard for many years* **in order that they could have a better life.**
   3 *I'm going early* **so I don't have to stand in a queue.** (NOT *in order I don't have to stand*)

We often express purpose with a simple infinitive (*to clean*) (4). In formal situations, we also use the phrases *in order to* (5) or *in order not to* (6). Purpose clauses are sometimes used at the beginning of sentences (7).

   4 *Just use soap and water* **to clean it.** • *I think the boy fell when he was running* **to catch the bus.**
   5 *They recommend using bleach* **in order to clean it thoroughly.** • *You must fight* **in order to win.**
   6 *I'll clean the grill outside* **in order not to make a mess in here.** (NOT *in order to not make*)
   7 **In order to/To prevent vandalism,** *all doors and windows must be locked securely.*

We sometimes form purpose clauses with *so as to* and *so as not to*.

   8 *It's designed that way* **so as to** *let in more light.* • *I'll put it near the door* **so as not to** *forget it.*

When we want to include a subject before the infinitive verb, we can begin a purpose clause with *in order for* and a noun phrase (9) or a pronoun (10).

   9 **In order for the team to succeed,** *they must work together.* (NOT *In order to succeed the team* ...)
   10 **In order for you to win,** *we will need to pray for a miracle.* (NOT *In order you to win* ...)

12 Complete each sentence in such a way that is as similar as possible in meaning to the sentence(s) above it.

1 You should plan to leave early tomorrow. You'll avoid traffic jams on the way to the airport.
   In order to ....

2 We had to account for every penny we spent so that no money would be wasted.
   In order that ....

3 There must be a good source of light or plants won't grow indoors.
   In order for ....

4 We waited a few minutes until the rain stopped. We didn't want to get wet.
   So as ....

13 Correct the mistakes in the use of conjunctions in these sentences.

1 Mrs Peters slipped quietly into the room at the back that nobody would notice her.

2 I don't like it when they spray those chemicals all over the place for kill insects.

3 In order to care people about another person, they must feel connected to that person.

4 I didn't say anything about Kevin's coming in late so as to not get him in trouble.

5 A stepladder is made of two parts joined at the top in order it can stand on its own.

6 We must keep our new designs secret in order not our competitors find and copy them.

Result clauses with *so, so … that, such … that*

We use result clauses beginning with *so* to describe effects or unintended outcomes. We put result clauses after main clauses (1), often separated by a comma in formal uses (2).

1 *I'm tired* **so I'm going to bed**. · *He missed the bus this morning* **so he was late for work again**.
2 *There has been a reduction in the oil supply and increased demand*, **so prices have risen**.

In formal situations, *so that* is sometimes used instead of *so* to introduce a result clause. In a result clause, *so that* ('as a result') doesn't mean the same as *so that* ('in order that') in a purpose clause.

3 *A tree had fallen during the storm*, **so that** *the road was blocked and we couldn't go anywhere.*
(NOT ~~in order that the road was blocked~~)

We can use an adjective (4), an adverb (5) or a quantifier (*few, little, many* or *much*) (6) between *so* and *that* to form a result clause. We often leave out *that* in informal uses.

4 *It was* **so nice (that) we ate lunch outside.** · *The puppy was* **so cute (that) she picked it up.**
5 *The lecturer talked* **so fast (that) none of us could understand him.**
6 *There were* **so many people (that) we had to wait.** · *I ate* **so much (that) I could hardly move.**

We can also use a noun phrase (*nice weather*) between *such* and *that* to introduce a result clause (7). We often leave out *that* in informal situations, but not from certain fixed expressions (*in such a way that*) (8).

7 *It was* **such nice weather (that) we ate lunch outside.** · *I got* **such a shock (that) I was speechless.**
8 *Try to think about these problems* **in such a way that you don't exaggerate their importance.**

We can say: *It's so nice that …* or *It's such nice weather that …* (NOT ~~It's so nice weather that~~ …)

14 Rewrite each pair of sentences as a single sentence, using *so* in a result clause.

1 They were feeling really tired. They went to bed early last night.

....

2 I wasn't able to do the homework. I forgot to take my textbook home with me.

....

3 Marjorie is in a popular TV show. People recognize her when she's out shopping.

....

4 We had to drink bottled water. They said the tap water wasn't safe to drink.

....

15 Add one of these clauses, changed to include *so … that* or *such … that*, to each of the following sentences.

That class was early   *We had a wonderful time on holiday*
The fire spread rapidly through their cabin   *Wendy's children had bad colds this morning*
✓ *The fog was thick*   *You and I don't have much money*

Example: *The fog was so thick (that)* you couldn't see your hand in front of your face.
1 .... they couldn't save any of their belongings.
2 .... she couldn't let them go to school.
3 .... we can just throw it away carelessly.
4 .... we didn't want to come home.
5 .... everyone had trouble staying awake in it.

Contrast clauses with *although*, *though*, *even though*, etc.

We use *although* ('despite the fact that') at the beginning of a clause which contains information that contrasts in an unexpected or surprising way with information in another clause.

    1 (The sun was shining. I expected it to be warm.) ***Although the sun was shining,*** *it was cold.*
      (Jim is ill. I expect he doesn't have to go to work.) *Jim has to go to work **although he's ill**.*
We can also use *but* to express contrast, but not with *although*: *Jim is ill, but he has to go to work.*
(NOT ~~Although Jim is ill, but he has to go to work.~~)

We often use *though* instead of *although* in informal situations (2). We can use *though* (not *although*) after adjectives or adverbs moved to the beginning of the clause (3).

    2 ***Though Kate's clever,*** *she isn't doing very well at school.* • *He has to go to work **though he's ill**.*
    3 ***Though*** *the test was **difficult**, we all passed.* → ***Difficult though*** *the test was, we all passed.*
In formal situations, *as* is also used in this structure: *Difficult as the test was, we all passed.*

When we want to emphasize a contrast, we can use *even though* when we are talking about past or present situations (4) and *even if* for future or possible situations (5). We don't use *even* with *although* or as a conjunction by itself.

    4 *Bill kept playing golf **even though it was raining**.* (NOT *… ~~even although it was raining.~~*)
    5 *Bill would play golf **even if it was snowing**.* (NOT *… ~~even it was snowing.~~*)
Subjunctive *were* is sometimes used after *even if*: *He would play even if it were snowing.*

In formal situations, other conjunctions such as *whereas* (6) and *while* (7) are sometimes used to express a contrast between two clauses. The phrase *much as* is also used in contrast clauses with verbs such as *like, hate* or *want* (8).

    6 *Boys were encouraged to be adventurous **whereas girls were always told to stay clean**.*
    7 ***While no one doubts his ability,*** *his arrogant attitude has been difficult to accept.*
    8 ***Much as I like music,*** *I can't listen to opera for long.* • ***Much as I want to,*** *I can't help you.*

We can use *despite the fact that* instead of *although* to introduce a contrast clause (9). We can also use the prepositions *despite* or *in spite of* plus gerunds instead of a clause with *although* (10).

    9 ***Despite the fact that he had lots of friends,*** *he still felt really lonely sometimes.*
  10 ***Despite studying hard,*** *I failed the test.* • *She wasn't satisfied **in spite of being paid extra**.*
      (NOT ~~Despite I studied hard, I failed. She wasn't satisfied in spite of she was paid extra.~~)

16 Complete each sentence in such a way that it is as similar as possible in meaning to the sentence above it.

1 I disagree with his point of view, but I understand why he thinks that way.
   Although ....

2 Jack is still unemployed in spite of applying for about a dozen different jobs.
   Though ....

3 While most people agreed that the car was a bargain, none of them wanted to buy it.
   Even ....

4 Though it seems unlikely, the children may not want to go to the zoo on Saturday.
   Unlikely ....

5 The old people didn't have very much money, but they were really generous.
   Despite ....

     But 12 Even if/though 192 Subjunctive 167, 186 The fact that 164 Though 210 While 197–8

Reduced adverbial clauses

An adverbial clause formed with a present participle is called a reduced adverbial clause (1).
We put *not* before the present participle in the negative (2). Reduced adverbial clauses are also called participle clauses and are typically used in formal situations.

1 When he looked outside, he saw the police car. → ***Looking outside,*** *he saw the police car.*
2 Because she didn't feel very well, she sat down. → ***Not feeling very well,*** *she sat down.*

We can form reduced adverbial clauses with *having* + past participle for an earlier action, usually instead of a past perfect (3). We use *being* + past participle instead of a passive (4).

3 After he had retired, Cecil decided to travel. → ***Having retired,*** *Cecil decided to travel.*
4 I was really quite flattered at first, because I was asked to work with one of the professors.
   → *I was really quite flattered at first,* ***being asked to work with one of the professors***.

We usually only use reduced adverbial clauses when the subjects of the main clause and the adverbial clause are the same (5). We avoid using reduced adverbial clauses when the subjects are different (6).

5 Because <u>it</u> was barking loudly, <u>the dog</u> scared us. → ***Barking loudly,*** *the dog scared us.*
6 Because <u>it</u> was barking loudly, <u>we</u> were scared. (NOT ~~Barking loudly, we were scared.~~)

We can also form reduced adverbial clauses by using subordinating conjunctions such as *before* and *as if* with a present participle.

7 Before you leave, switch off all the lights. → ***Before leaving,*** *switch off all the lights.*
8 He stood there, as if he was waiting for someone. → *He stood there,* ***as if waiting for someone***.
Note that *because* is not used in this way. (NOT ~~He stood there, because waiting for someone.~~)

When we use a subordinating conjunction such as *although, though, when* or *while* with an adjective or a prepositional phrase (9), or with the past participle of a passive (10), we can leave out the subject + *be*.

9 ***Although (they are) small,*** *terriers are tough.* • *Arnold studied Greek* ***while (he was) at Oxford***.
10 ***Though (it had been) broken,*** *it still worked.* • ***When (it is) seen from space,*** *the earth is blue.*
The past participle is sometimes used without a conjunction: ***Seen from space,*** *the earth is blue.*

---

17 Add reduced versions of these adverbial clauses to the following sentences (adapted from a newspaper article about problems in London's Underground railway system).

although it manages	*as if they were trying*	*until they make sure*	✓ *while they waited*
although they were frustrated	*once it has been broken*	*since it opened*	

Example: <u>While waiting</u> in line for buses during a recent one-day train strike, London's commuters displayed remarkable patience with their struggling Underground.

1 ...., most people just shrugged and went back to their newspapers, ... to ignore this latest inconvenience.

2 .... in 1863, the Underground has grown into a sprawling network of tracks, some of which are in desperate need of repair.

3 .... to cover its operating costs from fares, the Underground never seems to have enough money for long-term investment and maintenance.

4 The government's argument is that, ... into several private companies, each of the system's smaller parts will be better able to attract new investment.

5 Opponents of the government's plan to sell parts of the Underground say that they should not be allowed to proceed .... that all existing lines are safe for passengers.

Because 201   Passives 57   Present participle or gerund? 139   Reduced relative clauses 176

Tests

A Choose the word or phrase that best completes each sentence.

1 Players may not leave the area without permission _____ the game is being played.

   a despite   b during   c much as   d while

2 Remember to wear a helmet _____ your head is protected.

   a in order that   b so as   c that   d to

3 _____ they had been waiting in line all night, I was sure they'd get tickets.

   a as though   b because of   c since   d until

4 Sylvia said it was _____ lovely weather they all went swimming.

   a as   b as if   c so   d such

5 Once you _____ into a routine, you'll find the work is quite easy.

   a are settling   b have settled   c settled   d will settle

B Identify the one underlined expression (A, B, C or D) that must be changed in order to correct the sentence.

1 They <u>didn't</u> think he <u>had</u> been <u>to visit</u> his birthplace since he <u>is</u> a small child.
   A   B   C   D

2 Some British people put a 'GB' plate on the back of their car <u>so that</u> to show <u>that</u> the car is from
                                                                  A   B

   Great Britain <u>when</u> they drive to other countries, <u>even though</u> it seems rather odd.
                 C   D

3 <u>When cooking</u> previously frozen vegetables, use about half as much time <u>as you would</u> for fresh
   A   B

   vegetables <u>because becoming</u> softer <u>after they have been kept</u> in a freezer.
              C   D

4 <u>For</u> it was late, they stopped near a stream <u>in order to</u> rest the horses and <u>so as not to</u> get lost <u>while</u>
   A   B   C   D

   riding through the forest.

5 <u>Much as</u> I liked her paintings, I couldn't act <u>as</u> she was Picasso or someone like that <u>when</u> she
   A   B   C

   clearly was a beginner, <u>though</u> very good for a beginner, of course.
                           D

C Complete this text with the following words.

after   *as*   *because*   *to*   *when* (×2)

In Britain, (1) _____ you need legal advice, you go to see a solicitor. Solicitors spend most of their time in their offices (2) _____ their work mostly involves preparing legal documents, especially those involved in buying a house. They can, (3) _____ necessary, go to court with you, but, (4) _____ taking down details of a serious legal matter, they will often contact a barrister (5) _____ represent you in court.

(6) _____ you may have seen in films or on TV, barristers wear white curly wigs and black robes in court.

D Complete each sentence in such a way that it is as similar as possible in meaning to the sentence above it.

1 It was late and I was exhausted, so I went straight to bed.
Because _____

2 There will have to be a change in his attitude or he won't continue to work here.
In order for _____

3 From the way he talked, I thought he owned the restaurant.
He talked _____

4 Finish your homework, then you can go out.
You can't _____

5 I know he's your friend, but he can't sleep here.
Even _____

6 We left half an hour earlier than necessary because we didn't want to be late.
So as _____

E Choose one word or phrase from each pair to complete the text.

although	as easy as	as if	just	as much	despite	so that	though
and so	so easy	if	just as	as much as	despite the fact	whereas	even

(1) _____ a lot has been written and said about class differences in British society, they no longer mean (2) _____ they used to. Traditionally, the upper classes were wealthy and powerful (3) _____ the lower or working classes were poor. Nowadays, some of the upper classes may still seem to behave and speak (4) _____ their social status continues to be (5) _____ it was for their aristocratic ancestors, but it is no longer based on exclusive wealth and power. Maintaining large houses with lots of servants is not (6) _____ it used to be and, strange (7) _____ it may seem, the new owners of those large houses may speak with distinctly working-class or even foreign accents. (8) _____ that their parents may have been middle or working class, many of today's wealthy Britons achieved success based on education and enterprise, not birth and inheritance.

17 Connectors and focus structures

Connectors are words such as *consequently*, *however* and *so* and phrases such as *in addition*, *in fact* and *for example* which are used to link clauses and sentences. (*The Japanese economy has been very strong and **consequently** the yen has risen in value.* ***In addition***, *the dollar has continued to show weakness. The pound,* ***however***, *has remained steady.*)

Focus structures are also used to link sentences. One type of focus structure is called fronting. In **fronting**, one part of a sentence (*I can't eat <u>asparagus</u>*) is moved to front position in order to focus attention on that part. (*I can eat broccoli and carrots. <u>Asparagus</u> I can't eat.*)

Another type of focus structure is a **cleft sentence**. In a cleft sentence, we focus attention on one part of a sentence and put the other part of the sentence in a separate clause. We can begin a cleft sentence with *it* (***It's*** *<u>asparagus</u> I can't eat*) or *what* (***What*** *I can't eat is <u>asparagus</u>*).

1 Read through this text and find one connector in each paragraph.

A ALL THOSE PEOPLE WHO say that the weather hasn't been normal recently are right. However, since there is really no such thing as normal weather, they probably mean something else. If they mean that average summer temperatures have been getting warmer, then they are certainly correct. In fact, it is not just the summer temperature, but the general average temperature of the whole world that has been steadily moving up.

B The signs are everywhere. There are small signs. For example, butterflies in North America have moved about 60 miles north of where they used to live. There are also very large signs. Huge masses of ice in mountain glaciers and the Arctic are melting. The famous snow cap on Africa's Mount Kiliminjaro has almost disappeared. Actually, ice or snow doesn't really disappear, it turns into water, flows into the ocean and causes sea levels to rise.

C Why is this happening? One answer is that it could simply be part of a natural process. After all, there have been long periods of warmth in the past. So we could just be experiencing another warming trend. This kind of answer had more supporters a few years ago. What scientists now believe is that human activity is the cause. For more than two hundred years, humans have been gradually changing the atmosphere, mainly as a result of industrial pollution. We have created an atmosphere around the earth that, like a giant glass container, lets heat from the sun through and holds it inside.

D Will temperatures and sea levels keep rising? Should we just move to higher ground and throw away our winter coats? The answer depends on where you live. If you live on the coast of Florida, the answer is a definite yes. However, if you live in northern Europe, your temperatures may soon be on the way down. All that fresh water pouring into the Atlantic will change the circulation patterns in the ocean. As a consequence, the current of air that flows towards Europe will become much cooler. According to one prediction, winter in London is going to become much more like winter in Copenhagen

2 Choose one of the following as the final sentence of each of the paragraphs (A–D) above.

1 It may be a good idea to hold on to your coat. (...)

2 It's known as the greenhouse effect. (...)

3 It's called global warming. (...)

4 As a result, small islands in the Pacific are going under. (...)

Types of connectors and focus structures

Adverbs as connectors

The most common connectors are adverbs such as *however* or *then* which we can use to link a sentence (1) or clause (2) to a preceding sentence or clause. They are also called linking words.

   1 *We wanted to rent a flat near the university.* **However,** *they were all too expensive.*

   2 *The old woman poured two cups of tea,* **then** *I asked her if she remembered my grandparents.*

Others include: actually, also, finally, instead, later, meanwhile, secondly, so, therefore

We usually put adverbs used as connectors at the front of the sentence or clause (3). The only connectors we don't use in front position are *as well* and *too*. We can use them and other connectors in end position (4). We can also use connectors in mid position, after *be* or auxiliary verbs (5) and before the main verb (6). Not all connectors can be used in all possible positions.

   3 *I've been to Morocco several times.* **Actually,** *I've just come back from there.*

   4 *I spent a few days in Casablanca. I visited Rabat and Tangier* **as well.**

   5 *Don't forget your raincoat. You are* **also** *going to need an umbrella.*

   6 *Dave and Alice arrived with steaming hot coffee. They* **also** *brought fresh rolls.*

We don't usually put a connector between a verb and its object. (NOT ~~They brought also fresh rolls.~~)

Phrases as connectors

We use some prepositional phrases as connectors, usually in front position (7), but sometimes in mid (8) or end position (9). Not all prepositional phrases used as connectors can be put in all possible positions. We usually separate phrases used as connectors with commas.

   7 *The doctor will see you soon.* **In the meantime,** *could you please complete these forms?*

   8 *We have your application, but it's incomplete. You didn't,* **for example,** *include a photograph.*

   9 *One man lied about having a degree in English. He had never been to university,* **in fact.**

Others include: as a result, for a start, in addition, in conclusion, in other words, on the other hand

We can also use infinitive phrases such as *to begin with* as connectors, usually in front position.

   10 *I had a summer job in a factory, but I didn't enjoy it.* **To begin with,** *I had to start at six, which meant I was always tired.*

Others include: to conclude, to start with, to summarize, to sum up

Focus structures

We can use focus structures to link sentences. We can move one part of a sentence to front position to link that sentence more closely to the preceding sentence. This is called fronting.

   11 *I'd rather visit Paris than London these days.* (I don't like London as much as I used to.)

      → *London I don't like as much as I used to.*

We can also use focus structures to emphasize one part of a sentence, usually when we are making a contrast with, or adding to, information in a preceding sentence. Sentences like this, which begin with *it* (12) or *what* (13), are called cleft sentences.

   12 I didn't eat the strawberries. (Jackie ate them.) → **It** was *Jackie* who ate them.

   13 We didn't like the way he spoke. (We really didn't like his rude behaviour.) → **What** *we really didn't like was his rude behaviour.*

---

3 **Find examples of the following in the text on page 208:**

   1 a sentence with a connector in mid position: ....

   2 a focus structure beginning with *what*: ....

Connectors, prepositions and conjunctions

Connectors or prepositions?

Some connectors (*as a result, in addition*) are similar to complex prepositions (*as a result of, in addition to*). Instead of a connector (1), we sometimes use a complex preposition plus a noun phrase (2) or a pronoun (3) at the beginning of a sentence.

1 *As a result*, sea levels are rising. *In addition*, they discussed the situation in the Pacific.
2 *As a result of these changes*, sea levels are rising. (NOT *As a result of sea levels are rising.*)
3 *In addition to that*, they discussed the situation in the Pacific. (NOT *In addition that*, ...)

Other complex prepositions include: as an example of, in comparison to/with, in contrast to

We can also use a complex preposition plus a noun phrase or pronoun (4), or a similar connector (5), in end position.

4 *Malcolm went to Cambridge. Sarah chose Oxford instead of Cambridge.*
5 *He went to Cambridge. She chose Oxford instead.* (NOT ... *Oxford instead Cambridge.*)

Connectors or conjunctions?

We can use connectors such as *also* and *however* in a way that is similar to the coordinating conjunctions *and* and *but*. We use the connectors when we want to emphasize the type of connection, such as adding (6) or contrasting (7).

6 *Suzy's doing great these days. She's living in the country. She also has a new boyfriend.* •
   She's living in the country and she has a new boyfriend.
7 *I sometimes drink coffee in a restaurant. However, I prefer tea most of the time.* •
   I sometimes drink coffee in a restaurant, but I prefer tea most of the time.

We sometimes use coordinating conjunctions before connectors in the same clause when we want to emphasize the type of relationship, such as result (8) or contrast (9), between the clauses.

8 *She didn't sign the contract and consequently it isn't legal.* (NOT *consequently and*)
9 *They were trapped for two days, but nevertheless they survived.* (NOT *nevertheless but*)

We sometimes reduce clauses after coordinating conjunctions, but not after connectors.

10 *The show was supposed to start early, but didn't.* (NOT ... *however didn't.*)

Although connectors and conjunctions can both link clauses inside sentences, we usually use conjunctions to join clauses within the same sentence (11) and connectors to link sentences (12).

11 *You can stay here and help me or you can go inside, but you can't just sit watching TV.*
12 *We were working outside all day. Meanwhile, he was sitting inside watching TV.*

We can use *so* and *though* as connectors or as subordinating conjunctions. When used as conjunctions, *so* and *though* introduce an adverbial clause as part of a sentence (13). When used as connectors, they link one sentence to another (14).

13 *It was an interesting offer, though I couldn't accept it, so I said nothing.*
14 *I'm sure it was her car outside. So she must have been at home.* • *We really liked their new flat. It was lovely. It was very expensive, though.*

---

4 **Using information from the text on page 208, complete these sentences with connectors, prepositions or conjunctions.**

1 .... industrial pollution, the atmosphere has gradually changed.

2 .... small changes such as butterflies moving north, there are large changes such as glaciers melting .... flowing into the ocean. Sea levels are rising ....

Adverbial clauses 197 Complex prepositions 125 Coordinating and subordinating conjunctions 12

5 Choose one phrase from each pair to complete these sentences from a history text.

in addition	*in contrast*	*for example*	*as a result*
in addition to	*in contrast to*	*as an example of*	*as a result of*

The Spanish-American war was fought between Spain and the United States in 1898.
There were several reasons for US involvement. (1) . . . . , American investors were losing
money because of Spanish policies in Cuba. (2) . . . . the Spanish forces, the US navy was
very modern and powerful. (3) . . . . the war, Cuba became independent from Spain.
(4) . . . . , the United States gained control of Puerto Rico.

6 Complete this description with these words.

also   and   as a result   but   however   so

The Titanic was considered to be the fastest and most modern passenger ship of its day. It was
(1) . . . . believed to be unsinkable. During its first voyage in 1912, (2) . . . . ,
the ship hit an iceberg (3) . . . . sank. While the ship was slowly sinking, there was
time for the passengers to escape, (4) . . . . there were not enough lifeboats,
(5) . . . . hundreds of people drowned in the disaster. (6) . . . . , tough new
laws were introduced to make ships much safer.

7 Choose a sentence or clause (a–d) to follow each sentence or clause (1–4) and add these words.

and   but   instead   or   so (×2)   though

1 We loved playing in the snow. (. . .)
2 I liked the car . . . . my wife loved it. (. . .)
3 I didn't think the test was long
  . . . . difficult, (. . .)
4 There wasn't a flight available. (. . .)

a . . . . some of the students did.
b . . . . we went by train
  . . . .
c . . . . we bought it.
d It was really cold, ...

8 Editing. Correct the mistakes in the use of connectors in this text.

My friend Kazuko sometimes helps me with my English writing. She was born in Japan, ~~however,~~ but
she spent part of her childhood in America consequently her English is really good. She isn't like an
American, although. Americans seem to be very direct, in contrast this Kazuko is very indirect. As
example, she never tells me that I have made a mistake. Instead that, she points to a line and takes a
deep breath. She makes also a small 'tsss' sound. Alternatively, or she may say some part needs 'special
attention'. For her, nothing is ever wrong; it is simply 'not finished yet'. As a result this, I have not only
learned English from her, but I have also learned how to be helpful and patient. Nevertheless that, I
think that she will have to take a few deep breaths when she reads this. In other word, it is not
finished yet.

Adding and contrasting connectors

Adding connectors: *also, as well, too,* etc.

When we want to show that we are adding information, we can use *also* in front (1) or mid position (2), but not usually in end position. We use *as well* or *too* in end position (3).

1 *You mustn't forget to include the postcode.* **Also**, *make sure you provide a return address.*
2 *Carl is good at French. He's* **also** *studying French cooking. I think he* **also** *speaks Italian.*
3 *He speaks a little Spanish* **as well/too.** (NOT ~~He speaks a little Spanish also.~~)

In formal situations, we can use other connectors, typically in front position, to show that we are adding to (4) or supporting (5) ideas presented earlier.

4 *We are sending food and water.* **In addition**, *they will need things like tents and blankets.*
5 *If you're ready, you should go ahead without me.* **Besides**, *I'd rather stay at home tonight.*

Others used formally include: furthermore, indeed, likewise, moreover, similarly

We can use *in other words* (6) and *that is (to say)* (7) in front position when we want to show that information is being stated in another way.

6 *It's described as downsizing.* **In other words**, *people are losing their jobs.*
7 *He told me he wanted to join the army.* **That is (to say)**, *he wanted to wear a uniform and carry a gun.*

We can use connectors such as *in particular* (8), or *for example* and *for instance* (9), in front, mid and end positions when we want to show that we are adding more specific information.

8 *I enjoyed the book.* **In particular**, *I liked the details of life in Japan as it used to be.*
9 *William doesn't help with the housework. He has,* **for example**, *never washed the dishes.* • *This study of smoking habits is incomplete. There's no mention of teenagers,* **for instance**.

Contrasting connectors: *however, instead,* etc.

We can use *however* and *instead* when we want to show that we are creating a contrast and introducing information which is unexpected or contradictory. We usually put *however* (10) and *instead* (11) in front position, but they can also be used in mid and end positions (12).

10 *She had hoped Daniel would stay all weekend.* **However**, *he had to leave on Saturday.*
11 *He was supposed to stay here and help us move things.* **Instead**, *he went off to play golf.*
12 *Extra security precautions had been proposed earlier. They were,* **however**, *considered too costly at the time. A tightening of existing security measures was undertaken* **instead**.

Others used formally include: in contrast, nevertheless, on the other hand, rather, yet

Connectors used for adding or contrasting: *actually, in fact, after all*

We can use *actually* and *in fact* when we introduce information that adds something, often in support of a previous statement (13), or when the information contrasts with what was expected (14). We usually put both forms in front position, but they can also be used in end or mid position (15).

13 *I've known Henry Martin for years.* **Actually**, *we went to the same school.*
14 *Everyone thought the exam would be difficult.* **In fact**, *it turned out to be quite easy.*
15 *We went to the same school,* **in fact**. • *It* **actually** *turned out to be quite easy.*

We can use *after all* ('don't forget') in front or end position when we add information as a reminder (16). We can also use *after all* ('despite what was expected'), usually in end position, when we include information that contrasts with what was expected (17).

16 *I don't have to tell my parents everything.* **After all**, *I am over 21./I am an adult* **after all**.
17 *When I saw the rain, I didn't think we could go for a walk. Tony convinced me to go with him and we saw a beautiful rainbow. I'm so glad we decided to do it* **after all**.

 In addition (to) 125, 210 *Instead (of)* 125, 210

9 Using a dictionary if necessary, add the following words and phrases to the definitions in this paragraph.

facelift (×2)   forklift   lift (×2)   also (×2)   for example   similarly   that is

A (1) ...., which is (2) .... known as an elevator in the USA, is a machine that you stand in to go up and down inside a building. This word is (3) .... used for the action of taking someone somewhere in a car, described as 'giving someone a (4) ....'. Something rather different is meant by a (5) ...., which is an operation to make someone look younger by, (6) ...., removing fat or pulling the skin tighter. (7) ...., the process of improving the appearance of the outside of a building can be described as 'giving it a (8) ....'. A (9) .... is a vehicle with special equipment, (10) ...., two long metal prongs sticking out in front, which is used for lifting and moving heavy things.

10 Add one group of connectors (not necessarily in this order) to each of these paragraphs (adapted from a magazine article).

✓ *also / however / in other words   indeed / in fact / too   actually / also / in particular*

A Roger Goodman was really fit when he played rugby in school. He ~~also~~ stayed in good shape through university. Once he started working, things changed. He began eating a lot more and exercising a lot less. After a few years, his clothes were feeling tight and he was breathing really hard after running up stairs. He was 'out of shape'.

B Roger didn't think he had time for outdoor activities, so he decided to join a health club. Like a lot more men these days, he started thinking about cosmetic surgery to improve his appearance. He wanted to get rid of some of the wrinkles around his eyes. Cosmetic surgeon Dr Khalid Idris of Body Image in Highbury says, 'Our clients used to be mostly women. Now we have more men than women coming in for certain types of surgery.'

C The number of men seeking help from surgeons like Dr Idris has increased dramatically in recent years. It's a trend that started in the USA where cosmetic surgery is a $500 million business. The emphasis on looking young isn't limited to facelifts, but has created a huge demand for dental improvements and hair transplants.

11 Correct the mistakes in the use of connectors in these sentences.

1 I'm still studying European History. I'm hoping as well to take a British History class.

2 I'd rather have chicken than fish if that's okay. I don't like actually fish very much.

3 I don't mind correcting students' homework. It's part of my job after all that.

4 I wouldn't say that Adam is the best student. In addition, he's certainly not the worst.

5 Recycling has been successful in schools. On the other hand, young children now automatically put their empty bottles in the recycling bin, not the dustbin.

Result and time connectors

Result connectors: *so, therefore,* etc.

We can use *so* in front position to show that what follows is a result of, or is caused by, earlier events (1). We sometimes use *therefore* when we want to emphasize a logical or necessary result (2). *Therefore* is more formal than *so*.

 1 *We were moving some things out of the house when it started pouring with rain.* **So** *everything got very wet.*
 2 *The woman killed her husband and she intended to do it.* **Therefore** *she is guilty of murder.*

In formal situations, we can use *as a result,* usually in front position, to show that something is a direct result of earlier events.

 3 *There has been an increase in population and a shortage of housing.* **As a result**, *rents have gone up and fewer students can afford to live within walking distance of the college.*

Others used formally include: accordingly, as a consequence, consequently, hence, thus

Time connectors: *then, afterwards,* etc.

We can use *then* as a connector, usually in front position, to show that one action or situation is later than another (4) or follows logically from another (5). We sometimes use *then* at the beginning of a clause emphasizing what follows logically from a preceding *if*-clause (6).

 4 *We had unpacked everything for the picnic and had just sat down.* **Then** *it started to rain.*
 5 *Perhaps you could hire a car for a few days.* **Then** *you'd be able to go wherever you wanted.*
 6 *If we allow the terrorists to succeed,* **then** *no one will ever feel safe again anywhere.*

We can use other connectors such as *afterwards,* in front or end position, when we're talking about the time relationship between one sentence and another.

 7 *The film was based on Harris' first novel.* **Afterwards**, *the book became a bestseller.*

Others include: earlier, later, previously, subsequently

We can use *meanwhile* ('during that time') to show that two things are happening during the same period of time (8). We can also use *meanwhile* ('before that time') to talk about something happening between two points in time (9). We usually put *meanwhile* in front position.

 8 *My sister finished high school and got a good job.* **Meanwhile**, *I remained a poor student.*
 9 *Let's meet again tomorrow.* **Meanwhile**, *I'll get in touch with Craig about your proposal.*

Others include: in the meantime ('before that time'), simultaneously ('during the same time')

---

12 Choose a sentence or clause (a–f) to follow each sentence or clause (1–6) and add *so* or *then*.

 1 We got stuck in a bad traffic jam on the way to the concert. (...)
 2 I know you don't like green peppers. (...)
 3 If our operating budget is cut by 10%, (...)
 4 It was a terrible morning, with a lot of problems in the office. (...)
 5 A lot more people came to the meeting than they expected, so (...)
 6 The children have to do their homework every afternoon when they come home. (...)

 a .... at lunchtime I spilled some tomato soup down the front of my white shirt.
 b .... they can play or watch TV.
 c .... when we arrived, it had already started.
 d .... we really will have to reduce services.
 e .... I didn't put any in the salad.
 f .... the room was very crowded.

Result clauses 203   *So* 202–3, 210   *Then* after *if*-clauses 189   Time clauses 198–9

Listing connectors

We can use *first* (or *firstly*), *second* (or *secondly*), etc. in front position to show the order of things in a list or a sequence. We sometimes use *then* or *next* instead of *second(ly)*, *third(ly)*, etc.

1 *We really have to clean the house.* **First**, *we have to take out the rubbish.*
   Then/Second, *we'll have to wash all the dishes piled up in the kitchen sink.*
   Thirdly/Next *we really need to scrub the floor because it's so dirty.*

We can use *for a start* instead of *first(ly)* in front position to show that we are beginning a sequence of reasons to support or explain a preceding statement (2). We can use *finally* in front position to show that we are at the end of a list (3).

2 *I hated working there.* **For a start**, *everyone else was much older than me.*
Others include: first of all, in the first place, to begin with, to start with

3 **Finally**, *I must thank my parents for their years of patience and support.*

We can use a phrase such as *to sum up* when we are going to provide a summary of points already made (4).

4 **To sum up**, *they liked our ideas, but they want to know more about the costs involved.*
Others include: in brief, in conclusion, in short, in summary, to conclude, to summarize

13 Add these connectors to the following recipe.

finally   first   second   then (×2)

To make hot-baked chips for two, you'll need four large potatoes, the white of one egg, a quarter teaspoon of cayenne pepper and a pinch of salt. Slice each potato lengthwise, cut each slice lengthwise into long sticks. Mix the egg white, cayenne and salt in a bowl. Stir the potato sticks round in the mixture. Spread the coated potato sticks on a greased baking sheet and bake them in the oven at 170° for 35 minutes.

14 Write one of these connectors, or no connector, where appropriate, at the beginning of each of these sentences (adapted from a textbook).

as a result   ✓for a start   in short   secondly   so   then

Example: ....−......... Animal communication is different from human communication in two ways.
Example: For a start, ... Animal signals are always restricted to what is happening here and now.
1 .... When your dog comes to you and says, 'Woof!', it always means, 'I'm woofing now.' It doesn't mean, 'I woofed last night.'
2 .... However, humans can easily talk about last night and things that happened years ago.
3 .... They can go on to talk about what they'll be doing tomorrow or next year.
4 .... Humans are also capable of talking about what doesn't even exist.
5 .... They can refer to things like heaven and hell without ever having seen them.
6 .... Animal communication consists of a fixed number of signals and each signal is used for one particular thing or occasion.
7 .... Human communication, on the other hand, is very creative and humans are able to invent new words, as illustrated by 'woofing' in the last paragraph.
8 .... Human communication has special properties not found in animal communication.

Focus structures: fronting and inversion

We can focus attention on (or emphasize) one part of a sentence, such as the object, by moving it to front position. This is called fronting. We can use fronting, usually in formal situations, to link a sentence more closely to the preceding sentence (1) and to highlight a contrast (2).

1 She was coughing, sneezing and shivering. (He recognized these symptoms immediately.)
 → _These symptoms_ he recognized immediately.
2 We met the Greens. (We liked Mrs Green, but we really didn't care for her husband.)
 → _Mrs Green_ we liked, but _her husband_ we really didn't care for.

After fronting, we often put the verb or auxiliary verb before the subject. This is called inversion. We usually use inversion with verbs describing place or movement after prepositional phrases (3) or after adverbs such as _here_ and _there_ (4) in front position.

3 I was told to sit on a chair in the middle of the room. (An old woman stood behind the chair.)
 → _Behind the chair_ **stood an old woman**. • _Into the room_ **walked two men** wearing sunglasses.
4 _Here_ **comes the bride**. • _There_ **goes my bus**. (NOT ~~There my bus goes.~~)

We also use inversion after negative words (_neither, nor_) (5), phrases beginning with _not_ (6), and after adverbs such as _scarcely_ or _seldom_ (7) in front position.

5 I don't like it. _Neither_ **do my parents**. _Nor_ **does anyone** else that I've asked.
6 _Not until later_ **did we** notice the broken glass. • _Not only_ **was the car** old, it had no windows.
7 _Scarcely_ **had he** sat down when the phone rang. • _Seldom_ **have I** heard such nonsense.

We use inversion after _only_ with prepositional phrases (8) or time expressions (9) in front position.

8 I've looked for it in other places. _Only in Italy_ **can you** find this special kind of ice cream.
9 _Only after the test_ **will we** know if it worked. _Only then_ **can we** decide what to do next.

Inversion is also used after participles moved to front position, usually in narratives.

10 The bedroom was empty. _Lying on the bed_ **was a parcel**. _Attached to it_ **was a small note**.

15 Complete this text by adding one of these expressions in each space.

did she	_is it_	_it was_	_she was_	_she would_	_was something_
had she	_it is_	_here comes_	_was she_	_would she_	_was part_

Only occasionally (1) .... find herself reading someone else's newspaper, over their shoulder, as she sat in the station waiting room. Mostly (2) .... just not very interested, nor (3) .... willing to risk getting caught. Why (4) .... so embarrassing to get caught doing that, she wondered to herself. It isn't against the law or anything. But facing her today (5) .... that really caught her attention. One of our greatest fears in modern life, the headline said, was having to speak in public. The article offered ways to develop your confidence. Seldom (6) .... ever had to speak to an audience, but (7) .... her turn to give a ten minute presentation in her Spanish class that afternoon. Not only (8) .... have to speak to an audience, (9) .... have to do it in a foreign language. She felt the room getting hotter as she leaned forward to get a closer look. Suddenly blocking her view (10) .... of a large black beard and the big nose of the newspaper's owner. 'Oops. Oh, (11) .... my train,' she said quickly, as she stood up and stumbled towards the door. Public speaking isn't scary, she thought to herself, (12) .... public reading that makes me really nervous.

Focus structures: cleft sentences

When we want to focus attention on (or emphasize) one part of a sentence, we can use special structures called cleft sentences. In a cleft ('divided') sentence, we divide the sentence into two parts and focus attention on one part. This part is usually stressed in speech. Some cleft sentences begin with *it* and are called *it*-clefts (1). Others begin with *what* and are called *wh*-clefts (2).

    1 Martin + ate your pizza. → ***It** was <u>Martin</u> who ate your pizza.*
        Martin ate + your pizza. → ***It** was <u>your pizza</u> that Martin ate.*
    2 Anna really likes + chocolate ice cream. → ***What** Anna really likes is <u>chocolate ice cream</u>.*

It-clefts

We usually form *it*-clefts with *it* + *be* + an emphasized part + a relative clause beginning with *who* (3), *that* (4) or no relative pronoun (5).

    3 Someone said Ali phoned earlier. (Ali didn't phone. Alex phoned.) → *No, it wasn't <u>Ali</u> who phoned. It was Alex.*
    4 I'm not interested in anyone else. (I love you!) → *It's <u>you</u> that I love!*
    5 Don't you like vegetables? ~ No, I like most of them. (I hate onions.) → *It's <u>onions</u> I hate.*

We usually use *it*-clefts when we want to focus attention on a noun or pronoun, but we can also focus on other parts of a sentence such as an adverb (6) or an adverbial clause (7).

    6 You were supposed to be here yesterday. → *It was <u>yesterday</u> that you were supposed to be here.*
    7 Things got worse after Elaine left. → *It was <u>after Elaine left</u> that things got worse.*

Wh-clefts

We usually form *wh*-clefts with a *what*-clause + *be* + an emphasized part. The emphasized part can be a noun phrase (8) or a noun clause (9).

    8 I can't stop yawning. (I need a cup of coffee.) → *What I need is <u>a cup of coffee</u>.*
    9 They don't know if Richard's planning to stay here. (They're hoping that he'll leave soon.)
        → *What they're hoping is <u>that he'll leave soon</u>.*

We can also use *wh*-clefts to focus attention on verb phrases. We usually use a form of the verb *do* in the *what*-clause and the base form of the verb in the emphasized verb phrase (10). We sometimes use an infinitive in the emphasized verb phrase after *to do* in the *what*-clause (11).

    10 Alison has an unusual job. (She repairs old clocks.) → *What she does is <u>repair old clocks</u>.*
    11 David is ambitious. (He wants to study law.) → *What he wants to do is <u>(to) study law</u>.*

We sometimes use *all* ('the only thing') instead of *what* at the beginning.

    12 I'll stop yawning soon. (I just need a cup of coffee.) → ***All** I need is <u>a cup of coffee</u>.*

16 Complete each cleft sentence, emphasizing the underlined part, in such a way that it is as similar as possible in meaning to the sentence above it.

    1 <u>The cigarette smoke</u> is irritating my eyes.
        It ....

    2 <u>We</u> had to clean up all the mess.
        It ....

    3 Jimmy <u>watches TV in his room</u> instead of studying.
        What ....

    4 Scientists now believe <u>that human activity is the cause</u>.
        What ....

Tests

A Choose the word or phrase that best completes these sentences.

1 These plants usually flower in spring, _____ won't if there is frost.

   a but   b however   c nevertheless   d otherwise

2 I enjoyed reading the story. It was rather sad, _____ .

   a also   b but   c so   d though

3 Jasmine is working as a dental assistant. What she does is _____ people's teeth.

   a clean   b cleans   c cleaning   d to clean

4 Tickets are required for admission. _____ , those who don't have a ticket won't get in.

   a Consequently   b Rather   c Similarly   d Subsequently

5 Desert flowers can be invisible for years _____ appear suddenly after heavy rain.

   a actually, but   b alternatively or   c consequently and   d nevertheless, so

B Identify the one underlined expression (A, B, C or D) that must be changed in order to correct these sentences.

1 To begin with, she insisted that, in addition to her children, she should be allowed to bring their
     A   B

pets; that is, she wanted as well to bring a dog and two cats.
      C   D

2 For many years, coal was not only readily available, but it was also very cheap in comparison other
                     A   B   C

types of fuel and consequently it was used in all the factories.
              D

3 As a matter of fact, we had just heard about the problem and, because of that, we didn't stay
      A   B

actually in London very long afterwards.
  C   D

4 In conclusion, the new rules state that, in accordance with our agreement, workers who previously
    A   B   C

did extra work without extra pay must now receive overtime pay. As a result that those who are
                                                    D

asked to do extra work will receive additional payment.

5 In the meantime, some of us had to stay in the old building, though it was rather primitive.
    A   B

For a start, there was no hot water. In addition to there were cockroaches everywhere.
   C   B

C Choose the most appropriate phrase for each space in this text.

after all   for example   in addition   in the meantime   so

The difficulty of getting people to pay attention to the problem of rising sea levels is that it often has to compete with, (1) _____ , news of rising food prices or an increase in violent crime. (2) _____ , you are unlikely to worry about flooding in the future if, (3) _____ , you can't afford to eat or you're about to be shot. (4) _____ , most of us don't live anywhere near the sea. (5) _____ why should we worry about it?

D Complete each sentence in such a way that it is as similar as possible in meaning to the sentence(s) above it.

1 There wasn't any butter. We used margarine instead.
   Instead _____

2 You can only get dishes and bowls with this design in Poland.
   Only _____

3 We didn't discover the mistake until much later.
   Not _____

4 Flooding causes most of the damage in spring.
   It's _____

5 She left because he was so unpleasant.
   It was _____

6 I know that the main road is blocked.
   All _____

7 He went to the party by himself.
   What he _____

8 Doris is hoping to travel across Canada by train.
   What _____

E Complete this paragraph using only one word or phrase from each pair.

| afterwards | as a result of | in contrast | similarly | that | in the beginning | what |
| next | the result is | in particular | it's the same | that is | to begin with | why |

(1) _____ I'd like to do today is introduce some important terms that you will become familiar with during this class. (2) _____, there is the term 'greenhouse effect'. A greenhouse is a building with glass sides and a glass roof which trap heat from the sun and hold it inside the building. (3) _____, the polluted atmosphere surrounding the earth is now trapping and holding the heat of the sun, causing temperatures to rise. (4) _____, the polluted atmosphere is having the same kind of effect as a greenhouse. (5) _____, there is the term 'greenhouse gases'. These are the gases which are polluting the atmosphere. (6) _____, one gas called carbon dioxide, which is produced when things like coal and oil are burned, accumulates in the atmosphere and is a direct cause of the greenhouse effect. (7) _____ the greenhouse effect, we are now experiencing a phenomenon known as 'global warming', which is a more general term for increased world temperatures.

Answer key

Unit 1 Sentences

1 1 He was unconscious. (line 18)
OR Police praised the young teacher's quick thinking. (line 25)
OR The bus driver never regained consciousness. (line 29)
OR He was later pronounced dead at East Surrey hospital. (line 30)
OR 'That's a terrible tragedy. (line 36)
OR A local driving school has also offered him six free driving lessons. (line 41)
2 A young English teacher saved the lives of 30 students **when** he took control of a bus **after** its driver suffered a fatal heart attack. (line 1) OR Harvold, **who** has not passed his driving test, said, 'I realized (that) the bus was out of control **when** I was speaking to the students on the microphone.' (line 12)

2 1 after (OR when)   2 suffered (OR had)
3 hit (OR collided with)   4 before
5 died   6 but
7 was   8 praised
9 and   10 offered

3 1 He **was** unconscious. (line 18)
OR That**'s** a terrible tragedy. (line 36)
2 If he hadn't reacted quickly (line 26)
OR He **was later pronounced** dead at East Surrey hospital (line 30)
OR He **had worked regularly** with the school (line 31)
3 there **could have been** a terrible accident (line 27)
OR I hoped the driver **would** survive (line 34)

4 1 I was so relieved that **no one** else was hurt (line 33)
2 (he) was very well regarded by **staff.** (line 32)
OR He had worked regularly with the **school** (line 31)

5 1 won't be easy   2 Was Lord of the Flies
3 has pockets   4 doesn't interest me
5 isn't going to   6 None of you are
7 have I had   8 wasn't about dancing
9 Is Statistics   10 aren't made

6 1 was (c)   2 was (e)   3 is (a)   4 is (d)
5 are (b)

7 1 orchestra have   2 everybody has
3 Nobody … has   4 committee have
5 Darts has   6 teachers has/have
7 police have   8 eggs has

8 1 holdall   2 carry things
3 travel (OR are travelling) 4 hinge
5 swings   6 closes
7 hallucination   8 seeing things
9 hypocrite   10 pretends
11 behaves   12 hijacker
13 seizes   14 go
15 demand things

9 1 take (b) put it in   2 like (c) going to
3 wait (d) shivering   4 heard (a) believe it

10 1 gets, moves   2 rest, nap (OR nap, rest)
3 hibernate, eat   4 lie, fall
5 talks, happens   6 sing, go
7 snore, breathe

11 1 She whispered 'Good luck' to him.
2 The judge fined her £500 for speeding.
3 The farmer refused us permission to walk across his field (OR refused to give us permission OR refused to give permission to us)
4 James confessed (to me) that he took (OR had taken) Caroline's book.

12 1 reserved … keeping it for
2 transmitted … spread them to (OR spread … transmit them to)
3 retrieved … found them for (OR found … retrieved them for)
4 transferred … sells him to (OR sold … transfers him to)
5 required … offer them to

13 She explained us > She explained to us (OR She explained)
gave the following information half of the husbands > information to half
Your wife has described you a holiday trip to China > described a holiday trip to China to you
One of her friends told to her > told her
you think sounds like a really good idea > think (that) it sounds
you ask to her some questions > ask her some questions (OR ask some questions)
Your wife has suggested you a holiday trip to China > suggested a holiday trip to China to you
You don't like > You don't like it
You believe is a really bad idea > You believe (that) it is a really bad idea

you ask some questions her > ask her some
   questions (OR ask some questions)
The researcher didn't tell to the wives > tell the
   wives
the wives she said to the husbands > the wives
   what she said
decide the husbands thought it was a
   good idea > decide if (OR whether) the
   husbands thought

14 1 is (d) 2 look*(f) 3 feel (e) 4 appear
   (b) 5 sound* (a) 6 taste (c)
   *2 look *and* 5 sound *can be exchanged*

15 1 smelled OR tasted   2 tasted OR smelled
   3 get   4 seemed to make
   5 become   6 looked
   7 appeared to be   8 turned
   9 get   10 feel
   11 stay   12 turn

16 It appeared a big problem > appeared to be a
   big problem (OR seemed (to be) a big
   problem)
She went to be crazy > went crazy
she just decided to make blonde her hair >
   make her hair blonde
her hair turned into bright orange > turned
   bright orange
It also became orange her face > Her face also
   turned orange (OR It also made her face
   orange OR Her face also became orange)
She looked like really strange > looked really
   strange
Mona looked an orange balloon > looked like
   an orange balloon
Mona got to be very upset > got very upset
I just kept to be quiet > kept quiet
make it look like better > look better

17 the same subject [3]
   the same subject and verb [5]
   the same subject and auxiliary [4]
   the same verb and object after an auxiliary
      verb in later clauses [7]
   repeated objects and/or prepositional phrases
      from the first clause [6]
   an addition [8]
   an alternative [11]
   a combination [9]
   a combination of negatives [10]
   relative clauses [14]
   noun clauses [13]
   adverbial clauses [15]
   adverbial clauses at the beginning of complex
      sentences [16]

18 1 (c) or ... and   2 (d) or (OR and)

3 (a) but ... and   4 (b) and

19 1 stopped   2 we talked, he got
   3 she came, talked   4 It seemed, got, had
   5 came, we had   6 it stopped, seemed

20 1 heartbeat   2 or
   3 as   4 Heartbreak
   5 because   6 heart-throb
   7 who   8 and
   9 whom   10 heart attack
   11 which   12 and
   13 heartburn   14 which

21 1 which   2 who   3 live
   4 and   5 tell   6 if
   7 see   8 but   9 because
   10 don't like

Tests

A 1 d 2 b 3 b 4 d 5 c

B 1 C (contained)
   2 C (prefers)
   3 D (put £5 in)
   4 D (show it to me OR show me it)
   5 C (made all the young people happy)

C 1 begins in November   2 include fever
   3 catch the flu   4 give it
   5 sneezes

D 1 Nick admitted to one of the detectives that
      he had taken the cashbox.
   2 The police persuaded us that it was too
      dangerous and we were convinced.
   3 The frog suddenly turned into a prince
      after the princess kissed him.
   4 He told us that two hours wouldn't (OR
      won't) be enough to finish the job.
   5 Someone painted the wall white yesterday.

E 1 were ready   2 seemed quite satisfied
   3 stood alone   4 is better
   5 became clear

Unit 2 Tenses

1 1 Soon there **were** all kinds of forms available
      from Bullnotes ... (line 39)
   OR The big problem, they soon discovered,
      is that everyone wants these things ...
      (line 43)
   OR In what turned out to **be** a common
      experience ... (line 46)
   OR ... and there really won't **be** a problem
      with the letter of application. (line 58)

2 Choose one: For several years he will have been trying to turn a good idea… (line 3)

OR He won't **be** doing anything special … (line 5)

OR They **were** starting to make a small steady profit when they met Terry Lloyd. (line 18)

OR Terry had **been** creating home pages for his friends … (line 19)

OR They soon found that students **were** looking for more than lecture notes. (line 25)

OR They needed to do other things that they **weren't** learning in their classes. (line 26)

OR Imagine that you **are** applying for a scholarship. (line 27)

OR You have **been** trying to write a letter of application and you can't get it right (line 28)

OR You need an example of the kind of letter you **are** trying to write. (line 30)

OR 'I **am** writing this letter …' (line 35)

OR Dylan **was** working day and night … (line 41)

OR … he didn't think about what he **was** doing in terms of a business (line 42)

OR Dylan **is** still looking for a way to make Bullnotes work as a business, but these days he **is** always counting his pennies and he **is** having a hard time paying his bills. (line 52)

Choose one: For several years he will **have** been trying … (line 3)

OR … his business venture won't **have** made any money for most of the past year. (line 7)

OR When they started, it **had** seemed like such a great idea. (line 11)

OR Dylan and his friend, Michael Underwood, **had** been writing up their lecture notes … (line 12)

OR They **had** used that money to pay … (line 15)

OR Terry **had** been creating home pages for his friends … (line 19)

OR You **have** been trying to write a letter of application and you can't get it right. (line 28)

OR Or maybe someone **has** asked you to write a letter of recommendation. (line 31)

OR … whom I **have** known for … (line 36)

OR He **has** thought about taking a teaching job … (line 55)

In the following examples, *have* is a main verb, not an auxiliary verb:

they **had** a successful website … (line 48)

OR … he **is having** a hard time paying his bills. (line 54)

OR He **has** lots of experience now … (line 58)

2 1 B 2 E 3 D 4 A 5 C

3 Choose one from each list.
Imperative or infinitive: turn (A), celebrate (A), do (A, B, C), pay (B, D), make (B, D, E), become (B), Imagine (C), write (C), get (C), download (C), be (D), create (D), work (E)
Present simple: need (C)
Present simple +s in third person singular: is (A), wants (D), has (E)
Present continuous: are applying (C), am writing (C), is (always) counting (E), is having (E)
Present perfect: has asked (C), have known (C), has thought (E)
Present perfect continuous: have been trying (C)
Past simple: started (B), sold (B), met (B), showed (B), created (B), established (B), set (B), found (C), needed (C), were (D), didn't think (D), discovered (D), turned (D), tried (D), had (D), didn't (really) make (D), went (E), was (3D)
Past continuous: were starting (B), were looking (C), weren't learning (C), was working (D), was doing (D)
Past perfect: had seemed (B), had used (B)
Past perfect continuous: had been writing (B), (had been) selling (B), had been creating (B)
Future: will (soon) need (A), won't be (E), will have (A)
Future continuous: won't be doing (A)
Future perfect: won't have made (A)
Future perfect continuous: will have been trying (A)

4 A 1 is being 2 tell 3 says 4 has 5 is
B 6 look 7 are 8 live 9 move
   10 resemble
C 11 'm (OR are) looking 12 isn't
   13 Do … know 14 're (OR are) repairing
   15 's (OR is) using

5 1 has won … has said … hat-trick
2 also-ran … has taken … has not finished
3 has heard … has-been … has trained
4 no-show … has bought … hasn't come

6 1 have … known (c) 've (OR have) been
  2 (b) 've (OR have) … been swimming
  3 Have … completed (d) 've (OR have) done
  4 Have … shown (a) 's (OR has) been reading

7 She ~~is living~~ here since 1995 > She's (OR She
    has) lived OR She's (OR She has) been living
  she ~~has been going~~ back > she's (OR she has)
    gone back
  She's ~~having~~ an accent > She has an accent
  people who ~~are coming~~ from France > people
    who come from France
  I never ~~ask~~ her > I've (OR I have) never asked
    her
  if she ~~is speaking~~ French > if she speaks French
  She ~~is really liking~~ to go to the theatre > She
    really likes to go
  she ~~is inviting~~ me > she's (OR she has) invited
    me or she invited me
  In the short time I'm ~~knowing~~ her > I've (OR I
    have) known her
  we ~~become~~ good friends > we've (OR we have)
    become good friends

8 A 1 were listening 2 came
    3 said 4 were making
  B 5 broke 6 stole 7 was teaching 8 saw
  C 9 explained 10 understood
    11 was talking
  D 12 I didn't get 13 missed
    14 was wondering (OR wondered)

9 1 had been worrying (OR had worried)
  2 had planned (OR had been planning)
  3 had been
  4 had broken
  5 had caught
  6 had been living (OR had lived)
  7 had been taking (OR removing)
  8 had made
  9 had … removed (OR taken)
  10 had … had

10 we sometimes ~~stop~~ > we sometimes stopped
    (OR we would sometimes stop)
  If it wasn't ~~rain~~ > raining
  we just ~~sleep~~ outside > we just slept (OR we
    would just sleep)
  We really ~~enjoying~~ that > enjoyed
  If it ~~was rain~~ > was raining (OR rained)
  and ~~crawl~~ inside > crawled
  while we ~~sleep~~ in the tent > were sleeping
  I ~~think~~ > thought
  the ground ~~moving~~ under me > was moving
    (OR moved)
  I ~~sit~~ up > sat
  and I ~~realize~~ > realized

the tent ~~was try~~ to move > was trying
~~was hold~~ it in place > was holding
When we ~~get~~ outside > got
we ~~discover~~ > discovered
that we ~~stand~~ > were standing
our tent slowly ~~floats~~ away > was slowly
  floating
we ~~really surprised~~ > we were really surprised
then we ~~think~~ > thought
it ~~is~~ very funny > was

11 A 1 've (OR have) known 2 started
    3 've (OR have) … met
  B 4 Have … heard 5 have … become
    6 had
  C 7 told 8 've (OR have) had
    9 hasn't come

12 1 have … been   2 asked
  3 were   4 didn't seem
  5 did … say   6 told
  7 didn't know   8 didn't call
  9 've (OR have) had   10 haven't eaten
  11 's (OR has) made

13 1 needed (b) gave
  2 said (a) had talked
  3 came (d) hadn't finished
  4 (c) had worked

14 1 've (OR have) … heard   2 was
    3 had … reached   4 were
    5 hadn't … locked   6 didn't lock
    7 hadn't eaten*   8 went
    9 didn't eat*   10 was
    11 had cooked   12 have gone
    13 explained

*7 and 9 can be exchanged

15 to give or ask for information about the
    future [2]
  when we make promises, requests or threats [1]
  future actions in progress at a particular
    time [5]
  expressing plans or intentions [4]
  something will be completed by a particular
    time [7]
  lasting from a point before that time up to that
    future time [6]
  a prediction based on past experience or
    knowledge [10]
  in predictive conditionals [9]
  a prediction based on what we feel or think
    now [8]
  a past prediction about the future [11]
  a decision already made [12]
  a decision made at that moment [13]
  future events in a schedule or timetable [16]

future actions in clauses after subordinating
conjunctions [15]

a future action we have planned or
arranged [14]

16 1 will be (b) 'll (OR will) have been
2 will (d) Will … be
3 will be (a) 'll (OR will) have been
4 will be (c) 'll (OR will) have been

17 1 will have
2 wasn't going to stop (OR wouldn't stop)
3 don't start
4 'll be (OR 'm going) to be
5 'll give
6 make

18 1 or I ~~report~~ you > or I'll (OR I will)
report you
2 Let's get together for lunch sometime, ~~will~~
~~we?~~ > shall we?
3 'I ~~do~~ it!' > 'I'll do it!'
4 Pat McGuire ~~will spend~~ five years > will
have spent
5 ~~I'm~~ going to work > I was going
6 Do you think she'll ~~go~~ to bed already? >
she'll have gone
7 I guess ~~it's raining~~ later > it'll rain (OR it's
going to rain)
8 those that we think ~~about to~~ be available >
are about to (OR will OR are going to)
9 you'll ~~sit~~ on a plane > you'll be sitting
10 If ~~I'll finish~~ before you > If I finish
before you
I ~~wait~~ for you outside > I'll wait
11 ~~Will Stefan to get~~ these boxes later > Is
Stefan to get (OR Will Stefan get) these
boxes later
~~is to take~~ them now? > is he to take them
(OR will he take them OR is he taking them)
now?
12 before ~~it'll close~~ > before it closes
or the parcel ~~doesn't~~ arrive > or the parcel
won't arrive

Tests

A 1 c 2 a 3 d 4 b 5 c OR a

B 1 D (is having) 2 A (used to)
3 C (knew) 4 A (make) 5 C (had put)

C 1 was beginning 2 had peeped
3 was reading 4 had 5 thought

D 1 By the time we sell the car, we will have
spent £300 on repairs.
2 This is the first time I have (ever) had to
think about my health.

3 Juliet has been working (or has worked)
here for about six years.
4 It's even worse than I thought it would be.
5 It was Christmas when I (last) talked to my
parents.

E 1 is … happening
2 have been
3 be experiencing
4 had
5 believe
6 have … been changing OR have been …
changing
7 have created
8 lets
9 holds
10 Will … keep

Unit 3 Modals

1 1 we should never (line 6)
OR don't have to (line 48)
OR won't (line 64)
2 We **may** be told, for example, that we
should never open an umbrella indoors
because that **will** bring bad luck. (line 6)

2 1 E 2 C 3 D 4 A 5 B

3 We aren't told why or what kind of bad thing
might happen to us, but few of us **are going to**
try to find out. (line 10)
Others **will** say that seeing a black cat **is**
supposed to be lucky. (line 37)
This is usually heard when people talk about
their good luck or when they are hoping that
they **will be able to** get or do something they
want. (line 54)

4 1 be … have 2 be … be
3 be … have 4 have … have been

5 Prediction: But we would probably have been
asked to stop.
Willingness, habits and preferences: I would
have hated to have to buy a new one.
Ability: We could easily have chatted for
another hour.
Permission: Children may not be left alone in
the playground.
Possibility: I was glad that my old computer
could be repaired.
Necessity: They must be accompanied by an
adult.
Deduction: I guess he must have forgotten
about it.
Obligation: He should be helping you clear
out the garage.

6 1 will be (e) should be
2 going to (c) must be
3 can't (b) must have
4 ought (a) won't
5 may have been (d) able to

7 1 regrettable, should
2 advisable, shouldn't
3 inevitable, will
4 reluctant, wouldn't
5 inconceivable, can't
6 hypothetical, might

8 I ~~didn't could~~ do that > I couldn't do that
I knew I ~~will~~ have to quit my job > would have to
I ~~have~~ much less money > would have much less money
I ~~don't should~~ give up such a good job > I shouldn't
a young woman ~~supposed~~ to think > was (OR is) supposed to think
I ~~couldn't decided~~ > I couldn't decide
what I ~~ought do~~ > ought to do
she ~~should go~~ to university > she should have gone
I ~~should to give~~ it a try > I should give it a try
I ~~didn't should~~ be afraid > I shouldn't be afraid
she ~~may can~~ help me pay > she might be able to help me pay

9 1 will 2 would 3 I'd 4 I'm going to
5 would have 6 I was going to 7 Shall
8 you'll 9 won't 10 I'll

10 1 won't (OR will not) go … 'll (OR will) give
2 wouldn't start … pushed
3 'd (OR would) like … 'd (OR would)… have
4 'd (OR would) …play … will … stay
5 'll (OR will) …be … 'd (OR would) hate
6 won't (OR will not) need … 'll (OR will) have eaten (OR eat)
7 would be … wouldn't say

11 1 can't (OR cannot OR aren't able to) fly … can (OR are able to); swimming
2 unflappable … can (OR is able to) stay
3 numb … couldn't (OR wasn't able to) feel
4 illiterate … can't (OR cannot OR aren't able to) read
5 successful … been able to … tried OR has tried
6 managed … were able to … difficult

12 1 couldn't 2 could 3 could 4 can

13 1 may (c)   2 be allowed to (f)
3 Can (a)   4 be allowed to (e)
5 can (or may) (b)   6 be allowed to (d)

14 Of course, you ~~could~~ > you can
she ~~isn't being~~ able to do her own work > she isn't able to (OR she can't do)
she ~~can~~ have said > she could have said (OR she can say)
Sorry, but you ~~can not~~ > can't OR cannot
how ~~do they could do their work?~~ > how could they do their work? (OR how can they do their work?)
I knew that I ~~can~~ have tried > could have tried
I didn't think I'~~ll can~~ change how she behaved > I didn't think I could change

15 1 may have … absurd
2 may be … disqualified
3 undecided … may … may not
4 potential … might not
5 may not … feasible
6 theoretical … might

16 1 can pick
2 can't imagine
3 could be
4 couldn't be sent
5 could have been avoided
6 could have been saved

17 1 They ~~can~~ be going to > may / might / could
2 Someone ~~can~~ still be using > may / might / could
3 You ~~may~~ be hanged > might / could
4 These people ~~can~~ have > may / might
5 I ~~can~~ have finished > may / might / could … I ~~can~~ not > may / might
6 ~~May~~ someone tell me > Can / Could
7 we really ~~might~~ not believe > can't / cannot / could not / couldn't
8 if you ~~may~~ be willing > might
9 the weather ~~can~~ be > may / might / could
10 ~~May~~ the children > Could

18 1 extra … don't have to
2 step … have to
3 fruit … mustn't
4 must / have to … command
5 obligation … don't have to
6 duty-free … don't have to
7 taboo … mustn't
8 evil … have to

19 1 didn't have to … required
2 needn't have … unnecessary
3 mustn't … allowed
4 need to … official
5 having to … significant
6 must … impossible

20 1 so you ~~mustn't~~ clean them > don't have to clean

2 Everyone will ~~have got to~~ go > will have to go

3 I'll ~~need get~~ some aspirin > I'll need to get (OR I'll have to get)

4 I ~~must to~~ find a replacement > I must find (OR I have to find)

5 customers ~~needn't to~~ leave > don't need to leave (OR needn't leave)

6 we ~~had got to~~ take a taxi > we had to take

7 the one ~~to must have to tell~~ him > the one to have to tell him (OR the one who must (OR has to) tell him)

8 you ~~don't need be~~ over twenty-one > you don't need to (OR have to) be

9 we ~~must go~~ > we had to go

10 we ~~needn't have to wait~~ > we needn't have waited (OR we didn't need to wait)

21 1 (d) must   2 (c) must be   3 (e) must have
4 (a) can't have   5 (b) can't

22 1 must have taken
2 must have been
3 couldn't have done
4 couldn't have carried (OR couldn't carry)
5 must have put
6 must be losing

23 1 person   2 had better
3 umbrella   4 shouldn't
5 ladder   6 should be
7 should have   8 shoulder
9 ought not   10 mirror
11 cat   12 is supposed to

Tests

A 1 d   2 a   3 a   4 c   5 a

B 1 A (may)   2 D (ought not to be)
3 D (would)   4 C (can)   5 A (had)

C 1 may not be familiar
2 can be used
3 must be paid
4 won't be required
5 will be charged

D 1 Students are not allowed to park here. (OR Students are not permitted to park here.)

2 His trip may have been cancelled at the last minute.

3 She didn't enjoy having to get up at five every morning.

4 He couldn't have committed the crime, according to the report.

5 This shirt shouldn't have been (OR ought not to have been) put in the washing machine.

E 1 might*   2 couldn't
3 was able to   4 would
5 be able to   6 would*
7 be willing to 8 had to
9 should   10 was … going to

1 and 6 can be exchanged.

Unit 4 Negatives and questions

1 1 Is there anything else? (line 31)
Is it a weapon? (line 44)

2 She **wasn't** seriously injured, but it really frightened her and she **wouldn't** go out alone. (line 4)

2 1 G*   2 E   3 H*   4 F   5 D
G and H can be exchanged

3 1 She wasn't seriously injured, but it really frightened her and she **wouldn't** go out alone. (line 4)
OR For example, women with longer hair are more likely to be attacked than women whose hair is shorter or in a style that **can't** be grabbed. (line 28)

2 It's really more about awareness and how **not to be** an easy target. (line 25)
OR We advise women **not to go** alone to parking areas and garages … (line 39)

3 …we focus more on **not getting** into that kind of situation. (line 19)
OR We talk a lot about **not becoming** a victim …(line 23)

4 **Who** can take part? (line 10)

4 1 How **don't** you get into 'that kind of situation'? (line 22)

2 it isn't much of a weapon, **is it?** (line 45)

5 1 aren't … non-stick
2 isn't … non-resident
3 not … non-event
4 Non-refundable … doesn't
5 nondescript … no
6 non-stop … won't

6 1 Who isn't   2 Why don't   3 Where did
4 What do   5 When were   6 Whose … are

7 we ~~didn't really could~~ say much > we really couldn't say (OR we couldn't really say)
What ~~you think~~ is the best pet? > What do you think

226

I ~~not care~~ about pets > I don't care

Why ~~we have~~ pets? > Why do we have pets?

We ~~not need~~ them for anything > We don't need them

~~don't we?~~ > do we?

some people think dogs ~~not clean~~ > dogs aren't clean

so they ~~not~~ good pets > so they're not good pets (OR so they aren't good pets)

~~does he~~ > do they?

He didn't ~~answered~~ > He didn't answer.

she ~~could have not~~ a cat > she couldn't have a cat (OR she could not have a cat)

Why ~~do some people can't~~ have pets > Why can't some people have pets?

~~Do~~ some pets more expensive to keep > Are some pets

How ~~will be trained the pet?~~ > How will the pet be trained?

Who ~~is take care~~ of the pet > Who takes care of the pet? (OR Who will take care of the pet?)

8 1 (c) none   2 (d) none
    3 No (a) not   4 not (b) no

9 1 infrequent   2 doesn't
    3 carefree   4 nothing
    5 careless   6 not
    7 invisible   8 no one
    9 infallible   10 never
    11 indifferent   12 no

10 1 There has (OR There's) never been a better chance to make money on the stock market.
    2 We didn't notice until the next morning that she hadn't come home. (OR We didn't notice that she hadn't come home until the next morning.)
    3 No one (OR Nobody) warned us at any time about polluted water. (OR No one / Nobody warned us about polluted water at any time.)
    4 The janitor will say, 'Don't smoke in here,' won't he?

11 1 No sooner   2 had I   3 Not only
    4 were they   5 they were   6 I had
    7 nothing   8 no idea   9 Nor
    10 did I   11 Not until   12 did we

12 1 (d) Which   2 (f) What   3 (a) What
    4 (c) What   5 (b) Which   6 (e) Which

13 1 During which (B)   2 How often (C)
    3 What ... from (A)   4 With whom (C)
    5 Which of (B)   6 Where ... from (A)
    7 Who ... by (C)   8 What ... for (C)

14 1 Who   2 Who else
    3 What ... about   4 Whatever
    5 Where   6 How long
    7 Where exactly   8 Which ... in
    9 Where ... from   10 How ever

15 1 Who do you believe is responsible for the current conflict?
    2 Where did her father think she might have gone?
    3 When did the weather forecaster say the rain should stop?
    4 What do you imagine their new house is going to look like?

16 1 (c) Who   2 (e) Do ... Why
    3 (d) didn't ... did   4 (b) How
    5 (a) Does ... which

17 1 are you   2 He's   3 Is he
    4 he was   5 do I   6 you're
    7 you don't   8 was he   9 did he
    10 he did   11 I do   12 don't you

Tests

A 1 b   2 a   3 d   4 c   5 a

B 1 C (did he ask)   2 D (no longer take)
    3 D (didn't you)   4 C (do they)
    5 B (not an)

C 1 Aren't   2 what   3 no
    4 I'm not   5 Can't

D 1 Not only was the room cold, but it was also very damp.
    2 Who did your sister say she gave the money to?
    3 What does Andreas think has been stolen?
    4 She said, 'Why don't you (OR Why not) take the train instead of driving?'
    5 They asked me what his name was and where he lived.

E 1 Nothing   2 never   3 no
    4 What ... BA 21   5 Why ... Leisure
    6 Who ... Somebody else   7 Did ... Yes
    8 which ... London   9 Where ... New York
    10 How ... None

Unit 5 The passive

1 will find (line 28); were found (line 42) have been moving (line 23); had been moved (line 16)

2   1 have been … injured
    2 have been left
    3 was hit
    4 were (OR have been) destroyed
    5 were (OR have been) buried/trapped
    6 have blocked
    7 have had to be flown in
    8 are going to be felt

3   1 the apple blossoms that **are** always **shaken** loose from the trees (line 4)
       OR and **(are) blown** along the country roads (line 6)
       OR The scenes of devastation this morning **are described** by one rescue worker as 'like the end of the world' (line 21)
    2 The names of all victims **are being withheld** until their families can be notified (line 47)
    3 For as long as people can remember, small towns … **have been hit** by storms every spring (line 1)
       OR … the roads **have been blocked** by dozens of fallen trees (line 26)
       OR About 100 people **have been** seriously **injured** (line 50)
       OR more than 1,000 **have been left** homeless (line 51)
    4 the Clintons **were found** alive by rescuers this morning (line 42)
       OR Tragically, they **were** both **killed** when part of a wall crashed through the floor on top of them (line 45)
    5 Other buildings where tractors and equipment **were being stored** seem to have been completely blown away (line 18)
    6 Herds of cattle that **had been moved** into barns for safety are nowhere to be seen, nor are the barns (line 16)

4   1 being (c)   2 to be (e)   3 be (d)
    4 been (f)   5 be (a)   6 been (b)

5   1 were destroyed
    2 are expected
    3 were left
    4 are blocked (OR were blocked OR have been blocked)
    5 were knocked
    6 was flooded (OR is flooded)

    7 to be rescued
    8 are closed
    9 were injured (OR have been injured OR are injured)
    10 were reported (OR have been reported)

6   1 The house can't be seen from the street
    2 He said our papers wouldn't (OR won't) be corrected before Friday.
    3 The towels must have been taken out of the dryer.
    4 Your books aren't going to be stolen from this room.
    5 I didn't enjoy being told what to do all the time.

7   1 can be used
    2 is also called
    3 is believed
    4 may have been convicted
    5 have been shown
    6 had been sentenced
    7 was released
    8 has also been used
    9 would never have been solved

8   1 Erin was seen outside the theatre as she was waiting to go in. She had a new hairstyle.
    2 Karen feels sad because she wasn't promoted (OR hasn't been promoted) and she has to carry on as if nothing happened.
    3 The ball is thrown to Evans (OR Evans is thrown the ball). Evans tries to go past Jennings, but he is stopped (by Jennings). It's a foul.

9   1 impossible (a)   2 inexplicable (b)
    3 knowledgeable (b)   4 illegible (b)
    5 inaudible (a)   6 unspeakable (b)
    7 reusable (a), (b)

10 just after my younger sister ~~born~~ > was born
   Lots of people ~~were come~~ > came
   I ~~gave~~ the job > was given
   As each guest ~~was arrived~~ > arrived
   I ~~handed~~ boxes > was handed
   which ~~filled~~ with things > were filled
   that ~~wrapped~~ in Christmas paper > were wrapped
   I ~~told~~ which ones > was told
   and which ones ~~had to be place~~ > had to be placed (OR I had to place)
   So many presents ~~brought~~ for us > were brought
   the experience of ~~given~~ so much> being given

11 what is done, not who does it [1]

we don't know … who performed the actions [2]

the person or thing affected by the action [3]

that subject is the topic of two or more sentences [5]

several actions that affect the same subject in a single sentence [4]

rules and warning notices [9]

procedures, especially in research reports [7]

formal written reports [8]

to avoid personal commands [11]

to avoid implying that we are only talking about ourselves [10]

the speaker of statements and questions [13]

of orders and requests in infinitives [12]

to distance ourselves from the reported information [14]

not sure if the information is reliable [15]

a current report [17]

a report of something in the past [18]

12 You can only consult reference books in the library.

You must obtain special permission to use them outside the library.

You should return all books on time or you will have to pay a fine.

If you do not pay the fine, you will lose borrowing rights.

You may not borrow library books for others or give them to others.

If you lose a book, you must pay the cost of replacement.

13 1 are (OR were) said to be
2 were told not to use
3 is (OR was) reported to have died
4 wasn't mentioned … were received

14 It has been claimed that tasks cannot be used successfully with beginner level students.

The following study was designed so that that claim could be investigated.

Two groups of students were created, each with different proficiency levels.

They were given a task in which they were shown a set of pictures and asked to tell a story. (OR A task was given to them … a set of pictures was shown to them … they were asked)

They were recorded as they spoke and then their stories were examined.

15 1 is considered by
2 was established by
3 are filled with

4 are performed … were experienced by
5 were not written by

16 1 were defeated (d) reacted
2 were smashed (c) were stolen
3 get caught (b) get beaten up
4 were treated (a) were reported

17 1 opened   2 stopped
3 crashed   4 was knocked
5 was carried   6 ran
7 exploded   8 shook
9 was handed   10 get … injured

Agents: (5) the surging crowd, (6) I, (9) the old woman

Tests

A 1 d   2 a   3 c   4 c   5 c

B 1 C (married)
2 D (crashed)
3 B (with a special key)
4 C (being repaired OR which were being repaired OR which had been repaired)
5 B (was OR is located)

C 1 is experienced
2 was believed (OR considered)
3 were bitten by (OR had been bitten by)
4 could be cured by
5 was … recommended by
6 is … considered (OR believed)
7 may (OR might) be said

D 1 There's a saying that Rome wasn't built in a day.
2 The tests have been collected and the answers (have been) checked.
3 Death is more likely to be caused by a bee sting than a snake bite these days.
4 There were reported to be serious problems with the new design.
5 We weren't given instructions or shown what to do. (OR We were given no instructions … OR We weren't given any instructions …)

E 1 n   2 b   3 o   4 c   5 h   6 l   7 i   8 e

Unit 6   Articles and nouns

1 1 True   2 True   3 False   4 8 million
5 False   6 True   7 80 per cent   8 True

2 1 an accident (line 23)
2 the United States (line 10)

3 1 Europe (line 9)

2 a ... crash (line 11), a flight (lines 16, 17), a factor (line 19), a smoke hood (line 33), a fire (line 34).

3 the airport (line 6), the flight (lines 7, 19), the chance (line 10), the ... exit (lines 25, 26), the number (line 26), the ... door (line 28), the ... person (line 29), the plane (line 33), the hood (line 34)

4 car (line 4)

5 the ... forms (line 1), the ... planes (line 8), the ... jets (line 8), the ... airlines (line 9), the ... parts (line 15), the people (line 21)

6 ... jets (line 1), ... planes (lines 12, 13), accidents (line 14), seats (line 26), clothes (line 30), ... fibres (line 30), ... materials (line 31), ... gases (line 35)

7 The duration (line 18), the dark (line 27), the skin (line 32)

8 Flying (line 1), transportation (line 2), travelling (line 3), air (line 3), survival (line 22), cotton (line 31), wool (line 31), smoke (line 35).

4 when we mention them first [1]
when we think they are already known [2]
when we classify the kind of thing we're talking about [3]
any example of the kind of thing we're talking about [4]
the work they do [6]
the kind of beliefs they have [5]
in definitions [9]
in descriptions of particular features [8]
the type of thing mentioned [7]
the same ordinary things as we are in our daily lives [11]
in the physical world outside [10]
identify people by their jobs [12]
their unique roles in society [14]
with professional organizations [13]
inventions and musical instruments [16]
in generalizations [15]
prepositional phrases with *of* [19]
relative clauses [18]
superlative adjectives and emphasizing adjectives such as *main* or *first* [17]

5 1 the   2 the   3 –
4 –   5 the   6 the
7 the   8 an   9 a
10 the   11 the   12 the
13 a   14 a   15 a
16 –   17 –   18 a

6 1 (f) the   2 (d) a   3 (a) the
4 (e) the   5 (c) a   6 (b) the

7 1 a   2 the   3 –   4 a   5 the   6 –
7 a   8 the   9 –   10 The   11 a   12 –

8 I was starting to learn ~~the English~~ > learn English
He was from Cardiff in ~~the Wales~~ > in Wales
He was always making ~~the jokes~~ > making jokes
One day he ~~wrote words~~ > wrote the words
~~on blackboard~~ > on the blackboard
I offered to ~~answer question~~ > answer the question
changed to ~~the A~~ > changed to A (OR an A)
that ~~was good answer~~ > that was a good answer
he ~~changed letter~~ > changed the letter
happy ~~with new spelling~~ > happy with the new spelling
~~with the absolute confidence~~ > with absolute confidence
I looked round in ~~the confusion~~ > in confusion
it ~~needed second M~~ > needed a second M
it should have ~~the M~~ too > an M
nodded with ~~the smile~~ > with a smile
I still ~~remember terrible feeling~~ > I still remember the terrible feeling
feeling ~~of the embarrassment~~ > of embarrassment

9 1 a   2 a   3 a   4 one   5 a   6 a   7 a
8 a   9 –   10 –   11 a   12 –   13 a
14 one   15 a   16 a

10 1 an   2 –   3 –
4 –   5 –   6 an
7 –   8 a   9 a
10 a   11 –   12 –
13 a (OR the)   14 –   15 the
16 the (OR –)   17 –   18 –
19 the   20 the   21 –
22 –   23 –   24 a
25 the   26 the   27 –
28 –   29 the   30 –

11 1 –   2 –   3 a
4 a   5 one   6 one
7 an (OR –)   8 –   9 a (OR one)
10 one   11 the   12 a (OR the)
13 the (OR a)   14 a   15 the
16 the   17 the   18 a
19 the   20 the   21 a
22 one (OR –)   23 the   24 an
25 an   26 the   27 the
28 the   29 –   30 –

12 people, creatures and objects [1]
actions and events [2]
substances and materials [5]
abstract ideas, qualities and states [4]
activities [3]
a single thing [7]
a substance or general idea [8]
in phrases which are countable [10]
separate units or parts of nouns which are
   uncountable [9]

13 1 government   2 a country
       3 a … piece   4 toast
       5 – … bread   6 soup
       7 a mixture   8 cereal*
       9 nuts*   10 – … fruit
       11 milk   12 breakfast

8 and 9 can be exchanged

14 1 outskirts … are (e)   2 press is (d)
       3 clergy are (f)   4 Mathematics is (b)
       5 Binoculars are (a)   6 is (c) fortnight

15 a particular person or thing [1]
a common combination of things, not
   possession [2]
people and other living things [5]
groups and organizations [6]
times [7]
places [4]
as if it was a person [8]
when an object is described as 'having'
   something [9]
that noun is treated as known [11]
one of a larger number rather than a
   particular one [10]
when one thing is part of another [13]
when describing actions, ideas or
   processes [12]
when a long phrase is used for the
   possessor [14]
what they are for [16]
what they are made of [18]
what work they do [15]
what kind they are [17]
where and when they happen or are used [19]
in compound nouns [20]

16 1 Life's troubles
       2 worries of each day
       3 morning's special news
       4 world's problems
       5 woman's love
       6 Mother's Day

17 Part A
     1 consumer groups
     2 credit cards
     3 college student
     4 credit card offers
     5 application forms
     6 give-aways
     7 T-shirts
     8 bottom line
     9 high-risk borrowers
     10 credit rating
     11 interest rates
     12 sense of responsibility
     13 money matters
     14 buy-now-pay-later world
Part B
parents' willingness; children's credit card debt

18 1 a … job … an … restaurant … the pay
       2 an … bicycle … The shop owner
       3 the teacher … the board
       4 a film … The price

19 1 The   2 the   3 –
       4 –   5 The   6 the
       7 a   8 the   9 a
       10 the   11 the   12 the

20 1 a (d) the   2 – (j) the   3 the (f)
       4 one (g) –   5 a (a)   6 a (h)
       7 a (c)   8 a (i) –   9 (b)
       10 – (e) a

21 4 - 2 - 1 - 5 - 3 - 6 - 9 - 8 - 7

Tests

A 1 d   2 b   3 c   4 b   5 b

B 1 B (are > is)   2 D (the tennis)
      3 B (a research)   4 C (pairs of trousers)
      5 C (CD's > CDs)

C 1 a   2 the   3 a   4 –
      5 a   6 a   7 the   8 –

D 1 Yesterday, a masked man robbed a woman
        outside a (OR the) post office.
      2 In business news, the Bank of England is
        raising (OR will raise) interest rates by one
        and a half per cent.
      3 Yesterday's news of the murder of a priest in
        Kent (has) shocked the community.
      4 Reviewers have criticized a new account of
        Scottish history by an English writer.

E 1 the middle of the century
      2 The urgency of the challenges
      3 the authors of the report (OR the report's
        authors)

4 Sims' (OR Sims's OR The Sims) organization
5 the health of the earth (OR the earth and the health of)
6 the group's latest report
7 the world's population (OR the population of the world)
8 the destruction of the environment

Unit 7 Determiners and quantifiers

1 1 all these changes (line 27)
  2 all cars (lines 11, 17, 53)

2 1 C 2 E 3 D 4 A 5 B

3 1 that car (line 16)
    this area (line 20)
    those old farms (line 22)
    these changes (line 27)
    or those Saturday trips (line 37)
  2 **Choose one from four of these sets:**
    My grandfather (lines 1, 5, 30, 39) OR my grandmother (lines 2, 7, 27) OR my eyes (line 3) OR my grandparents (lines 19, 25) OR my driveway (line 50)
    their voices (line 4) OR their lifetimes (line 20)
    our return (line 37) OR our accident (line 38) OR our driveway (lines 42, 45)
    his thoughts (line 43) OR his window (line 48)
    your house (line 51)

4 1 a little, much
  2 each, every, one
  3 a few, both, many, several, ten

5 **Choose four:**
  a lot of other cars (line 8)
  Both of my grandparents (line 19)
  lots of new houses (line 23)
  one of them (line 26)
  some of the problems (line 31)
  one of those Saturday trips (line 37)

6 A 1 these 2 my 3 those 4 his
  B 5 this 6 that 7 our 8 a few
  C 9 much 10 the 11 his 12 some
  D 13 some 14 thirty 15 most
      16 a little
  E 17 a 18 both 19 each 20 half

7 1 minority … a few
  2 maximum … much
  3 quota … many
  4 unanimous … every
  5 lottery … any
  6 majority … most

8 One of boys fell > One of the boys
  twisted the ankle badly > twisted his ankle
  Most them stayed > Most of them
  with injured boy > with the injured boy
  while two the older boys left > two of the older boys
  this two boys didn't know > these two boys
  walking round in big circle > in a big circle
  for a few hour > a few hours
  back with his friends > their friends
  each boys had brought some water > each boy (OR each of the boys)
  all them managed to survive > all of them (OR they all) managed

9 with plural and uncountable nouns [1]
  as pronouns [2]
  talking about something specific [3]
  in positive sentences [5]
  in questions or offers expecting positive answers [4]
  in sentences with a negative element [7]
  in questions when no specific answer is expected [6]
  in if-clauses [9]
  'it doesn't matter which one' [8]
  a large amount or number [10]
  an approximate number or percentage [12]
  a person, place, or thing whose identity is unknown [11]
  to emphasize 'not any' [13]
  before subject nouns [14]
  before singular and plural nouns [16]
  as a pronoun and with of-phrases [15]

10 1 (c) any 2 (f) any 3 (b) no
   4 (e) any 5 (a) some 6 (d) some

11 1 There was some woman here yesterday asking if we had any old clothes, but I told her we didn't (have any).
   2 Some (OR Some of the) information in that newspaper article was incorrect. There aren't any wolves or bears in Scotland.
   3 I've managed to find some dry paper to start a fire, but I can't light it. Don't you have any matches?
   4 I'm sure I made some mistakes when I was typing. If you find any mistakes, please correct them.

12 1 some 2 no 3 any 4 some 5 any
   6 no 7 some 8 any 9 no 10 any

13 1 empty … none
   2 uninhabited … some … none
   3 some … any … extinct
   4 no … scoreless
   5 dead … no

14 1 (b) whole   2 (d) half
3 (a) both   4 (c) All

15 1 all   2 no   3 none of   4 one of
5 Both of   6 both   7 all of
8 half   9 whole   10 one of

16 1 each pair   2 twins … neither
3 choice … either   4 couple … neither
5 quarterly … every   6 doubles … each

17 1 There hasn't been much discussion of the
new road, but (many (of the)) older village
residents are against it.
2 Did you ask how much these postcards cost?
How many (of them) are you going to buy?
3 I'll be (much) later today because I have so
many different places to go to and there's so
much traffic in town.
4 I asked my classmates if they did much (of
the) homework and many (of them) said
they didn't do much (of it) unless there was
a test.

18 1 many   2 Many   3 much of   4 many of
5 Many … much   6 many of

19 1 (d) most of   2 (f) more of
3 more (a) more   4 most (c) most
5 most of (b)   6 (e) more of

20 1 much   2 many   3 more   4 many
5 more   6 more   7 much

21 1 few (d) a few   2 a little (e) a few of
3 (b) a little of   4 few (a) little
5 a little (c) a few

22 1 a quarter of   2 Once a
3 two-fifths of an   4 twice as
5 twenty per cent of the   6 four times the

23 1 little   2 a few   3 fewest
4 fewer   5 fifty per cent

Tests

A 1 c   2 c   3 b   4 c   5 c

B 1 D (some of their friends)
2 C (either colour OR either of the colours)
3 C (a little information OR some
information)
4 A (all of them OR they all)
5 A (most of Europe)

C 1 a lot of   2 both   3 some
4 neither   5 the   6 a little

D 1 Not many people are willing to help others.
2 Half the report (OR Half of the report) has
been written already.

3 No explanation was given (to us) for the
delay.
4 All of us want to live forever.

E 1 Most of
2 a great deal of (OR more)
3 two-thirds of
4 twelve times
5 few
6 many
7 fewest
8 a third of
9 ninety per cent of
10 more of (OR a great deal of)

Unit 8 Pronouns, substitution and ellipsis

1 1 **it**'s as if you've known each other all your
lives (line 25)
2 **She** took his right hand and placed **it**
against hers, palms touching (line 32)

2 1 D   2 C   3 E   4 A   5 B

3 1 They, we (C)
2 hers, mine, yours* (E)

*Note that his in his right hand (E) is a determiner, not a
pronoun.*

4 You meet **someone** for the first time, and it's
as if you've known each other all your lives.
(line 24)
Everything goes smoothly. (line 26)

5 1 yours   2 they   3 his
4 it … him   5 that … this

6 1 You know that you shouldn't use a phone
while you're driving.
2 I heard that they're going to demolish this
old factory so (that) they can build a new
school.
3 If you're self-indulgent, you allow yourself
to do or have too much of what you like.
4 I think that we shouldn't criticize when
we're not sure of our facts. (OR I think that
you shouldn't criticize when you're not sure
of your facts.)

7 1 A disguise … something … no one
2 Camouflage … something … everything
3 A mirage … something … nothing

8 she ~~played it~~ (OR ~~she played it~~)> played them
~~for we~~ to learn the words > for us
~~hers~~ favourite songs > her

233

no really understood the words > no one (OR nobody)

but every talked > everyone (OR everybody)

about different something > about something different

in his groups > their

And no ones were > no one (OR nobody) was

were trying > was

to practise his English > their

one song that went like that > this

what your want > you

what your need > you

That was interesting words > Those were

I did learn somethings > something (OR some things)

9 1 (c) himself   2 (a) yourself (or yourselves)
3 (d) myself   4 (b) them

10 1 you   2 yourself   3 it   4 itself   5 we
6 ourselves   7 they   8 themselves

11 1 by herself
2 about himself
3 for themselves
4 with me
5 near you

12

1 each	2 other	3 yourself
4 you	5 each*	6 other's*
7 one*	8 another's*	9 one
10 another	11 each	12 the other

*the combinations 5 plus 6 and 7 plus 8 can be exchanged

13 1 express themselves
2 hurt herself
3 blamed each other (OR blamed one another OR each blamed the other)
4 agree with each other (OR agree with one another)
5 meet each other's (OR meet one another's)

14 1 It really annoys everyone that Tony never helps with the cleaning.
2 It can be a big disadvantage not having a car.
3 It's very important in my job to see potential problems in advance.
4 It was a complete mystery why she left so suddenly.
5 It must have been a shock to discover that your passport was missing.
6 It always amazes me that people can eat such unhealthy food and live so long.

15 1 there was snowing > it was snowing (or there was snow)
2 It isn't much time left > There

3 There certain to be questions > There are certain
4 It was said to be hundreds of people stranded > There were said to be hundreds of people stranded (OR Hundreds of people were said to be stranded)
5 A lot of fat and sugar is in pies > There's a lot of fat and sugar in pies
6 Everyone found very amusing > found it very amusing
7 They viewed it offensive > viewed it as offensive
8 there were found no survivors > no survivors were found (OR there were no survivors found)

16 1 (d) any   2 ones (c) ones
3 some (b) them   4 one (a) it

17 they started looking for it > one
some ones were really expensive > some were
But she kept looking for it > one
She eventually found a second-hand > a second-hand one
so she bought right way > bought it right away
every had fallen for the same trick > every one (OR everyone OR each one)

18 1 so   2 so ... so   3 so ... do it
4 does so   5 done it   6 to do so

19 1 one   2 so   3 –   4 –
5 one   6 ones   7 –

20 a repeated subject [5]
a repeated subject and auxiliary [4]
a repeated subject and verb [6]
after *then* and *yet* [8]
after subordinating conjunctions [7]
repeated objects [10]
or preposition phrases [9]
the object from second or later clauses [11]
a repeated verb phrase [13]
after *be* as a linking verb [12]
after infinitive *to* [15]
or *not to* [14]
we can also leave out *to* [16]
when both clauses have the same structure [17]
when the subject is a pronoun [18]
when we ask [19]
or report questions [20]

21

1 litter	2 –	3 –
4 waste	5 them	6 –
7 –	8 pollution	9 –
10 them	11 rubbish	12 they
13 –	14 them	

22
1 train
2 Boston
3 no one was
4 wouldn't tell us what
5 the others hadn't
6 didn't
7 I sat in the back
8 she didn't want to

23 He put the money on the table and ~~he~~ sat down. He sat in his hot clothes and ~~he~~ felt heavy. The woman looked over at him and ~~she~~ smiled. Her smile said she was in charge and she could take his money if she wanted ~~to take his money~~. Of course she could ~~take his money~~, he thought, but obviously she didn't want to ~~take his money~~ yet. The smile lingered for a moment or two longer, then ~~it~~ disappeared and ~~it~~ was replaced by a dark stare.

'I asked you to pay me a thousand and you agreed ~~to pay me a thousand~~. This is only five hundred.'

'You'll get your thousand. I'll give you half ~~of your thousand~~ now and I'll give you the other half ~~of your thousand~~ later when I get the orchid.'

'I could get the orchid and ~~I could~~ find someone else who'd want to buy it.'

'You won't ~~find someone else who'd want to buy it~~. Nobody else is even looking for this orchid.'

The dark stare wanted to stay, but ~~it~~ was slowly replaced by half a smile. It said she would give me half of the smile now and the other half ~~of the smile~~ later.

Tests

A 1 d   2 b   3 b   4 c   5 c

B 1 B (with her)
2 C (the other)
3 D (she tastes it)
4 B (regarded it as an opportunity)
5 B (a knife was discovered)

C 1 do something   2 them myself
3 someone else   4 do it

D 1 It should have been useful having wealthy parents, but they didn't actually support her.
2 They don't like each other. (OR They don't like one another.)
3 I'm sure there will be someone at the airport to meet you.
4 It would not be a good idea to go swimming out in the ocean by yourself.

5 There were said to be thousands of people affected by the rail strike.

E 1 she   2 me   3 myself   4 him
5 anyone   6 ours   7 that   8 himself
9 one   10 anywhere   11 it

Unit 9 Adjectives and adverbs

1 1 very important (line 15)
OR really bad (line 34)
2 large heavy wooden wardrobes (line 33)

2 1 best   2 very (OR really)   3 important
4 diagonally   5 directly   6 horizontal
7 small   8 large (OR heavy OR wooden)
9 pointed   10 Blue   11 soft   12 natural

3 Restrictive: main (line 16)
Intensifying: perfect (line 5)

4 **Choose one example of each type.**
Opinion: comfortable, harmonious, beneficial, important, best, better, easier, bad, vulnerable, restless, negative, soothing, peaceful
Size: small, large
Physical quality: heavy, soft
Age/Time: ancient, modern, contemporary
Shape: pointed, horizontal
Colour: blue, brown

5 **Choose one example of each type.**
Location: outdoor
Origin/Course: Chinese
Material: wooden
Type: agricultural, physical, horizontal, natural
Purpose: relaxing

6 ancient Chinese (OR large wooden OR heavy wooden OR soft natural)

7 1 The flags of Britain and the USA both have red**,** white **and** blue designs.
2 He described the wonderful, friendly, outgoing people who worked in the little Italian café.
3 You immediately notice the large plastic vases with pink **and** purple flowers on every table.
4 There are many industrial **and** agricultural applications of the new chemical compounds.
5 What are the cultural**,** religious **and** historic origins of these current regional conflicts?

8
1 The entire German team played well.
2 The wine made a small red stain.
3 There's nothing new in the main Christian values.
4 You'll need comfortable leather hiking boots.
5 It has a long pointed stem with tiny pink flowers.
6 The windows are in huge circular wooden frames.
7 They are the major northern industrial nations.
8 ✓
9 They found a beautiful antique rocking chair.
10 Her mother was alone in the total chaos.
11 ✓
12 We like recent American economic policies.

9
1 large	2 rare
3 black	4 white
5 similar	6 small
7 hard	8 shiny white*
9 bluish-grey*	10 great
11 thin*	12 sharp*
13 cool	14 northern
15 large	16 tropical
17 juicy	18 yellow
19 prickly	

*8 and 9 can be exchanged; *11 and 12 can be exchanged*

10
1 Italian and Greek*
2 great little outdoor
3 carefree, crazy, happy (in any order)
4 older English
5 southern European*
6 cheap Spanish
7 big square plastic
8 sour and twisted (OR twisted and sour)

* *1 and 5 can be exchanged*

11
1 irritating (d)
2 worried (c)
3 exhausted (b)
4 astonishing (a)

12
1 bored	2 interesting	3 annoying
4 amazed	5 interested	6 annoyed
7 amazing	8 boring	

13
1 home-made	2 long-distance
3 peace-keeping	4 never-ending
5 well-educated	6 funny-looking
7 white-washed	

14 the poor and ~~weaks~~ > weak
The situation is ~~appalled~~ > appalling
without seeing ~~a homeless~~ > a homeless person (OR the homeless)
The ~~unemployeds~~ stand around > unemployed
The old and sick ~~receives~~ no help > receive
Why are we no longer ~~shocking~~ > shocked
~~Does~~ the Japanese > Do
and the ~~Canadian~~ have the same problems > Canadians
The unthinkable ~~have~~ happened here > has

15
1 We thought we had started our hike early, but other people had already left the campsite (OR had left the campsite already).
2 The workers usually get paid weekly, but they haven't been paid for last week yet (OR they haven't yet been paid for last week).
3 The students still hadn't completed all their work when they had to leave here yesterday.
4 Alice lived here recently, but she doesn't live here any more.
5 We used to hardly ever hear them (OR We hardly ever used to hear them), but they've become really noisy lately (OR but lately they've become really noisy).

16
1 always	2 only	3 outside
4 today	5 no longer	6 twice
7 sometimes	8 recently	9 ever
10 yet		

17
1 The couple had got married very recently (OR had very recently got married).
2 The baby looks exactly like her mother.
3 He isn't only an athlete, he's a scholar too!
4 Wait for us, we're coming now.
5 Lunch is almost ready.
6 Wear this silly hat. It's only for fun.

18
1 I completely forgot my brother's birthday yesterday. (OR Yesterday I completely forgot my brother's birthday. OR I forgot my brother's birthday completely yesterday.)
2 The piano is really large and our doorway isn't wide enough.
3 We enjoyed the trip very much, but it was too expensive. (OR We very much enjoyed the trip.)
4 I'll read the report carefully tomorrow. (OR I'll carefully read the report tomorrow. OR Tomorrow I'll read the report carefully. OR Tomorrow I'll carefully read the report.)

19 1 Traditionally (c) completely
2 only (a) of course
3 carelessly (f) even
4 Individually (e) enough
5 casually (b) very
6 extremely (d) angrily

20 1 Actually   2 certainly
3 very*   4 seriously
5 unfortunately   6 completely*
7 of course   8 probably
9 uncontrollably   10 still
11 Apparently   12 nervously
3 and 6 can be exchanged

21 1 longer … more likely (OR likelier) … best
2 oldest (OR eldest) … taller … fast
3 new … better-behaved (OR more well-behaved) … earlier
4 best-known … shorter … easier (OR most beautiful … more different … quicker)
5 different … most beautiful … quickest (OR short … well-known … easiest OR easy … well-known … shortest)
6 well … worst … least skilled

22 1 the best   2 as quickly as
3 more easily   4 faster
5 better   6 less beneficial*
7 more wasteful*   8 smaller
9 the most important   10 puzzled
6 and 7 can be exchanged

23 they put the ~~good looking~~ of all the people > best-looking
were not attractive as those > not as attractive
the people in Group A were warm > warmer
kind > kinder
exciting > more exciting
and sensitive than those in Group B > more sensitive
Group A would find high-paid jobs > higher-paid
have successful marriages > more successful
and lead happy lives than Group B > happier
to have appealing personalities > more appealing
and to be socially skilled than the Group B women > more (OR better) socially skilled
but also to be vain > vainer (OR more vain)
materialistic > more materialistic
snobbish > more snobbish
and likely to get divorced than them > more likely
Group A would be bad parents than Group B > worse

Tests

A 1 c 2 b 3 b 4 a 5 c

B 1 D (six feet deep)
2 B (some soldiers who were afraid)
3 C (I usually drink)
4 A (remove 'very')
5 B (Italians)

C 1 already … never   2 just … further
3 longer … reading   4 Eventually … easier
5 Suddenly … short   6 round black

D 1 Everyone thought the event was well-organized and exciting.
2 The earlier you leave here, the quicker you'll get there.
3 Mark is not as good a cook as David.
4 I'm looking for a fairly long green woollen scarf.

E 1 only   2 earlier   3 yet
4 acutely   5 pleased   6 young
7 Japanese   8 coloured   9 certainly
10 far

Unit 10 Prepositions

1 **Choose four:**
At the same time (line 10)
in the Christmas break (line 16)
at night (line 28)
during the weekend (line 28)
until 3 a.m. (line 31)
on Friday and Saturday nights (line 31)

2 1 against
2 out of
3 during
4 in exchange for (OR for)
5 in
6 for
7 than
8 at
9 during
10 with
11 according to
12 of

3 1 we talked to (d)
2 of them (a)
3 apart from working (b)
4 in which today's students struggle (c)

4 1 at six in the morning
2 on her birthday next Saturday
3 in September every year

4 at night in winter

5 on Christmas Day in the past

6 at four o'clock on Friday afternoon

7 at sixty-five in 2005

8 on the fourth of July in 1776 (OR on the fourth of July, 1776 OR in 1776 on the fourth of July)

5 1 expiry date   2 during   3 deadline
   4 in   5 by   6 curfew
   7 after   8 at   9 until
   10 in

6 1 waiting ~~since~~ an hour > for (OR waiting an hour)
   ~~till~~ his next meeting > before

2 My sister ~~works~~ > has worked (OR has been working)
   since ~~after~~ 2003 > since 2003 (OR since before 2003)

3 received in this office ~~until~~ 9 a.m. > by (OR before)
   ~~in~~ the first of March > on

4 appointments ~~in~~ every morning > appointments every morning
   see you ~~on~~ next Monday morning > see you next Monday morning

7 1 on (d) in   2 at (c) in
   3 in (a) at   4 on (b) in

8 1 The meeting focused **on** economic problems **in** developing countries **in** South-East Asia.

2 You can either stand **at** the bar or sit **at** a table **in** most pubs **in** Britain.

3 We were depending **on** my brother to meet us **at** the exit door after the concert.

4 The children were laughing **at** something they had seen **in** a cartoon.

9 1 under … overcoat
2 overpopulation among
3 overlap between
4 overalls over
5 above … overflow
6 below … overhead

10 1 to   2 from   3 out of   4 towards
   5 across*   6 along*   7 to*   8 past

*5, 6 and 7 can be exchanged

11 1 through … to   2 along … towards
   3 out of … from

12 1 towards   2 over   3 on   4 through
   5 along   6 from   7 into   8 towards

13 1 of the door with a screwdriver
2 with American history by reading
3 with some friends of ours
4 by scoring … of the match
5 with the yellow lampshade … with a cheque

14 1 rice except   2 omelettes without
   3 fish besides   4 meal except
   5 fruit except for   6 ice cream with
   7 bread without   8 pizza, minus

15 1 You have to fill in this form and send it back with your payment.

2 My dad has given up his attempt to get the university to do away with tuition fees.

3 We had to cut back on our spending after we found out that our rent was going up.

4 Please go along with local customs at the temple and take off your shoes (OR take your shoes off) before going in.

16 1 Push away   2 Stand up
   3 raise … up*   4 breathe out
   5 bend … down   6 breathe in
   7 lift … up*   8 go back

* 3 and 7 can be exchanged

17 1 B   2 A   3 B   4 B   5 A
   6 A   7 A or B   8 B

Tests

A 1 a   2 a   3 c   4 d   5 c

B 1 C (instead of)   2 C (~~on~~ every day)
   3 B (in)   4 D (over)
   5 D (out of OR in)

C 1 away   2 from   3 to
   4 in   5 out of   6 for

D 1 During August this building will be closed for renovation.

2 Besides shopping, what else did you do when you were in Rome? (OR Besides shopping when you were in Rome, what else did you do?)

3 Apart from the apple I gave you earlier, haven't you eaten anything else today?

4 Without more financial support we won't be able to do much.

E 1 By   2 past   3 At
   4 under   5 towards   6 with
   7 into   8 of   9 along
   10 across

Unit 11 Infinitives and gerunds

1 helped hundreds of people to stop **smoking** (line 11)
and **avoiding** social situations (line 17)
situations that will make her want **to smoke** (line 18)
many people continue **smoking** (line 23)
Encourage her **to avoid** stressful situations (line 25)

2 1 kick the habit (line 5)
   2 doing yoga (line 27)
   3 (going) cold turkey (line 34)
   4 over the counter (line 42)

3 1 want to become (2)
   2 makes them experience (1)
   3 to stop doing (3)
   4 of treating (1) (OR for controlling (2) OR without needing (4))

4 1 to be … having   2 to have … being
   3 to have … having 4 to have … to be

5 1 to have finished (4)
   2 to be studying (1)
   3 to have been living (2)
   4 to be done (4)
   5 to have been constructed (3)
   6 having slept (1)
   7 being killed (2)
   8 having been built (3)

6 1 Your homework was supposed to have been (OR to be) done before you went out.
   2 I wanted to thank her for having taken (OR for taking) the time to help me.
   3 They complained about not having been (OR not being) told about the changes.

7 1 travelling   2 meeting
   3 to have visited   4 to have been doing
   5 being held   6 to have been based
   7 to be using   8 to be burning
   9 to have been built 10 not to have seen

8 1 hope (OR am hoping) to visit
   2 invited … to stay
   3 wants … to spend
   4 enjoy taking
   5 imagine … making
   6 love to be

9 1 allow … to take
   2 forget to send
   3 meant to tidy
   4 prefer not to talk (OR prefer not talking)

5 avoid trying to drive
6 forced … to stop playing

10 encouraged me ~~take~~ > to take
advised me ~~remember~~ > to remember
remember ~~clean~~ the bathrooms > to clean
likes ~~clean~~ bathrooms > cleaning (OR to clean)
I didn't mind ~~do~~ it > doing
I was first starting ~~learn~~ > to learn
I could practise ~~speak~~ English > speaking
I enjoyed ~~try~~ > trying
~~try improve~~ my English > trying to improve
I didn't want ~~work~~ > to work
I don't regret ~~do~~ it > doing
I decided ~~study~~ harder > to study
and try ~~get~~ a better job > to get

11 1 It's essential to plan ahead in my kind of job. (OR It's essential in my kind of job to plan ahead.)
   2 Jessica was disappointed not to see any of her friends at the shopping centre.
   3 It was so good of Christopher to come to our rescue when our car broke down.
   4 Those huge buses aren't easy to drive along narrow winding roads.

12 1 idea … studying
   2 plan … to take
   3 problem keeping
   4 place to stay
   5 information … reserving
   6 task … to phone
   7 someone to ask
   8 cost … renting

Tests

A 1 d 2 c 3 b 4 a 5 d

B 1 A (learning)   2 D (refused to help)
   3 B (to wait)   4 A (visiting)
   5 D (of doing)

C 1 assumed to be
   2 heard … sneeze (OR sneezing)
   3 remembered … telling
   4 allowed to go
   5 smell … burning.

D 1 A place to park is sometimes hard to find.
   2 Is it really necessary to keep all these old files?
   3 It would be a mistake for him to buy a new car now.
   4 Amy still remembers being bitten by a dog when she was very young.
   5 The boy denied having done anything

wrong. (OR The boy denied doing anything wrong.)

E 1 trying   2 to look
    3 to do   4 to regain
    5 stopping   6 to keep (OR to have kept)
    7 starting   8 losing
    9 putting   10 going

Unit 12 Reporting

1 1 He would just nod and **say**, 'Thanks for coming round,' (line 56)

    2 those who had opinions mostly **said** that it was a strange story (line 49)

2 1 C   2 D   3 B   4 F   5 A   6 E

3 1 put (line 10) (OR call out (line 13))

    2 grumbled (line 22)

4 1 comma
    2 quotation mark
    3 comma
    4 quotation mark
    5 quotation mark
    6 quotation mark

5 'Susanna,' Mrs Alder called out, 'I'd like you to come and meet Michael.' A girl appeared in the doorway. 'How do you do?' she said. 'Nice to meet you,' he mumbled. 'Please don't call him "Michelle" or "Mikey" or any other silly names,' warned Mrs Alder as she swept out of the room. 'Have you read "Harry Potter"?' Susanna suddenly said. 'What one?' he asked. 'Oh, no, you little Mickey Mouse,' she said as she came into the room, 'you must say "Which one?", not "What one?", if you're going to survive here.' (OR … into the room. 'You must …)

6 1 He said that he left (OR had left) his jacket there the day before (OR the previous day).

    2 The reviewer wrote that Carlin's new book was the funniest thing he or she had ever read.

    3 She said that they wouldn't eat it then, but they might have it for lunch the next day (OR the following day).

    4 He advised us that we should take as much water as we could carry.

    5 You told me that you had to (OR must) get something to eat or you would faint.

    6 CompCo is reporting that demand for new computers in the UK is declining.

    7 She asked if she should get rid of those old boxes in the cupboard.

7 1 was   2 could   3 is
    4 has   5 are   6 can't
    7 won't   8 would   9 will
    10 live   11 can   12 lived
    13 were   14 had

8 1 I mentioned to Mr Brody that there was something wrong with the lights.

    2 I reminded Julia that she and her friends had to tidy up after the party.

    3 He warned me (OR you/him/her/us/them) not to touch any of the wires.

    4 He denied doing anything wrong. (OR He denied that he had done anything wrong. OR He denied that he did anything wrong. OR He denied having done anything wrong.)

9 1 shouting
    2 had mentioned (OR mentioned)
    3 wondered
    4 talk
    5 asked
    6 told
    7 explained
    8 claim
    9 begged
    10 thought.

10 I can't ~~agree them~~ > agree with them

and offered ~~me to help~~ > to help me

I ~~explained them~~ > explained to them

that I ~~can't~~ get the wheel off > couldn't

One of them ~~told that~~ > told me that (or said that)

and ~~assured that~~ > assured me that

He even suggested ~~me to stand~~ > standing (OR that I (should) stand)

~~warned me watch out~~ > warned me to watch out (OR warned me that I should watch out)

~~joked~~ the small wheels > joked about

~~I spoke them thanks~~ > I thanked them. (OR I told them, 'Thanks.' OR I said, 'Thanks' to them.)

They ~~refused take~~ > refused to take

I ~~offered pay them~~ > offered to pay them

11 1 One of the defendants called out that he (OR she) was not guilty.

    2 Her statement that she'd been adopted really surprised us.

    3 I agree with the students' argument that the cost of tuition has increased too much.

    4 No one believed his claim that he was not a thief. (OR his claim not to be a thief.)

12 1 (c) whether 2 (a) who
  3 (d) where 4 (b) that

13 1 One of the visitors asked about whether there would be a fridge in the hotel room. (OR … asked if there would be … OR … asked whether there would be …)
  2 He asked me why I did that (OR why I was doing that OR why I had done that OR why I had to do that) and I pointed out that it was part of my job.)
  3 She asked me what to do next (OR what she should do next) and my response was that she should (OR could) get some chairs.
  4 Her explanation that no one asked her (OR had asked her) whether or not she had a degree was incredible. (OR if she had a degree or not OR whether she had a degree or not)

14 1 why she wasn't sleeping
  2 that there was a 'moster' under her bed.
  3 what a 'moster' was
  4 if (OR whether) she had seen the monster
  5 (that) she hadn't, but (that) she knew it had big teeth.
  6 where it had come from

15 1 The professor asked her students not to eat or drink during lectures. (OR The professor asked her students if they would not eat or drink during lectures.)
  2 The guard ordered the prisoner to stand up when the judge came in.
  3 The worker asked to leave early on Friday. (OR The worker asked (his boss) if he could leave early on Friday.)
  4 Scott's mother recommended applying to several universities. (OR Scott's mother recommended (that) he (should) apply to several universities.)

16 1 to place her napkin in her lap (OR that she should / must place her napkin in her lap OR that she place her napkin in her lap)
  2 not to rest her elbows on the table (OR that she should / must not rest her elbows on the table OR that she not rest her elbows on the table)
  3 to chew her food with her mouth closed (OR (that) she should / must chew her food with her mouth closed)
  4 not to talk with her mouth full (OR (that) she shouldn't / mustn't talk with her mouth full)
  5 not to put a lot of food on her plate all at once (OR that she shouldn't / mustn't put a lot of food on her plate all at once OR that

she not put a lot of food on her plate all at once)
  6 not to take more food until it is offered (OR that she shouldn't / mustn't take more food until it is offered OR that she not take more food until it is offered)
  7 should / must ask somebody
  8 if they would (please) pass the salt (OR to (please) pass the salt)

17 1 recommendation that we (should) take the early flight to Glasgow.
  2 belief that a perfect life can be achieved.
  3 diagnosis … that I had an ear infection.
  4 sorry that she lost her temper.
  5 positive that we would all pass the exam.
  6 aware that dogs weren't allowed there.

Tests

A 1 b 2 d 3 b 4 c 5a

B 1 D (would be able)
  2 C (agreed with me)
  3 C (encouraged her not to quit)
  4 A (inquired about whether)
  5 B (offered to bring OR offered to bring us)

C 1 tell 2 asked 3 explained* 4 hadn't said
  5 hadn't spoken 6 replied* 7 pointed out
  8 talk (OR talked)
*3 and 6 can be exchanged

D 1 Mrs Dalloway said she would buy the flowers herself.
  2 She asked Henry if he had left (OR left) his keys in the door.
  3 There was an announcement that the strike was over.
  4 His only comment was that he would return the following day (OR the next day OR the day after).
  5 His statement that he wouldn't do it surprised us.
  6 I remember one time when my aunt told me not to talk with my mouth full. (OR … my aunt told me that I mustn't (OR shouldn't) talk with my mouth full.)
  7 They invited me (OR us) to stay at their house.

E 1 (that) he would be here by eight o'clock
  2 if she knew where Rob was
  3 (that) she thought he had gone out about half an hour earlier
  4 apologized (OR said that he was sorry)
  5 that he had forgotten that he had promised to take his mother into town that morning

Unit 13 Noun clauses

1 1 One of the individuals typically insists **that** he or she will not stop doing something despite the fact **that** it is a source of conflict. (line 46)

OR Sometimes one of them will say **that** he or she actually prefers it **that** the other has separate interests. (line 49)

*NOT: ~~On the basis of their study, the researchers have concluded **that** a modern marriage may begin with passionate love, but its survival depends a lot on 'companionate love', a feeling that includes affection, caring and friendship.~~ (line 62)

The second that (= which) is a relative pronoun introducing a relative clause, not a noun clause. See page 164.

2 It makes you wonder **if** getting married is worth the effort. (line 7)

2 1 T 2 T 3 F 4 F 5 F 6 F

3 1 that it was one of their best memories (line 32)

OR that he or she will not stop doing something (line 47)

OR that he or she actually prefers it that the other has separate interests. (line 49)

2 **the case** that marriage has become a gamble (line 9)

OR **one indication** that the couple speaks with a single voice (line 24)

OR … **the fact** that it is a source of conflict (line 48)

3 **likely** that a marriage will end in divorce (line 6)

OR **delighted** that so many of their couples stayed together (line 20)

OR **obvious** that these individuals had really different views about marriage (line 57)

4 what advice they would give to younger people thinking about getting married (line 52)

5 to what makes a successful marriage (line 12)

4 2 We **learned** that pineapples don't grow on trees. (7)

3 No one **noticed** that the keys were missing. (7)

4 She could never **anticipate** what he might want. (8)

5 I'll **show** you how it works. (10)

6 He **screamed** that he hated school. (9) (OR She **said** she felt that everyone was against her. (9) OR He **told** me that he loved me. (10))

7 Ewan **suggested** that we should leave early. (8)

8 They **consider** it an offence when women go out in public without covering their heads. (12) (OR We **thought** it odd that no one called us. (13) OR Many people **regard** it as a really bad idea that the police have started carrying guns. (14))

5 1 It doesn't surprise me at all that they don't have any money left.

2 It just astonishes me that children would rather sit watching TV instead of playing outside.

3 It has never been explained why the government didn't act immediately to stop the movement of all animals.

4 It wasn't clear whether Nicole's father had been for or against her marriage, but he did participate in the wedding ceremony.

6 1 what   2 it   3 that
4 that   5 it   6 that
7 Whether   8 that   9 where

7 1 **That** Mr Baker complained about the noise was predictable, but we assured **him (that)** it wouldn't happen again. (OR **It was predictable that** Mr Baker complained about the noise, but we assured **him (that)** it wouldn't happen again.)

2 The headmaster warned **us** (OR **me** or **you**) during our meeting **that** some teachers wouldn't like **it that** (OR **the fact that**) their classrooms had suddenly been changed.

3 They told me about **what** Geoff had said, but I thought **it** strange **(that)** he didn't mention money.

4 The police regarded **it as** suspicious **that** the dead woman's husband had recently taken out a life insurance policy in her name.

5 The prosecutor showed the jury how **the crime could** have been committed by Feldman, but he didn't convince **them** (OR **the jury**) that Feldman was guilty.

8 1 His explanation that he had been stuck in traffic for over an hour didn't sound right.

2 Their discovery that the boy suffered from asthma changed their attitude.

3 The belief that there are aliens from outer space living among us is quite widespread.

9 1 with the view that
2 to the fact that
3 conclusion was (that)
4 against the idea that
5 example of
6 Despite the fact that
7 belief that
8 in agreement that

10 1 premonition … that … which/that
2 Scepticism … that … that
3 Superstition … that … which/that
4 Déjà vu … that … which/that

11 raise ~~issues how~~ equality can be > issues of
(OR about OR with regard to) how
~~the fact which~~ women don't have > the fact
that
based on ~~the belief people's~~ attitudes can be
changed > the belief that people's
~~the assumption other~~ peaceful changes > the
assumption that other
~~in spite of it is~~ largely controlled by men > in
spite of the fact that it is

12 1 We were afraid (that) our old car might
break down.
2 I was completely surprised that (OR when OR
by the fact that) Karen suddenly decided to
quit her job.
3 Sean was absolutely sure (that) the test
would be easy.

13 1 unlikely (that)   2 aware of how
3 surprising when   4 glad that
5 embarrassed by what   6 amazed (that)

14 in *that*-clauses (1)
the negative subjunctive (2)
instead of the present subjunctive (3)
after verbs expressing orders (6)
rules (5)
suggestions (4)
in a reported order (7)
not in a reported statement (8)
after nouns expressing orders (11)
rules (10)
suggestions (9)
after adjectives expressing what is necessary
(12)

15 1 crucial (d) (should) not be disturbed
2 stipulates (OR stipulated) (c) (should) have
3 recommends (OR recommended) (f)
(should) spend
4 suggestion (a) (should) be given
5 requirement (b) (should) be worn
6 insists (OR insisted) (e) (had) arrested

16 A 1 what they're thinking
2 what happened that day
3 who their best friends are
B 4 that women are less likely than men
5 that men get the impression
6 that women never tell jokes
C 7 if men and women talk equally
8 people think
9 the women talked more
D 10 that men think
11 women talk a lot
12 that they hear women

17 1 that there was another world
2 (that) Columbus reached Iceland
3 he could reach China
4 that Columbus wasn't the first European
5 (that) Columbus's visit to Iceland gave him
the confidence
6 there would eventually be a place to land

Tests

A 1 c   2 d   3 a   4 d   5 b

B 1 A (That Sandra … OR The fact that Sandra
…)
2 D (~~which~~ > that)
3 A (I heard ~~about~~ that)
4 B (like > like the fact OR like it)
5 B (~~remind that~~ > remind us OR me OR you,
etc. that)

C 1 idea of **how** categorization works
2 we take it for granted **that** categories have
3 and **that** all members of a given category
4 we see **that** it is
5 it is not surprising **that** we hold

D 1 He didn't conceal the fact that his parents
weren't English.
2 It has always been a big mystery to me why
anyone would want to jump out of a plane
and put their trust in a parachute.
3 Our expectation was that no one would be
there.
4 Bridget was sorry that her comments had
upset Mark's mother.
5 Despite the fact that these apples don't look
very nice, they're delicious.

E 1 noticed (that)   2 know if
3 reason to when   4 argue (that)
5 concedes that   6 That emotion
7 rule out that   8 view that
9 feel (that)   10 unfair that

Unit 14 Relative clauses

1 which sank in 1718 (line 5)
OR who was the most notorious pirate of his day (line 6)
whose real name was Edward Teach (line 8)
OR whatever they captured from these enemies of the queen (line 13)
when the European powers declared peace (line 15)
OR what they knew best (line 19)
OR which had the speed and power (line 22)
OR which they renamed 'Queen Anne's Revenge' (line 25)
that he needed (line 31)
OR whose huge black beard was twisted into long tails (line 34)
OR who carried several guns and swords in belts (line 35)
OR (which were) slung across both shoulders (line 36)
OR that he could use (line 38)
when he was killed in a sea battle with two British ships (line 41)
OR which had been sent (line 42)
OR (that) we still have today (line 46)

2 1 whose   2 who
3 that (OR which)   4 who (OR whom)
5 that (OR which)   6 which
7 when   8 that (OR which)
9 – (OR that OR which)

3 … all (that) he needed (line 31)
… fuses (that) he could use to ignite cannons during an attack (line 38)

4 Defining: which had the speed and power (line 22)
which had been sent (line 42)
Non-defining: which sank in 1718. (line 5)
which they renamed 'Queen Anne's Revenge' (line 25)

5 1 who   2 who   3 that
4 which   5 (that)   6 who
7 which   8 who   9 that
10 whom

6 1 that (OR which) uses exaggerated actions, often involving accidents
2 who controls a sports game
3 in which each competitor takes part in three different sports
4 from whom you rent a room or flat (OR that (OR who) you rent a room or flat from)

5 , the largest part of which is below the surface of the water,
6 , some of which are poisonous,
7 , which consists of nine islands,
8 , whom (OR who) most people know as Mark Twain,

7 ~~a letter said~~ I had been terminated > a letter that (OR which) said
the letter, ~~that~~ came from the university, > which
termination (~~means~~ 'the end') > which means
~~which it felt~~ really weird > which felt
that I could be fired from it > that I could be fired from (OR from which I could be fired)
I was just ~~a student didn't~~ have a job > a student who (OR that) didn't
it was ~~an error had~~ been caused > an error that (OR which) had
I wasn't ~~the only one had~~ been terminated > the only one who (OR that) had
A lot of ~~other people didn't~~ have jobs > other people who (OR that) didn't

8 1 memo … sent … working
2 mermaid … having
3 jigsaw … printed … cut
4 shadow … caused … standing

9 1 parked outside … sitting in it
2 standing on the bed … covered with feathers
3 starting at 8 p.m. … based on a true story
4 accused of crimes committed during the war
5 not having children … going out to concerts and the theatre

10 For all you food lovers ~~who will be~~ sitting at home and ~~who will be~~ looking for something ~~that is~~ interesting on TV this afternoon, there's a fabulous new TV show ~~which is~~ called 'The Asian Kitchen', ~~which has been~~ created and ~~which has been~~ produced by Mary Sah, ~~which begins~~ beginning at 4.30 this afternoon. Among the dishes ~~which will be~~ featured will be Saucy Tofu, ~~which consists~~ consisting of tofu squares ~~which have been~~ dipped in a special batter, ~~which have been~~ deep-fried and ~~which have been~~ covered in a creamy peanut sauce, and Evil Shrimp, ~~which is~~ made with hot peppers, ~~which have been~~ sauteed with other vegetables and ~~which are~~ served with shrimp ~~which are~~ sizzling in a shallow pool of red curry. It's the most delicious thing on TV today!

11 to refer to people [1]

for organizations [3]

and places [2]

things that are part of [4]

or belong to [5]

of which after a noun when we talk about things [7]

the noun plus *of* at the end [6]

after personal pronouns [9]

and indefinite pronouns [8]

followed by *who* or *that* [12]

after quantifiers [11]

12 1 whose parents are dead

2 who doesn't care about money

3 whose wood (OR the wood of which OR of which the wood) is strong and durable

4 from whose upper windows (OR from the upper windows of which) large flags were hanging

5 who have completed their questionnaires

6 many of whose paintings look like large comic strips

13 1 before which you must complete something

2 for whose moral education you have promised to be responsible (OR whose moral education you have promised to be responsible for)

3 whom (OR who) you look up to

4 through which you look (OR which you look through OR that you look through OR – you look through)

14 about a ~~situation which~~ those > a situation in which (OR a situation where)

~~those want~~ to fight > those who want

a person ~~who the~~ house > whose

house is made of ~~glass, it's~~ something > glass, which is

~~something is~~ easily broken > something which (OR that) is

the person you threw the stone ~~at him~~ > the person at whom you threw the stone (OR the person whom you threw the stone at OR the person (who) you threw the stone at)

~~the meaning of it~~ I looked up > the meaning of which OR whose meaning

similar ~~to you have~~ > to those you have (OR to those that you have OR to those which you have)

for ~~anyone is~~ critical > anyone who is

15 1 when 2 where 3 how

4 what 5 how 6 why

16 1 Prison … where

2 motive … why

3 crime … which

4 Revenge … that … what

5 Quarantine … when

17 1 (d) however 2 (c) whatever

3 (a) whenever 4 (e) whichever

5 (b) whoever

18 1 whatever 2 that 3 where

4 which 5 what 6 when

7 whichever 8 how 9 why

Tests

A 1 a 2 b 3 c 4 d 5 b

B 1 C (who, because *that* is not used in a non-defining clause describing a person)

2 C (along which something slides)

3 C (that OR no relative pronoun, because *when* is not used after 'every time')

4 C (which made, because reduced relatives are not used for sudden actions)

5 D (all that, because a quantifier used as a pronoun takes *that*, not *which*)

C 1 whose 2 that OR which

3 where OR in which 4 What

5 which

D 1 Elizabeth is the name from which Betty is derived. (OR Elizabeth is the name (that/which) Betty is derived from.)

2 India is where her parents were born. (OR India is the place/country where/in which her parents were born.)

3 Hemingway is the author whose short stories I liked best.

4 Whatever I do, her parents will never like me.

5 I was at the first lecture during which he talked about humanism. (OR I was at the first lecture, when/where/in which he talked about humanism.)

E 1 (that is/which is) often told to children

2 who sells a cow

3 (which/that) his mother thinks are worthless

4 which grow very quickly

5 (that is/which is) called a beanstalk

6 where (OR in which or above which) he discovers a giant

7 from whom he steals some things (OR that/who he steals some things from)

8 suspecting (OR who suspects) something is wrong

9 which he then cuts down

10 who is chasing him

Unit 15 Conditionals

1 1 if she caught a cold (line 46)
2 if I put a huge swimming pool in front of my house (line 26)
OR If I went to all that trouble (line 29)
OR If you were in my situation (line 41)

2 1 (Cathy) 2 (Erin) 3 (Anna)
4 (Dave) 5 (Belinda)

3 1 If she has a cup of coffee, she always wants to smoke a cigarette (line 7)
OR If she catches a cold, she goes to bed immediately (line 50)
2 If she had a cigarette in her hand, she was cool. (line 3)
3 If you are successful, it will be because of hard work. (line 12)
OR If you don't have a struggle, you won't experience the triumph. (line 18)
OR If you build it, they will come. (line 24)

4 1 was (f) 2 come (d) 3 is (a)
4 is (e) 5 don't (b) 6 is (c)

5 1 if I put a huge swimming pool in front of my house, people would think I was crazy. (line 26)
OR If I went to all that trouble, I'd put the pool at the back of my house. (line 29)
OR If I were you, I'd sell it. (line 33)
OR If you were in my situation, I would help you out. (line 41)
2 If he had wanted to sell his car, he would have done that already. (line 36)
OR If he had worked harder at school, he would have had some kind of career by now. (lines 39)

6 1 If I knew Jason's phone number, I could tell him what happened.
2 If she had prepared for the test, she would (OR could OR might) have passed.
3 If you had warned us about the bad weather, I would (OR could OR might) have brought a raincoat.
4 If I was in your situation, I would (OR might) start looking for another job.

7 1 were
2 would start
3 wanted*
4 could do
5 started
6 would contribute
7 had started

8 could have paid*
9 would have contributed*
10 decided*
11 would cost
12 would end up

*3 and 10 can be exchanged. *8 and 9 can be exchanged.

8 he ~~always fall~~ asleep > always fell (OR would always fall OR always used to fall)
his feet ~~are~~ near the fire > were
his slippers usually ~~start~~ to smoke > started (OR would start)
my grandmother ~~has to~~ rush over > had to (OR would have to)
my father ~~sit~~ in that chair > sits
he immediately ~~go~~ to sleep > goes
and ~~start~~ snoring > starts
My mother ~~get~~ really annoyed > gets
if that ~~happen~~ > happens
if I ~~take~~ … ~~happen~~ to me > if I take … will happen (OR if I took … would happen OR if I were to take … would happen)
I ~~don't~~ have this dilemma > wouldn't
my older brother ~~doesn't move~~ away > hadn't moved
If he ~~stays~~ > had stayed
he ~~is given~~ the chair > would have been given
and I ~~am not faced~~ with the problem > wouldn't be faced (OR wouldn't have been faced)
If I ~~move~~ > moved
the chair ~~fit~~ > would (OR could) fit
~~Do~~ I really have a problem > Would
if I ~~settle~~ > settled
and ~~give~~ in > gave
But who ~~wake~~ me … if my slippers ~~catch~~ > would wake … caught (OR will wake … catch)

9 1 he … rather 2 he … prefer
3 he'd … have 4 he … wants
5 he'd … chase

10 A number of idioms have come from the game of cricket. **If** something is described as *not cricket*, it means that it is not fair or honourable. **If** someone is *on a sticky wicket*, they are in a difficult situation. (OR Someone is *on a sticky wicket* **if** they are in a difficult situation.) This is because balls do not bounce very well **if** the ground near the wicket is sticky (wet and muddy). **If** it is said that someone had *a good innings*, it means they had a long life or career.

11 1 If they took the test earlier today, they won't get the results until tomorrow.

2 If it isn't going to be a problem, I'd like to leave my bike in the hallway tonight.

3 If William sent the letter last week, it would have arrived by now, I'm sure.

4 If it was a terribly cold day outside, we would stay in bed until noon.

5 If the neighbour's dog hadn't started barking at 4 a.m., I wouldn't be so tired now.

6 I wouldn't feel so full now if I hadn't eaten so much at lunch.

7 If Sarah has completed all her work already, we can let her leave early today.

8 If you didn't watch television as a child, you probably won't know why some of these people from old TV programmes are famous.

12 typical patterns in the present (1)
the past (2)
to express rules (5)
habits (4)
correlations, such as scientific observations (3)
when we are explaining how to do something (6)
for plans (8)
predictions (9)
to ask about future events (11)
to make requests (10)
completely imaginary situations (14)
potential outcomes of a course of action (15)
willingness to do something, despite lack of ability (13)
express regret (17)
assign blame (18)

13 1 (predictive, 9)
2 (factual, 3)
3 (hypothetical, 15)
4 (factual, 5)
5 (counterfactual, 16)
6 (factual, 6)
7 (hypothetical, 13)
8 (counterfactual, 18)

14 1 had asked (c)   2 was (a)
3 don't want (e)   4 hadn't forgotten (b)
5 need (d)

15 1 If that's your goal
2 if the only measure of success was becoming a doctor
3 If you tried as hard as you could
4 If it's complete
5 If not
6 If you've done your best

16 1 Unless she comes soon, we'll have to leave without your friend. (OR Unless your friend comes soon, we'll have to leave without her.)

2 Whether Andy's ready or not, we're going to start playing. (OR Whether or not Andy's ready, we're going to start playing.)

3 They'll only let you take books out of the library if you're a registered student.

4 Even though our team played really well, we didn't win the game.

17 1 unless   2 If only
3 even though   4 whether or not
5 only if   6 If it isn't

18 A Simple: 2 Given,   5 Suppose,
   6 Supposing,   8 What if,   9 With
B Exclusive: 3 Providing that/provided that,
   7 as long as/so long as
C Exceptional: 4 otherwise,   10 Without

Tests

A 1 b   2 a   3 d   4 d   5 c

B 1 A (was)   2 D (will)   3 C (had)
4 B (~~will~~ get)   5 C (if ~~only~~)

C 1 If   2 will   3 didn't   4 if
5 was   6 throw   7 if

D 1 Unless someone is willing to help, the party is not likely to (OR will not) happen.

2 If only she had been wearing (OR had worn) a crash helmet, she would (OR might OR could) have escaped injury.

3 Even though she could be very difficult, I still loved her.

4 Whether you like the idea or not, we're leaving tomorrow.
OR Whether or not you like the idea, we're leaving tomorrow.

5 I'm sorry, but if the traffic hadn't been so bad, I wouldn't have arrived late.

E 1 If anyone asked me
2 if he wins
3 If he does that
4 if he loses
5 If that happens to him
6 If that is the result
7 If he doesn't really fight
8 unless he's an idiot

Unit 16 Adverbial clauses

1 A so she tried to take good care of his proud creation (line 5)

B Before he began his career with the national weather service (line 7)

OR Although he'd had to give up his artistic ambitions (line 9)

C because there was all that cement in the soil (line 16)

OR when he was mixing the cement, sand and water (line 18)

D When there was a spell of warm summer weather (line 23)

OR Before Emily could get to them (line 27)

E when Emily had to go out and sweep the whole country every morning (line 30)

OR If it wasn't wet (line 31)

OR When it rained a lot (line 34)

F Even though it wasn't really cold during most of the winter (line 37)

OR as if it had been carved from a large flat slab of marble by an expert hand (line 43)

2 1 T   2 F   3 F   4 F   5 T   6 T

3 1 After her husband passed away (line 1)

2 because there was all that cement in the soil (line 16)

3 When there was a spell of warm summer weather (line 23)

4 Even though it wasn't really cold during most of the winter (line 37)

5 as if it had been carved from a large flat slab of marble by an expert hand (line 43)

4 1 When I was standing at the bus stop in the rain, I watched Maurice drive by in his new car.

2 As the skin starts to turn yellow, you'll know that the fruit is getting ripe.

3 While we're eating (OR having OR at) lunch, we shouldn't talk about anything to do with work.

4 Just as I was getting out of the shower, the phone rang in the other room.

5 1 When   2 When OR While

3 As   4 As OR When OR While

6 1 prediction … before   2 skewer … while

3 postscript … after   4 blender … until

7 1 have been   2 'll be   3 've been   4 'll be

5 will be   6 've been   7 've been   8 will be

8 1 (c) as if   2 (a) as   3 (d) as if   4 (b) as

9 1 They all behaved as though nothing had happened.

2 It was still just as I remembered it.

3 It tastes as though it was made yesterday.

4 you try to do as well as they have done.

5 hidden in the forest, just as the guidebook had described it.

6 you think it isn't as much as it really is

10 1 As it's a holiday, all the banks will be closed on Monday.

2 Since she had an operation on her foot, she has had to use crutches.

3 While we're all together today, we should decide on a date for the Christmas party.

4 Now that he has finished his exams, I wonder what he'll do next.

11 1 (c) because   2 (b) as if

3 (a) Because   4 (d) as if

12 1 In order to avoid traffic jams on the way to the airport, you should plan to leave early tomorrow.

2 In order that no money (would) be wasted, we had to account for every penny we spent.

3 In order for plants to grow indoors, there must be a good source of light.

4 So as not to get wet, we waited a few minutes until the rain stopped.

13 1 ~~that~~ nobody would notice her > so (OR in order) that

2 ~~for~~ kill insects > to

3 ~~In order to care people~~ about another person > In order for people to care

4 ~~so as to not~~ get him in trouble > so as not to

5 ~~in order it~~ can stand > in order that it can stand (OR in order for it to stand)

6 ~~in order not our competitors find~~ > in order that (OR so that) our competitors don't find

14 1 They were feeling really tired, so they went to bed early last night.

2 I forgot to take my textbook home with me, so I wasn't able to do the homework.

3 Marjorie is in a popular TV show, so people recognize her when she's out shopping.

4 They said the tap water wasn't safe to drink, so we had to drink bottled water.

15 1 The fire spread so rapidly through their cabin (that)

2 Wendy's children had such bad colds this morning (that)

3 You and I don't have so much money (that)

4 We had such a wonderful time on holiday (that)

5 That class was so early (that)

16 1 Although I understand why he thinks that way, I disagree with his point of view. (OR Although I disagree with his point of view, I understand why he thinks that way.)

2 Though he has applied for about a dozen jobs, Jack is still unemployed.

3 Even though most people agreed that the car was a bargain, none of them wanted to buy it. (OR Even though none of them wanted to buy it, most people agreed that the car was a bargain.)

4 Unlikely though it seems, the children may not want to go to the zoo on Saturday.

5 Despite the fact that the old people didn't have very much money, they were really generous. (OR Despite not having very much money, the old people were really generous.)

17 1 Although frustrated … as if trying

2 Since opening

3 Although managing

4 once broken

5 until making sure

Tests

A 1 d 2 a 3 c 4 d 5 b

B 1 D (was)

2 A (~~so that~~ OR *replace* 'so that' *with* 'in order')

3 C (because they become)

4 A (Because)

5 B (as if OR as though)

C 1 when 2 because 3 when
4 after 5 to 6 As

D 1 Because it was late and I was exhausted, I went straight to bed.

2 In order for him to continue to work here, there will have to be a change in his attitude.

3 He talked as if (OR as though) he owned the restaurant.

4 You can't go out until you finish (OR have finished) your homework.

5 Even though he's your friend (OR Even though I know he's your friend), he can't sleep here.

6 So as not to be late, we left half an hour earlier than necessary.

E 1 Although 2 as much as 3 whereas
4 as if 5 just as 6 as easy as 7 though
8 Despite the fact

Unit 17 Connectors and focus structures

1 A then (line 7)
   OR In fact (line 7)

B For example (line 12)
   OR also (line 14)
   OR Actually (line 18)

C After all (line 24)
   OR So (line 25)

D However (line 41)
   OR As a consequence (line 45)

2 1 (D) 2 (C) 3 (A) 4 (B)

3 1 There are **also** very large signs. (line 14)

2 What scientists now believe is that human activity is the cause. (line 29)

4 1 As a result of (OR Because of OR As a consequence of)

2 In addition to (OR As well as) … and … as a result (OR as a consequence OR as well OR too)

5 1 For example 2 In contrast to
3 As a result of 4 In addition

6 1 also 2 however 3 and
4 but 5 so 6 As a result

7 1 (d) though 2 and (c) so
3 or (a) but 4 (b) so … instead

8 in America ~~consequently~~ her English > in America. Consequently, her English (OR in America and consequently her English OR in America, so consequently her English)
She isn't like an American, ~~although~~ > though
seem to be very direct, ~~in contrast this~~ Kazuko > seem to be very direct. In contrast, Kazuko (OR seem to be very direct. In contrast to this, Kazuko OR seem to be very direct, but in contrast, Kazuko)
~~As example~~ > For example,
~~Instead that~~ > Instead (OR Instead of (doing) that)
She ~~makes also~~ a small > also makes
a small 'tsss' sound. ~~Alternatively, or~~ she may say > a small 'tsss' sound or she may say (OR a small 'tsss' sound. Alternatively, she may say OR a small 'tsss' sound. Or she may say)

As a result this > As a result (OR As a result of this)

Nevertheless that > Nevertheless (OR Despite that OR In spite of that)

In other word > In other words

9 1 lift 2 also 3 also
   4 lift 5 facelift 6 for example
   7 Similarly 8 facelift 9 forklift
   10 that is

10 A **However**, once he started working, things changed. (OR Once he started working, **however,** things changed. OR Once he started working, things changed, **however.**)
In other words, he was 'out of shape'. (OR He was, **in other words**, 'out of shape'. OR He was 'out of shape', **in other words.**)
B **Also**, like a lot more men these days, he started thinking about cosmetic surgery. (OR Like a lot more men these days, he **also** started thinking about cosmetic surgery.)
In particular, he wanted to get rid of some of the wrinkles around his eyes. (OR He wanted, **in particular,** to get rid of some of the wrinkles around his eyes. OR He wanted to get rid of some of the wrinkles around his eyes, **in particular.**)
Actually, now we have more men than women coming in for certain types of surgery. (OR Now we **actually** have more men than women coming in for certain types of surgery. OR Now we have more men than women coming in for certain types of surgery, **actually.**)
C *__Indeed__, the number of men seeking help from surgeons like Dr Idris has increased dramatically in recent years. (OR The number of men seeking help from surgeons like Dr Idris has *__indeed__ increased dramatically in recent years.)
*__In fact__, the emphasis on looking young isn't limited to facelifts, but has created a huge demand. (OR The emphasis on looking young isn't limited to facelifts, but *__in fact__ has created a huge demand. OR The emphasis on looking young isn't limited to facelifts, but has *__in fact__ created a huge demand but has created a huge demand for dental improvements and hair transplants **too.**)

*Indeed *and* in fact *can be exchanged*

11 1 I'm hoping as well to take a British History class. > I'm hoping to take a British History class as well.
   2 I don't like actually fish very much. > Actually, I don't like fish very much. (OR I don't actually like fish very much. OR I don't like fish very much, actually.)
   3 It's part of my job after all that. > after all
   4 In addition, he's certainly not the worst. > However, (OR Nevertheless, OR On the other hand, OR Yet)
   5 On the other hand, young children now automatically put their empty bottles in the recycling bin, not the dustbin. > For example (OR For instance OR In particular OR In fact)

12 1 (c) So 2 (e) So 3 (d) then
   4 (a) Then 5 (f) So 6 (b) Then

13 To make hot-baked chips for two, you'll need four large potatoes, the white of one egg, a quarter teaspoon of cayenne pepper and a pinch of salt. **First**, slice each potato lengthwise, **then** cut each slice lengthwise into long sticks. **Second**, mix the egg white, cayenne and salt in a bowl. **Then** stir the potato sticks round in the mixture. **Finally**, spread the coated potato sticks on a greased baking sheet and bake them in the oven at 170° for 35 minutes.

14 1 – (OR So)
   2 –
   3 Then(,) they can go on to talk about what they'll be doing tomorrow or next year.
   4 –
   5 As a result, they can refer to things like heaven and hell …
   6 Secondly, animal communication consists of a fixed number of signals …
   7 –
   8 In short, human communication has special properties …

15 1 *did she 2 she was
   3 was she 4 is it
   5 was something 6 had she
   7 it was 8 *would she
   9 she would 10 was part
   11 here comes 12 it is

1 and 8 can be exchanged

16　1　It's the cigarette smoke that's irritating my eyes.

　　2　It was us who (OR that) had to clean up all the mess.

　　3　What Jimmy does is watch TV in his room instead of studying.

　　4　What scientists now believe is that human activity is the cause.

Tests

A　1 a　2 d　3 a　4 a　5 a

B　1　D (a dog and two cats as well.)

　　2　C (in comparison to OR in comparison with)

　　3　C (actually stay in London)

　　4　D (As a result, OR As a result of that,)

　　5　D (In addition to that, OR In addition,)

C　1　for example　　　2　After all

　　3　in the meantime　4　In addition

　　5　So

D　1　Instead of (using) butter, we used margarine.

　　2　Only in Poland can you get dishes and bowls with this design.

　　3　Not until much later did we discover the mistake.

　　4　It's flooding that causes most of the damage in spring. (OR It's in spring that flooding causes most of the damage.)

　　5　It was because he was so unpleasant that she left.

　　6　All I know is that the main road is blocked.

　　7　What he did was go to the party by himself.

　　8　What Doris is hoping to do is to travel across Canada by train.

E　1　What　　　　　2　To begin with

　　3　Similarly　　4　That is

　　5　Next　　　　　6　In particular

　　7　As a result of

Exit Test

There are four spaces in each of the following paragraphs.
Choose the best answer (a, b, c or d) for each space.

1 After police arrested a man for breaking into a supermarket, they discovered that the thief was actually a teenage girl dressed as a man. Although they informed (1) _____ she didn't have to (2) _____ them anything, the girl confessed (3) _____ she had done it (4) _____ her family because they had no money and they were hungry.

1 a) her that	b) that	c) that her	d) to her that
2 a) admit	b) explain	c) report	d) tell
3 a) that	b) that to them	c) them that	d) them to that
4 a) by	b) for	c) that	d) to

2 It was (1) _____ late and I was beginning to (2) _____ tired, so I asked Rachel to finish her drawing and tidy up. She held the drawing up for me to see. It (3) _____ a big black dog that (4) _____ sitting at a table.

1 a) becoming	b) being	c) getting	d) going
2 a) feel	b) feel as	c) feel it	d) feel to be
3 a) looked	b) looked as	c) looked for	d) looked like
4 a) seemed	b) seemed like	c) seemed to be	d) seemed was

3 The residents of Montclair valley are (1) _____ only upset about some recent changes, but they're also very angry because (2) _____ consulted. Some families have lived and (3) _____ crops in the valley for many years, (4) _____ now their way of life is being threatened by developers who plan to build hundreds of new houses in the area.

1 a) both	b) either	c) neither	d) not
2 a) wasn't	b) weren't	c) it wasn't	d) they weren't
3 a) grew	b) grow	c) growing	d) grown
4 a) after	b) before	c) but	d) or

4 Because it (1) _____ a lot recently, I (2) _____ out as much and I suspect you will have been (3) _____ why I haven't been in touch. I'm sorry about the long silence, but I (4) _____ to phone you this week and maybe we can arrange to meet for lunch on Friday or Saturday.

1 a) has been raining   b) is raining   c) rain   d) rains

2 a) am not going   b) don't go   c) haven't gone   d) never go

3 a) believing   b) knowing   c) realizing   d) wondering

4 a) am promising   b) have been promising   c) have promised   d) promise

5 My grandfather said that when he (1) _____ up, he lived on a farm. During the summer, he (2) _____ to get up early every morning and work all day on the farm. He said that most people (3) _____ to go away on holiday, as they do now. But he (4) _____ feeling unhappy or deprived or anything like that because all of his friends were in the same situation.

1 a) had been growing   b) had grown   c) was growing   d) was grown

2 a) had been   b) has   c) was having   d) would have

3 a) didn't use   b) haven't used   c) wasn't used   d) weren't used

4 a) didn't remember   b) hadn't been remembering   c) hadn't remembered   d) wasn't remembering

6 As soon as the war was over, the refugees (1) _____ to go back to the villages they (2) _____ about five years earlier. When they arrived, they (3) _____ that other groups from the east had moved into the ruined houses and (4) _____ rebuilding them.

1 a) have tried   b) had tried   c) tried   d) were tried

2 a) have left   b) had left   c) leave   d) were left

3 a) have found   b) had found   c) found   d) were found

4 a) are   b) have   c) had   d) were

7 Paul and Jack meet in the corridor as Jack is locking his office door.

Paul: Oh, hello. I (1) _____ put this report in your mailbox, but perhaps you'd rather take it now.

Jack: Oh, thanks. Actually, I (2) _____ have lunch right now, but if you put it in my mailbox, I (3) _____ it as soon as I (4) _____ back.

1 a) 'll   b) 'm going to   c) shall   d) was going to

2 a) 'll   b) 'm going to   c) shall   d) would

3 a) 'll be reading   b) 'll have read   c) 'll read   d) read

4 a) get   b) 'll be getting   c) 'll get   d) 'll have got

8 I'm not sure where Karen is. She (1) _____ have been waiting outside her house this
   morning so that we (2) _____ give her a lift to work, but she wasn't there. Of course,
   she might (3) _____ sleeping and didn't hear us. If she had decided to take the bus, she
   (4) _____ arrived by now. I hope she isn't sick.

   1 a) may   b) must   c) ought   d) should
   2 a) can   b) can be   c) could   d) could have
   3 a) be   b) been   c) have   d) have been
   4 a) will be   b) will have   c) would be   d) would have

9 Don't you hate it when people say things like 'Let's be careful, (1) _____ we?'? It always
   sounds to me as if two of us (2) _____ to do something together, but in fact the other
   person (3) _____ doing anything. (4) _____ prefer it if they just said, 'You
   should be careful', because that's what they really mean.

   1 a) will   b) would   c) shall   d) should
   2 a) are going   b) will   c) will be   d) would
   3 a) won't   b) won't be   c) won't have   d) won't to
   4 a) I'd   b) I'll   c) I'm   d) I've

10 The best summer holiday I (1) _____ was when I was ten and I went to stay
    with my grandparents for a few weeks. At that time they were living in the country and
    (2) _____ still go for long walks through the woods. I (3) _____ to climb trees
    and run around with their dog. I (4) _____ go near the lake by myself, but
    my grandfather sometimes took me fishing there.

   1 a) am remembering   b) can remember   c) must remember   d) was remembering
   2 a) can   b) could   c) may   d) might
   3 a) could   b) could be   c) could have   d) was able
   4 a) can't   b) may not   c) might not   d) wasn't allowed to

11 Tommy, (1) _____ better slow down and wait for the rest of us. I'm sure we have lots
    of time, so we (2) _____ to run. We don't (3) _____ stop and buy tickets and
    there are still lots of people on the platform, so the train (4) _____ come yet.

   1 a) you'd   b) you'll   c) you're   d) you've
   2 a) aren't need   b) don't need   c) needn't   d) needn't have
   3 a) have to   b) have got to   c) must   d) must have to
   4 a) can't   b) can't be   c) can't have   d) couldn't

12 Joe has just returned to the computer lab where Sam works.

Joe: Who (1) _____ been using my computer?

Sam: I have (2) _____ idea. But these computers are for any student who wants
to use them, (3)_____?

Joe: Of course. But (4) _____ you see me doing my work on that machine before
lunch? I hope it hasn't all been lost.

1 a) has   b) has he   c) have   d) have they
2 a) no   b) no longer   c) not   d) not an
3 a) aren't they b) can't it   c) don't they   d) isn't it
4 a) aren't   b) didn't   c) don't   d) haven't

13 Liz is helping Sue clean out her flat.

Liz: Did you want to keep all these old books or (1) _____?

Sue: I'm not sure. They look interesting, but (2) _____ of them would be
worth anything.

Liz: So, (3) _____ of them do you think (4) _____ going to keep?

1 a) no   b) none   c) not   d) nothing
2 a) none   b) no one   c) not any   d) nothing
3 a) for what b) for which   c) what   d) which
4 a) are   b) are you   c) you   d) you are

14 The Star Tree hotel chain is in financial trouble and some of their smaller hotels are going
to have (1) _____. Rising costs (2) _____ for recent losses and many smaller
hotels (3) _____ to have been losing money for many years. No buyer has yet
(4) _____ for the properties.

1 a) been sold   b) being sold   c) sold   d) to be sold
2 a) are being blamed   b) blamed   c) have blamed   d) to be blamed
3 a) are reported   b) are reporting c) been reported d) have reported
4 a) been found   b) being found   c) found   d) to be found

15 'The Waste Land' is (1) ——————— title of (2) ——————— poem by T.S. Eliot, first published in 1922. (3) ——————— style of the poem has had a great influence on (4) ——————— modern poetry.

1 a) a   b) an   c) the   d) -
2 a) a   b) an   c) the   d) -
3 a) a   b) an   c) the   d) -
4 a) a   b) an   c) the   d) -

16 'I don't call this (1) ——————— progress,' says Bob Harding, owner of (2) ——————— small business in the city centre. He complains that an hour and fifteen minutes (3) ——————— become his typical commuting time every morning. 'It used to take only twenty minutes. There's just too much (4) ——————— now.'

1 a) a   b) one   c) the   d) -
2 a) a   b) an   c) the   d) -
3 a) are   b) has   c) have   d) is
4 a) car   b) cars   c) motor   d) traffic

17 I'm really enjoying my new job. All of (1) ——————— people I work with are friendly and I haven't had (2) ——————— problems so far. The best part is that I get paid (3) ——————— two weeks instead of waiting (4) ——————— month between pay days like in my last job.

1 a) that   b) the   c) them   d) -
2 a) any   b) much   c) some   d) no
3 a) all   b) both   c) each   d) every
4 a) a whole   b) the whole of   c) whole   d) whole of

18 Last year we had (1) ——————— more rain in the early spring and it made (2) ——————— in the garden grow better. We probably had three or four (3) ——————— strawberries as we're getting this year. I checked the strawberries in the garden this morning, but there (4) ——————— that were ripe.

1 a) a large number of   b) a lot of   c) many   d) much
2 a) all   b) each   c) every   d) everything
3 a) time as many   b) time as much   c) times as many   d) times as much
4 a) was only a little   b) was only little   c) were only a few   d) were only few

19 I was sitting at my desk when there was a loud crash as something came flying through the window. At first I thought it was a rock, but then I realized it was a cricket ball. I picked up the ball and put it on the desk beside (1) _____. Two young boys appeared outside the broken window. They said they were sorry, but then they started arguing, with each blaming (2) _____ for causing the accident. Then suddenly one of them asked if (3) _____ could have the ball back. I said, 'I don't think (4) _____. Not until you pay for this broken window.' They looked at me, then at each other, and then they both started running.

1 a) me   b) mine   c) my   d) myself
2 a) another   b) one other   c) other   d) the other
3 a) it   b) then   c) they   d) -
4 a) it   b) so   c) that   d) -

20 Although they were described as the (1) _____ designs in many years, there isn't (2) _____ about the latest line of shoes from Santorelli. As one of the most famous designers (3) _____ Italy, Salvatore Santorelli is expected to do (4) _____ simply repeat the previous year's successful formula of 'smart, but casual' sandals in a range of pastels.

1 a) first Italian new b) first new Italian c) new first Italian d) Italian first new
2 a) anything new very b) anything very new c) new anything very d) very new anything
3 a) by   b) in   c) of   d) to
4 a) as much as   b) more than   c) the best   d) the most

21 I remember when we stayed (1) _____ New York (2) _____ a few days (3) _____ last summer. It was really hot, even (4) _____ night, and I just felt miserable.

1 a) at   b) in   c) into   d) -
2 a) by   b) during   c) for   d) in
3 a) at   b) on   c) in   d) -
4 a) at   b) by   c) during   d) in

22 When we were students, my friends and I rented a cabin (1) _____ the mountains
    so that we could go hiking. It only cost us £25 for the whole week, not (2) _____
    food, of course. One day, my friend Daniel got tired and stopped to rest, saying he'd catch
    (3) _____ later, but when he still hadn't returned to the cabin (4) _____
    late afternoon, we started getting worried. Luckily, he met some men who were hunting in
    the area and they brought him back to the cabin before it got dark.

1	a) above	b) in	c) on	d) over
2	a) include	b) included	c) includes	d) including
3	a) up us	b) up with us	c) us up	d) with us up
4	a) by	b) during	c) in	d) since

23 When I visit big cities like Paris, I usually avoid (1) _____ to the most famous places
    because I really hate crowds. But it was no use (2) _____ that to my friend Tatjana
    because she was really eager (3) _____ the Mona Lisa in the Louvre and she refused
    (4) _____ outside while she went in.

1	a) go	b) going	c) gone	d) to go
2	a) trying explain	b) trying to explain	c) to try explaining	d) to try to explain
3	a) for see	b) to see	c) in seeing	d) seeing
4	a) letting me to wait	b) letting me wait	c) to let me to wait	d) to let me wait

24 At a time when it has become so important (1) _____ in school, we shouldn't be
    (2) _____ to learn that more students are cheating than ever before. With so many
    of them anxious about (3) _____, students also now seem to believe that those who
    cheat are unlikely (4) _____.

1	a) succeed	b) succeeding	c) success	d) to succeed
2	a) surprise	b) surprised	c) surprises	d) surprising
3	a) fail	b) failed	c) failing	d) to fail
4	a) to catch	b) to be catching	c) to be caught	d) to have caught

25 There was one student who asked about (1) _____ it was okay to use a dictionary
    during the exam and I had to tell her (2) _____ it. Then she started arguing
    (3) _____ me that her teacher always allowed her to use it in class. I had to
    remind (4) _____ was an exam, not a classroom exercise.

1	a) if	b) that	c) whether	d) why
2	a) don't use	b) no use	c) no using	d) not to use
3	a) about	b) for	c) to	d) with
4	a) her it	b) that	c) that it	d) -

26 Andrew Murphy, former managing director of Delco Electronics, has pleaded 'Not Guilty'
to charges (1) _____ £5 million from the company. He claims not to know where
(2) _____. He has suggested that an accountant (3) _____ the money.
Investigators consider (4) _____ anyone else in the company could have
committed the crime.

1 a) stealing   b) that he stole c) to have stolen d) which he stole
2 a) did go the money b) did the money go c) the money went d) went the money
3 a) is taking   b) should take   c) takes   d) took
4 a) it unlikely that b) that it unlikely c) that unlikely d) unlikely that

27 I've been looking for a special kind of brown cheese (1) _____ made in Norway, but
(2) _____ name I can't remember. There was one woman I talked (3) _____
in the Gourmet Experience shop on King Street (4) _____ said they could order it
for me if I could give her more information about it.

1 a) it   b) that's   c) was   d) which
2 a) what   b) which   c) where   d) whose
3 a) to   b) to her   c) to whom   d) -
4 a) what   b) who   c) whom   d) -

28 The term 'organic' can only be used to describe food (1) _____ in situations
(2) _____ no artificial chemicals have been used. Anyone (3) _____
fertilizer (4) _____ containing chemicals to make tomatoes grow bigger, for
example, is certainly not growing them organically.

1 a) grown   b) that growing c) where growing d) which grown
2 a) how   b) that   c) where   d) which
3 a) use   b) used   c) uses   d) using
4 a) what   b) when   c) which   d) -

29 (1) _____ their hair wasn't actually very long, rock groups such as the Beatles and the Rolling Stones were often criticized as 'long-haired' or 'needing haircuts' when they first became popular during the early 1960s. At that time men were also considered effeminate if they (2) _____ long hair. The opposite was true for men who grew a beard (3) _____, of course, it was allowed to grow too long. Beards grow faster than hair and need more care. In fact, if the average man never trimmed his beard, it (4) _____ to nearly ten metres in his lifetime. Now, that's a lot of hair!

1 a) Even though   b) If only   c) Unless   d) Whether
2 a) had   b) have   c) will have   d) would have
3 a) if   b) if not   c) only if   d) unless
4 a) grew   b) has grown   c) will grow   d) would grow

30 I know you're anxiously waiting to find out if I passed my exams, but I haven't heard anything yet. Perhaps I'll get the news today when the post (1) _____. I promise I (2) _____ you as soon as I get the news. It's three weeks (3) _____ I took the exams, but my teacher warned me that they sometimes don't announce the results until more than a month (4) _____.

1 a) comes   b) came   c) is coming   d) will come
2 a) call   b) called   c) 'll call   d) 'm calling
3 a) later   b) once   c) since   d) when
4 a) has passed   b) is passing   c) passed   d) will pass

31 (1) _____ in most other sports players are usually trying to get the most goals or points (2) _____ win, the opposite is true in golf. In a game of golf, it is the lowest score that wins. Each player must try to get his or her ball in the hole (3) _____ as few shots as possible. For each hole there is a given number of shots called 'par'. (4) _____ a player uses one shot less than par, it's called a 'birdie' and one more than par is called a 'bogey'.

1 a) Even although   b) In spite of   c) Instead of   d) Whereas
2 a) for   b) in order to   c) so that   d) such that
3 a) use   b) uses   c) used   d) using
4 a) As   b) Since   c) When   d) While

32 (1) _____ our flight from London to Toronto was delayed because (2) _____
bad weather, we missed our connection to Vancouver and had to spend six hours in the airport
(3) _____ for the next flight. (4) _____ being delayed, we still had a good trip
and didn't feel too jet-lagged when we arrived.

1 a) After	b) Although	c) If	d) So that
2 a) it	b) of	c) the	d) -
3 a) have waited	b) waited	c) waiting	d) were waiting
4 a) Although	b) As	c) Despite	d) Unless

33 What the recent use of DNA testing has shown (1) _____ eyewitness testimony may
not always be reliable. (2) _____, an eyewitness testified that he saw Gilbert Medeiros
with Angela Anderson shortly before the young woman was murdered and, (3) _____
that testimony, Medeiros was convicted and sent to prison. Not until much later
(4) _____ discovered through DNA testing that someone other than Medeiros had
been responsible for Anderson's death.

1 a) is it	b) is that	c) it is	d) that is
2 a) For example	b) In addition	c) On the other hand	d) Therefore
3 a) afterwards	b) as a consequence	c) as a result of	d) subsequently
4 a) it was	b) they	c) was	d) was it

34 Do you sometimes feel anxious or irritable when you're driving? It may be the smell inside
your car (1) _____ is determining how you feel. A recent study of American drivers
found that the smell of peppermint or cinnamon improved their performance by reducing
anxiety more than 20 per cent. Alertness (2) _____ increased by almost 30 per cent.
(3) _____, the smell of cakes or fast food made drivers more irritable and caused
them to speed, probably because those smells stimulate hunger (4) _____ make
drivers more anxious to get where they're going sooner.

1 a) it	b) that	c) what	d) which
2 a) also	b) as well	c) besides	d) moreover
3 a) In conclusion	b) In contrast	c) In other words	d) In particular
4 a) and	b) as a result of	c) consequently and	d) however didn't

Key to the exit test

Following the answers are page numbers in brackets where you can find information on the grammar points being tested.

1 1 a (8)
2 d (8)
3 a (8)
4 b (8)

2 1 c (10)
2 a (10)
3 d (10)
4 c (10)

3 1 d (12)
2 d (12)
3 d (12)
4 c (12)

4 1 a (18)
2 c (18)
3 d (17, 18)
4 d (18)

5 1 c (20)
2 d (20)
3 a (20)
4 a (20)

6 1 c (22, 23)
2 b (22, 23)
3 c (22, 23)
4 d (22, 23)

7 1 d (24)
2 b (24)
3 c (24)
4 a (24)

8 1 d (30)
2 c (29)
3 d (30)
4 d (30)

9 1 c (32)
2 a (32)
3 b (32)
4 a (33)

10 1 b (34)
2 b (34)
3 d (34)
4 d (35)

11 1 a (41)
2 b (38)
3 a (38)
4 c (40)

12 1a (45)
2 a (45)
3 a (46)
4 b (46)

13 1 c (48)
2 a (48)
3 d (50)
4 d (52)

14 1 d (58)
2 a (57, 58)
3 a (57, 63)
4 a (57, 58)

15 1 c (78)
2 a (70)
3 c (70)
4 d (72)

16 1 d (74)
2 a (74)
3 b (75)
4 d (74)

17 1 b (83, 84)
2 a (86, 90)
3 d (84)
4 a (88)

18 1 d (90)
2 d (88, 89)
3 c (93)
4 c (92)

19 1 a (100)
2 d (100)
3 c (106)
4 b (105)

20 1 b (112)
2 b (112, 118)
3 b (120)
4 b (120)

21 1 b (128, 130)
2 c (126, 127)
3 d (126)
4 a (126, 127)

22 1 b (128, 129)
2 d (125)
3 b (134)
4 a (126, 127)

23 1 b (142)
2 b (142, 145)
3 b (144)
4 d (139, 143)

24 1 d (144)
2 b (144)
3 c (144)
4 c (140, 144)

25 1 c (154)
2 d (156)
3 d (152)
4 a (152)

26 1 b (164)
2 c (161)
3 d (161, 167)
4 a (162)

27 1 b (173)
2 d (178)
3 a (173, 179)
4 b (173)

28 1 a (176)
2 c (180)
3 d (176, 178)
4 d (176)

29 1 a (192)
2 a (185)
3 d (192)
4 d (186)

30 1 a (198)
2 c (199)
3 c (198, 199)
4 a (199)

31 1 d (202)
2 b (202, 203)
3 d (205)
4 c (198, 201)

32 1 a (197, 199)
2 b (197)
3 c (205)
4 c (204)

33 1 b (217)
2 a (209)
3 c (210, 214)
4 d (216)

34 1 b (217)
2 a (212)
3 b (212, 215)
4 a (210)

Appendix: regular and irregular verbs

Regular verbs

We add **-ed** (1) or simply **-d** (2) to the base form of regular verbs to make the past simple and past participle forms.

    1 *I asked him, but he hasn't answered yet. • We wanted to know. • I have waited patiently.*

    2 *They agreed that it was a good idea. • That's why we have continued. • She hasn't smiled much.*

Before adding **-ed** to some verbs, we double the final consonant (after a single written vowel, in stressed syllables).

    3 *She had planned to visit us and regretted that poor health had stopped her.*

    Others include: *dragged, occurred, permitted, preferred, ripped, robbed, slipped, trimmed.*

    Note that *cancelled, travelled*, etc. in British English are *canceled, traveled*, etc. in American English.

We change the final **-y** (after a consonant) to **-i-** before **-ed** in some verbs.

    4 *Have you tried to get a scholarship? ~ I applied for one, but they haven't replied yet.*

    Others include: *carried, copied, cried, hurried, identified, implied, studied, testified, worried.*

Irregular verbs

We use special forms for the past simple of some verbs.

    5 *We saw Jack Brown yesterday. • I forgot I had your keys. • They understood what I taught them.*

We add **-en** (6) or **-n** (7) to the base form of some verbs to make the past participle.

    6 *Where have you been? • Have you eaten anything? • I had hidden it, but it had fallen out.*

    7 *I haven't seen that film. • Have you known him a long time? • They've driven up from London.*

We use the base form of some verbs for the past simple and past participle.

    8 *Yesterday I hit my forehead on the shelf and cut it, but it hasn't hurt too badly today.*

    Others include: *bet, burst, cost, forecast, let, put, quit, ride, set, shut, split, spread, thrust.*

Some verbs are used with both regular and irregular forms.

    9 *Have you burned/burnt the toast? • I dreamed/dreamt about you. • He spilled/spilt some milk.*

    Others include: *kneeled/knelt, leaped/leapt, learned/learnt, lighted/lit, speeded/sped.*

    Note that the **-ed** forms are becoming more common, especially in American English.

Common irregular verbs

basic form	past simple	past participle	basic form	past simple	past participle
be	was, were	been	light	lit	lit
become	became	become	lose	lost	lost
begin	began	begun	make	made	made
bend	bent	bent	mean	meant	meant
bet	bet	bet	meet	met	met
bite	bit	bitten	pay	paid	paid
blow	blew	blown	put	put	put
break	broke	broken	read	read	read
bring	brought	brought	ride	rode	ridden
build	built	built	ring	rang	rung
burst	burst	burst	rise	rose	risen
buy	bought	bought	run	ran	run
catch	caught	caught	say	said	said
choose	chose	chosen	see	saw	seen
come	came	came	sell	sold	sold
cost	cost	cost	send	sent	sent
cut	cut	cut	set	set	set
dig	dug	dug	shake	shook	shaken
do	did	done	shine	shone	shone
draw	drew	drawn	shoot	shot	shot
drink	drank	drunk	show	showed	shown
drive	drove	driven	shut	shut	shut
eat	ate	eaten	sing	sang	sung
fall	fell	fallen	sink	sank	sunk
feed	fed	fed	sit	sat	sat
feel	felt	felt	sleep	slept	slept
fight	fought	fought	slide	slid	slid
find	found	found	speak	spoke	spoken
fly	flew	flown	spend	spent	spent
forget	forgot	forgotten	spit	spat	spat
forgive	forgave	forgiven	split	split	split
freeze	froze	frozen	spread	spread	spread
get	got	got	stand	stood	stood
give	gave	given	steal	stole	stolen
go	went	gone	stick	stuck	stuck
grow	grew	grown	strike	struck	struck
have	had	had	swear	swore	sworn
hear	heard	heard	sweep	swept	swept
hide	hid	hidden	swim	swam	swum
hit	hit	hit	take	took	taken
hold	held	held	teach	taught	taught
keep	kept	kept	tear	tore	torn
kneel	knelt	knelt	tell	told	told
know	knew	known	think	thought	thought
lay	laid	laid	throw	threw	thrown
lead	led	led	understand	understood	understood
leave	left	left	wake	woke	woken
lend	lent	lent	wear	wore	worn
let	let	let	win	won	won
lie	lay	lain	write	wrote	written

Glossary

This is a list of grammar terms with explanations of what they mean. Words printed in blue in the explanations are themselves grammar terms and can be found in their own place in the glossary. Numbers following the explanations are numbers of the pages in the text where you will find more information.

action verb: a verb used to describe what we do or what happens (*I ate lunch.*). Compare **state verb**. 3

active: a form of the verb used to say what the subject does (*A thief stole my car.*). Compare **passive**. 57

adjective: a word such as *new* or *good-looking* used to modify a noun (*Jill's new boyfriend is good-looking.*). 111–14

adverb: a word such as *really* or *recently* used to modify a verb, adjective, adverb or sentence (*I met him recently and he's really good-looking.*). 116–18

adverbial: an adverb (*later*), prepositional phrase (*in town*) or adverbial clause (*after I finish work*) used to provide additional information in a clause or a sentence (*I'll meet you in town later after I've finished work.*). 3

adverbial clause: a clause typically introduced by a subordinating conjunction such as *because* and providing information such as when or why something happens (*I can't go out because I have to study.*). 197

agent: the person or thing that does or causes the action, typically the subject in active sentences (*Dickens wrote Oliver Twist.*). 64

article: a word used as a determiner before a noun, either as the definite article (*the*) or the indefinite article (*a/an*) (*The car had a flat tyre.*). 69–70

attributive adjective: an adjective used before a noun (*She had red hair and green eyes.*). Compare **predicative adjective**. 112

auxiliary verb: a form of *be*, *do*, *have* or a modal used with a main verb to form different tenses, negatives and questions (*Have you eaten yet?*). 3, 17

bare infinitive = base form 17

base form: the form of a verb such as *be* or *eat*, as listed in a dictionary. 17

clause: a group of words including a subject and a verb that forms a simple sentence (*She left yesterday.*) or is part of a complex sentence (*She left before you came.*) or compound sentence (*She left and I'm glad.*). 3, 11

cleft sentence: a structure in which a sentence (*I'm not supposed to drink coffee.*) is divided into two parts and attention is focused on one part, using an it-cleft (*It's coffee that I'm not supposed to drink.*) or a wh-cleft (*What I'm not supposed to drink is coffee.*). 217

collective noun = group noun 75

common noun: a noun which is not the name of anyone or anything (*The car had a flat tyre.*). Compare **proper noun**. 69

comparative: an adjective or adverb with -er (*healthier*) or *more/less* (*less expensive*), often followed by *than*, used to say that something has more or less of a quality than another (*Fish is **healthier** and **less expensive** than meat*.) Compare **superlative**. 120

complement: a word or phrase used after a linking verb, typically describing the subject (*She is **a student** so she isn't **rich**.*). 10

complex preposition: a preposition that consists of two or more words (***In addition to** me, there were three other people waiting **in front of** the entrance.*). Compare **simple preposition**. 125

complex sentence: a sentence with two or more clauses joined by a subordinating conjunction such as *because*, *before*, etc. (*I went to bed **because** I was tired.*). Compare **compound sentence**. 12

compound adjective: an adjective that consists of two words joined by a hyphen (*a **good-looking** person*, *a **home-cooked** meal*). 114

compound noun: two or more words used together as a noun to refer to a person or thing (*a **bus driver**, an **application form***). 78

compound sentence: a sentence with two or more clauses joined by a coordinating conjunction (*and, but, or*) (*Dave read a magazine **and** I went to bed.*). Compare **complex sentence**. 12

compound-complex sentence: a sentence with three or more clauses joined by both a coordinating conjunction and a subordinating conjunction (*Dave read a magazine **and** I went to bed **because** I was tired.*). Compare **complex sentence** and **compound sentence**. 12

conditional: a structure in which one clause, typically beginning with *if*, is presented as a condition for something in another clause (*If I have time, I'll help you.*). 185–6

conjunction: a word such as *and*, *but*, or that links words, phrases or sentences (*It's late **and** I want to go home.*). 2, 197, 210

connector: a word (*however*) or phrase (*in addition*) typically used to link sentences and sometimes clauses (*They didn't win. **However**, they played better than last week. **In addition**, they scored two goals.*). 209–10

continuous: a form of the verb using *be* + present participle (*The baby **is sleeping**.*). 17

contracted form: a short form of a word (*I've, he's, she'd, we'll, they won't*). 24, 29

coordinating conjunction: *and*, *but*, or (*I'll write **or** I'll call you.*). Compare **subordinating conjunction**. 12

copula or **copular verb** = **linking verb** 10

countable noun: a noun that can be singular (*book, child*) or plural (*books, children*) and used to refer to people or things as separate individuals. Compare **uncountable noun**. 74

counterfactual conditional: a type of unreal conditional used to talk about an imaginary connection between two events that never happened (*If you had been born in the Middle Ages, you would have had a harsh life*). 186

defining relative clause: a relative clause used to identify or classify people or things (*Do you know the man **who lives upstairs**?*). Compare **non-defining relative clause**. 174

definite article: *the* (*Can you see **the** moon?*). Compare **indefinite article**. 69-70

demonstrative pronoun: one of the words *this, that, these, those* used instead of a noun phrase (*I like **these** better than **those**.*). 83, 98

demonstratives: the words *this, that, these* or *those* used as a determiner before a noun (***this** book*) or as a pronoun instead of a noun phrase (*I don't like **that**.*). 83, 98

determiner: a word used before a noun such as an article (*a/an, the*), a demonstrative (*this, that, these, those*) or a possessive (*my, your, his, her, its, our, their*) (*A friend sent me **this** funny card for **my** birthday.*). 83

direct object: a word or phrase identifying the one(s) affected by the action of the verb (*I dropped **the ball**.*). Compare **indirect object.** 8

direct speech: the original words of a speaker, usually presented in quotation marks, in a report of what was said (*He said, '**I'm tired.**'*). Compare **indirect speech.** 149

ellipsis: leaving out words or phrases instead of repeating them (*Sue came in and _ sat down.*). 106

empty object *it*: the word *it* in direct object position, not used to refer to anything (*I hate **it** when I miss the bus.*). 102, 162

empty subject *it*: the word *it* in subject position, not used to refer to anything (***It** was nice to go for a walk even though **it** was raining.*). 102, 162

empty subject *there*: the word *there* in subject position, not used to refer to anything (***There** isn't any food left.*). 103

equative: an adjective or adverb in the structure (*not*) *as ... as*, used to say that something is similar (or not) to another in some way (*Your jacket is **as** big **as** my coat.*). 120

ergative: a transitive verb used without an object, typically used to say that an event simply happens, without an agent (*The door suddenly **opened**.*). 64

factual conditional: a type of real conditional used to express a fixed connection between two events now, in the past or always (*If the fruit is soft, it's ready to eat.*). 185

first conditional = predictive conditional 185

focus structure: a structure such as fronting or a cleft sentence used to focus attention on one part of a sentence (***Tea** I can drink. It's **coffee** I'm not supposed to drink.*). 216–17

fraction: a word or phrase such as *half* or *two-thirds* used as a quantifier with *of* before a determiner or pronoun to describe a part of something (***Two-thirds** of the students are from Europe.*). 93

fronting: a structure in which one part of a sentence (*I can't drink coffee*) is moved to front position (***Coffee** I can't drink because it gives me a headache.*). 216

generic noun: a noun used in making a general statement about something, not about a specific example (***Women** live longer than **men**.*). 75

generic pronoun: a pronoun such as *one, they, we* or *you* used with the meaning 'people in general' (***They** say **you** can't teach an old dog new tricks.*). 97

gerund: a word with the same form as the present participle, but used as a noun (*I enjoy **walking**.*). 139

group noun: a noun such as *committee* or *team* used to talk about a group of people as a single unit (*The Olympic **committee** chooses the national **team**.*). 75

hypothetical conditional: a type of unreal conditional used to express a distant and unlikely connection between one imaginary event and another (*If I had a lot of money, I'd buy a Mercedes.*). 186

imperative: the base form of the verb, typically used to give orders (*Stop!*). 17

indefinite adverb: an adverb such as *anywhere* or *everywhere* used to talk about places in a very general way (*I've looked **everywhere**, but I can't find my notebook **anywhere**.*). 98

indefinite article: *a/an* (*Would you like **an** apple or **a** banana?*). Compare **definite article**. 69–70.

indefinite pronoun: a pronoun such as *someone* or *anything* used to talk about people and things in a very general way (***Someone** called earlier, but they didn't say **anything**.*). 98

indirect object: a word or phrase used after a verb such as *give* or *send*, identifying the one(s) receiving something. (*I gave **Bob** some money. I sent a letter to **them**.*). Compare **direct object**. 8

indirect question: a version of a previous question, not the exact words, presented in a noun clause as a report of a *wh*-question (*He asked **what we were doing**.*) or a yes/no question (*He asked **if we were from Sweden**.*). 52, 154

indirect speech: a version of a previous utterance, not the exact words, presented in a noun clause as a report of what was said (*He said **that he was tired**.*). Compare **direct speech**. 150

infinitive: *to* plus the base form of a verb (*I'm hoping **to win**.*). 139

-*ing* form = **gerund** 139

intransitive verb: a verb that never has an object (*I can't **sleep**.*). Compare **transitive verb**. 6

inversion: a structure in which a verb or auxiliary verb is put before the subject (*Into the room **walked two men**.*). 216

inverted commas = **quotation marks** 149

it-cleft: a structure in which a sentence (*I'm not supposed to drink coffee.*) is divided into two parts, the first part with *it* + *be* + an emphasized element and the second part as a relative clause (*It's coffee (that) I'm not supposed to drink.*). Compare **wh-cleft**. 217

linking verb: a verb such as *be, become, seem*, used with a complement, typically describing the subject (*She **is/seems** unhappy.*). 10

linking word = **connector** 209

main verb: the verb in a clause (*Did you **follow** that? I **understood** what she **said**.*). Compare **auxiliary verb**. 45–6

mass noun = **uncountable noun** 74

mixed conditional: a type of conditional in which there is an unusual combination of tenses in the two clauses (*If you saw the film, you'll remember the battle scene.*). 188

modal: an auxiliary verb such as *can, could, must*, used with the base form of a verb to say what is possible, permitted, necessary, etc. (*You **must** leave now.*). Compare **phrasal modal**. 29

multiplier: a word or phrase such as *twice* or *five times* used as a quantifier before a determiner to say how often or how much more something is (*They pray **five times** a day.*). 93

negative: a sentence or clause with an auxiliary verb plus *not* or *n't* and a main verb (*I **don't** care.*). 45

negative adverb: a word or phrase such as *never* or *no longer* used as an adverb (*He **never** studies.*). 48

nominal clause = **noun clause** 161

non-count noun = **uncountable noun** 74

non-defining relative clause: a relative clause used to provide extra information, typically separated by commas (*My friend John, **who lives upstairs**, has a cat.*). Compare **defining relative clause**. 174

non-finite form = **base form** 17

noun: a word used for someone or something, either as a common noun (*book, courage*) or a proper noun (*Shakespeare, Denmark*). 69

noun clause: a *that*-clause (*I know **that it's late**.*) or a *wh*-clause (*I didn't know **what you were doing**.*) used like a noun phrase. 161–2

noun phrase: a phrase in which the main word is a noun and which is used as a subject or an object (***Their new flat** is really big so they're having **a party** for **sixty people** on **Saturday night**.*). 96

object: a noun, noun phrase or pronoun used as the direct object (*He took **the money**.*), indirect object (*I gave **him** the money.*) or after a preposition (*He took it with **him**.*). 8, 125

object pronoun: a personal pronoun (*me, you, him, her, it, us, them*) used as an object (*James gave **them** to **me**, not **her**.*). 97

pair noun: a noun used for something made of two matching parts such as *scissors* or *trousers*. 75

parenthetical noun clause: a noun clause used after a noun to provide extra information, typically separated by commas, dashes or brackets (*His first suggestion, **that we should go to Manchester**, wasn't very popular.*). 164

participle: a form of the verb, either the present participle (*breaking, repairing*) or the past participle (*broken, repaired*). 17, 220

participle adjective: an adjective derived from a present participle (*surprising*) or a past participle (*shocked*) (*She seemed **shocked** by the **surprising** news.*). 114

participle clause = **reduced adverbial clause** 205

particle: a preposition (*on*) or adverb (*away*) combined with a verb as a phrasal verb (*He put **on** his jacket and walked **away**.*). 134

passive: a form of the verb with *be* plus the past participle of a transitive verb, used to say what happens to the subject (*My car **was stolen**.*). Compare **active**. 57

past continuous: a form of the verb using *was* or *were* + present participle (*The baby **was sleeping**.*). 17, 20

past participle: the form of a verb such as *broken, repaired*, used in the perfect (*I had **broken** my watch.*) and the passive (*It was **repaired**.*). 17, 220

past perfect: a form of the verb using *had* + past participle (***Had you forgotten** anything?*). 17, 20

percentage: a phrase such as *ten per cent* (*10%*) used as a quantifier with *of* before a determiner or pronoun to describe a part of something (***Ten per cent** of the population is living in poverty.*). 93

perfect: a form of the verb using *have* + past participle (***Have you forgotten** anything?*). 17

personal pronoun: one of the subject pronouns (*I, you, he, she, it, we, they*) or object pronouns (*me, you, him, her, it, us, them*). 97

personification: the treatment of an abstract idea or a thing as if it was a person (***Death's cold hand*** *touched his shoulder.*). 76

phrasal modal: a phrase such as *be able to, be going to* or *have to* used instead of a modal (*We **have to** wait for Cathy.*). Compare **modal.** 28

phrasal verb: a verb + particle combination such as *sleep in* or *put on* (*He **put on** his shoes.*). 134

pluperfect = **past perfect** 20

possessive determiner: *my, your, his, her, its, our, their.* Compare **possessive pronoun.** 83

possessive noun: a noun plus an apostrophe with s (*Lee's car*) or without s (*Jones' house*). 78

possessive pronoun: *mine, yours, his, hers, ours, theirs.* Compare **possessive determiner.** 83, 97

possessive: a word such as *my, your, their* used as a determiner before a noun (***my*** *chair,* ***your*** *money*) and *mine, yours, theirs* used as a pronoun instead of a noun phrase (*I found **mine**, but I couldn't find **yours**.*). 83, 97

predicative adjective: an adjective used after a linking verb (*Her hair was **red** and her eyes were **green**.*). Compare **attributive adjective.** 112

predictive conditional: a type of real conditional used to express a likely connection between one event and another possible event (*If I have time, I'll help you.*). 185

preposition: a word such as *at* and *on*, or a phrase such as *in front of*, used before a noun, noun phrase or pronoun in a prepositional phrase (*I'll meet you **at** noon **on** Friday **in front of** the library.*). 125

prepositional phrase: a preposition plus a noun, noun phrase or pronoun (*on the table, in front of me*). 125

present continuous: a form of the verb using *am, is* or *are* + present participle (*The baby **is sleeping**.*). 17, 18

present participle: the form of a verb such as *sleeping*, used in the continuous (*Is he **sleeping**?*). Compare **past participle.** 17

present perfect: a form of the verb using *has* or *have* + past participle (***Have** you **forgotten** anything?*). 17, 18

progressive = **continuous** 17

pronoun: a word such as *she, anything* or *herself* used instead of a noun or noun phrase (*Molly is very old and **she** can't do **anything** by **herself**.*). 97–8, 100

proper noun: a noun with a capital letter used as the name of someone or something (***Elsa*** *is from* ***Switzerland**.*). Compare **common noun.** 69

quantifier: a word such as *many* and *some* or a phrase such as *a few* and *a lot (of)* used to talk about quantities (***Some*** *people have* ***a lot of*** *money.*). 84

question: a sentence with an auxiliary verb before the subject and main verb, used as a **wh-question** (*When did he leave?*) or a **yes/no question** (*Did he leave?*). 45

question tag: an auxiliary verb plus a subject pronoun used as a short form of a question added after a statement (*He hasn't left yet, **has he**? He's still here, **isn't he**?*). 46

quotation marks: a pair of marks ('...' or "...") inside which we put direct speech, special words or phrases, and titles (*'I'm tired,' he said.*) (*Have you read 'Animal Farm'?*). 149

real conditional: a type of conditional in which the events happen, have happened or are likely to happen. (*If I open the door, the cat will run out.*). Compare **unreal conditional**. 185

reciprocal pronoun: *each other, one another.* 100

reduced adverbial clause: an adverbial clause formed with a participle or a subordinating conjunction plus a participle (*(Before) leaving the house, he switched off the lights.*). 205

reduced negative: a short form of a negative, typically formed with a conjunction plus *not* (*Do you want this or not? If not, can I have it?*). 48

reduced relative clause: a relative clause formed with a participle and no relative pronoun (*I saw some people waiting outside.*). 176

reflexive pronoun: *myself, yourself, himself, herself, itself, ourselves, yourselves, themselves.* 100

relative clause: a clause typically introduced by a relative pronoun and used to provide additional information about a noun phrase in a preceding clause (*I was in a bus which was packed with children who were making a lot of noise.*). 173–4

relative pronoun: the words *who, whom, which, that* used to introduce a relative clause (*I have a friend who can fix computers.*). 173

rhetorical question: a sentence in the form of a question used to make a statement. (*Who cares?*). 52

reported speech = indirect speech 150

reporting verb: a verb such as *say* or *reply* used with direct speech (*He said, 'Hello.'*) or indirect speech (*I replied that I was busy.*). 149–52

second conditional = hypothetical conditional 186

simple preposition: a preposition that is a single word such as *at, during, in, without.* Compare **complex preposition**. 125

simple sentence: a single clause with a subject and a verb (*Mary sneezed.*) which may also include an object and an adverbial (*We ate lunch in a café.*). Compare **compound sentence** and **complex sentence**. 3

split infinitive: an infinitive with an adverb between *to* and the verb (*I want to really understand him.*). 139

state verb: a verb used to describe a state, not an action (*I know that he has a lot of money.*). Compare **action verb**. 3

subject: a noun, noun phrase or pronoun typically used before a verb to identify who or what performs the action of the verb (*Tony lost his keys and I found them.*). 4

subject pronoun: a personal pronoun (*I, you, he, she, it, we, they*) used as subject (*He wants to get married and she doesn't.*). 97

subject-verb agreement: the relationship of singular subject with singular verb (*He is eating lunch.*) or plural subject with plural verb (*They are eating lunch.*). 4

subjunctive: a special use of the base form of a verb in a noun clause, sometimes called the present subjunctive (*They have proposed that taxes be increased.*). Also the use of *were* in a noun clause after the verb *wish* (*I wish I were older*) and in a hypothetical conditional (*If I were you, I'd complain*), sometimes called the past subjunctive. 167, 186

subordinating conjunction: a word or phrase used to introduce an adverbial clause (*because*), a noun clause (*that*) or a relative clause (*who*) (*I didn't know **that** you were the person **who** called me **because** you didn't leave your name.*). Compare **coordinating conjunction**. 12, 197

substitution: the use of words such as *one*, *ones*, *so* and *do so* instead of repeating a word, phrase or clause (*I have a black pen, but I need a red **one**.*). 104

summary report: a short report using a verb that summarizes what was said (*He apologized.*). 152

superlative: an adjective or adverb with *-est* (*fastest*) or *most/least* (*most expensive*) after *the*, used to say that something has the most or the least of a quality (*He wants to get **the fastest** and **most expensive** car in the world.*). Compare **comparative**. 120

tag question = question tag 46

tense: the relationship between the form of the verb and the time of the action or state it describes. 17

that-clause: a type of noun clause beginning with *that* (*I thought **that I had made a mistake**.*). 161

third conditional = counterfactual conditional 186

three-word verb: a phrasal verb plus a preposition (*You should **hold on to** that book.*). 134

transitive verb: a verb used with an object (*I **dropped** the ball.*). Compare **intransitive verb**. 6

Two-word verb = phrasal verb 134

uncountable noun: a noun that can only be singular and used to refer to things such as activities (*research*), ideas (*honesty*) and substances (*rice*), but not separate individuals. Compare **countable noun**. 74

unreal conditional: a type of conditional in which the events have not happened, are not likely to happen or are imaginary (*If you had asked me earlier, I would have helped you.*). Compare **real conditional**. 186

verb: a word used in a clause to describe the action (*eat, steal*) or state (*belong, understand*) of the subject (*He **stole** something that **belonged** to me.*). 3, 11

verb with object = transitive verb 6

verb without object = intransitive verb 6

wh-clause: a type of noun clause beginning with a *wh*-word such as *what* or *whether* (*I don't know **what she wants**.*) (*I can't remember **whether she likes tea or coffee**.*). 161

wh-cleft: a structure in which a sentence (*I'm not supposed to drink coffee.*) is divided into two parts, one part as a clause typically beginning with *What* (*What I'm not supposed to drink*) and the other part *be* + an emphasized element (*What I'm not supposed to drink is coffee.*). Compare **it-cleft**. 217

wh-question: a question beginning with *What, Who, When, How much*, etc. (*When did he leave?*). Compare **yes/no question**. 45

wh-word: a word such as *what, who, where, how much*, etc. used at the beginning of a *wh*-question or a *wh*-clause (***Where** have you been?*)(*I don't know **what's** wrong.*). 45, 161

yes/no question: a question beginning with an auxiliary verb or *be*, typically answered with *Yes* or *No*. (*Did he leave?*). Compare **wh-question**. 45

zero conditional = factual conditional 185

Index

References in this index are to page numbers. Those in **bold** are the main entries.